Web Page Design
with XHTML/CSS

Alec Fehl

Asheville-Buncombe Technical Community College

LABYRINTH
L E A R N I N G ™

Web Page Design with XHTML/CSS
by Alec Fehl

LABYRINTH
L E A R N I N G ™

Labyrinth Learning
PO Box 20820
El Sobrante, California 94803
800.522.9746
On the Web at lablearning.com

President:
Brian Favro

Chief Operating Officer:
Ted Ricks

Series Editor:
Russel Stolins

Acquisitions Editor:
Jason Favro

Managing Editor:
Laura A. Lionello

Production Manager:
Rad Proctor

Editorial/Production Team:
DocumentJones, ICC-MacMillan,
Joy Robinson, and Sheryl Trittin

Indexing: Joanne Sprott

Cover Design:
Seventeenth Street Studios

ITEM: 1-59136-129-X
ISBN-13:   978-1-59136-129-9

Manufactured in the United States of America.

10 9 8 7 6 5 4 3 2

Web Page Design
with XHTML/CSS

Contents in Brief

UNIT 2 BEYOND THE BASICS

UNIT 3 APPENDICES

Table of Contents

Summary of Quick Reference Tables

Preface

What Is Covered: In *Web Design with XHTML/CSS* students learn how to create a professional website. In Unit 1, students learn the fundamentals of website planning and design. They write valid XHTML code, experiment with CSS, and learn about software tools. Students also work with text structures and make their web pages accessible to search engines, screen readers, and other user agents. Additional topics in this unit include image file formats, basic image editing techniques, acquiring and adding images, adding backgrounds, and creating hyperlinks. In Unit 2, students work with data and layout tables, add color to pages via HTML attributes and CSS, style text, and learn about the CSS box model. Other topics in this unit include the CSS float property, forms, information about web-hosting companies, and migrating websites created with outdated code to valid XHTML 1.0 transitional and CSS.

What Is Different: For more than a decade, Labyrinth has been working to perfect our *unique instructional design*. The benefit of our approach is that learning is faster and easier for students. Instructors have found that our approach works well in self-paced, instructor-led, and "blended" learning environments. The Labyrinth approach has many key features, including the following:

■ *Concise concept discussions* followed by Hands-On exercises that give students experience with those concepts right away.

■ *Figures* are always in close context with the text so no figure numbers are necessary.

■ *Quick Reference* sections summarize key tasks with generic steps that will work without repeating an exercise. These can be particularly useful during open-book tests.

■ *Hands-On exercises* are carefully written and repeatedly tested to be absolutely reliable. Many exercise steps are illustrated with figures to make them easier to follow.

■ *Skill Builder exercises* provide additional practice on key skills using less detailed exercise steps as the student progresses through the lesson.

We are now expanding our book list by adapting this approach to teaching other application programs in addition to Microsoft® Office, including Intuit® QuickBooks®, Adobe Photoshop Elements®, Macromedia® Dreamweaver®, digital photography, and more.

Comprehensive Support: This course is also supported on the Labyrinth website with a comprehensive instructor support package that includes detailed lesson plans, PowerPoint presentations, a course syllabus, extensive test banks, and more. Our unique WebSims allow students to perform realistic exercises with the web, email, and application program tasks that would be difficult to set up in a computer lab.

We are grateful to the many teachers who have used Labyrinth titles and suggested improvements to us during the 10 years we have been writing and publishing books. *Web Page Design with XHTML/CSS* has benefited greatly from the reviewing and suggestions of Jay Goldberg, Jupiter Community High School, Adult Education Department (Jupiter, FL); Bill Lewallen, Vision Magic (Palm Springs, CA); Isaac Snowden, Berkeley Adult School (Berkeley, CA); John Thacher, Gwinnett Technical College (Lawrenceville, GA); Lynne Weldon, Aiken Technical College (Aiken, SC); and Kathy Yeomans, Ventura Adult & Continuing Education (Ventura, CA).

How This Book Is Organized

The information in this book is presented so that you master the fundamental skills first, and then build on those skills as you work with the more comprehensive topics.

Visual Conventions

This book uses many visual and typographic cues to guide you through the lessons. This page provides examples and describes the function of each cue.

Anything you should type at the keyboard is printed in this typeface.

Tips, Notes, and Warnings are used throughout the text to draw attention to certain topics.

These margin notes indicate shortcut keys for executing a task described in the text.

Quick Reference tables provide generic instructions for key tasks. Only perform these tasks if you are instructed to do so in an exercise.

This icon indicates the availability of a web-based simulation for an exercise or other online content. You many need to use a WebSim if your computer lab is not set up to support particular exercises.

Hands-On exercises are introduced immediately after concept discussions. They provide detailed, step-by-step tutorials so you can master the skills presented.

The Concepts Review section includes both true/false and multiple choice questions designed to gauge your understanding of concepts.

Skill Builder exercises provide additional hands-on practice with moderate assistance.

Assessment exercises test your skills by describing the correct results without providing specific instructions on how to achieve them.

Critical Thinking exercises are the most challenging. They provide generic instructions, allowing you to use your skills and creativity to achieve the result you envision.

About the Author

Alec Fehl (BM, Music Production and Engineering, and MCSE A+, NT-CIP, ACE, ACI certified) has been a technical writer, computer consultant, and web application developer since 1999. After graduating from the prestigious Berklee College of Music in Boston, he set off for Los Angeles with the promise of being a rock star. After 10 years gigging in L.A., teaching middle school math, and auditioning for the Red Hot Chili Peppers (he didn't get the gig), he and his wife Jacqui moved to Asheville, North Carolina, where Alec now teaches computer classes at Asheville-Buncombe Technical Community College. Recently Alec was named 2007 Adjunct Teacher of the Year at AB-Tech Community College. Alec is a co-author of Labyrinth's *Microsoft Office 2007: Essentials* and *Computer Concepts and Windows XP/Vista* and author of *Microsoft PowerPoint 2007: Comprehensive*.

Unit 1

Basic Skills

In this unit, you will learn the fundamentals of website planning and design as you explore the differences between how web pages display in different browsers. While focusing on the separation of structure from presentation, you will begin writing valid XHTML code and experimenting with CSS. You will learn about a variety of software tools, which aid in the manual coding process. Once you are comfortable with the foundational concepts, you will work with text structures—including headings, paragraphs, and lists—as you work towards making your web pages accessible to search engines, screen readers, and other user agents. Once the text is in place, you will learn about image file formats, basic image editing techniques, and how to acquire images for your website. With this knowledge, you will then add images and backgrounds to your pages. Finally, you will work with hyperlinks to link pages, create email links, and link to other documents and rich media.

LESSON 1

Introducing Web Technologies

In this lesson, you will learn about technologies and nomenclature common to working with websites. You will learn the importance of testing your web pages in a variety of browsers. You will also learn to plan a site's purpose, basic layout, and page hierarchy as you become familiar with design standards.

LESSON OBJECTIVES

After studying this lesson, you will be able to:

- Differentiate between a web page and a website
- Identify various types of software used to deliver and view web pages
- Plan and wire frame a website
- Recognize industry standard layout principles

Case Study: Planning a Website

Haylie—an origami artist who sells her paper creations for weddings, corporate functions, and personal collections—wishes to create a website for her new home business, Folding Under Pressure. After researching web technologies to learn how websites work, she decides to start sketching out the page structure to get an idea for what creating her site will encompass.

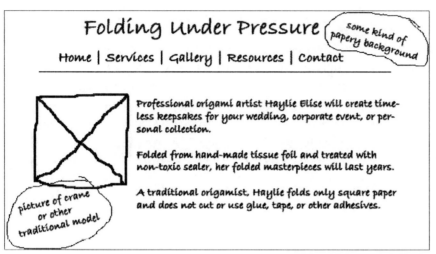

This is Haylie's hand sketch of one possible web page layout.

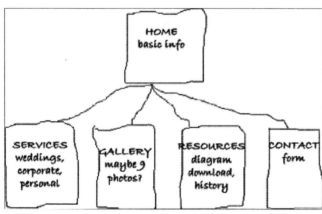

A hand sketch of the page hierarchy helps to define page function.

Learning About the Web

Many different entities and technologies are involved in making websites work. There are individual web pages. There are collections of pages known as websites. There is software to share, view, and create websites. Finally, there are organizations that, to a degree, regulate the Internet.

Web Page Defined

A *web page* is simply a document displaying text, images, video, or other media that you view in a *web browser* (software, such as Internet Explorer). A web page, though able to display graphics and video, is comprised of nothing more than text, meaning one may be created by typing words in a text editor like Notepad. Every web page actually has two "views." There is the view you see in a web browser, which displays the text, images, video, and other media. Then there is the source code view, or the raw code that was typed to create the web page. The source code is viewable in any text editor. Typing the source code necessary to create a valid web page is simple. You just need to know the secret language of HTML, which you will begin learning in Lesson 2, Working with HTML, XHTML, and CSS. Some of the source code text is special code that tells a web browser to display the web page content in certain colors or to display an image, video, or other media object.

This is a web page as viewed in a web browser.

This is the same page, but viewed in a text editor. An HTML web page is nothing more than text.

```
<html>
<head>
<title>Energy Information Administration - EIA - Official Energy
Statistics from the U.S. Government</title>
<meta name="description" content="Energy Information Administration -
EIA - Official Energy Statistics from the U.S. Government">
<link rel="stylesheet"
href="http://www.eia.doe.gov/styles/eia_sitewideF.css" type="text/css">
</head>

<body bgColor="#ffffff" leftMargin="0" topMargin="0" marginwidth="0"
marginheight="0">
<script language="JavaScript">InsertEIAHeaderCode();</script>
<table width="95%"  border="1" bordercolor="#FFFFFF" cellpadding="0"
cellspacing="0">
  <tr>
    <td height="52" colspan="2" bordercolor="#FFFFFF"> <img
src="http://www.eia.doe.gov/images/eia_picts3.jpg" width="1028"
height="50" alt="various energy pictures as top page border">
```

Website Defined

A *website* is a collection of web pages that deal with a similar subject. For example, rather than having a single web page with so much text that users have to continually scroll down, the website developer may decide to create several individual web pages, each with only a little text. These pages will then be linked together in such a way that users can jump back and forth between them. The collection of these related web pages is a website.

Site Root

All pages in a website must reside in the same folder, referred to as the *site root*. The site root folder may be further organized with subfolders to hold images, media, or web pages for different sections of the site. You may physically name the site root folder anything you like, such as My Website, Site Files, MyCompany.com, or any other name you like. However, this folder is always referred to generically as the site root.

Normally, there are at least two copies of the site root. One copy, called the *local site root,* resides on your computer. When a web page needs to be updated, you edit the file in the local site root. A second copy of the site root, called the *remote site root,* resides on the web server. It is the files in the remote site root that users see when they browse to your website. By keeping these two site roots separate, you can perform updates to web pages in the local site root and check them over before transferring the files to the web server, where users will actually see the updates. You will learn how to transfer files between the local and remote site roots in Lesson 13, Putting It on the Web.

The Internet and Internet Services

When one computer can communicate directly with another computer, they are "networked." Computer networks can contain as few as two computers or as many as millions of computers. The Internet is a worldwide network of computers—meaning that there are millions of computers connected to each other.

The World Wide Web (WWW) is not the Internet. The World Wide Web, or just the web as it is now most commonly called, is one of the many services available on the Internet. The web is used to share websites. Other Internet services include email (used to exchange electronic messages with others), remote administration (used to work with files and programs on a remote computer), and File Transfer Protocol (also known as FTP; used to transfer files across a network). There are many more services available on the Internet, but the web is perhaps the most popular.

Governing Bodies

While there is no organization policing content, there are organizations involved with regulating some aspects of the Internet and the web.

The *Internet Assigned Numbers Authority* (IANA) is responsible for the allocation of Internet Protocol (IP) addresses and the data in Domain Name System (DNS) root nameservers. Whoa! Don't worry. IP addresses and DNS are covered in Lesson 13, Putting It on the Web. For now, just understand the IANA is one of the bodies governing the Internet. IANA is actually operated by the *Internet Corporation for Assigned Names and Numbers* (ICANN). You can find more information at www.iana.org or www.icann.org.

To put it simply, there is no single organization in charge of regulating or policing the content on the Internet, but IANA (which is operated by ICANN) is responsible for keeping things in working order.

Learning About Web Browsers

A *web browser*, also known as a *web client*, is a type of software that allows you to connect to a website and view web pages. There are many different types of web browsers. The most popular web browsers include the following:

- Microsoft Internet Explorer (Win)
- Apple Safari (Win and Mac)
- Mozilla Firefox (Win and Mac)

 NOTE! *Microsoft Internet Explorer for Macintosh is officially discontinued as of 2006. Apple Safari (beta) is currently available for Windows. A final version may even be released by the time this book is published.*

Browser Compatibility

As all web browsers are slightly different and it is impossible to know which browser a potential visitor to your website is using, it is important that you test your web pages in as many browsers as possible. A web page will look one way in Internet Explorer but may look slightly (or significantly) different in Firefox. It's not important that your pages look identical in all browsers, but it is vitally important that all the information you want displayed appears correctly in all browsers. Web pages can also vary greatly when displayed in different versions of the same web browser, such as Internet Explorer 5.5 compared to Internet Explorer 6 or 7. To ensure your web pages function in more than just one browser, you should install various browsers on your computer and test your web pages in each. Installing multiple web browsers is covered in Lesson 3, Using Workspace Tools.

A web page displayed in Microsoft Internet Explorer 6

The same web page displayed in Microsoft Internet Explorer 5.5

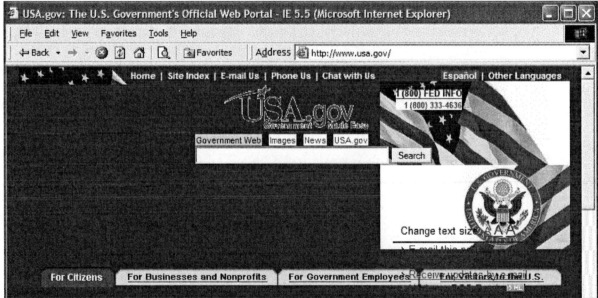

This web page is not even usable in Internet Explorer 5.5!

Standards Compliance

Not all browsers render pages the same way because not all browsers are truly standards-compliant. The World Wide Web Consortium (W3C) recommends standards for HTML authors, and browser manufacturers can choose to adhere to those standards or not in addition to adding support for their own proprietary codes. The result is a variety of browsers that interpret HTML code differently. By writing your code in accordance with the standards set forth by the W3C, your code will be more easily understood and edited by other developers— and you stand a better chance of the page functioning as expected in the largest number of browsers. In fact, the W3C offers free online validation tools that can be used to verify that your code is standards-compliant. You will learn about these validation tools later in this book.

Storing Your Exercise Files

Throughout this book you will be referred to files in a folder that corresponds to the lesson number you are studying (for example, "the Lesson 01 folder"). You can store your exercise files on various media, such as a USB flash drive, the My Documents folder, or a network drive at a school or company. Appendix A, Storing Your Exercise Files provides detailed instructions on downloading and unzipping the exercise files to your storage location.

  Hands-On 1.1   **Compare Browser Rendering**

In this exercise, you will compare the same web page in a variety of browsers to see that different browsers can render the same page differently.

Before You Begin: *If you have not done so already, please turn to the Downloading the Student Exercise Files section of Appendix A, Storing Your Exercise Files for instructions on how to retrieve the student exercise files for this book from the Labyrinth website and unzipping the files to your file storage location for use in this and future lessons.*

1. Open your Lesson 01 folder and double-click the file named compare_browser_rendering.htm.

NOTE! *Throughout this book, filenames will be referred to with their filename extensions. Your computer may be configured to hide filename extensions (the default setting in Windows). Your file may display as simply compare_browser_rendering.*

Your default web browser launches and displays the page.

2. Follow the prompts on the web page to complete this exercise.

Introducing Design Standards

While there is no right or wrong way to design a web page, there are strong choices and poor choices. Strong choices include those that aid in the overall usability of your site (so users don't get lost or frustrated trying to locate information on your site). Additionally, the presence of certain elements such as a *masthead* or *navigation bar* has become an unofficial standard, as these are things users expect to see. Similarly, other elements and concepts that were once popular, such as *splash pages*(which are discussed later in this lesson), should now be avoided because they detract from the user's experience and slow their browsing.

As an XHTML coder, you may not even be designing anything yourself; instead, you may farm out all of your graphic design to an artist and then recreate their vision with XHTML code and the artwork they provide. Even so, you should still know about a few basic concepts, such as:

- Usability
- Accessibility
- Standardized design layouts
- Consistency in design
- Breaking the rules
- Working with multiple layouts
- Relevancy of graphics
- Mystery meat navigation
- Splash pages

Usability

Usability refers to how easy it is for people to use your website. Google is a prime example of a usable site. No fancy bells or whistles. No animation. No snowflakes falling from the top of the screen. No background music. The site is just a few lines of text and a search box—plain and simple. And Google is one of the most visited websites on the Internet.

Many website owners (and designers) make the mistake of designing their sites for themselves rather than for the people who will be visiting the sites. As a developer, you must walk a very fine line between keeping your client happy while steering them away from poor design choices. A client may think it's "really cool" to have a three-minute video playing on the homepage. But people visiting the site will quickly lose interest waiting for it to download. Additionally, users will feel their time is wasted on subsequent returns to the site if they have to watch the movie again.

Web Images Video News Maps Gmail more ▾   iGoogle | Sign in

Google™

Advanced Search
Preferences
Language Tools

[Google Search]   [I'm Feeling Lucky]

Advertising Programs - Business Solutions - About Google

Make Google Your Homepage!

©2007 Google

The sparsely designed but easy to use Google website is one of the most popular on the Internet.

Accessibility

Usability should not be confused with *accessibility*. Accessibility refers to how easily your site can be accessed by people with disabilities (visual, auditory, physical, speech, cognitive, or neurological), or by people using alternative devices to browse your site such as screen readers, mobile phones, or personal digital assistants (PDAs). In fact, the 1998 amendment to section 508 of the Federal Rehabilitation Act requires that all federal agencies make their electronic and information technology available (accessible) to people with disabilities. Government sites require it by law. Other websites should just do it because it is a good professional practice. Throughout this book, you will learn how to increase your page's accessibility. Following are three basic items to remember, which will improve accessibility as you work through this book (these will make more sense once you have worked through later lessons, but keep them in the back of your head for now):

- ■ **Alt attribute**—Use the alt attribute for all images in order to provide a text alternative. This is required by XHTML. You will learn more about this in Lesson 6, Working with Images.

- ■ **Link text**—Use text in your hyperlinks that makes sense if read out of context. For example, "click here" makes no sense if read alone. "Send us email" makes more sense. You will learn more about this in Lesson 7, Working with Hyperlinks.

- ■ **Organization**—Use structural elements such as headings, paragraphs, and lists to define the document. You will learn more about this in Lesson 4, Working with Text.

Standardized Design Layouts

Users expect to see things in the same location no matter what website they visit. Typically, your eyes gravitate to the top or left side of a web page when looking for hyperlinks to click to go to other pages. Similarly, the area at the top of a web page (the masthead) is normally reserved for a company logo, name, slogan, and other branding elements. When the main navigation on a web page appears underneath all the content, users can become frustrated and leave your site, never to return.

TIP! *The word "branding" is used throughout the advertising world in print, web, and other promotional materials when referring to a company's identity and name recognition.*

Placing the navigation towards the bottom of the page reduces a page's usability. Not all users will immediately see the navigation because they are used to seeing navigation on top. Users with a smaller screen may need to scroll to see the navigation, reducing the page usability even further.

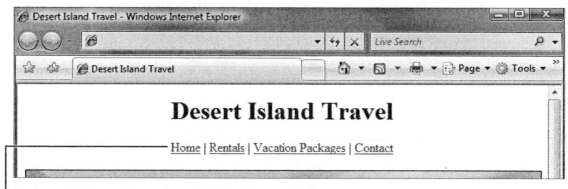

Placing navigation at the top (or to the left) of the document ensures that all users will see it regardless of their screen size.

Consistency in Design

Users shouldn't have to learn how your site works with every new page. They don't like it when each page looks completely different. Users like to know where everything is, no matter what page they are on. Keep the layouts of your pages similar so users can easily navigate your pages and find the content they need. Navigation elements, branding, and other information should be displayed consistently throughout all pages. When the location of navigation bars or other elements changes, users get confused and frustrated and they are less likely to return to your site. Similarly, colors and layout should be consistent so users know they are still on the same website.

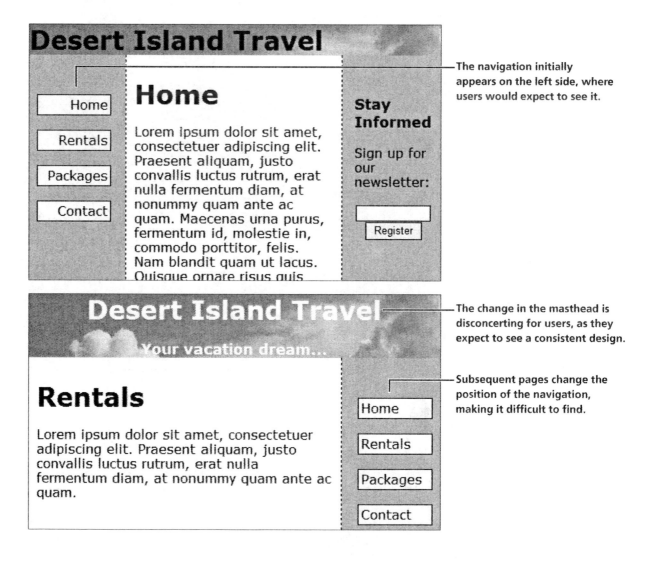

The navigation initially appears on the left side, where users would expect to see it.

The change in the masthead is disconcerting for users, as they expect to see a consistent design.

Subsequent pages change the position of the navigation, making it difficult to find.

Multiple Layouts

The exception to this rule is designing one layout for the homepage and another layout for all the rest of the pages, sometimes called the *inner pages* (the pages viewable once users have passed your homepage and are inside the meat of your site).

The homepage has a layout that differs from the rest of the pages.

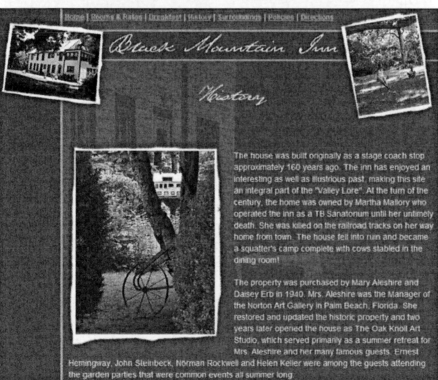

All other pages share a common layout.

Relevancy of Graphics

New designers often make the mistake of putting "cool" images on their sites just because they (or the client) like the images. Graphics should have relevance to the site content and should be used only when they enhance the design. Graphics should not distract the user from the content. In the old days of HTML, *spacer GIFs* were often used to help create a layout. Spacer GIFs are transparent images, usually 1 pixel by 1 pixel, which could be stretched via HTML attributes to be any height or width. Because they are transparent, they don't display in the browser, but they act as shims and create space—pushing elements over or down. Nowadays, these nonessential graphics are frowned upon in favor of accomplishing the same spacing with CSS paddings and margins.

 TIP! *Even if graphics are relevant, don't overdo it. Too many graphics on a page distracts from the text. Many sites place banner advertisements at the top of a page with several more down the sides. It may be necessary to balance your layout between income-generating banner ads and usability.*

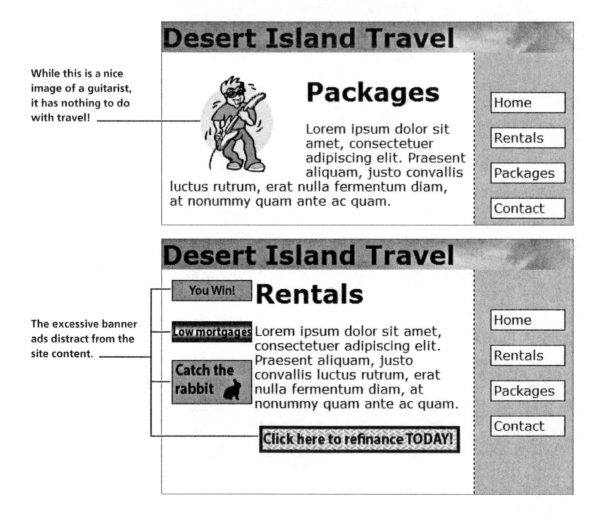

While this is a nice image of a guitarist, it has nothing to do with travel!

The excessive banner ads distract from the site content.

Mystery Meat Navigation

Navigation links should clearly indicate their function. For example, a link to a Contact page should read "contact" or something similar. Some designers think it is very artistic to have elaborate graphic buttons that don't indicate their linked page until the user points to them. While this may look cool to the designer, this is not user-friendly. When navigation links fail to identify their linked pages, they are referred to as *mystery meat navigation*. This type of navigation is a poor design choice because even though it may look artsy to the designer, it is not usable by the people visiting the site.

The stylized design may look cool to the website owner, but users have no idea where each button will take them until they point to it or click.

Only when users point to a button do they have any indication of where that link will go. This is not user-friendly.

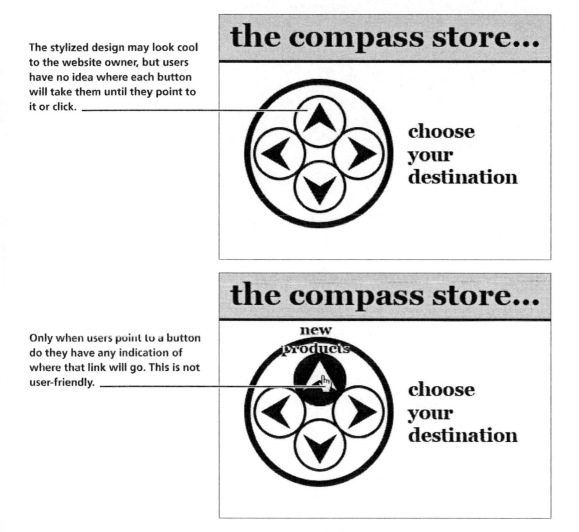

Splash Pages

A *splash page* is one that contains no real content, but rather a large picture or embedded media file meant to capture the user's attention. Time has proven that splash pages lose more attention than they get. And they are an annoyance to most users. Most splash pages have a "welcome" or "click to enter" link so users can enter the rest of the site, which contains the actual content. Not only are these pages a waste of time for users (Why click to enter the site? Why not just display content on the homepage right away?), but they can hurt search engine rankings. Remember that search engines look primarily for text on the page. A big picture or video file won't be recognized by a search engine, screen reader, or other alternative device as valid content. It is better to include actual content on your homepage, even if it is a short paragraph.

This splash page provides no useful content, just an annoying additional link users must click to gain access to real information.

Breaking the Rules

Remember that there is no list of rules that state "you must always do this" or "you must never do that" when designing a web page. However, there are certain design features that are generally accepted as providing a high level of usability and accessibility. It is okay to design against these unofficial standards as long as the following are true:

- You know you are breaking the rules

- You are breaking the rules for a specific purpose (the client demands it, the site is for a very targeted user group, or some other compelling reason)

- You can clearly articulate your reasons for breaking the rules

UNOFFICIAL "RULES" FOR DESIGNING A WEBSITE

Rule	Example
Adhere to "standardized" layouts	Place the company branding at the top and place navigation towards the top or down the left side.
Maintain a consistent design across all pages	Place masthead, navigation, footer, and other elements in the same location on all pages. Use the same color scheme on all pages.
Graphics should be relevant and not overwhelming	Use graphics that enhance the design and are relevant to the content. Do not use so many graphics on a page that the images distract from the text.

UNOFFICIAL "RULES" FOR DESIGNING A WEBSITE (CONTINUED)

Rule	Example
Avoid mystery meat navigation	Navigation links and buttons should clearly indicate the page or section to which they link.
Avoid splash pages	Do not design a homepage with only visual content and an "enter" link.
Break the rules	Break the rules only when you can clearly articulate your reasons for doing so.

 Hands-On 1.2   Identify Poor and Strong Usability Features

In this exercise, you will explore a website with very poor usability features. You will then view a redesign of the website that is much more usable.

Navigate a Site with Poor Usability

1. Open your Lesson 01 folder, if necessary, and double-click the file named poor_usability.htm.
   Your default web browser launches and displays the page.

2. Navigate the site as best you can, then either create a blank word processing document in your Lesson 01 folder named **Poor Usability** or obtain a worksheet from your instructor.

3. Answer the following questions in your Poor Usability document:
   - Was this site easy to navigate? Why or why not?
   - Did you feel like you were on the same website as you navigated from page to page? Why or why not?
   - Describe any changes you would make to the homepage.
   - Describe any changes you would make to the Contact page.
   - Describe any changes you would make to the Gallery page.
   - Describe any changes you would make to the Specials page.
   - Describe any changes you would make to the Privacy page.

4. Close your browser.

Navigate a Site with Strong Usability

5. Open your Lesson 01 folder, if necessary, and double-click the file named strong_usability.htm.
   Your default web browser launches and displays the page.

6. Navigate the site as best you can, then create a blank word processing document in your Lesson 01 folder named **Strong Usability**.

7. Answer the following questions in your Strong Usability document:
   - Was this site easy to navigate? Why or why not?
   - Did you feel like you were on the same website as you navigated from page to page? Why or why not?
   - Describe any changes you would make to the homepage.
   - Describe any changes you would make to the Contact page.
   - Describe any changes you would make to the Gallery page.
   - Describe any changes you would make to the Specials page.
   - Describe any changes you would make to the Privacy page.

8. Close your browser and your Lesson 01 folder.

Planning a Website

The first step in creating a website is to plan. Some questions to ask yourself (or your client) are:

- Why do you think you need a website?
- What do you want to accomplish with the website?
- Who will be using your website?

Being able to clearly articulate the answers to these questions will help you when designing the site because you will have a clear understanding of the purpose and target audience (the people you want to draw to your site). The more planning done up front, the less time and money will be wasted later by making huge modifications to near-complete web pages and graphics.

Statement of Purpose

Knowing why, or if, you need a website can save a lot of wasted time. If your reason for having a website is "because everyone else has one," your time and money may be better spent doing something other than creating a website! Every website-development project should start with a *statement of purpose*. This can be as short as a single sentence or as long as a few pages. It is simply a statement that outlines the general purpose of the website. It is a good idea to also state what the website will not do so the website owner isn't surprised by "missing functionality" when the website is completed.

A statement of purpose also helps to keep the project on track and helps to prioritize time and money. As clients, designers, artists, programmers, family, and friends all begin to voice opinions during the development of a site, their ideas can be checked against the statement of purpose to determine if what they want is within the defined purpose of the site.

Example

The following is a statement of purpose for a flower shop's website:

The purpose of our website is to promote our business by displaying several photo galleries of our flower arrangements. The website will also act as a sales tool. We can direct clients to specific web pages while on the phone to discuss flower arrangement options. It will not be possible to place online orders.

 Hands-On 1.3   **Write a Statement of Purpose**

In this exercise, you will write a statement of purpose for Folding Under Pressure, for your own site, or for a site provided by your instructor. Ask your instructor or choose one of the following options to complete.

Option 1: Write a Statement of Purpose for the Folding Under Pressure Site

1. Haylie's origami business, Folding Under Pressure, is considering developing a website. She sells her folded works mainly as wedding centerpieces and table decorations, as corporate convention gifts, and to personal collectors. She has many photos of her work. She would also like to educate people on the history of origami. In a word processing document, write a statement of purpose for the potential Folding Under Pressure website. Be sure to state two or three things that the website will accomplish and at least one thing the website will not do. Save your document as **Statement of Purpose FUP** in your Lesson 01 folder.

Option 2: Write a Statement of Purpose for an Existing Site

2. Find an existing website or browse to one suggested by your instructor. Study the homepage and a few inner pages until you are comfortable with the site's navigation, functions, and purpose. Imagine that the website does not yet exist and, in a word processing document, write a statement of purpose for the website. Be sure to state two or three things the website will accomplish and at least one thing the website will not do. Save your document as **Statement of Purpose ES** in your Lesson 01 folder.

Option 3: Write a Statement of Purpose for Your Own Site

3. Imagine a website you would like to create yourself. In a word processing document, write a statement of purpose for the website. Be sure to state two or three things the website will accomplish and at least one thing the website will not do. Save your document as **Statement of Purpose Mine** in your Lesson 01 folder.

Organizing Page Content

The next step after writing a statement of purpose is to begin organizing your content into categories or pages. Imagine what links (buttons) you might have in your site's navigation bar. An online store may include Home, Products, and Contact Us while a website that offers online guitar lessons may have categories of Home, Styles, and Instructors. Your website content should dictate your categories, which can then be used as your main links. Making a list of main categories and the content planned for each category is a good way to get a feel for how many pages your site will encompass. The Folding Under Pressure website can be organized as follows:

- **Home**—Basic information about the company

- **Services**—Detailed information about each of the services offered

- **Gallery**—Variety of photos of Haylie's origami

- **Resources**—Origami history, rules, styles, and diagram downloads for users wanting to try folding paper themselves

- **Contact**—Online form for users to send inquiries

Page Hierarchy

Navigating a website is an example of *nonlinear branching*. Starting from the homepage, users can browse to any page they like by clicking a link. They do not have to view the pages in a specific order, as if navigating pages along a straight line. This concept of nonlinear branching means users should be able to get to any page on your site from any other page. (This is true of relatively small sites. Larger sites consisting of hundreds of pages are not likely to allow browsing to any page from any page.) Making a sketch of your page hierarchy will help you when designing the layout because it will show you how many pages your site will have, and thus how many main navigation links you need. This is also the time to decide if there is too much content on a single page. Of course, "too much" is subjective. However, it is generally accepted that about two to three screen lengths of content is about all users can take in. Any more than that and the page becomes overwhelming.

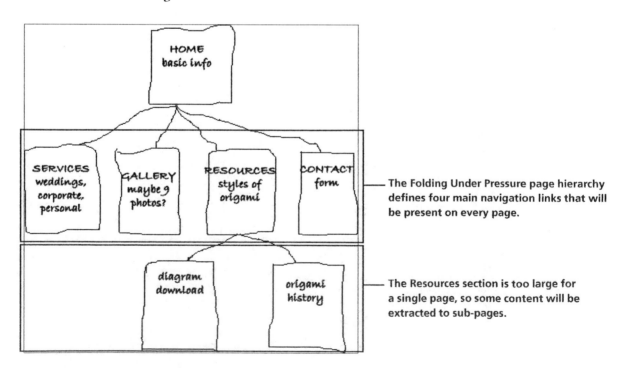

The Folding Under Pressure page hierarchy defines four main navigation links that will be present on every page.

The Resources section is too large for a single page, so some content will be extracted to sub-pages.

Wire-framing

In web design, a *wire frame* is a rudimentary visual representation of a web page. It shows the basic layout of page elements and can be used by a graphic artist to design the artwork for a website. A wire frame can be created with a pencil and paper or with a computer drawing program such as Adobe® Photoshop®, Fireworks®, or Illustrator®.

The wire frame for the Folding Under Pressure homepage

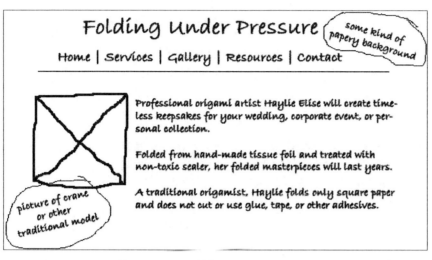

The graphic artist's composite rendering of the actual web page based on the wire frame

Hands-On 1.4   Create a Wire Frame

In this exercise, you will create a wire frame of an alternate homepage design.

1. Sketch an alternate layout for the Folding Under Pressure homepage. You may use pencil and paper or a computer drawing program. Here are some suggestions for altering the wire frame shown earlier in this lesson:

   ■ Place the navigation links elsewhere on the page, like down the side. Be sure they are still located in a place where users will find them!

   ■ Alter the placement of the text and the graphic, or include more graphics on the page.

   ■ Use artwork in conjunction with, or instead of, the text navigation links.

   ■ Change the masthead.

2. If you chose to use a computer drawing program, save your drawing as **Wire Frame** in your Lesson 01 folder.
   You now have a solid understanding of what goes into planning and designing a website!

Concepts Review

True/False Questions

1. A web page is a collection of individual files.   TRUE   FALSE

2. The web and the Internet are the same thing.   TRUE   FALSE

3. The Internet offers many services, including email and the web.   TRUE   FALSE

4. The IANA and ICANN are responsible for policing content on the Internet.   TRUE   FALSE

5. A web browser and a web client are the same thing.   TRUE   FALSE

6. If your web page looks good in Internet Explorer, it will look good in any other TRUE   FALSE
   browser.

7. You should vary the design and layout of every page on your website to keep it inter-   TRUE   FALSE
   esting for users.

8. Writing a statement of purpose can help keep a project on track and can help priori-   TRUE   FALSE
   tize time and money during development.

9. Splash pages are popular among users because they set the mood for a site.   TRUE   FALSE

10. To say that a site is accessible means that it is easy to use and navigate.   TRUE   FALSE

Multiple Choice Questions

1. What does section 508 of the Federal Rehabilitation Act require?
   a. All federal agencies must maintain a website.
   b. The websites of all federal agencies must make their online content accessible to people with disabilities.
   c. Navigation links must appear on the left side or at the top of federal websites.
   d. Graphics must be limited to no more than 10 per page for the benefit of users on slower dial-up Internet connections.

2. Who or what is responsible for regulating the content appearing on public websites?
   a. IANA
   b. ICANN
   c. The Federal Rehabilitation Act
   d. No one is responsible for regulating website content.

3. Which statement best describes the difference between usability and accessibility?
   a. Usability refers to your site's ability to make its content available to people with disabilities. Accessibility refers to how easy it is for people to navigate your site and find the information they need.
   b. Accessibility refers to your site's ability to make its content available to people with disabilities. Usability refers to how easy it is for people to navigate your site and find the information they need.
   c. Accessibility refers to adhering to standardized design practices. Usability is mandated by federal guidelines.
   d. Usability and accessibility refer to the same thing; the terms can be used interchangeably.

4. When sketching a wire frame, where should the branding go?
   a. Footer
   b. Main content area
   c. Masthead
   d. Sidebar

Skill Builders

Skill Builder 1.1   Pre-plan a Website

In this exercise, you will create a statement of purpose and page hierarchy for a new website.

Statement of Purpose

A client who sells homemade candy bars, Ramble on Chocoholics, has come to you with the following needs for a website: 1) Build company name recognition so people know what Ramble On Chocoholics is; 2) Sell candy bars online; 3) Make sure users of the site can easily find all products; 4) Make sure people with disabilities can use the website and buy the candy bars.

1. Create a word processing document named **sb-Candy Plan** in your Lesson 01 folder and write a statement of purpose for the Ramble On Chocoholics website.

Page Hierarchy

2. Based on your statement of purpose and the client's needs, create a list of at least three other pages for the website and state what content will appear on each of these pages. Write this information below the statement of purpose in the sb-Candy Plan document.

Skill Builder 1.2   Create a Wire Frame

In this exercise, you will create a wire frame for Ramble On Chocoholics.

Before You Begin: You must complete Skill Builder 1.1 before beginning this exercise.

1. Based on your statement of purpose and page hierarchy from the last exercise, sketch a wire frame of a proposed homepage. Remember that the homepage should capture the interest of a user while selling the company product. Don't forget the design standards you learned about in this lesson.

2. You may sketch your wire frame by hand, but if you choose to create it with a computer drawing program, save it to your Lesson 01 folder as **sb-Candy WF**.

Skill Builder 1.3   Check Browser Rendering

In this exercise, you will explore ways to test page designs in multiple browsers when you have only a single browser installed.

Some websites offer a service where you enter a URL to a web page and they create screen shots of the page in a variety of browsers so you can see how your page looks in different browsers. One such free service is BrowserShots.org.

1. Launch a web browser and navigate to **browsershots.org**.

2. Read about their free service and browse their screenshots and current queue.

3. Use your favorite search engine to find at least two other websites that offer similar services.

4. Create a blank word processing document in your Lesson 01 folder named **sb-Browser Shots**. Answer the following questions in your document:

   ■ In your own words, describe the service that browsershots.org and other sites like it provide.

   ■ Do you think this is a worthwhile service? Why or why not?

   ■ Provide the URLs for at least two other websites that offer a service similar to browsershots.org. Are these sites also free? How do they compare to browsershots.org?

5. Save and close your document when you are finished.

Assessments

Assessment 1.1   Write a Statement of Purpose

In this exercise, you will write a statement of purpose.

1. Think of a website you would like to create for your business or organization: a band, a little league team, etc. Write a statement of purpose that clearly states what the website should do and what it will not do. Type your statement of purpose in a word processing document. Save the document as **as-My Statement** in your Lesson 01 folder.

Assessment 1.2   Organize Content and Create Page Hierarchy

In this exercise, you will organize site content and sketch the page hierarchy.

Before You Begin: *You must complete Assessment 1.1 before beginning this exercise.*

1. Based on your statement of purpose from the last exercise, create a list of categories for your web content. Save your list as a new word processing document named **as-My Content** in your Lesson 01 folder. Keep the following points in mind:
   - These categories should translate to individual pages.
   - You may consider creating a few sub-pages if one area has a lot of content.
   - Be sure to explain what content each category/page will hold.

2. Sketch a diagram showing how the pages relate to each other.

Assessment 1.3   Create a Wire Frame

In this exercise, you will create a wire frame of your proposed layout.

Before You Begin: *You must complete Assessment 1.2 before beginning this exercise.*

1. Use the following guidelines to sketch a wire frame of the layout for the homepage you defined in the last exercise:
   - Include a masthead with the appropriate elements and don't make it too big.
   - Include navigation links where users will find them.
   - Include a sample of actual content so as not to accidentally create a splash page.

2. If your design calls for the homepage to have one design and all other pages to have a different design, create a wire frame for the "inner pages."

3. If you have created this in a computer drawing program, save it as **as-My Wire Frame** in your Lesson 01 folder.

Critical Thinking

Critical Thinking 1.1   Research Web Browsers

Use a search engine such as Google and search for a term such as **web browser comparison**.

Answer the following questions in a word processor document, saving it as **ct-Web Browsers** *in your Lesson 01 folder:*

1. Are there more web browsers available than just Microsoft Internet Explorer and Mozilla Firefox? (Be sure to state your source of information.)

2. Which is the most widely used web browser? (Be sure to state your source of information.)

3. Why is it recommended to test your web pages in a variety of web browsers?

4. If you were to have three web browsers on your personal computer for testing the web pages you create, which web browsers would you choose to install? Why?

Critical Thinking 1.2   Identify Poor Design Techniques

In this exercise, you will research poor design techniques.

1. Create a blank document with a word processor or spreadsheet program that contains a table with 11 rows and 3 columns.

2. Type the following as column headers in the cells across the top row:
   - **Live Example URL**
   - **Design Element**
   - **Why It Is a Poor Choice**

3. Save the blank document to your Lesson 01 folder as **ct-Bad Web Design**.

4. Launch your web browser and navigate to Google.com or another search engine.

5. Search for the phrase **bad web design**.

6. Visit at least three of the sites found by the search engine and read about poor web design techniques.

7. Return to the search engine and search for **bad web design examples**.

8. In your ct-Bad Web Design document, describe 10 examples of poor design choices by completing the table you created at the beginning of this exercise:
   - **Live Example URL**—Record the URL to the web page with the poor design choice. (You can copy the URL from the address bar of your web browser and paste it into the table in your document.)
   - **Design Element**—Describe the poor design feature.
   - **Why It Is a Poor Choice**—Describe why you believe this to be a poor design choice.

9. Save and close your document when you are finished.

Working with HTML, XHTML, and CSS

In this lesson, you will get a brief history and the basic concepts of HTML, XHTML, and CSS. You will learn to differentiate between a document's structure and presentation and to identify which languages to use for creating structure and presentation. You will view existing HTML code and even create your first web page.

LESSON OBJECTIVES

After studying this lesson, you will be able to:

- Describe the differences between HTML, XHTML, and CSS
- Differentiate between structure and presentation
- Write basic HTML code
- Create a valid XHTML document structure

Case Study: Learning a New Language

Haylie has ordered business cards featuring her website address. Now she would like to start learning how to create a simple web page. She begins by researching the terms HTML, XHTML, and CSS. Once she has learned the differences between these languages, she will begin working on a test document using XHTML and CSS before delving into the design of her actual website. She has enlisted the help of her friend Miguel, a graphic artist, to help with the design on her website.

```
<!DOCTYPE html PUBLIC "-//W3C//DTD XHTML 1.0 Transitional//EN"
"http://www.w3.org/TR/xhtml1/DTD/xhtml1-transitional.dtd">
<html xmlns="http://www.w3.org/1999/xhtml">
<head>
<title>My First Web Page</title>
<style type="text/css">
<!--
body {
   background-color: #FFFFCC;
}
p {
   font-family: Arial, Helvetica, sans-serif;
   font-size: 100%;
   color: #000000;
}

-->
</style>
</head>

<body>
<h1>Hello world!</h1>
<p>This is my first Web page.</p>
</body>
</html>
```

This is an example of the XHTML and CSS code Haylie will use to create a simple web page.

Presenting the Past, Present, and Future of HTML

Several languages are used to create web pages. The first was HTML, or Hypertext Markup Language. Development on HTML stopped in 1999 and focus has shifted to XHTML (Extensible Hypertext Markup Language) and CSS (Cascading Style Sheets). HTML allowed web developers to structure their documents with elements such as headings and paragraph text. It also allowed developers to control the appearance, or presentation, of documents such as text size and color. At its most basic, XHTML combines with CSS in an attempt to separate structure from presentation, with XHTML controlling the structure and CSS controlling the presentation. HTML, XHTML, CSS, structure, and presentation are discussed throughout this lesson.

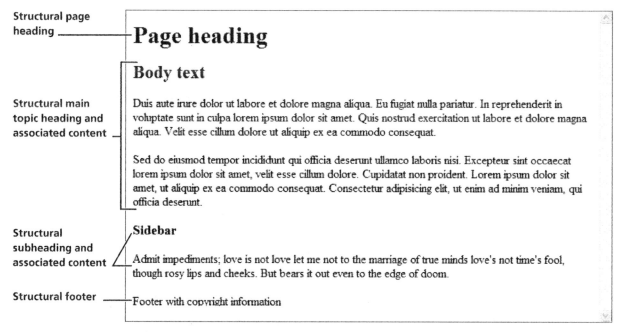

Structural page heading

Structural main topic heading and associated content

Structural subheading and associated content

Structural footer

XHTML strives to define the structure of a document without adding presentational markup.

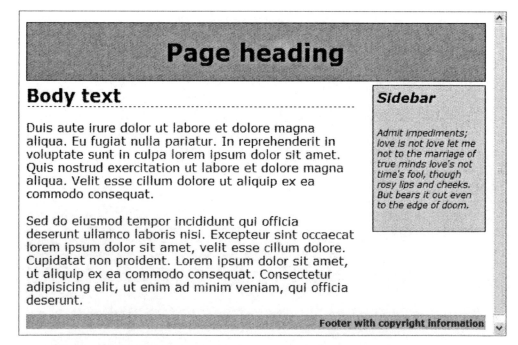

This is the same XHTML document with CSS code added to style the document visually.

HTML

Let's look at HTML word by word. *Hypertext* refers to hyperlinks—the things you click to navigate from one web page to another. Hyperlinks may be text or graphics. *Markup* refers to structured *syntax* (the rules for a computer language). In HTML, the syntax requires angle brackets and quotation marks being in the correct places. Put these together and you have a powerful *language* with which to create web pages.

The Early Years

HTML was created by Tim Berners-Lee in 1990 to help researchers and scientists communicate and exchange data. In 1996, the World Wide Web Consortium (W3C) took over maintaining and developing the HTML specification. Several versions of HTML have been standardized, with version numbers such as HTML 3.2, HTML 4.0, and HTML 4.01. Each subsequent version added functionality, such as the ability to create tables or numbered lists or to center text on a page. The last version of HTML, HTML 4.01, was published in 1999.

Viewing the HTML of an Existing Web Page

Although HTML is being phased out in favor of XHTML (which will be discussed later), HTML forms the basis of XHTML and is, therefore, a good thing to study first. When looking at the HTML code of a web page, you will see bits and pieces of what is displayed on the web page itself—along with other text that is part of the HTML syntax. Don't worry about all that stuff in the angle brackets, like <html>, <head>, <title>, and the others. We'll get to those later in this lesson. Remember, we're just getting started. For now, just realize that there is text in the HTML source code that displays in the browser window.

This HTML code...

...produces this web page.

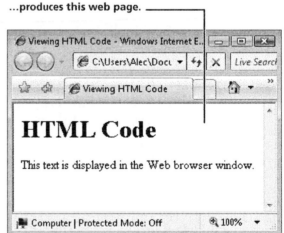

No Special Software Required

An HTML document is a plain text document. Therefore, you don't need any fancy software to create one. Windows users can use the Notepad program that comes free with Windows. Macintosh users can use SimpleText (in OS9 and earlier) or TextEdit (in OS X). While these text editors will do the job, there are other options that we will discuss in Lesson 3, Using Workspace Tools.

Never Use a Word Processor

Don't use a word processor like Microsoft Word or WordPad to type your HTML! Word processors can add formatting characters to your saved document that will render your HTML document invalid. Use a regular, plain, "vanilla" text editor like Notepad (Win) or TextEdit (Mac). In fact, even copying and pasting from a word processing document to a text document can result in invalid HTML.

 TIP! *If you are using TextEdit on a Mac, be sure to set the proper option to save your files as plain text.*

⌐HTML code typed in a word processor looks fine initially, but...

```
<body>

<p align="center">This text was typed in a word processor,
then pasted into Notepad. Notice what has happened to the
quotation marks in the opening P tag at the beginning of this
paragraph.</p>
```

⌐...when pasted into a text document, characters such as the quotation marks can become corrupt.

```
<body>
<p align=█center█>This text was typed in a word
processor, then pasted into Notepad. Notice what has
happened to the quotation marks in the opening P tag at
the beginning of this paragraph.</p>
```

The HTML Language

The HTML language is made up of elements, which are identified by tags. Elements include headings, paragraphs, tables, lists, or anything else that represents a structure. Tags identify the beginning and end of an element. An opening tag, which begins an element, looks like this: `<tagname>`. A closing tag, which ends an element, looks like this: `</tagname>`. Notice that the only difference is that the closing tag contains a forward slash. And there's no such tag as the `<tagname>` tag. We're just using it as an example!

About Tags

Tags can be likened to parentheses in mathematical operations. Just as the parentheses in the mathematical statement 3+(4x5) instruct you to multiply 4x5 first, the HTML tags tell the browser when to start and stop a certain element. An opening tag such as `<b>` instructs the browser to start displaying text as bold while the closing tag `</b>` tells the browser to stop displaying bold. In other words, the `<b>` and `</b>` tags mark the beginning and end of a **bold** element. You will see this example again later in this lesson.

Main Elements of HTML Documents

An HTML document is defined by three main elements that outline the structure of any web page. They are the HTML, HEAD, and BODY elements. The HEAD and BODY elements are both contained, or *nested,* inside the HTML element. Remember, we'll get to the other elements (TITLE, H1, and P) later in this book.

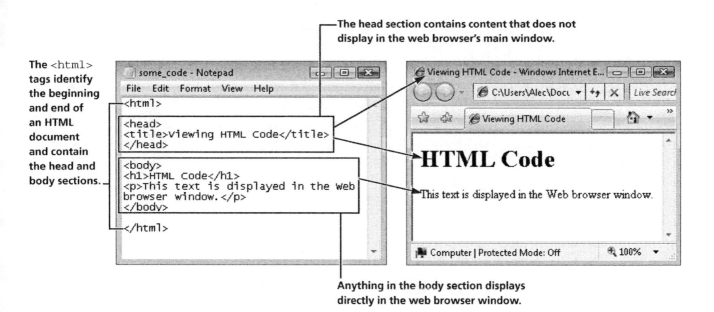

The head section contains content that does not display in the web browser's main window.

The `<html>` tags identify the beginning and end of an HTML document and contain the head and body sections.

Anything in the body section displays directly in the web browser window.

Elements and Tags

As elements and tags are so closely related, the terms are often used interchangeably. However, remember that tags define where an element begins and ends. Any tag that has an associated closing tag is called a *container tag*. In the preceding example, all of the tags are container tags. Notice that the opening `<html>`, `<head>`, `<title>`, `<body>`, and `<p>` tags all have an associated closing tag. Additionally, container tags surround (or contain) other bits of text or code. The opening tag tells the browser to start doing something while the closing tag tells the browser to stop. For example, the line `<b>This is bold</b> but this is not bold` tells the browser when to start displaying text as bold and when to stop displaying text as bold. (Technically, the opening `<b>` tag creates a bold *element* while the closing `</b>` tag ends the bold element.) Not all tags are container tags. We'll look at the non-container type (called *replacement tags*) later in this book.

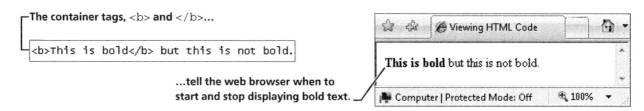

The container tags, `<b>` and `</b>`...

...tell the web browser when to start and stop displaying bold text.

Using Attributes and Values

An HTML element can be modified with an attribute-value pair. For example, you have seen that the `<h1>` tag creates a structural page heading. You can modify that page heading by centering it using the "align" attribute with a value of "center."

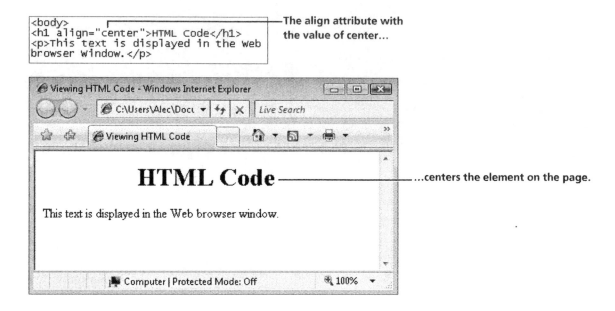

```
<body>
<h1 align="center">HTML Code</h1>
<p>This text is displayed in the web
browser window.</p>
```
The align attribute with the value of center...

...centers the element on the page.

Not all elements can use the same attributes. See Appendix D, Working with HTML/XHTML Tags and Attributes for a list of supported attributes.

 ## Hands-On 2.1   View Sample HTML Code

In this lesson, you will view the HTML code of a web page.

1. Start Internet Explorer.
   Your browser opens and your default homepage is displayed.

2. Press and hold Ctrl while tapping the letter O, then release Ctrl to open the Open dialog box.

 TIP! *In the future, this command will be displayed like this: Use Ctrl + O.*

   The Open dialog box appears, allowing you to browse to a file to open.

3. Click Browse and navigate to your Lesson 02 folder.

4. Select the hello.htm document, click Open, and click OK.
   The web page displays in your browser window.

5. Follow these steps to display the source code for the web page:

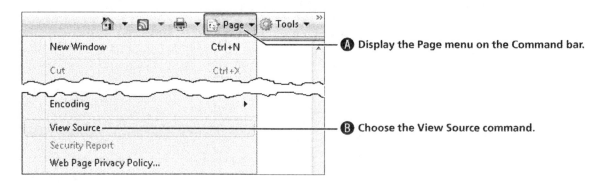

Ⓐ Display the Page menu on the Command bar.

Ⓑ Choose the View Source command.

NOTE! *From this point forward, this type of command will be written like this:*
Choose Page→View Source from the Command bar.

If you are running Win Vista, a security prompt may appear. This helps protect the computer from a virus running a command without your knowledge. This warning appears in Win Vista depending on the computer configuration; it does not appear in Win XP.

6. Click Allow, if you are using Win Vista, and a security warning dialog appears. If you are not running Win Vista, continue with the next step.

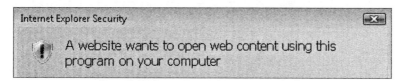

Notepad, or your computer's default text editor, opens and displays the HTML code for the web page.

7. Start Microsoft Word, WordPad, or another word processor and create a blank word processing document in your Lesson 02 folder named **Tags**.

8. In your Tags document, create one list of all the container tags you see in the HTML code. Create another list of all the tags that are not container tags.

9. Save and close your Tags document.

10. Close Notepad. Choose No if you are prompted to save any changes.

11. Close Internet Explorer.

Understanding the Language of XHTML

There are several versions of Extensible Hypertext Markup Language, but it is basically HTML with a few stricter rules.

- A Title element (created by `<title>` tags in the head section) is required.

- All elements must be properly nested.

- All elements must be closed with the appropriate closing tag.

- All tags and attributes must be typed in lowercase letters.

- All attributes require values contained inside quotes.

There are a few more rules you will learn throughout the lesson, and a more complete list is provided later in this book. For now, let's look at this short list in a little more detail.

Title Element

A title element, created by opening and closing title tags, must be present in the head section towards the top of the document. Visually, this creates the text in the web browser's title bar. A title element looks like this:

```
<title>Welcome to My World</title>
```

Proper Nesting

You can use the <b> tag to make text appear bold and the <i> tag to make text appear italic. Again, as these tags add presentation markup to your page, it is best to use CSS for making text bold and italic (if the visual presentation is your goal). However, these tags make for a great example of proper nesting. When elements are properly nested, there is clearly an outer tag and an inner tag, such as:

```
<b><i>This is bold and italic</i></b>
```

Notice the <i></i> element is completely nested inside the <b></b> element. That satisfies the proper nesting requirement. However, this code...

```
<b><i>This is bold and italic</b></i>
```

...is no good! The tags are crisscrossed with no clear outer or inner element.

The order of the elements doesn't matter. For example, reversing the bold and italic elements would be just fine, as long as they were still properly nested, so this...

```
<i><b>This is bold and italic</b></i>
```

...is perfectly acceptable.

Closing Tags

XHTML requires all tags to be closed. For example, in HTML, you could get away with starting a paragraph with the <p> tag, not closing it, and starting a new paragraph:

```
<p>This is the first paragraph.
<p>And this is a second paragraph.
```

This breaks the rules of XHTML. Valid XHTML code looks like this:

```
<p>This is the first paragraph.</p>
<p>And this is a second paragraph.</p>
```

Lowercase Tags

Properly written XHTML must use lowercase letters for all tags. It is not uncommon to view the source of a web page and see HTML code like this:

```
<BODY>
<H1>My Page</H1>
<P>This is my web page
</BODY>
```

However, that is not valid XHTML code as the tags are not lowercase. Valid XHTML looks like this:

```
<body>
<h1>My Page</h1>
<p>This is my web page</p>
</body>
```

Quoted Values

While this was accepted in HTML...

```
<h1 align=center>This headline is centered</h1>
```

...it is not valid XHTML code. All values must be "quoted" as in:

```
<h1 align="center">This headline is centered</h1>
```

Additionally, HTML allows for attributes without values, such as the code to create a checked checkbox: `<input type="checkbox" CHECKED>`

That is not valid XHTML because the CHECKED attribute is uppercase and does not have a value and because the INPUT element is not closed. Valid XHTML looks like this:
`<input type="checkbox" checked="checked" />`

Note that the INPUT element does not have a true closing tag. There is no such thing as `</input>`. To satisfy the XHTML requirement that all elements are closed, the opening tag itself is closed at the end with a slash. You'll learn more about these types of tags, called replacement tags, throughout this book.

XHTML Versions and the DOCTYPE Declaration

So why use XHTML rather than HTML? The simple answer is "because the World Wide Web Consortium says so," but there are other reasons, too. XHTML is also valid *XML*, another markup language, and as such can be integrated more easily into advanced applications. Additionally, there may come a time when web browsers no longer support HTML. Granted, that may not be for another 10 years or more, but any industry professional needs to stay current with the industry standards—and XHTML is the current standard.

The following table lists the current XHTML version specifications and the purpose of each.

XHTML VERSIONS

Version	Purpose
XHTML 1.0 transitional	Same as HTML 4.01, but with stricter rules; allows developers with HTML skills to transition their web pages from HTML to XHTML; also allows the use of older tags not supported by stricter versions of XHTML (deprecated tags)
XHTML 1.0 strict	Similar to XHTML 1.0 transitional, but forbids deprecated tags; any tag attributes have also been removed
XHTML 1.0 frameset	Used to create framed pages
XHTML 1.1	Similar to XHTML 1.0 strict, but with deprecated features removed
XHTML 2.0	Still in development

 NOTE! *As XHTML 1.0 transitional is the easiest to learn and implement, this is the version on which this book will focus. Learning XHTML 1.0 transitional first also builds a foundation upon which you can delve further into XHTML 1.0 strict or understand and maintain older HTML documents.*

XHTML Version Identification

You must identify which version of XHTML your web page uses. This is the job of the DOCTYPE declaration, which is a small bit of mandatory code at the very top of your web pages. The DOCTYPE declaration states what version of XHTML your page is coded with, and the web browser (or other user agent) uses this information to determine how to display the code. If you have the XHTML 1.0 strict DOCTYPE at the top of your page but you've written XHTML 1.0 transitional code, your web page may not display as expected (if at all). The DOCTYPE declaration for XHTML 1.0 transitional looks like this:

```
<!DOCTYPE html PUBLIC "-//W3C//DTD XHTML 1.0 Transitional//EN"
"http://www.w3.org/TR/xhtml1/DTD/xhtml1-transitional.dtd">
```

While the code can span a single line, it is normally broken into two lines for readability. Note that the DOCTYPE declaration breaks a few rules of syntax that apply to other elements. For example, the tag name is uppercase and there is no closing tag or closing slash in the opening tag.

 NOTE! *The DOCTYPE declaration tag must start with an exclamation mark, the word DOCTYPE must be capitalized, and there is no closing slash. This is contrary to the rules for all other tags. It's an odd tag, but the specification requires it to be this way.*

xmlns Attribute

XHTML requires the opening <html> tag to include the xmlns attribute. The purpose of this attribute is fairly complex and is related to the XML document specification. Suffice it to say, this is required for valid XHTML so your documents better have it! The complete xmlns attribute-value pair for XHTML documents looks like this:

```
<html xmlns="http://www.w3.org/1999/xhtml">
```

Character Encoding and Meta Tags

For a web browser to display the correct characters (such as letters from the English alphabet) it needs to know what character encoding to use. This is typically done with a <meta> tag. The <meta> tag is somewhat of a general-purpose tag that can hold all sorts of information, like search engine keywords, a description of the web page, the name of the web page author, and more. Technically, <meta> tags are said to hold *meta-data* (information about the document itself). Some web pages may have 5, 10, or more <meta> tags. The old style character set used by web pages was the ISO-8859-1 character set, which supported all characters in the English language. However, as the Internet grew to truly world-wide proportions, this character set was no longer sufficient as it didn't support characters from other languages. The UTF-8 character set is the preferred character encoding today, and your web pages will not validate without a character encoding declaration. (You will learn more about validation in Lesson 14, Migrating and Troubleshooting.) The following character encoding statement should appear beneath the <title> tag in the <head> section of your web pages.

```
<meta http-equiv="Content-Type" content="text/html; charset=utf-8" />
```

QUICK REFERENCE: BASIC XHTML RULES

XHTML Rule, Example

- The DOCTYPE declaration must be present at the top of the document to identify which version of which language was used to code the web page.

```
<!DOCTYPE html PUBLIC "-//W3C//DTD XHTML 1.0 Transitional//EN"
"http://www.w3.org/TR/xhtml1/DTD/xhtml1-transitional.dtd">
```

- The HTML tag must include the xmlns attribute.

```
<html xmlns="http://www.w3.org/1999/xhtml">
```

- The Title element must be present in the head section.

```
<title>My Page Title</title>
```

- Character encoding must be present.

```
<meta http-equiv="Content-Type" content="text/html; charset=utf-8" />
```

- Tags must be properly nested.

```
<b><i>The italic tag is completely nested inside the bold tag</i></b>
```

QUICK REFERENCE: BASIC XHTML RULES (CONTINUED)

XHTML Rule, Example

- All elements must be closed.

```
<b>This element is closed</b>
```

- All attributes must be lowercase.

```
<p align="center">This tag's align attribute is lowercase.</p>
```

- All attributes must have a quoted value.

```
<p align="center">This tag's align attribute contains a value in quotes.</p>
```

 Hands-On 2.2   **Create the XHTML Structure**

In this exercise, you will create a blank XHTML 1.0 transitional document with the structures in place, ready to accept content.

Before You Begin: *Remember that characters to type look like this:* **Type this text**. *Keys to press but not type out look like this:* Enter Spacebar.

1. Choose Start→All Programs→Accessories→Notepad.

2. Type the DOCTYPE declaration to define the document as an XHTML 1.0 transitional document as shown. Be very careful to type all the slashes and capital letters exactly as indicated!

 TIP! *You must always type code exactly the right way. There is no room for error!*

```
<!DOCTYPE html PUBLIC "-//W3C//DTD XHTML 1.0 Transitional//EN" Enter
"http://www.w3.org/TR/xhtml1/DTD/xhtml1-transitional.dtd">
```

Entering the code on two lines isn't required, but it does make reading the code easier.

3. Tap the Enter key twice to create some space in your code.

4. Type the complete opening html tag:

```
<html xmlns="http://www.w3.org/1999/xhtml">
```

5. Tap the Enter key twice to create some space in your code.

6. Type the entire head section, which includes the required title element:

```
<head> Enter
  <title>My First XHTML Page</title> Enter
  <meta http-equiv="Content-Type" content="text/html; charset=utf-8" /> Enter
</head>
```

7. Tap the Enter key twice to create some space in your code.

8. Complete the document by typing the body element and closing html tag:

```
<body>Enter Enter
</body>Enter Enter
</html>
```

Your XHTML code should look like the following example.

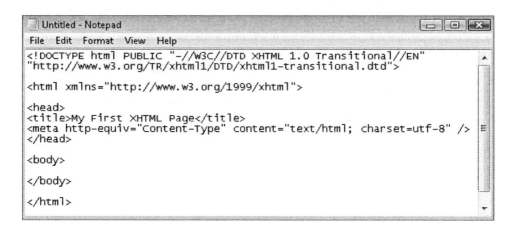

```
<!DOCTYPE html PUBLIC "-//W3C//DTD XHTML 1.0 Transitional//EN"
"http://www.w3.org/TR/xhtml1/DTD/xhtml1-transitional.dtd">

<html xmlns="http://www.w3.org/1999/xhtml">

<head>
<title>My First XHTML Page</title>
<meta http-equiv="Content-Type" content="text/html; charset=utf-8" />
</head>

<body>

</body>

</html>
```

9. Choose File→Save As from the menu bar to open the Save As dialog box.

10. Navigate to your Lesson 02 folder.
    In the next step, you will type not only the filename, but also a filename extension. You will learn about web page file extensions later in this lesson.

11. Type **my_xhtml.htm** as the filename and click Save.
    You have now finished entering the structural tags for your first XHTML web page!

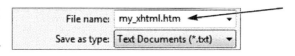

Completing Your First XHTML Page

When you type XHTML code manually, as opposed to using specialized web design software like Adobe Dreamweaver® or Microsoft FrontPage® (which you will learn more about in the next lesson) that lets you create web pages like a page layout program, it's called *hand coding* or *manual coding*. A popular practice for hand coding an XHTML page is to start with the required structural tags—DOCTYPE, html, head, title, body—and to then go back and fill in the content later. This ensures you don't forget to close one of these major sections because you are so wrapped up in typing the content. This is what you just finished doing in the last exercise. It is also common practice, as you saw in the previous exercise, to incorporate double spaces between the sections to make the code easier to read and edit.

TIP! *Remember that you should always use a text editor like Notepad (Win) or SimpleText/TextEdit (Mac) and not a word processor like Microsoft Word or WordPad. Word processors add formatting to your document, which invalidates the XHTML; text editors do not.*

In this exercise, you will add body content to the web page that will be displayed in the web browser window. Remember that everything you have typed so far is necessary to tell the web browser how you plan to build the web page and how it should be displayed in the browser window.

1. Click in the space between the opening and closing body tags and type the following page heading: **\<h1\>Hello World!\</h1\>**

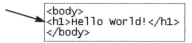
```
<body>
<h1>Hello world!</h1>
</body>
```

Be careful to type the closing tag correctly. Don't forget the slash!

2. Tap [Enter].

3. Type the following to create paragraph text: **\<p\>This is my first hand coded page.\</p\>**

```
<body>
<h1>Hello world!</h1>
<p>This is my first hand coded page.</p>
</body>
```

4. Choose File→Save from the menu bar (or [Ctrl]+[S] from the keyboard).

Previewing Your Page

You will want to test your page as you type your code. It is easier to find mistakes when you do a little at a time rather than trying to find an error in a large, completed document. Which page below would you rather try to troubleshoot?

```
<!DOCTYPE html PUBLIC "-//W3C//DTD XHTML 1.0 Transitional//EN"
"http://www.w3.org/TR/xhtml1/DTD/xhtml1-transitional.dtd">

<html xmlns="http://www.w3.org/1999/xhtml">

<head>
<title>My First XHTML Page</title>
</head>

<body>
<h1>Hello world!</h1>
<p>This is my first hand coded page.</p>
</body>

</html>
```

Testing your page incrementally makes finding errors easier.

Waiting until a page is complete before testing can make identifying errors difficult.

```
<!DOCTYPE html PUBLIC "-//W3C//DTD HTML 4.01 Transitional//EN" "http://www.w3.org
xml:lang="en" xmlns="http://www.w3.org/1999/xhtml"> <!-- Metadata --> <head><t
web Portal</title><meta content="USA.gov: Home page of the U.S. Government's offi
transactions, services, and information. It provides direct online access to fede
                    " name="description"><meta content="US Government, Firstgov, first
us gov, government forms, government auctions, portal, government jobs, governme
information, federal, state, local, tribal, USA, services, home" name="keywords">
name="classification"><meta content="Global" name="distribution"><meta content="S
content="public domain" name="copyright"><meta content="en" name="language"><meta
http-equiv="Content-Type"><meta content="Vignette Content Management, V7 (raz)" n
17:37:25 GMT" name="Generated"><link href="http://www.usa.gov/rss/updates.xml" re
and Features" type="application/rss+xml"><link href="http://www.usa.gov/rss/FAQs.
Government Questions from USA.gov" type="application/rss+xml"><script language="J
type="text/javascript"></script><script language="JavaScript" src="/js/en/trigger
type="text/javascript"></script><script language="JavaScript" src="/js/en/stdLaun
type="text/javascript"></script><script language="JavaScript" type="text/javascri
language="JavaScript" src="/js/en/main_Audience_Script.js" type="text/javascript"
src="/js/font_Size_Main_Utility.js" type="text/javascript"></script><script langu
src="/js/en/font_Size_Css.js" type="text/javascript"></script><noscript><link hre
rel="stylesheet" type="text/css"><link href="/styles/en/localized.css" media="scr
type="text/css"></noscript><link href="/styles/main_print.css" media="print" rel=
end Metadata --> <body> <!-- skip nav -->    <div id="skip"><a href="#skip_conten
border="0" height="1" src="/images/clearpix.gif" width="1"></a><a href="#skip_rig
special features" border="0" height="1" src="/images/clearpix.gif" width="1"></a>
nav -->   <div id="hp_Top_Nav">   <!-- either link box or short text for the top na
Languages -->    <div id="non_Languages"><img alt="The United States Flag" border=
src="/images/flag_HP_Top.jpg" width="140"><a href="/index.shtml" title="Home">Hom
href="/Site_Index/index.shtml" title="Site Index">Site Index</a> | <a
href="http://origins.usa.gov/external/external.jsp?url=http://www.firstgov.go
title="E-mail Us">E-mail Us</a> | <a href="/Contact/Directories.shtml"
href="http://origins_usa_gov/external/external.jsp?url=http://answers_firstgov_go
```

Another common practice when hand-coding is to have your file open twice: once in the text editor where you type your code and another in the web browser so you can preview your work as you go. The Windows taskbar at the bottom of the screen makes it easy to switch between these two windows.

The same page is open in both Notepad and Internet Explorer.

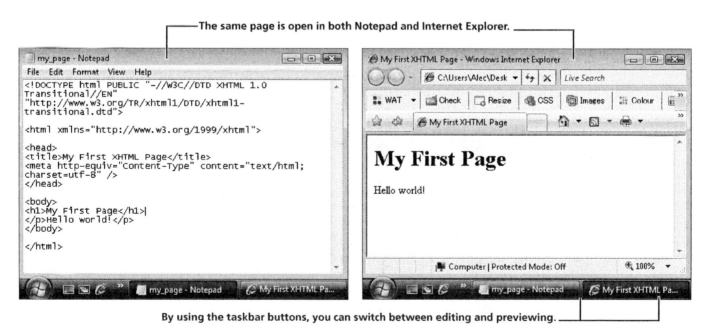

By using the taskbar buttons, you can switch between editing and previewing.

Hands-On 2.4 **Preview Your Page**

In this exercise, you will preview your page in a browser and then switch back and forth between Notepad and Internet Explorer as you make page changes.

Preview Your Page

1. Start Internet Explorer.
   Internet Explorer opens and your default homepage is displayed.

2. Use Ctrl+O to open the Open dialog box.
   The Open dialog box appears, allowing you to browse to where your file is located.

3. Click Browse and navigate to your Lesson 02 folder.

4. Select your my_xhtml.htm document, click Open, and click OK.
   The web page displays in your browser window.

5. Notice where the content displayed in the browser window came from.

The title displayed in the browser window came from the `<title>` tag in the `<head>` section.

The page heading came from the `<h1>` tag.

The body text came from the `<p>` tag.

Switch Between Windows

6. Click the my_xhtml – Notepad button on the taskbar.

NOTE! *Your taskbar may look different based on the version of Windows you are using and the shortcuts displayed on your Quick Launch toolbar. This example is from Win Vista.*

7. Locate the `<h1>` tag and click between the 1 and the >.

8. Tap the Spacebar and type **align="center"**. Your code should look like this:

```
<h1 align="center">Hello World!</h1>
```

Notice that you do not type the period after the quotation mark following the word center!

9. Save your changes.

10. Click the Internet Explorer button on the taskbar to return to the Internet Explorer window.

11. Tap the F5 function key on the keyboard to refresh the page.
The page heading, Hello World!, becomes centered on the page because of the `align` *attribute. The* `align` *attribute is an example of presentational code and, as such, should really be moved to CSS code. You will learn how to do this later in this book.*

12. Click the my_xhtml – Notepad button on the taskbar at the bottom of your screen to return to Notepad.

Naming Web Pages

There are a few simple rules to follow when you create your web pages. Using appropriate file-names will ensure your pages are accessible to all web browsers and will make maintaining your website much easier. How will it make maintenance easier, you ask? Patience! That comes later in Lesson 7, Working with Hyperlinks.

Placeholder Documents

It is a common practice to create blank placeholder documents at the beginning of a web design project. This way, if content is added to a page, hyperlinks can be tested without resulting in errors. You should have a good idea of which pages need to be created if you have created a statement of purpose, wire frame, and site hierarchy as discussed in Lesson 1, Introducing Web Technologies. Before creating any pages, however, you need to understand the importance of proper file-naming.

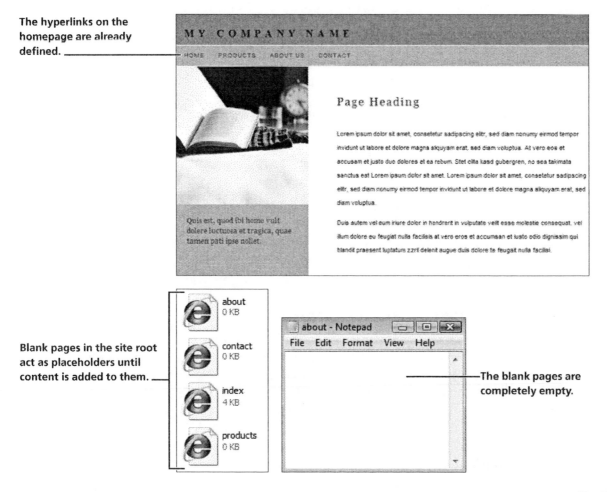

The hyperlinks on the homepage are already defined.

Blank pages in the site root act as placeholders until content is added to them.

The blank pages are completely empty.

Standard Naming Conventions and Best Practices

There are some simple rules and good habits to remember when creating web pages. Follow these simple steps to ensure that your web pages work in any browser and on any web server. While these are not requirements, they are good habits.

- **Use only lowercase letters, like mypage.htm.** Many web servers are computers running a UNIX or Linux operating system, and these operating systems are case-sensitive. In other words, Mypage.htm and mypage.htm are two completely different files and can reside in the same location. (This is not possible on Windows because Windows will see these as the same file.) Using lowercase letters all the time ensures that any hyperlinks you create reference the correct page rather than a similarly named page with a capital letter.

- **Do not use spaces.** If your filename needs two parts, use the underscore character, like `my_file.htm`. Spaces in filenames are not allowed on computers running the UNIX operating system, and many web servers are UNIX computers.

- **Filenames should be relatively short.** A poor choice for a filename may be `my_first_web_page_using_pure_html_coding.htm`. A better choice would be `first_page.htm`. The longer a filename, the more likely you are to mistype it when creating hyperlinks in your HTML code, and the more likely users are to mistype it in a web browser's address bar.

- **Use only letters, numbers, and the underscore character.** Other characters are not supported by the UNIX operating system.

These rules apply to all files residing inside your site root folder. However, the site root folder itself does not have to adhere to these rules, as only the files inside will be served on the web.

Web Page Names to Avoid

Just as there are best practices for naming web pages, there are also practices that can cause trouble. The following table gives examples and explains potential problems.

POOR WEB PAGE NAMES		
Poor Choices for Filenames	**Why These Are Poor Choices**	**Better Choices for Filenames**
live@five.htm	Uses a character other than a letter, number, or underscore	live_at_five.htm
Contact Us.htm	Contains capital letters and a space	contact_us.htm
Home.htm	Contains a capital letter	home.htm
our_newest_products.htm	Too long	new_products.htm

Default Documents

A web server is a computer that stores web pages and makes them available on the Internet. Any computer can become a web server if web server software is installed. (You will learn about web server software in Lesson 13, Putting It on the Web.) When a user browses to your website, the web server software on the computer housing your website must decide which of your many web pages to display first. The web server knows which page to display first based on the names of all your files. There is a setting within the web server software called the *default document*. This setting determines which file is displayed first based on filenames. The two most popular settings for this include *index.htm* and *default.htm*.

TIP! *Unless otherwise instructed by your web-hosting company, you should name your homepage (the page that displays first when someone browses to your website) index.htm or default.htm.*

No Default Document

If no pages in your website are named in accordance with the default document setting on the web server, users are likely to see a permissions error or other unexpected page when they browse to your website.

Index of /test

Name	Last modified	Size	Description
Parent Directory		-	
Connections/	29-Sep-2006 23:11	-	
mmServerScripts/	04-May-2007 23:04	-	
notes/	04-Jul-2007 11:05	-	
home.php	20-Jun-2006 13:45	18K	
images/	29-Sep-2006 23:11	-	
includes/	04-May-2007 23:10	-	
login.php	20-Jun-2006 13:45	18K	
media/	12-Jul-2007 16:40		
page2.php	31-Aug-2006 17:50	446	
products.php	22-Jun-2007 21:51	10K	
styles/	29-Sep-2006 23:11	-	
test_form.php	22-Jun-2007 21:51	7.4K	

Apache/2.0.48 (Win32) PHP/4.3.4 Server at localhost Port 80

In many cases, if no default document is present, users will see a directory listing (a list of all the files and folders in the site root).

Red Hat Enterprise Linux **Test Page**

This page is used to test the proper operation of the Apache HTTP server after it has been installed. If you can read this page, it means that the Apache HTTP server installed at this site is working properly.

If you are a member of the general public:

The fact that you are seeing this page indicates that the website you just visited is either experiencing problems, or is undergoing routine maintenance.

If you would like to let the

If you are the website administrator:

You may now add content to the directory /var/www/html/. Note that until you do so, people visiting your website will see this page, and not your content. To prevent this page from ever being used, follow the

In other cases, the web server displays a default test page if no default document is present.

.HTM or .HTML?

A web page's file extension identifies it as a web document to a web browser, so a valid file extension *must* be part of the filename. You may have seen some web pages end with an .htm file extension while others end with .html. You may even have noticed some ending with completely different file extensions like .php, .asp, .cfm, or .jsp. These letters indicate that a language other than HTML was used to create the web page. This course focuses on the HTML (and XHTML) language; therefore, all of your files will end with either .htm or .html. Either will work; just stay consistent. The difference between .htm and .html is similar to addressing an envelope and using either *street* or the abbreviation *st*. They mean the same thing.

 TIP! *Use .htm as the extension for your web pages as it saves you time and energy not having to type the additional l at the end. Web developers like to save every millisecond possible!*

Folders and Directories

As your website will be stored in a single folder, the site root, with possible subfolders for images, media, and other site assets, you need to be sure you understand the vernacular of the computer profession. The terms *folder* and *directory* mean the same thing. At some point, you may need to call a web server administrator for tech support, and if they tell you that you need to make a change to a file in the cgi-bin directory, you'll need to know that just means the folder named cgi-bin. Average computer users tend to use the term *folder* while *directory* is most often used by computer professionals or power users. The naming of folders/directories should follow the same guidelines used for naming files.

 Hands-On 2.5   **Name Web Files**

In this exercise, you will save a copy of an open web document with an appropriate filename.

1. Choose File→Save As from the menu bar.

2. If necessary, navigate to your Lesson 02 folder.

3. In the File Name box, change the name of the file to **index.htm** and click Save.
   The my_xhtml.htm file is closed and Notepad displays the index.htm file.

Introducing CSS

A *Cascading Style Sheet* (CSS) is a block of code written in the CSS language that defines how elements display visually on a web page (the "presentation"). The word *sheet* implies the code resides in a separate file. While that is often the case, it is not always true. Cascading style sheets can consist of code embedded directly in an HTML document (as you will see in the next exercise). XHTML is supposed to define the document structure: page headings, body text, what's a footer, etc. CSS is supposed to define the appearance: fonts, font size, colors, and even placement of certain elements. However, this doesn't always happen. Originally, HTML allowed for styling of text with the `<font>` tag and aligning of elements with the `<center>` tag. As XHTML 1.0 transitional was designed to help transition a page from HTML to XHTML, these older constructs are still supported—but every effort should be made to avoid them. There are also elements that aren't officially deprecated, but should be avoided.

Deprecated Elements

A *deprecated element* or *deprecated tag* is one that still works but is being phased out and will most likely cease to function in future versions of standards-compliant web browsers, handheld devices, and other user agents. Such tags include the `<font>` tag, used for styling text; the `<s>` and `<strike>` tags, which create strikethrough text; the `<u>` tag, which underlines text; and the `<center>` tag, which centers elements on a page. These tags should be avoided and CSS used instead. In fact, many of these tags are not valid for XHTML 1.0 strict.

Other Tags to Avoid

While not officially deprecated, the `<b>` and `<i>` tags should be avoided and replaced with the `<strong>` and `<em>` tags, respectively, for accessibility reasons. If a web page is accessible, it means the content can be accessed by anyone. This includes the visually impaired, search engine spiders, and portable Internet devices such as cell phones—just to name a few. Consider the following scenario.

Your page content includes the text "Our weekend sale is happening now!" You want the word *sale* to really stand out, so you surround it with the `<b>` tag.

Surrounding the word *sale* in `<b>` tags...

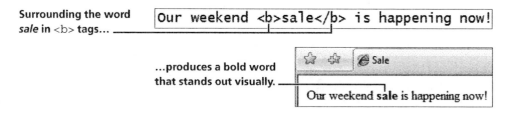

...produces a bold word that stands out visually.

However, a visually impaired user browsing your web page with a screen reader (software that reads web pages aloud) can't see the bolded word. The screen reader software reads the sentence with no emphasis, and search engines don't know that *sale* is an important word because the `<b>` tag, like the `<i>` tag, is for visual styling only.

Using <strong> instead of <b> (and <em> instead of <i>) results in the same visual display but causes the screen reader to read the text with a different emphasis on the bolded or italicized word. Search engines also realize that these affected words are to be emphasized. If you simply want to affect the visual style of a word, it is still better to use CSS rather than any tag that implements visual presentation.

CSS is covered more fully in Lesson 9, Introducing CSS and Color, but let's type some CSS code so you can get a sneak peek of what's to come.

 Hands-On 2.6   Add CSS to Your Page

In this exercise, you will add some basic CSS formatting to your document.

1. Locate the closing </title> tag in the <head> section, click immediately after it, and tap Enter.

2. Type the following text to create a CSS block in the <head> section, using Enter where appropriate:
   Be sure to type this exactly as it appears with the colons and semicolons. Mistyping a single character can break your web page!

```
<style type="text/css">
body {
background: yellow;
font-family: arial;
color: darkred;
}
</style>
```

3. Save your changes to the web page.
   The changes to the page won't display properly in step 4 unless you save them in Notepad first.

4. Make the Internet Explorer window active and tap the F5 key to refresh the page.
   The page refreshes to display your new formatting: a yellow background, red text, and a different font.

5. Close Internet Explorer.

6. Close Notepad.

Summarizing HTML, XHTML, and CSS

HTML is the basic language used to create web pages. As you know, it has been replaced by XHTML. Where HTML allows the developer to define document structure in addition to defining the visual presentation, XHTML strives to only define document structure and leaves the visual presentation to CSS.

QUICK REFERENCE: OUTLINING BASIC HTML TAGS

Tag	What It Does / Code

DOCTYPE	Defines the version of HTML/XHTML used to code the web page.
	`<!DOCTYPE html PUBLIC "-//W3C//DTD XHTML 1.0 Transitional//EN"`
	`"http://www.w3.org/TR/xhtml1/DTD/xhtml1-transitional.dtd">`

HTML	Defines the document as an HTML document and identifies its namespace. `<html xmlns="http://www.w3.org/1999/xhtml"></html>`
Head	Defines the head of the document, which holds primarily meta-data. `<head></head>`
Title	Creates the document title, which is displayed in the web browser title bar. `<title></title>`
Meta	Provides information to search engines and general instructions to the web browser. `<meta ...attributes-and-values... />`
Body	Holds the content that is displayed in the main browser window. `<body></body>`
Bold	Visually formats text as bold. `<b></b>`
Strong	Visually formats text as bold and structurally flags text as important. `<strong></strong>`
Italic	Visually formats text as italic. `<i></i>`
Emphasis	Visually formats text as italic and structurally flags text as emphasized. `<em></em>`
Heading	Structurally defines a heading. Visually enlarges and bolds text. `<h1></h1>`
Paragraph	Structurally defines paragraphs. Visually adds top and bottom margins. `<p></p>`

Concepts Review

True/False Questions

1. HTML is set to replace XHTML as the preferred language for coding web pages.   TRUE   FALSE

2. It is okay to use a standard word processor such as WordPad or Microsoft Word to author HTML files.   TRUE   FALSE

3. You use HTML tags to create elements.   TRUE   FALSE

4. Container tags have an opening tag and an associated closing tag.   TRUE   FALSE

5. Attributes can be used within opening tags to modify an element.   TRUE   FALSE

6. Tags cannot be nested inside each other.   TRUE   FALSE

7. HTML allowed tags to be uppercase or lowercase while XHTML requires them to be uppercase only.   TRUE   FALSE

8. You use CSS to visually format a web page.   TRUE   FALSE

9. Deprecated tags are tags that have recently been introduced into XHTML and, as such, may not be fully supported in all web browsers.   TRUE   FALSE

10. It is a good practice to name your web pages with short, descriptive filenames that use underscores instead of spaces.   TRUE   FALSE

Multiple Choice Questions

1. Miguel has transferred his website to a server and is receiving reports from people trying to use the website that they are seeing a strange error message instead of the homepage. What is the most likely cause of this problem?

    a. Miguel has failed to name his homepage index.htm, default.htm, or whatever the default document setting is on the web server.

    b. Miguel has named his web pages with the .html filename extension rather than .htm.

    c. All the users reporting the problem are browsing to the wrong website.

    d. The users are using an unsupported web browser.

2. Which one of the following names is the most recommended format for a web page?

    a. Contact Us.htm

    b. contactUs.html

    c. contact_us.htm

    d. contact us.htm

3. Which group of elements/tags is required for a valid XHTML document?

    a. DOCTYPE declaration, HTML tags, HEAD tags, TITLE tags, and BODY tags

    b. DOCTYPE declaration, HTML tags, HEAD tags, CSS tags, and BODY tags

    c. DOCTYPE declaration, META tags, HEADING tags, TITLE tags, and BODY tags

    d. HEADING tags, PARAGRAPH tags, and BODY tags

4. What is the proper nesting sequence for the following tags?

    a. `<b><i>This is bold and italic</b></i>`

    b. `<i><b>This is bold and italic</i></b>`

    c. `<b></b>This is bold and italic<i></i>`

    d. `<b><i>This is bold and italic</i></b>`

Skill Builders

Skill Builder 2.1   Create an XHTML Document Structure

In this exercise, you will create a blank XHTML document with the correct structure ready to receive content.

1. Launch Notepad and immediately save the blank document to your Lesson 02 folder as **sb_2.htm**.

 TIP! *One last reminder: Type all code exactly as it is written here.*

2. Type the following DOCTYPE declaration:

```
<!DOCTYPE html PUBLIC "-//W3C//DTD XHTML 1.0 Transitional//EN" Enter
"http://www.w3.org/TR/xhtml1/DTD/xhtml1-transitional.dtd"> Enter
```

3. Type the complete html, head, and body structures:

```
<html xmlns="http://www.w3.org/1999/xhtml"> Enter
<head> Enter
<title>Skill Builder 2</title> Enter
<meta http-equiv="Content-Type" content="text/html; charset=utf-8" /> Enter Enter
</head> Enter
<body> Enter Enter
</body> Enter
</html>
```

4. Save your document.

5. Minimize Notepad and navigate to your Lesson 02 folder.

6. Double-click your sb_2.htm file to view it in a web browser.
   The file opens in your default web browser since you designated it as an .htm file.

7. Verify the title, Skill Builder 2, appears across the top of the web browser window and that nothing appears in the main window of the web browser.

Skill Builder 2.2   Add Body Content

In this exercise, you will add body content that will display in the browser window.

Before You Begin: You must complete Skill Builder 2.1 before beginning this exercise.

1. Switch to Notepad, click in the space between the opening and closing body tags to place your cursor, and type the following:

```
<h1>The Blue Period</h1>  Enter
<p>The page is blue.<br />The text is blue.<br />
I <strong><em>love</em></strong> blue!</p>
```

Notice you tapped the Enter *key only once. Depending on your settings in Notepad, the text between the opening and closing paragraph tags may not fit on a single line and may automatically wrap. That's okay.*

2. Save your changes.

3. Return to the browser window and tap the F5 function key to refresh the page. *Your page should resemble the following figure.*

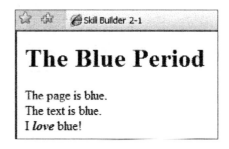

Skill Builder 2.3   Add CSS Formatting

In this exercise, you will add visual formatting with CSS.

Before You Begin: You must complete Skill Builder 2.2 before beginning this exercise.

1. Switch to Notepad, click in the space between the meta tag and the closing head tag, and type the following to start the CSS code block:

   `<style type="text/css">` `Enter`

2. Type the following to color the page background light blue and the text dark blue:

   `body {` `Enter`
   `background: lightblue;` `Enter`
   `}` `Enter` `Enter`
   `p {` `Enter`
   `color: darkblue;` `Enter`
   `}` `Enter` `Enter`
   `</style>`

3. Save your changes.

4. Return to the web browser and tap the `F5` function key to refresh the page.
   The page color and paragraph text color change to the colors you specified in your CSS.

5. Close your web browser.

6. Close Notepad.

Assessments

Assessment 2.1   Create an XHTML Document

In this exercise, you will create an XHTML document.

1. Launch Notepad and immediately save the blank document to your Lesson 02 folder as **as_2.htm**.

2. Type the complete DOCTYPE declaration for an XHTML 1.0 transitional document and tap Enter twice.

3. Type the opening html tag and tap Enter twice. (Don't forget the xmlns attribute!)

4. Type the complete head section. Be sure to include the following:
   - Give the document a title of **Assessment 2**.
   - Include the character encoding meta tag.

5. Type the correct code to display the following page heading, paragraph text, and line breaks.

> # Things I Like About Eggs
>
> They come in all different shapes
> They come in all different colors

6. Save your changes and preview your page in your browser.

Assessment 2.2   Add CSS Visual Formatting

In this exercise, you will create an XHTML document.

Before You Begin: You must complete Assessment 2.1 before beginning this exercise.

1. Switch to Notepad and add the opening and closing <style> tags to the appropriate location within the head. Be sure to include the type attribute in the opening <style> tag.

2. Create a CSS rule for the body that specifies the page background color as lightgreen and the text color as darkcyan.

3. Save your changes.

4. View the page in a web browser and verify the colors have been applied.

Critical Thinking

Critical Thinking 2.1   Create an XHTML Document

In this exercise, you will create an XHTML document complete with CSS formatting.

1. Start Notepad and save the blank file to your Lesson 02 folder with an appropriate file-name for a homepage. (Be sure not to overwrite the index file that already exists! Use another name appropriate for a homepage.)

2. Create the XHTML structure, including the DOCTYPE, html tags, complete head section, and an empty body section. Be sure to create an appropriate title to display in the web browser window.

3. In the body section, create a page heading with text of your choice.

4. Create a paragraph of text consisting of at least four sentences. Insert the appropriate code to force a line break after one of the sentences.

5. In the appropriate location in the head section, create a block of CSS code to give the page a silver background with green text.

6. Save your changes and preview your page in a browser.

7. Close your browser and Notepad.

LESSON 3

Using Workspace Tools

In this lesson, you will learn about software that is useful for coding web pages. You will also learn about software that enhances web browser functionality for HTML coders. By using software specific to writing HTML, you benefit from features such as line numbering and syntax coloring, which reveals errors as you type and makes correcting mistakes as you go easier. You will also learn the importance of knowing how to write your own HTML even though there is software that writes it for you.

LESSON OBJECTIVES

After studying this lesson, you will be able to:

- Describe the difference between page-centric and site-aware software
- List key features of a typical HTML editor
- Describe reasons for understanding HTML even though some software writes it for you
- Identify various browser tools and add-ons

Case Study: Using the Right Tool for the Right Job

As Haylie now understands how unforgiving XHTML is when it comes to making small mistakes such as forgetting a quotation mark or neglecting to close a tag, she researches alternatives to Notepad that may help to identify coding errors on the fly. Also, knowing that browsers render web pages differently, she learns what software she needs to install to be able to check her web pages in a variety of popular browsers.

HTML editors, such as Notepad2, offer syntax coloring and line numbering.

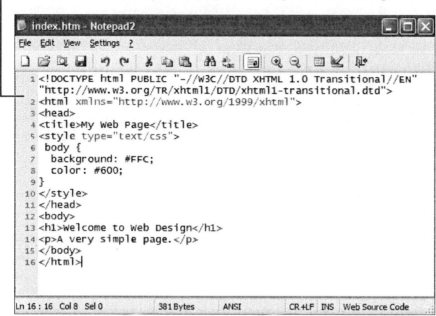

The Web Developer toolbar for the Firefox browser offers tools for working with XHTML and CSS.

Introducing Website Development Tools

There are hundreds of software programs that help web developers work and produce output more efficiently. There is software that aids in hand-coding, software that will write all of the code for you, software to work with images, and software to help you complete just about any other web-related task.

Page-centric vs. Site-aware Software

Some programs, such as Notepad, allow you to work with web pages as if they were disjointed individual files with no relationship to other HTML documents. Other more advanced programs help you maintain consistency throughout all pages in a particular website. Basic text editors like Notepad are considered *page-centric* because they treat each web page as an individual entity with no knowledge of related pages. Other *site-aware* software, like Adobe Dreamweaver or Microsoft Expression® (the replacement for Microsoft FrontPage), can help you maintain links between pages or consistency in layout and design because these programs are able to recognize full websites—not just individual web pages—and are aware that certain web pages are related to each other.

Text Editors

In the beginning, there were text editors. Windows users had Notepad and Macintosh users had SimpleText. These programs allowed web developers to hand code their HTML with no bells or whistles. If you weren't extremely focused and careful, it was difficult to catch any typos in your code as these text editors simply displayed black text on a white background. The nice thing about these editors was they forced you to be conscientious about your code. Today, many web developers still prefer to use Notepad over more advanced software.

On the Macintosh, SimpleText was replaced by TextEdit in OS X. TextEdit is more similar to WordPad than Notepad in that it can read and write Rich Text documents, which can include basic text formatting similar to that of a word processor.

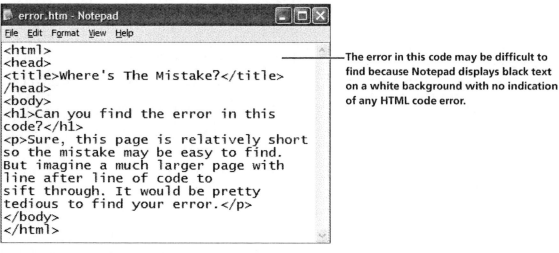

The error in this code may be difficult to find because Notepad displays black text on a white background with no indication of any HTML code error.

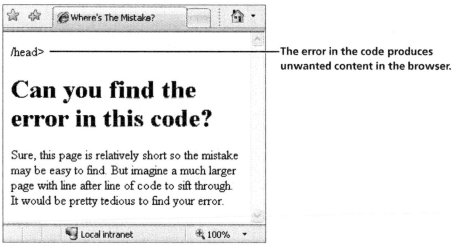

The error in the code produces unwanted content in the browser.

 Hands-On 3.1   Identify Errors with a Text Editor

In this exercise, you will try to identify the error in a web document by using Notepad.

View the Page in a Browser

1. Open a folder window to the Lesson 03 folder of your file storage location.

2. Open the error.htm file.

   Your web browser launches and displays the page. The large paragraph should be in a gray box with a black border. Depending on your browser, the page may not display properly because there is an error in the code.

   For example, Internet Explorer displays the page incorrectly and you see the results of the code error. The Safari browser (Mac) displays a blank page. If you had opened this page in Firefox, the page would display with the border and formatting intact as Firefox is able to overcome this particular error in coding. This is just another example of how important it is to test your pages in multiple browsers.

View the Code in Notepad

3. Choose Start→All Programs→Accessories→Notepad.

4. If necessary, maximize 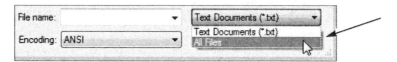 the Notepad window.

5. Choose File→Open from the menu bar and navigate to your Lesson 03 folder.

6. Change the file type filter to show all files and then open the error.htm file.

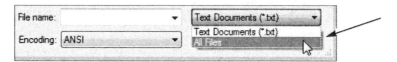

The same file is now open in both your web browser and in Notepad. You can now make edits in Notepad and refresh the web browser to see your changes.

7. Look through the code and try to locate the error.
Unless you have previous experience with HTML, this will be next to impossible as Notepad gives no indication as to where an error might be.

Fix the Error

8. Locate the title tags towards the top of the document.
Notice that the closing title tag is missing its closing angle bracket.

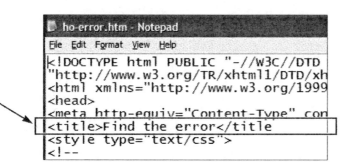

9. Type the **>** symbol at the end of the line so the line reads as follows:

```
<title>Find the error</title>
```

10. Choose File→Save from the menu bar to save your changes.

11. Click the browser button in the taskbar at the bottom of your screen to return to the web browser.

12. Tap the [F5] function key at the top of your keyboard to refresh the page.
The page now displays as expected. Leaving out even a small thing such as an angle bracket can cause your web pages to display improperly.

13. Close the browser.

14. Close Notepad.

Using HTML Editors

The next step up from a basic text editor is an HTML editor. The name HTML editor is more of a generic term because HTML editors can create HTML, XHTML, CSS, and documents in other web languages such as JavaScript and PHP. They are an improvement to text editors in that they offer line numbering and syntax highlighting as basic features, and most HTML editors offer many more advanced features.

Line-numbering

Line numbering simply lists line numbers down the left column of the document, making it easy to find a specific location. For example, a poorly coded page may result in a browser displaying an error similar to "Error on line 23 at character 14." With Notepad, you would have to count down to line 23, then over to the fourteenth character. With an HTML editor and line numbering, locating a specific line of code is easy.

Syntax-coloring

Syntax coloring (or syntax highlighting) color-codes as you type. This makes it easy to spot errors. Rather than producing only black text, an HTML editor may display all HTML tags in blue, attributes in green, attribute values in red, and regular page text in black. If all of the text after a certain point suddenly turns a color other than what it should be, you know you have a typo somewhere.

Syntax highlighting has identified an error by coloring the <h1> tag red. That indicates an error somewhere above line 6. (At line 5, the opening body tag is missing its closing angle bracket.)

 You can see a color version of this figure on the web page for this book.

POPULAR HTML EDITORS

HTML Editor	Operating System	Basic Features
Notepad2 (free)	Win	Line numbering, syntax coloring
Crimson Editor (free)	Win	Line numbering, syntax coloring, auto-indent, macro recording, spell check, and more
TextPad	Win	Line numbering, syntax coloring, macro recording, spell check, clip library, and more
BBEdit	Mac	Line numbering, syntax coloring, spell check, code collapse, code clippings, and more
Bluefish	Linux	Line numbering, syntax coloring, auto tag closing, FTP support, and more
Quanta Plus	Linux	Line numbering, syntax coloring, highly customizable, and more

 Links to some popular text editors are on the web page for this book.

Free Editors

Different HTML editors have different features. Notepad2 is a very basic editor that offers line numbers and syntax coloring—and that's about it. Crimson Editor offers more features, including a nice feature where it automatically indents as you type CSS code. Both Notepad2 and Crimson Editor are free, and links to the developer websites appear on the web page for this book.

Commercial Editors

The choice of many web professionals who hand code is BBEdit from Bare Bones Software. (Sorry, Windows users; BBEdit is for Macintosh only.) Other Windows alternatives include TextPad, CoffeeCup HTML Editor, and UltraEdit. Features and interfaces vary greatly, so try one of the free ones or download a trial of a commercial editor until you find one you are comfortable with. A Google search for *html editor* should bring up about 130 million results. Remember, an HTML editor is not required to create web pages. You can get by just fine with Notepad. But line numbers and syntax coloring will make errors easier to spot.

 TIP! *The author of this book recommends Notepad2 or Crimson Editor for their ease of use and cost (free!).*

Notepad2 offers only basic features, but it is simple to use.

```
index.htm - Notepad2

File   Edit   View   Settings   ?

1 <!DOCTYPE html PUBLIC "-//W3C//DTD XHTML 1.0 Transitional//EN"
    "http://www.w3.org/TR/xhtml1/DTD/xhtml1-transitional.dtd">
2 <html xmlns="http://www.w3.org/1999/xhtml">
3 <head>
4 <title>My Web Page</title>
5 <style type="text/css">
6  body {
7    background: #FFC;
8    color: #600;
9 }
```

Crimson Editor offers more features than Notepad2, as evidenced by its extensive menu bar and toolbar.

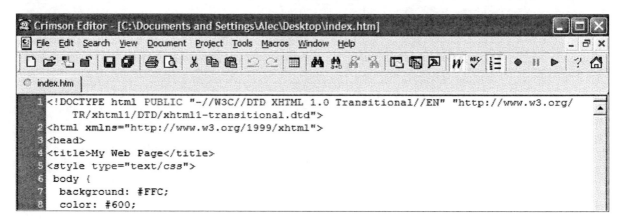

 Hands-On 3.2A **Use Syntax Coloring**

In this exercise, you will use an HTML editor to see how syntax coloring works.

Before you begin: *If your computer has Crimson Editor installed, proceed with this exercise. If your computer does not have Crimson Editor installed, skip this version of the exercise and perform the steps in Hands-On 3.2B on page 73.*

Start Crimson Editor and Create a Blank Document

1. Choose Start→All Programs→Crimson Editor→Crimson Editor.
   The Crimson Editor software launches. Recent documents may have been automatically opened.

2. Choose File→Close All from the Crimson Editor menu bar if any documents have automatically opened.

3. Choose File→New from the menu bar.
   A new file has been created, but Crimson Editor does not know how to apply syntax coloring because it doesn't know what type of document it is.

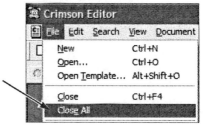

4. Choose Document→Syntax Type→HTML from the menu bar.

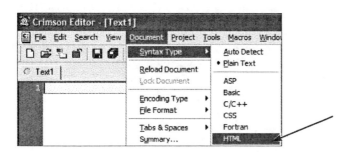

Crimson Editor now knows this is an HTML file and will apply the proper syntax coloring.

Type Code

5. Type the following code:

```
<!DOCTYPE html PUBLIC "-//W3C//DTD XHTML 1.0 Transitional//EN" Enter
"http://www.w3.org/TR/xhtml1/DTD/xhtml1-transitional.dtd"> Enter
```

A valid XHTML document must begin with a DOCTYPE declaration. Although the code is a single line of code, it is normally broken up across two lines for readability.

6. Type **<html xmlns="http://www.w3.org/1999/xhtml">** Enter.
Notice the angle brackets are black while the tag name, html, is blue.

7. Type the following code:

```
<head> Enter
<title>Syntax Coloring</title> Enter
```

You will now type the code for a meta tag and make an intentional mistake.

8. Type the following code:

```
<meta Spacebar name=
```

Name *is colored red. Crimson Editor colors attributes red. Remember that in XHTML, all attribute values must be enclosed in quotations.*

9. Type **"description**.
Your code should look like this:

```
<meta name="description
```

The word description *is colored purple. Crimson Editor colors attribute values purple. However, notice you have intentionally failed to type the closing double quotation mark.*

10. Type Spacebar **content="Test for syntax coloring"** Spacebar **/>**.
Your code should look like this:

```
<meta name="description content="Test for syntax coloring" />
```

The word content *should be red because it's an attribute of the meta tag, and the phrase* Test for syntax coloring *should be purple because it's a value. The colors are off because there is an error in the code.*

11. Locate the word *description* and type a double quotation mark (") after it.
Your code should look like this:

```
<meta name="description" content="Test for syntax coloring" />
```

The syntax coloring indicates the code is valid. Both attributes, name *and* content, *are red and the quoted values are purple.*

12. Choose File→Exit from the menu bar. Choose No when prompted to save changes.
Skip the next version of this exercise and continue reading the Using GUI Workspaces section on page 75.

Hands-On 3.2B   Use Syntax Coloring

On the Web

In this exercise, you will use an HTML editor to see how syntax coloring works.

Before You Begin: If your computer has Crimson Editor installed, skip this version of the exercise and perform the steps in Hands-On 3.2A on page 71. If you have already completed that exercise, continue reading Using GUI Workspaces section on page 75.

Start Crimson Editor and Create a Blank Document

1. Launch Internet Explorer, navigate to **labpub.com/learn/wdhtml**, and click the Hands-On 3.2B Use Syntax Coloring Link.

2. Choose Start→All Programs→Crimson Editor→Crimson Editor.
The Crimson Editor software launches. Recent documents may have been automatically opened.

3. If any documents have automatically opened, choose File→Close All from the Crimson Editor menu bar.

4. Choose File→New from the menu bar.
A new file has been created, but Crimson Editor does not know how to apply syntax coloring because it doesn't know what type of document it is.

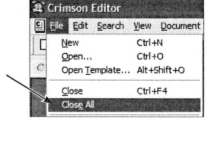

5. Choose Document→Syntax Type→HTML from the menu bar.

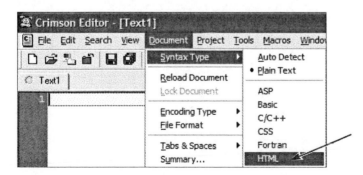

Crimson Editor now knows this is an HTML file and will apply the proper syntax coloring.

Type Code

6. Type the following code:

```
<!DOCTYPE html PUBLIC "-//W3C//DTD XHTML 1.0 Transitional//EN" [Enter]
"http://www.w3.org/TR/xhtml1/DTD/xhtml1-transitional.dtd"> [Enter]
```

A valid XHTML document must begin with a DOCTYPE declaration. Although the code is a single line of code, it is normally broken up across two lines for readability.

7. Type **<html xmlns="http://www.w3.org/1999/xhtml">** [Enter].
Notice the angle brackets are black while the tag name, html, is blue.

8. Type the following:

```
<head> [Enter]
<title>Syntax Coloring</title> [Enter]
```

You will now type the code for a meta tag and make an intentional mistake.

9. Type the following code:

```
<meta [Spacebar] name=
```

Name is colored red. Crimson Editor colors attributes red. Remember that in XHTML, all attribute values must be enclosed in quotations.

10. Type **"description**.
Your code should look like this:

```
<meta name="description
```

The word description *is colored purple. Crimson Editor colors attribute values purple. However, notice you have intentionally failed to type the closing double quotation mark.*

11. Type [Spacebar] **content="Test for syntax coloring"** [Spacebar] **/>**.
Your code should look like this:

```
<meta name="description content="Test for syntax coloring" />
```

The word content *should be red because it's an attribute of the meta tag, and the phrase* Test for syntax coloring *should be purple because it's a value. The colors are off because there is an error in the code.*

12. Locate the word *description* and type a double quotation mark (**"**) after it.
Your code should look like this:

```
<meta name="description" content="Test for syntax coloring" />
```

The syntax coloring indicates the code is valid. Both attributes, name *and* content, *are red and the quoted values are purple.*

13. Choose File→Exit and answer No when prompted to save changes.

14. Close Internet Explorer.

Using GUI Workspaces

A GUI (Graphical User Interface) web-development program is one that lets you create web pages without having to write any code yourself. You simply type just as you would in a word processor and drag pictures onto the document and the software writes all the HTML code for you in the background. These programs offer a "code view" screen so you can always get to the raw code and make manual edits, but knowledge of HTML is not necessary to use one of these programs.

The industry standard GUI web-development software is Adobe Dreamweaver, but Adobe GoLive®, Microsoft FrontPage, and Microsoft Expression are popular as well. These programs are sometimes referred to as WYSIWYG (What You See Is What You Get, pronounced "wissy-wig") editors.

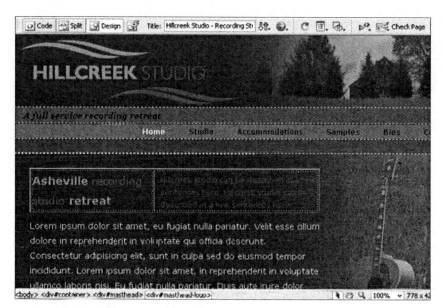

WYSIWYG programs like Adobe Dreamweaver allow you to create web pages in a visual-design mode.

They also allow access to the raw HTML code.

```
   1  <!DOCTYPE html PUBLIC "-//W3C//DTD XHTML 1.0 Transitional//EN"
      "http://www.w3.org/TR/xhtml1/DTD/xhtml1-transitional.dtd">
   2  <html xmlns="http://www.w3.org/1999/xhtml">
   3  <head>
   4  <meta http-equiv="Content-Type" content="text/html; charset=utf-8" />
   5  <title>Hillcreek Studio - Recording Studio Asheville</title>
   6  <link href="styles/base.css" rel="stylesheet" type="text/css" media="screen"/>
   7  <link href="styles/home.css" rel="stylesheet" type="text/css" media="screen"/>
   8  <link href="styles/print.css" rel="stylesheet" type="text/css" media="print"/>
   9  </head>
  10
  11  <body>
  12  <div id="container">
  13    <div id="mastheadtext">
  14      <h1>Hillcreek Studio, Asheville, NC</h1>
  15    </div>
  16    <div id="masthead">
  17      <div id="masthead-logo"></div>
  18    </div><div id="tagline">
  19      <h1>A full service recording retreat</h1>
  20    </div>
  21    <div id="topnav">
  22      <ul>
  23        <li><a href="index2.php" class="selected">Home</a></li>
  24        <li><a href="studio.php">Studio</a></li>
  25        <li><a href="accommodations.php">Accommodations</a></li>
```

Knowledge of HTML Is Necessary

While knowledge of HTML is not *required* when using a WYSIWYG tool, it is *necessary* in order to use the tool efficiently and effectively. Yes, you can buy some software and have it write all your HTML code for you while you blissfully ignore the details. But if there are ever problems with the page or you use the software to open an existing web page created by someone else, you may have a need to manually edit the code. Additionally, you will be able to use the software more efficiently if you understand what it is doing for you. Even if you use one of these programs that writes all the code for you, the importance of understanding exactly what code the software is writing for you cannot be stressed enough.

Working with Browser Tools

You saw in Lesson 1, Introducing Web Technologies that different browsers may render web pages differently. Therefore, you must check your pages in a variety of browsers to ensure they function. And while you are using a browser to check your pages, you can turn your browser into a development tool (rather than just a viewing tool) by installing some free web browser add-ons.

Multiple Browsers

To test your web page in a variety of browsers, you need access to a variety of browsers. For example, you may want to test your web page in Internet Explorer 6, Internet Explorer 7, Firefox 1.x, Firefox 2.x, Netscape 8.x, and Netscape 9.x. This is easy for non-Microsoft browsers such as Firefox or Netscape because you can install multiple versions into different folders on your hard drive and use them all. But Microsoft limits the Windows operating system to having a single version of Internet Explorer installed. This leaves you with several options for testing your pages in multiple versions of Internet Explorer.

- **Purchase multiple computers and install a different Microsoft browser on each.** This is costly, requires a lot of physical space for all those computers, and can become a management nightmare with so many computers to maintain.

- **Use a program like the free Microsoft VirtualPC.** VirtualPC lets you install multiple versions of Windows on the same computer. These versions of Windows run in a "virtual machine," like a computer within a computer. Each version of Windows can run a different version of Internet Explorer. This is also costly as you still need a legal license to install all those versions of Windows. It also requires significant hard drive space.

- **Use the free MultipleIE software from TredoSoft.** This software automates the installation of Internet Explorer 3.0, 4.01, 5.01, 5.5, and 6.0 onto a computer already running Internet Explorer 7 (IE7). These previous versions are installed in "standalone" mode, meaning they don't interfere with the default installation of IE7 and all versions can be run at the same time. There is no need for multiple computers or multiple installations of Windows. A link to the developer website is available from the web page for this book, and installation instructions are included in Appendix B, Outlining Useful Development Resources.

 TIP! *Do not attempt to install MultipleIE on Win Vista as Internet Explorer 4–6 will not run on Win Vista. If you have Win Vista, consider installing VirtualPC instead.*

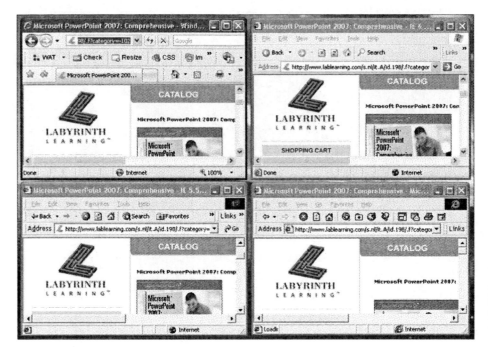

The same computer can run Internet Explorer 3, 4, 5, 6, and 7 concurrently with TredoSoft's MultipleIE.

Which Browsers to Test

The most popular web browsers currently in use include the following:

- Internet Explorer 6 (Win)
- Internet Explorer 7 (Win)
- Firefox (Win and Mac)
- Safari (Mac, though at the time of this writing, a beta version of Safari for Win is available)

There are a variety of sources for web browser statistics on the Internet, and while their numbers all vary, the four browsers mentioned previously are consistently at the top of all the lists. Links to the download pages for these browsers are available on the web page for this book.

Toolbars

There are a number of add-ons (or extensions) users can install to add functionality to a web browser. For web developers, perhaps the most useful are the Web Accessibility Toolbar for Internet Explorer and the Web Developer toolbar for Firefox. Both of these toolbars add functionality to the browser, allowing the user to toggle CSS on and off, validate the page code, outline page elements, and more. These features can be useful when developing or troubleshooting a page. Links to the download pages for these toolbars appear on the web page for this book.

Firefox with the Web
Developer toolbar

The same page in Firefox
with all CSS disabled via
the Web Developer toolbar

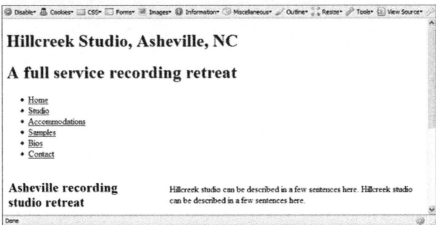

Internet Explorer 7 and the
Web Accessibility Toolbar
set to highlight all
Heading elements

Hands-On 3.3 **Use a Browser Toolbar**

In this exercise, you will use the Firefox browser and the Web Developer toolbar to explore several features helpful to Web developers.

Before You Begin: The Firefox browser and the Web Developer toolbar add-on should be installed. Your computer must also be connected to the Internet. Skip this exercise if you don't have this browser and toolbar add-on.

Open a Web Page

1. Choose Start→All Programs→Mozilla Firefox→Mozilla Firefox to launch the Firefox browser.
   You may need to check with your instructor if Firefox is not available from your Start menu. The Web Developer toolbar should appear towards the top of the browser window by default. If it doesn't, perform step 2. If the Web Developer toolbar does display, skip to step 3.

2. If necessary, choose View→Toolbars→Web Developer Toolbar to display the Web Developer toolbar.
   You will see the Web Developer toolbar displayed across the top of the web page.

3. Choose File→Open File from the menu bar.

4. Navigate to your Lesson 03 folder and open the explore_toolbar.htm file.

5. Choose View Source→View Source from the right side of the Web Developer toolbar.

   The XHTML source code opens in a new window. Note the DOCTYPE declaration at the top of the page declares this page uses XHTML 1.0 Strict (not Transitional). This will be important towards the end of this exercise.

6. Close the window displaying the XHTML code.
   The web page displaying CSS formatting reappears. In the next step, you will disable the CSS formatting to see how the page looks to search engines, screen readers, and other devices that ignore CSS.

Work with CSS

7. Choose CSS→Disable Styles→All Styles from the Web Developer toolbar:

The styles are disabled and you are left viewing the unformatted structural XHTML. Note the keyboard shortcut for this command: Ctrl + Shift + S. *It is a useful one!*

8. Choose CSS→Disable Styles→All Styles from the Web Developer toolbar to turn the styles back on.

Use Structural Tools

9. Choose Information→Display DIV Order from the Web Developer toolbar.

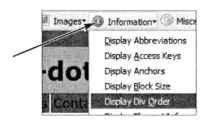

Each DIV tag is outlined in red and is numbered in the order it appears in the XHTML code. This is helpful in determining the structural outline of an existing page.

10. Choose Information→Display DIV Order from the Web Developer toolbar to toggle this option off.

Identify Deprecated Code

11. Choose Outline→Outline Deprecated Elements from the Web Developer toolbar.

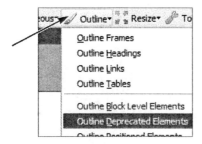

The text in the footer at the bottom of the page, Exploring a Toolbar, *is outlined because it uses the deprecated* `<font>` *tag to color the text black. This option is useful in locating deprecated code that should be updated.*

12. Choose Outline→Outline Deprecated Elements from the Web Developer toolbar to toggle this option off.

Validate Code

Remember, earlier in this exercise you learned that this document declared XHTML 1.0 Strict.

13. Choose Tools→Validate Local HTML from the Web Developer toolbar.

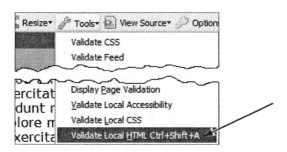

This option uploads a copy of the current page to the online validator at w3.org. The validator opens in a new tab. Note that the page has failed XHTML 1.0 strict validation because of the use of the deprecated `<font>` *tag. If the DOCTYPE declared XHTML 1.0 transitional, the page would have passed validation because the deprecated* `<font>` *tag is allowed in XHTML 1.0 transitional.*

14. Close the Result for webdeveloper tab.

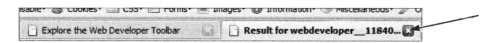

There are many other features of the Web Developer toolbar, and similar features exist for the Web Accessibility Toolbar for Internet Explorer. Take some time at home or in the computer lab to explore them.

15. Close the Firefox window.

Concepts Review

True/False Questions

1. Page-centric software helps maintain links between web pages in the same site and consistency in design and layout.　TRUE　FALSE

2. Text editors offer the ability to format text, such as bold, italic, or underlined styles.　TRUE　FALSE

3. Syntax coloring is useful in identifying errors in the HTML code as you type it.　TRUE　FALSE

4. HTML editors are very expensive with their high cost outweighing their features; therefore, you should use a text editor to hand-code your web pages.　TRUE　FALSE

5. Notepad2 and Crimson Editor are examples of WYSIWYG editors.　TRUE　FALSE

6. If you use a program such as Adobe Dreamweaver, which creates all the HTML code for you, it is not necessary to understand HTML yourself.　TRUE　FALSE

7. The Windows operating system allows you to install multiple web browsers from different manufacturers.　TRUE　FALSE

8. The Windows operating system allows you to install multiple versions of Internet Explorer.　TRUE　FALSE

9. If your web page displays correctly in Internet Explorer, there is no need to check it in other browsers.　TRUE　FALSE

10. After all code has been written, a browser toolbar can be helpful in identifying errors in the page.　TRUE　FALSE

Multiple Choice Questions

1. Which of the following programs is considered a text editor?
   a. Notepad
   b. TextEdit
   c. Dreamweaver
   d. FrontPage

2. What makes an HTML editor different from a text editor?
   a. The ability to format text as bold, italic, or underlined.
   b. The ability to select a word or phrase and apply a color to text.
   c. Features such as syntax coloring, which helps you identify coding errors.
   d. The ability to read and write HTML documents.
   e. All of the above

3. Which of the following tools should be part of an HTML author's arsenal?
   a. HTML editor with syntax coloring
   b. Multiple web browsers
   c. Web browser toolbars with features such as CSS toggling, code validation, and element outlining
   d. All of the above

4. Miguel is trying to locate an error in his HTML code that is causing a web page to display incorrectly. Upon opening his file in a program that supports syntax coloring, he sees that all of the tags at the top of the document are blue, but then turn red towards the middle of the document. Where is the most likely location of the error?
   a. Within the first tag that has turned red
   b. Immediately after the first tag that has turned red
   c. Immediately before the first tag that has turned red
   d. In the opening DOCTYPE declaration

Skill Builders

Skill Builder 3.1   Identify and Fix Code Errors

In this exercise, you will locate and fix several code errors.

Before You Begin: Check with your instructor to see if you should use a text editor with no syntax coloring, such as Notepad, or an HTML editor with syntax coloring, such as Notepad2 or Crimson Editor. If you use Notepad or another editor without line numbers, you will have to count the lines yourself. Use Internet Explorer for this exercise. If you use Firefox or another browser, the errors may not display as indicated in the exercise.

View a Page with Minor Errors in a Browser

1. Navigate to your Lesson 03 folder and double-click the sb_3_1_error.htm file to open it in your default browser.
   The page does not display as it should. HTML code is actually displayed in the browser window.

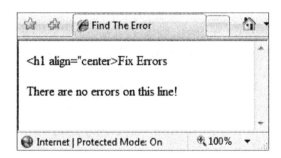

Fix the Errors

You may need to review the basic rules of XHTML from Lesson 2, Working with HTML, XHTML, and CSS to catch all the errors.

2. Launch your file editor: Notepad, Notepad2, Crimson Editor, or whatever editor your instructor prefers.

3. Choose File→Open and navigate to your Lesson 03 folder.

4. Open the file sb_3_1_error.htm.
   There are several errors in this document. You will fix them all.

5. Create a blank word processing document and save it to your Lesson 03 folder as **sb-3-1-errors**. Use this word processing document to record your answers throughout this exercise.

6. Locate the DOCTYPE declaration at the top of the page. Remember that this is a long line that may actually wrap to two or more lines in your editor's window. Describe the error in your word processing document and then fix it in the document.
   Be sure to number the response in your word processing document as number 6.

7. Locate the HTML tag and examine the xmlns attribute. Does the xmlns attribute have the correct value? Describe the error in your word processing document and then fix it in the document.
   Be sure to number the response in your word processing document as number 7.

8. Save your changes and use the taskbar to return to the browser.

9. Tap the [F5] function key to refresh the page and see the effects of your changes.
   The two errors you fixed had no effect on the rendering of the page.

10. If fixing these two errors had no effect on how the page displays in the browser, was it really necessary to fix these? Why or why not? Answer these questions in your word processing document.
    Be sure to number the response in your word processing document as number 10.

11. Use the taskbar to return to your editor.

12. Line 9, which begins with an <h1> tag, contains an error. Describe the error in your word processing document and then fix it in the document.
    Be sure to number the response in your word processing document as number 12.

13. Line 13 contains a single error. Describe the error in your word processing document and then fix it in the document.
    Be sure to number the response in your word processing document as number 13.

14. Save your file.

View the Fixed Page

15. Using the taskbar, return to your web browser and tap the [F5] function key to refresh. Your page should resemble the following figure.

 # Assessments

Assessment 3.1   Compare Text and HTML Editors

In this exercise, you will compare the pros and cons of text editors compared to HTML editors.

Before You Begin: Create a blank word processing document in your Lesson 03 folder and save it as **as-3-1-editors**. *Use this word processing document to type your answers to steps 1–6 in this exercise.*

1. List at least three benefits of using a plain text editor such as Notepad.

2. List at least three benefits of using an HTML editor that, at the very least, features line numbering and syntax coloring.

3. Describe at least one problem with using a plain text editor such as Notepad.

4. Describe at least one problem with using an HTML editor that, at the very least, features line numbering and syntax coloring.

5. If you were teaching a class in HTML coding, would you prefer your students used a text editor or an HTML editor. Why?

6. If you got a job involving a lot of hand coding of HTML, would you prefer to use a text editor or an HTML editor? Why?

Critical Thinking

Critical Thinking 3.1   Research Freeware Safety

Several free programs were mentioned in this lesson, including Notepad2, Crimson Editor, Firefox, Web Accessibility Toolbar, Web Developer toolbar, and MultipleIE. Knowing that real dangers of virus and spyware infestation can occur by installing software written by unscrupulous programmers, you need to make absolutely certain any freeware you are about to install is safe and free of malware.

Using your favorite search engine, Google Groups, or another web forum, research the safety of these programs and report your findings in a word processing document. Name the document **ct-3-1-freeware**. Be sure to include the source(s) of your information. The document should address the following topics:

- Are there any risks to downloading and installing a freeware program?

- If there are any risks, describe them.

- Describe how you would research the safety of a freeware program you were considering to download and install.

Critical Thinking 3.2   Compare HTML Editors

This lesson mentioned a few HTML editors, including Notepad2, Crimson Editor, and BBEdit. There are many more HTML editors available with a variety of features at a variety of costs.

Using your favorite search engine, Google Groups, or another web forum, find and compare at least three HTML editors not mentioned in this lesson. Answer the following about each of the three programs you found, and use a word processor or spreadsheet program to create a table in which to display your data. Save your file to your Lesson 03 folder as **ct-3-2-compare**.

- Name of the software

- Developer

- Homepage

- Supported platforms (Win, Mac, Linux)

- Cost

- Basic features

- Unique features (What makes this particular HTML editor different from others?)

LESSON 4

Working with Text

In this lesson, you will learn about the details of coding text with HTML. You will maintain structure in your document by utilizing headings, paragraphs, lists, and divisions. You will increase your web page's accessibility to search engines, screen readers, and other alternate devices. Additionally, you will create a solid foundation on which to implement CSS visual formatting. You will also denote emphasized text and insert special characters with HTML character codes.

LESSON OBJECTIVES

After studying this lesson, you will be able to:

- Use white space effectively to make code easier to edit
- Structure page text with headings, paragraphs, lists, and other structural markup
- Insert non-alphanumeric characters with character codes
- Differentiate between block level and inline elements

Case Study: Using Text

As Haylie begins to develop content for the site, Miguel starts working on the homepage. His first task is to add text to the homepage. Knowing that CSS code will be added to the page later to apply visual formatting, Miguel concentrates on the document structure by using headings, paragraphs, and other HTML tags.

While not visually formatted with color or graphical elements, the document structure is easy to discern. Search engines, screen readers, and text-only browsers would have no trouble accessing the page.

Controlling White Space and Line Breaks

Text that is close to the edge of a document can be difficult to read. When lines of text are close to each other, text blocks can be difficult to read. Using white space and line breaks can help make your code easier to work with and cause no negative effect on how the page is rendered in a browser.

White Space: The Friend You Can Ignore

White space in HTML code is the space between characters. It can occur horizontally between letters and words, or vertically between sentences and paragraphs. However, white space as it exists in the HTML code is rendered differently from what you might expect when viewed in a browser. In fact, white space is largely ignored by the browser, but can make your HTML code easier to read and edit.

Notepad: The white space between the lines of text makes the HTML code easy to read and edit.

Internet Explorer: The white space is ignored when rendered in the browser. All three lines of text appear on a single line with no extra space between the words *I*, *like*, and *eggs*.

A *lot* of white space was added between each word of the second line to prove a point.

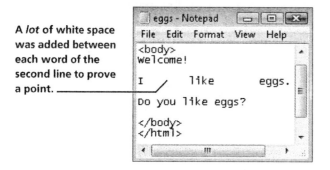

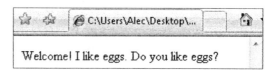

HTML vs. XHTML

The abbreviations HTML and XHTML are often used interchangeably. This makes sense most of the time as XHTML is based on HTML. However, there are times when it is not correct to say HTML when you really mean XHTML, or vice versa. Throughout this book, the terms HTML and XHTML are used somewhat interchangeably when appropriate.

Label	Applies to	Example
HTML	■ HTML 4.01 ■ XHTML 1.0 transitional ■ XHTML 1.0 strict	■ **HTML ignores white space:** Applies to HTML 4.01, XHTML 1.0 transitional, and XHTML 1.0 strict
XHTML	■ XHTML 1.0 transitional ■ XHTML 1.0 strict	■ **All tags must be closed in XHTML:** Applies to XHTML 1.0 transitional and strict ■ **The type attribute is forbidden in XHTML 1.0 strict:** Applies only to XHTML 1.0 strict

Only when something is unique to one version or the other will a clear distinction be made. For example, *XHTML 1.0 strict does not allow deprecated tags or presentational markup.*

Hands-On 4.1   Use White Space

In this exercise, you will examine how white space appearing in HTML code is rendered in a browser.

Create an XHTML 1.0 Transitional Page and View White Space in Notepad

1. Start Notepad and open the homepage-text.txt file from your Lesson 04 folder.
   You will wrap structural tags around the existing content to create a valid XHTML 1.0 transitional document.

2. At the top of the document, type the following DOCTYPE declaration for XHTML 1.0 transitional:

```
<!DOCTYPE html PUBLIC "-//W3C//DTD XHTML 1.0 Transitional//EN" Enter
"http://www.w3.org/TR/xhtml1/DTD/xhtml1-transitional.dtd"> Enter
```

⚠ **TIP!** *Remember that you must be a perfectionist when you type XHTML code. There is no room for mistakes!*

3. Type the remaining required structural tags at the top of the document:

```
<html xmlns="http://www.w3.org/1999/xhtml"> Enter
<head> Enter
<title>Folding Under Pressure - Home</title> Enter
<meta http-equiv="Content-Type" content="text/html;charset=utf-8" /> Enter
</head> Enter
<body> Enter
```

The top of your document should resemble the following figure.

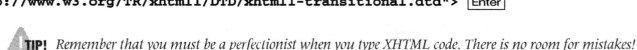

```
index - Notepad
File  Edit  Format  View  Help
<!DOCTYPE html PUBLIC "-//W3C//DTD XHTML 1.0 Transitional//EN"
"http://www.w3.org/TR/xhtml1/DTD/xhtml1-transitional.dtd">
<html xmlns="http://www.w3.org/1999/xhtml">
<head>
<title>Folding Under Pressure - Home</title>
<meta http-equiv="Content-Type" content="text/html;charset=utf-8" />
</head>
<body>

Folding Under Pressure

Home - Gallery -  How To - Resources - Contact
```

4. Tap Ctrl + End to scroll to the bottom of the document and close the BODY and HTML tags.

```
</body> Enter
</html>
```

The bottom of your document should resemble the following figure.

```
Folding Under Pressure Copyright 2007
Last updated July 1, 2007


</body>
</html>
```

5. Choose File→Save As to save a copy of the original file as an HTML document in your Lesson 04 folder as **index.htm**.

File name: | index.htm

You named the file index.htm because it will be the homepage. Note how the text is easy to read as each heading and paragraph is clearly separated by vertical white space.

6. Minimize ▬ Notepad to display your Desktop.

View White Space in a Browser

7. Open your Lesson 04 folder in a folder window.

8. Open the index.htm file. If necessary, maximize ▣ the browser window.
The file opens in your default browser. All the text runs together because white space is ignored.

Replacement Tags and Line Breaks

You can force the browser to display text on a new line by using a line break. The line break is an HTML tag that is a type of *replacement tag*. A replacement tag is one that is replaced at *runtime* (when viewed in a browser) by something else. In the case of the line break tag, it is replaced by an actual line break. Replacement tags don't have a separate closing tag like <body> and </body> or <title> and </title> have. However, XHTML requires that every tag is closed. Replacement tags integrate a closing statement inside the tag by adding a forward slash at the end, as in <br />. The white space between the "r" and the "/" is optional;
 is also valid. However, the additional space makes the code a bit easier to read.

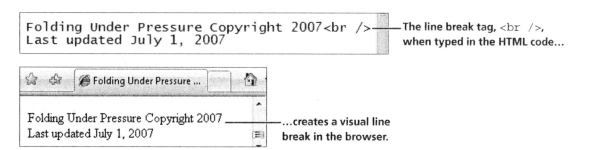

```
Folding Under Pressure Copyright 2007<br />
Last updated July 1, 2007
```
— The line break tag, <br />, when typed in the HTML code...

Folding Under Pressure ...

Folding Under Pressure Copyright 2007
Last updated July 1, 2007
— ...creates a visual line break in the browser.

Paragraphs

Structurally, labeling something as a paragraph indicates body text. Most of the text on a typical page will be paragraph text. The paragraph tag is a container tag, so an opening <p> and a closing </p> are required in XHTML. Any text contained within the tag is considered part of the paragraph. You can have as many paragraph tags on the page as you want, with each set defining a new paragraph. Visually, paragraphs create double spaces as they have inherent top and bottom margins.

Paragraph tags create document structure...

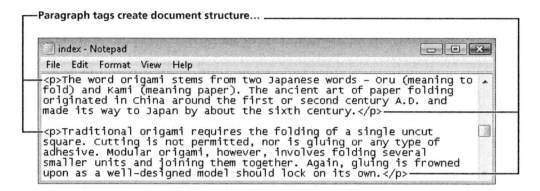

...and visually create double spaces between paragraphs.

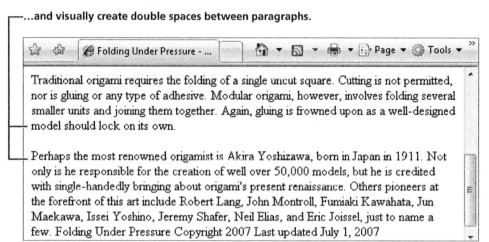

Line Breaks vs. Paragraphs

Remember that the goal of XHTML is to create structure. While you can use two line breaks next to each other to create the same visual double space created by a paragraph, you would have failed to create a solid document structure if the lines of text were in fact different paragraphs.

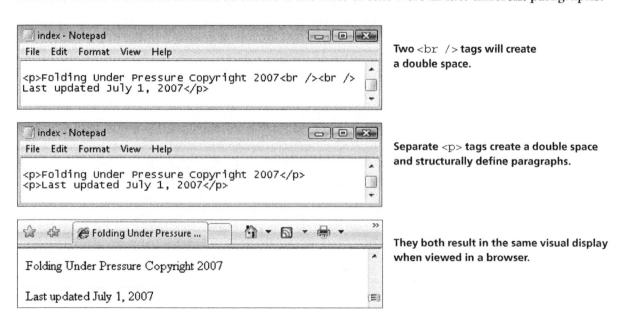

Two `<br />` tags will create a double space.

Separate `<p>` tags create a double space and structurally define paragraphs.

They both result in the same visual display when viewed in a browser.

!TIP! *Use distinct paragraphs rather than multiple line breaks.*

Nesting Paragraphs

Nesting paragraphs is not legal in HTML. In other words, you should never have one paragraph inside another, as in the following code:

```
<p>This is a paragraph
<p>This is a nested paragraph</p>
</p>
```

Even though the tags are properly nested and properly closed, the nesting of paragraph tags is not allowed. Some browsers may let you get away with it, but your page may not display as intended or even function in other browsers.

 ## Hands-On 4.2   Add Paragraphs and Line Breaks

In this exercise, you will add paragraphs and line breaks to the web page.

Add Paragraphs

1. Make Notepad the active window. Scroll to the top of the document, if necessary.

2. Follow these steps to create a paragraph:

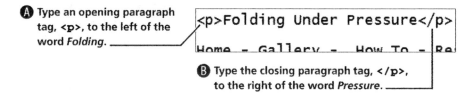

A Type an opening paragraph tag, **<p>**, to the left of the word *Folding*.

```
<p>Folding Under Pressure</p>
Home - Gallery - How To - Re
```

B Type the closing paragraph tag, **</p>**, to the right of the word *Pressure*.

3. Enclose what will later become the navigation bar, *Home – Contact – How To – Resources – Contact*, inside paragraph tags.

   <p>Home - Gallery - How To - Resources - Contact**</p>**

4. Continue adding opening and closing paragraph tags throughout the rest of the document. The following table shows the first few words of each paragraph (the last two lines should be contained in a single paragraph):

The Artist	Traditional origami requires...
Haylie Elise has been...	Perhaps the most...
The Art	Other pioneers...
The word origami...	Folding Under Pressure...

5. Verify that every block of text begins with an opening paragraph tag and ends with a closing paragraph tag. The following figure shows just a portion of the document (your text may appear different than the figure).

```
<p>Home - Gallery -  How To - Resources - Contact</p>

<p>The Artist</p>

<p>Haylie Elise has been folding paper for as long as she can remember. She brings simple
traditional origami models to life and folds the complex creations of modern origami masters.
Haylie's folded masterpieces are available for your wedding, corporate event, personal
collection, or other gathering. She lives in Asheville, NC, with her pet goldfish Gunter.
(But pieces can be shipped anywhere in the world!)</p>

<p>The Art</p>

<p>The word origami stems from two Japanese words - Oru (meaning to fold) and Kami (meaning
paper). The ancient art of paper folding originated in China around the first or second
century A.D. and made its way to Japan by about the sixth century.</p>
```

6. Use ⌈Ctrl⌉+⌈S⌉ to save your changes.

7. Make the browser window active.
The web browser displays the old version of your document before your changes. You must refresh the page to see your changes.

8. Tap the ⌈F5⌉ function key to refresh the page.
The browser displays your paragraphs and the content is no longer a single large block.

9. If necessary, scroll to the bottom of the web page and notice the copyright appears on a single line.

Add a Line Break
Now, you will break up the copyright text to display on two lines, but remain as a single paragraph.

10. Make the Notepad window active.

11. Use ⌈Ctrl⌉+⌈End⌉ to jump to the bottom of the code and find the last paragraph containing the copyright information.
The HTML code displays this on two separate lines, but the browser ignores white space. You must instruct the browser to begin a new line.

12. To the right of the word Pressure, at the bottom of the document, type the code for a line break.

```
<p>Folding Under Pressure<br />  ◄————————————————
Copyright 2007 Last Updated July 1, 2007</p>
```

13. Save your changes.

14. Make the web browser window active.

15. Tap ⌈F5⌉ to refresh the page and see your changes.
The copyright paragraph now displays on two separate lines.

Using Headings

Just as not all words in a newspaper article or a book are paragraph text, not all words on a web page are paragraph text. Structurally, a heading introduces a topic or section of your page. Visually, headings are made larger and bolder than other text. Of course, the visual presentation of headings, like everything else, can be customized later with CSS.

Heading Styles

There are six different heading styles (and six corresponding heading tags) in HTML, and you may have as many of each as you like on your page. This is so you can structure a page with headings, subheadings, subheadings of headings, and so on. For example, the main heading at the top of a web page may be the largest heading style, while all paragraphs are introduced by a subheading.

Heading Tags

Heading tags, like paragraph tags, are container tags; therefore, a closing heading tag should always be present. Heading tags are numbered, with <h1> being the largest and <h6> being the smallest. A common mistake is to open with one heading size, but close with another.

```
<h1>This is a heading 1 style</h2>
```

This heading started as an <h1>, but was closed as an <h2>. This is invalid markup and may result in the entire page being rendered as a large heading.

Six headings and a paragraph in HTML

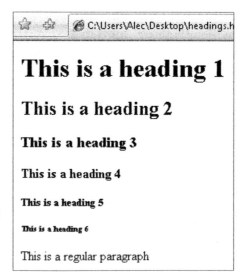

H1 is the largest and
H6 is the smallest

Tiny Headings

You may be asking yourself why you would ever want to use Headings 4–6 if they are the same size or smaller than a regular paragraph. Aren't headings supposed to be big? Remember that XHTML deals with structure. CSS deals with visual formatting. If you had a web page that displayed an outline for a book, you may easily have six levels of headings, subheadings, and sub-sub-sub-sub-subheadings. These heading tags create the document structure. You can always use CSS to make your headings look any way you like. You could even make an H6 larger than an H1 with CSS!

Block Level and Inline Elements

You can think of a heading as a special kind of paragraph—one that informs the reader a new topic or section is about to begin. Both headings and paragraphs are *block-level elements*. This means that no other block-level element can be on the same line (share the same horizontal space).

With HTML, you cannot have a heading or paragraph on the same line as another heading or paragraph. Conversely, the strong, emphasis, and line break tags create *inline elements*. An inline element can be on the same line as other inline- or block-level elements. For example, a line break can occur inside a paragraph or heading and a word inside a paragraph can be strong or emphasized.

Nesting Headings and Paragraphs

Recall that headings and paragraphs are block-level elements. The HTML specification says that some, but not all, block-level elements may contain other block-level elements. This is where you need to get into the real nitty-gritty of the HTML specification. *Some* block-level elements may contain other block-level elements, but that is not true for all block-level elements. Providing a complete list of which block-level elements can contain which other block-level elements at this point would be getting ahead of ourselves. Instead, let's focus on the rules for headings and paragraphs. (You will learn about lists and DIVs later in this lesson.)

- Headings may not contain other headings, paragraphs, lists, or DIVs.

- Paragraphs may not contain other paragraphs, headings, lists, or DIVs.

Non-examples

The following code examples are not valid because they incorporate illegal nesting.

```
<p><h1>My Heading</h1>My paragraph text…</p>
<h1>My heading<h2>My subheading</h2></h1>
```

Examples

The following are examples of valid code.

```
<h1>My Heading</h1><p>My paragraph text…</p>
<h1>My heading</h1><h2>My subheading</h2>
```

In this exercise, you will add heading tags to your document.

Add a Heading

1. Make the Notepad window active.

   The first block of text in the <body>, Folding Under Pressure, states the topic of the entire page. It should be the largest heading possible.

2. Use Ctrl + Home to jump to the top of the document, then follow these steps to change the first paragraph tags to heading tags:

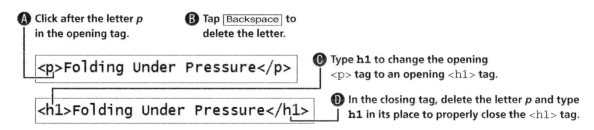

Ⓐ Click after the letter *p* in the opening tag.

Ⓑ Tap Backspace to delete the letter.

```
<p>Folding Under Pressure</p>
```

Ⓒ Type **h1** to change the opening <p> tag to an opening <h1> tag.

```
<h1>Folding Under Pressure</h1>
```

Ⓓ In the closing tag, delete the letter *p* and type **h1** in its place to properly close the <h1> tag.

Add Subheadings

The page also contains two main sections of text: one about the artist *and one about the* art.

3. Locate the block of code <p>The Artist</p> and change the <p> tags to <h2> tags, using the steps described in step 2.

   ```
   <p>Home - Gallery - How To - Resources - Contact</p>

   <h2>The Artist</h2>

   <p>Haylie Elise has been folding paper for as long as she can
   remember.
   ```

4. Locate the block of code <p>The Art</p> and change the <p> tags to <h2> tags, using the steps described in step 2.

   ```
   <h2>The Art</h2>
   ```

5. Choose File→Save and then make the web browser window active.

6. Tap the F5 function key to refresh the page.

   Your page should resemble the following figure.

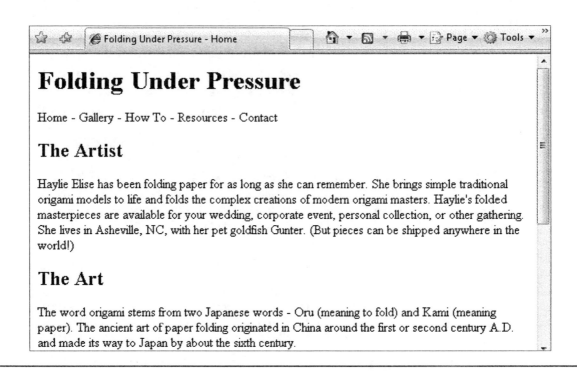

Just Because You Can Doesn't Mean You Should

While XHTML strives to remove all presentational formatting, remember that there are different versions of XHTML. XHTML 1.0 transitional allows presentational markup so authors of HTML (which explicitly allowed presentational markup) could start to transition to XHTML. XHTML 1.0 strict does not allow most presentational markup. While this book uses the XHTML 1.0 transitional version, the ultimate goal is to move all presentational markup to CSS and eventually write standards-based XHTML 1.0 strict code.

TIP! *Even though XHTML 1.0 transitional allows presentational markup, it should be avoided if possible as you strive for XHTML 1.0 strict.*

Paragraph and Heading Presentation

You are likely to work with existing pages that are valid XHTML 1.0 transitional and include presentational markup, so you should be able to recognize this code when you encounter it. Paragraph and heading tags each support the *align* attribute, which can be used to horizontally position content on a page.

The heading and paragraph tags support the align attribute.

The align attribute horizontally centers this heading within the width of the browser window.

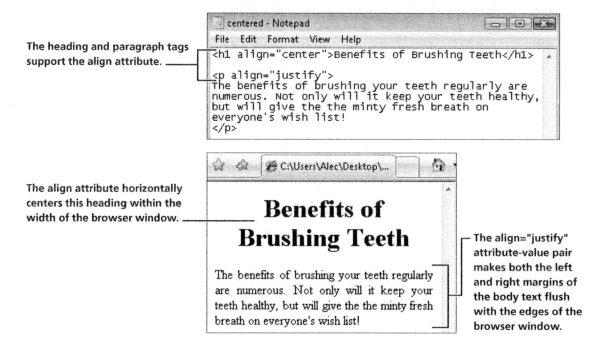

The align="justify" attribute-value pair makes both the left and right margins of the body text flush with the edges of the browser window.

Getting Equivalent Results with CSS

This same result can be accomplished through CSS, and has the added benefit of clearly separating structure from presentation as you strive for the stricter standards.

CSS can accomplish the same presentational result as HTML attributes.

The browser display is identical whether CSS or HTML attributes are used.

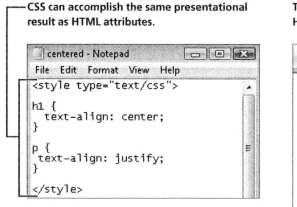

You will learn more about CSS and how to accomplish defining the visual presentation of your pages later in this book.

Formatting Characters

From the beginning of this book you've been encouraged to separate structure from presentation. But you've just seen that some structural elements do come with their own basic visual formatting—such as top and bottom space around paragraphs or larger bolder heading text. Other structural elements can make text look bold or italic without being considered visual formatting.

Strong and Bold Text

When you see bold text in print, what do you think? How do you read the bolded words? If you really think about it, you will realize that visually bold text often carries a structural meaning—namely something that says, "This text should be read louder and stronger because it's **really important**." In the old days, HTML authors would use the now-deprecated bold (<b>) container tag, but that just added visual formatting. A search engine or screen reader didn't know that text was to be read louder or given more importance. The strong (<strong>) container tag visually formats text the same way as the bold tag, but adds that missing piece of structure. Search engines and screen readers know that the <strong> tag carries special meaning and that the text contained within the tag is to be given more importance than other text.

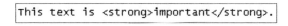

The <strong> tag is a container tag. It instructs the browser when to start and when to stop displaying text as strong.

Visually, the <strong> tag makes text bold. Because it carries special structural meaning as well, it is preferred to the deprecated <b> tag.

Emphasized and Italicized Text

Just as the <strong> tag structurally implies importance and visually displays as bold, the emphasis tag (<em>) implies emphasis and displays visually as italic. The now-deprecated italic tag (<i>) is similar to the <b> tag in that it made text look italic, but carried no meaning for search engines, screen readers, or other alternative devices. Use the <em> container tag to indicate emphasis and display as italic.

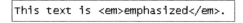

The <em> tag instructs the browser when to start and when to stop displaying text as emphasized.

Visually, the <em> tag makes text italic. Because it carries special structural meaning as well, it is preferred to the deprecated <i> tag.

Strong Emphasis

Both the `<strong>` and `<em>` tags create inline elements as opposed to block-level elements. Text surrounded by the `<strong>` or `<em>` tags does not take up the full width of the browser window and can appear on the same line (inline) as other text and other elements. Inline elements can be nested safely inside other tags, and even inside each other, providing they are properly closed.

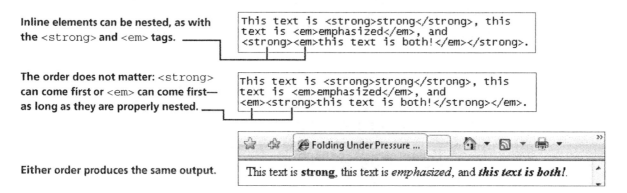

Inline elements can be nested, as with the `<strong>` and `<em>` tags. —

```
This text is <strong>strong</strong>, this
text is <em>emphasized</em>, and
<strong><em>this text is both!</em></strong>.
```

The order does not matter: `<strong>` can come first or `<em>` can come first— as long as they are properly nested. —

```
This text is <strong>strong</strong>, this
text is <em>emphasized</em>, and
<em><strong>this text is both!</strong></em>.
```

Either order produces the same output.

☆ ☆ 🌐 Folding Under Pressure ... 🏠 ▾ 🔖 ▾ 🖨 ▾ »

This text is **strong**, this text is *emphasized*, and ***this text is both!***.

 Hands-On 4.4   Create Strong and Emphasized Text

In this exercise, you will use the `<strong>` *and* `<em>` *tags to create strong and emphasized text.*

Create Strong Text

1. Make the Notepad window active.

2. If necessary, use ⌃Ctrl+⌂Home; locate the paragraph under the heading The Artist.

3. Follow these steps to make Haylie's full name bold and important:

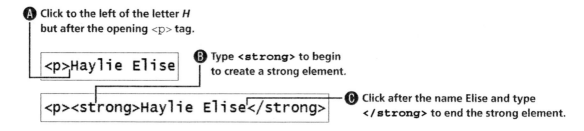

Ⓐ Click to the left of the letter *H* but after the opening `<p>` tag.

`<p>Haylie Elise`

Ⓑ Type `<strong>` to begin to create a strong element.

`<p><strong>Haylie Elise</strong>`

Ⓒ Click after the name Elise and type `</strong>` to end the strong element.

Create Emphasized Text

4. Locate the last sentence in the same paragraph (the sentence inside parentheses).

5. Follow these steps to emphasize the sentence, but not the parentheses:

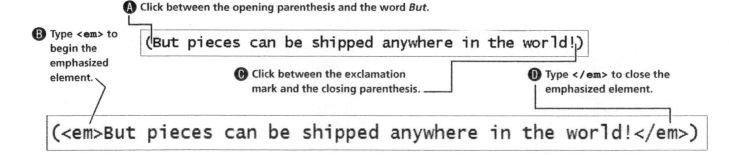

Ⓐ Click between the opening parenthesis and the word *But*.

Ⓑ Type `<em>` to begin the emphasized element.

`(But pieces can be shipped anywhere in the world!)`

Ⓒ Click between the exclamation mark and the closing parenthesis.

Ⓓ Type `</em>` to close the emphasized element.

`(<em>But pieces can be shipped anywhere in the world!</em>)`

6. Locate the first paragraph under the section The Art.

7. Using the steps outline in step 5, make the two Japanese words, *Oru* and *Kami*, emphasized.

```
<em>Oru</em> (meaning to fold) and <em>Kami</em>
```

Create Strong Emphasized Text

8. If necessary, scroll down and locate the third paragraph in the *The Art* section.

9. Using the steps outlined above, make the name Akira Yoshizawa strong and emphasized. You can begin with either the \<strong\> tag or the \<em\> tag. It doesn't matter—as long as the tags are properly nested.

```
is <strong><em>Akira Yoshizawa</em></strong>, born in Japan
```

View Your Changes

10. Save your changes and then make the web browser window active.

11. Tap the F5 key to refresh the page.
    Your page should now resemble the following figure.

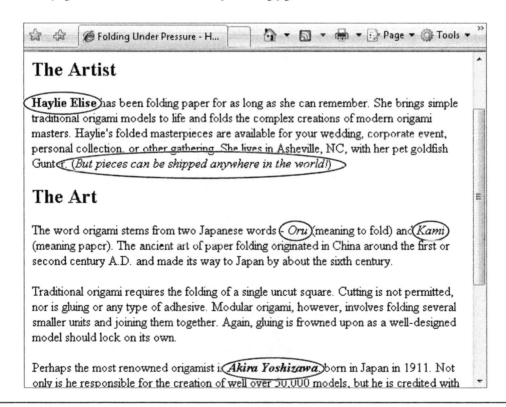

Inserting Special Characters

A computer keyboard contains alphanumeric characters plus a few others characters, such as @ and %. But what if you want to use characters that don't appear on your keyboard, such as the copyright symbol or accented characters? The answer lies in HTML character codes.

HTML Character Codes

An HTML character code is a special code you type that looks a bit odd in the HTML code but is rendered by the browser as a special character. HTML character codes always begin with an ampersand (&) and always end with a semicolon (;). The other characters you type between the & and ; determine what is actually displayed in the browser; for example, the code `&copy;` will display the copyright symbol. The code `&frac12;` will display the fraction one-half. A complete list of character codes can be found in Appendix C, Working with Character Codes in this book, but a list of a few characters appears in the following table.

QUICK REFERENCE: SELECTED HTML CHARACTER CODES

Symbol	Name	HTML Character Code
©	Copyright	`&copy;`
®	Registered trademark	`&reg;`
&	Ampersand	`&amp;`
™	Trademark	`&trade;`
÷	Division sign	`&divide;`
ü	Lowercase u with umlaut	`&uuml;`

Hands-On 4.5   Create HTML Character Codes

In this exercise, you will add special characters with HTML character codes.

1. Make the Notepad window active to edit the index.htm page.

2. Use Ctrl + Home to jump to the top of the page and locate the first paragraph in The Artist section, if necessary.

3. Follow these steps to add an umlaut to the goldfish's name:

Ⓐ Locate the next to last sentence starting with "She lives...."

```
gathering. She lives in Asheville, NC, with her pet goldfish
Gunter. (<em>But pieces can be shipped anywhere in the
world!</em>)</p>
```

Ⓑ Click in the name Gunter between the letters *u* and *n* and tap Backspace to delete the letter *u*.

Ⓒ Type the following: `&uuml;`   `G&uuml;nter`

4. If necessary, scroll to the bottom of the document and locate the word *copyright* in the last paragraph.

5. Double-click the word *copyright* to select it and tap ⌐Backspace⌐ to delete it.

6. Type the following: **©** ⌐Spacebar⌐
Your code should resemble the following.

```
<p>Folding Under Pressure &copy; 2007<br />
```

7. Save your changes and make the web browser window active.

8. Tap the ⌐F5⌐ key to refresh the page.
Your page should resemble the following figures.

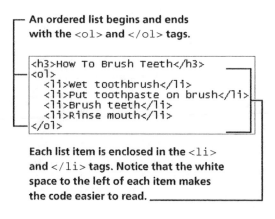

Working with Lists

HTML offers tags to create three different types of lists: ordered lists, unordered lists, and definition lists. As the names imply, these tags are used to create lists of items. The type of list you create is determined by the list content. Each type of list is not only structural, but it carries with it basic formatting to set it apart from headings and paragraphs. Lists are block-level elements and cannot be nested inside heading or paragraph tags, or vice versa.

Ordered Lists

Use an ordered list when listing items where the order is important, as in a set of instructions or steps to complete a specific task. You may be familiar with ordered lists in Microsoft Word, where they are called numbered lists. An ordered list begins with the code to start the list (an `<ol>` tag). This is followed by the code to create each item in the list (an `<li>` tag). Finally, the list is ended. Like other container tags, each item in the list and the list itself must be closed. The following code creates a list of basic instructions that should be followed in a specific order.

An ordered list begins and ends with the `<ol>` and `</ol>` tags.

```
<h3>How To Brush Teeth</h3>
<ol>
  <li>Wet toothbrush</li>
  <li>Put toothpaste on brush</li>
  <li>Brush teeth</li>
  <li>Rinse mouth</li>
</ol>
```

Each list item is enclosed in the `<li>` and `</li>` tags. Notice that the white space to the left of each item makes the code easier to read.

How To Brush Teeth

1. Wet toothbrush
2. Put toothpaste on brush
3. Brush teeth
4. Rinse mouth

Ordered lists are indented slightly to the right and are numbered by default.

Unordered Lists

Use an unordered list when listing items where the order is not important, as in a list of items to take on vacation or a list of random chores. Another term you may be familiar with for an unordered list is a bulleted list. The code for an unordered list is almost identical to that of an ordered list, except it uses the <ul> tag instead of the <ol> tag. The following code creates a list of items where the order of these items is not important.

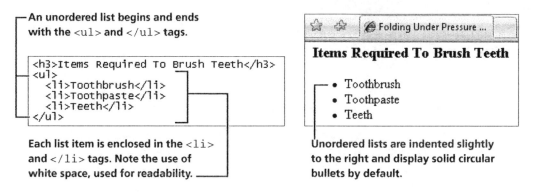

An unordered list begins and ends with the <ul> and </ul> tags.

```
<h3>Items Required To Brush Teeth</h3>
<ul>
    <li>Toothbrush</li>
    <li>Toothpaste</li>
    <li>Teeth</li>
</ul>
```

Each list item is enclosed in the <li> and </li> tags. Note the use of white space, used for readability.

Items Required To Brush Teeth

- Toothbrush
- Toothpaste
- Teeth

Unordered lists are indented slightly to the right and display solid circular bullets by default.

Definition Lists

Definition lists differ from ordered and unordered lists in that they require more tags and items appear in groups. Imagine a series of headings and paragraphs where each heading may have one or several paragraphs. A definition list behaves in a similar way. The structure of a definition list includes:

- The definition list itself, which begins and ends with <dl> and </dl> tags.

- A term, similar to a heading, that is defined by <dt> and </dt> tags.

- A definition, similar to a paragraph, which is defined by <dd> and </dd> tags.

Definition lists, as the name implies, are useful when creating a list of words and definitions. But if you're creative, you can find other uses for them, too, as shown in the following figure.

A definition list begins and ends with the
`<dl>` and `</dl>` tags.

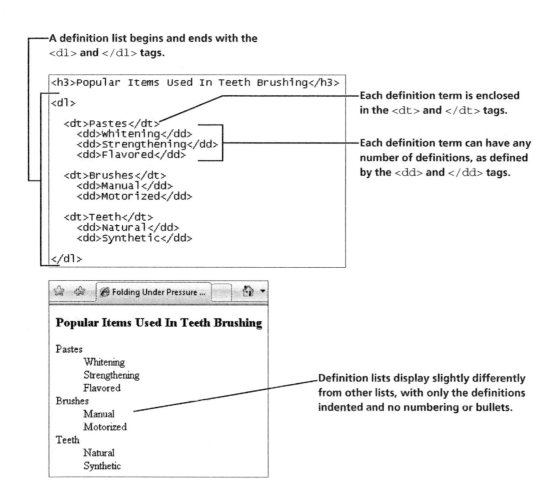

```
<h3>Popular Items Used In Teeth Brushing</h3>

<dl>

  <dt>Pastes</dt>
    <dd>Whitening</dd>
    <dd>Strengthening</dd>
    <dd>Flavored</dd>

  <dt>Brushes</dt>
    <dd>Manual</dd>
    <dd>Motorized</dd>

  <dt>Teeth</dt>
    <dd>Natural</dd>
    <dd>Synthetic</dd>

</dl>
```

Each definition term is enclosed
in the `<dt>` and `</dt>` tags.

Each definition term can have any
number of definitions, as defined
by the `<dd>` and `</dd>` tags.

Popular Items Used In Teeth Brushing

Pastes
    Whitening
    Strengthening
    Flavored
Brushes
    Manual
    Motorized
Teeth
    Natural
    Synthetic

Definition lists display slightly differently
from other lists, with only the definitions
indented and no numbering or bullets.

 Hands-On 4.6   **Create Unordered Lists**

In this exercise, you will add an unordered list to your page.

1. Make Notepad the active window.

2. Scroll down to the last paragraph in the *The Art* section, if necessary.

3. Delete everything in the paragraph (not in the document) after the word *include* and type a colon (**:**).

```
<p>Other pioneers at the forefront of this art include:</p>

Folding Under Pressure Copyright 2007
Last updated July 1, 2007
```

4. Click after the closing `</p>` tag and tap [Enter].

```
of this art include:</p>
07
```

Lists cannot be nested inside a paragraph.

5. Type the following to create an unordered list:

```
<ul> Enter
Spacebar Spacebar <li>Robert Lang</li> Enter
Spacebar Spacebar <li>John Montroll</li> Enter
Spacebar Spacebar <li>Fumiaki Kawahata</li> Enter
Spacebar Spacebar <li>Eric Joissel</li> Enter
</ul>
```

The spacebar adds white space to make the code easier to read.

6. Save your work and make the web browser window active.

7. Tap the F5 key to refresh the page.
Your page should resemble the following figure.

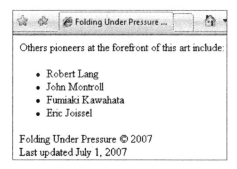

Nesting Lists

While lists cannot be nested inside headings or paragraphs, they can be nested inside each other—and they can be mixed-and-matched when nested. For example, you can have an ordered list nested inside an unordered list. The key to nesting lists is to insert the entire code block for the nested list between the opening `<li>` and closing `</li>` tags of a list item in the parent list, as in the following figures.

```
<h3>Items required To Brush Teeth</h3>

<ul>
  <li>Toothbrush</li>
  <li>Toothpaste
    <ul>
      <li>mint</li>
      <li>cinnamon</li>
      <li>orange-vanilla</li>
    </ul>
  </li>
  <li>Teeth</li>
</ul>
```

Lists can be nested inside each other. White space makes the code easier to read.

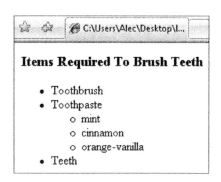

Nested lists are automatically indented and receive a different bullet style or number style from that of the parent list.

List Properties

Ordered and unordered lists support a variety of attributes that affect the display of list items. You can make an ordered list start with a specific number and have it display numbers, Roman numerals, or letters next to ordered list items. For unordered lists, you can display closed circles, open circles, or squares next to unordered list items. However, it is best to leave this presentational code to CSS whenever possible.

QUICK REFERENCE: LIST ATTRIBUTES

Tag	Attribute/Example	Values
OL	type `<ol type="A">`	■ 1—Uses numbers; default ■ A—Uses uppercase letters ■ a—Uses lowercase letters ■ I—Uses uppercase Roman numerals ■ i—Uses lowercase Roman numerals
OL	start `<ol start="6">`	■ An integer—Specifies the starting number for the entire list
UL	type `<ul type="circle">`	■ disc—Closed circle; default ■ circle—Open circle ■ square—Closed square
LI	type `<li type="a">`	■ 1, A, a, I, i, disc, circle, or square—Overrides the setting in the list
LI	value `<li value="3">`	■ Integer—Overrides the default number

The attribute/value `start="4"`, in combination with the type set to lowercase, specifies starting on the fourth letter *d*.

The attribute/value `type="a"` specifies lowercase letters.

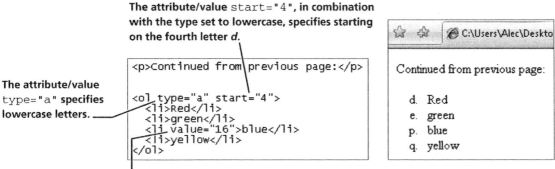

```
<p>Continued from previous page:</p>

<ol type="a" start="4">
  <li>Red</li>
  <li>green</li>
  <li value="16">blue</li>
  <li>yellow</li>
</ol>
```

C:\Users\Alec\Deskto

Continued from previous page:

d. Red
e. green
p. blue
q. yellow

The *value* attribute in the <li> tag specifies a new starting value for the remaining list items. The value *16* corresponds to the 16th letter in the alphabet, *p*.

NOTE! XHTML 1.0 strict *forbids the type, start, and value attributes in the UL, OL, and LI tags. The type attribute can easily be replaced with CSS, but the start and value attributes are much more difficult and CSS alternatives are not supported in all browsers. For XHTML 1.0 transitional, it is far easier (and still valid) to use the start and value attributes rather than recreate the result with CSS.*

Defining Document Structure

At their most basic, most documents can be defined with three main structural regions.

- **Masthead**—Located at the top of the page; normally includes the company name, tagline, logo, and other branding elements

- **Content**—The main body of the document

- **Footer**—Located at the bottom of a document; normally includes less important information, text for search engine optimization, or information required by law but of little interest to most users

In addition, web pages typically have a section of hyperlinks called the navigation bar, or navbar. This is a fourth generic region for web pages.

Structural Regions Are Not Tags

These regions are not to be confused with HTML structural tags like HTML, HEAD, and BODY. The masthead, content, and footer regions are not tags; they are generic terms that can apply to a web page just as easily as they can apply to a magazine layout or brochure. With web documents, regions such as these can be defined with <div> tags.

Structuring with DIV Tags

The division (<div>) tag is a block-level container element and normally cannot share a line with any other element, like another DIV (although it is possible to override this with advanced CSS). DIV elements are normally used to separate sections of content from each other for structural purposes. They make formatting your document later with CSS much easier.

DIV tags are one of those special block-level elements that can contain other block-level elements. While DIV tags cannot be nested inside heading, paragraph, or list elements, all of these elements can be nested inside a DIV. And other DIVs can be nested inside a DIV.

DIV tags separate sections of content.

```
index - Notepad
File  Edit  Format  View  Help

<div id="masthead">
<h1>The Toothbrush Place</h1>
<h3>Your Teeth Are Our Business</h3>
<hr/>
</div>

<div id="content">
<p>Brush at least twice a day if you
</div>

<div id="footer">
<p><em>All rights reserved. &copy; 2
</div>
```

It is easy in most cases to simply look at a document and determine where DIV tags should be inserted.

The Toothbrush Place

Your Teeth Are Our Business

Brush at least twice a day if you want to keep your choppers...

All rights reserved. © 2007

Identifying DIVs

DIV tags that identify unique sections of a document should be uniquely labeled. For example, the DIV tag that identifies a document's masthead may be labeled as "masthead" while another DIV that identifies the document's footer is identified as "footer." The key here is *unique*. Structurally, there would be only one masthead and only one footer.

id Attributes

All tags, not just DIV tags, can be uniquely identified by adding an id attribute with a unique value. Remember that with XHTML, all attributes must be lowercase and all attributes must have an associated quoted value. In the case of a masthead, the code may look like this:

```
<div id="masthead">...masthead content...</div>
```

The id attribute uniquely identifies the masthead section, and no other tag in the document can use id="masthead". Not only does the id aid in defining the document structure, but it can be used later in conjunction with CSS to apply visual formatting. For example, your CSS code can instruct the browser to "make all text in the masthead red and bold." You will see how to do this later in the book when you work with CSS.

Id Attribute Value Rules

A few important rules limit the possible values for the id attribute.

- Id values must begin with a letter or the underscore character.

- Id values cannot contain spaces.

Naming DIV Tags

Note there is nothing special about the words masthead, navbar, content, or footer as the values for the id attribute. These are generic terms that clearly define document regions. You can just as easily use the words branding, navigation, maintext, and bottomcontent to uniquely label your DIVs. However, the names you choose should describe the structural contents of the DIV tag. For example, `id="redText"` is a poor choice as it describes the visual formatting of the contents and not the structure of the contents. A better choice would be `id="intro"` or `id="mainContent"`.

 Hands-On 4.7   **Finalize the Document Structure with DIV Tags**

In this exercise, you will add DIV tags to isolate and identify the various sections of the document.

Visually Pinpoint DIVs

1. If necessary, scroll to the top of the web page in your browser.

2. Mentally identify the following four regions of the page: masthead, navbar, content, and footer.

Create DIV Tags

3. Make Notepad the active window in order to edit the index.htm page.

4. Scroll to the top of the document, if necessary.

5. Follow these steps to identify the entire masthead with a DIV tag:

Ⓐ Click to the left of the opening `<h1>` tag, type `<div id="masthead">`, and tap Enter.

```
<div id="masthead">
<h1>Folding Under Pressure</h1>
</div>
```

Ⓑ Click after the closing `</h1>` tag, tap Enter, and type `</div>`.

By typing the DIV tags on their own lines, you have used white space to make the HTML code easier to read and edit.

6. Using the steps detailed in step 5, identify the entire navigation bar with a DIV tag.

```
<div id="navbar">
<p>Home - Gallery - How To - Resources - Contact</p>
</div>
```

7. Using the steps detailed in step 5, identify the beginning of the main content section.

```
<div id="content">
<h2>The Artist</h2>
```

8. Using the steps detailed in step 5, identify the end of the main content section.

```
<li>Eric Joissel</li>
</ul>
</div>
```

9. Using the steps detailed in step 5, identify the footer.

```
<div id="footer">
<p>Folding Under Pressure Copyright 2007<br />
Last updated July 1, 2007</p>
</div>
```

10. Save your changes.
    Although you have made changes to the document, there should be no visual changes when viewed in the browser. Your DIV tags have simply aided in defining the structure of the document—and will help with future CSS formatting.

11. Make the web browser window active.

12. Tap the F5 key to refresh the page. Your page's display should not have changed at all.

13. Close your web browser.

14. Close Notepad.

Summarizing Tags

The following table lists the tags presented in this lesson. Remember that XHTML 1.0 transitional supports all the tags and attributes that HTML 4.01 supports, so even presentational markup is officially valid. However, in the quest to separate structure from presentation and eventually create valid XHTML 1.0 strict code, most attributes presented in this lesson should be avoided in favor of CSS.

QUICK REFERENCE: STRUCTURING TEXT WITH TAGS				
Tag	XHTML Code	Container or Replacement	Block or Inline	Attributes/Use CSS Instead?
Emphasis	`<em></em>`	Container	Inline	No attributes
Heading	`<h1></h1>` through `<h6></h6>`	Container	Block	align (use CSS)
Line break	` `	Replacement	Inline	No attributes
List item	`<li></li>`	Container	Block	type (use CSS) value
Ordered list	`<ol></ol>`	Container	Block	type (use CSS) start
Paragraph	`<p></p>`	Container	Block	align (use CSS)
Strong	`<strong></strong>`	Container	Inline	No attributes
Unordered list	`<ul></ul>`	Container	Block	type (use CSS)

# Concepts Review

True/False Questions

1. Tapping the [Enter] key while typing HTML code will result in the browser displaying a line break. TRUE FALSE

2. The best way to create space between paragraphs is to use multiple `<br />` tags. TRUE FALSE

3. There are six heading styles in HTML, with `<h1>` being the largest and `<h6>` the smallest. TRUE FALSE

4. In XHTML you should always use the `<b>` tag instead of the `<strong>` tag. TRUE FALSE

5. You should use an `<ol>` when creating a list of items where the order is important. TRUE FALSE

6. You should use DIV tags to define major regions of your document, and the DIV tags can contain headings, paragraphs, and lists. TRUE FALSE

7. Most documents contain the general masthead, content, and footer regions. TRUE FALSE

8. Use the `<masthead>` tag to define the masthead of an HTML document. TRUE FALSE

9. A list created with `<ul></ul>` tags can be displayed with letters, numbers, or Roman numerals. TRUE FALSE

10. Id attributes must be unique throughout any single document. TRUE FALSE

Multiple Choice Questions

1. Consider the following statements. Who is correct?
   - Vincent says that HTML forbids presentational markup of any kind and that all presentational formatting must be defined via CSS.
   - Elza says HTML allows presentational formatting but XHTML forbids it.
   - Sabra says most presentational markup is only forbidden in XHTML strict; HTML and XHTML transitional allow it completely.

   a. Vincent is correct.
   b. Elza is correct.
   c. Sabra is correct.
   d. No one is correct.

2. Tran has tried to create a numbered list of driving directions, but they display on his page with bullets instead of with numbers. What has he done wrong?

a. He failed to set the type attribute in his `<ul>` tag to `type="1"`.

b. He failed to set the number attribute in his `<ul>` tag to `number="1"`.

c. He used the `<ul>` tag instead of the `<ol>` tag.

d. Tran has done nothing wrong. HTML can only display lists with bullets.

3. Cheyenne is trying to display the registered trademark symbol (®) on her web page. She has typed the code `$reg;` but it is not working. What has she done wrong?

a. She used the dollar sign (`$`) instead of the ampersand (`&`).

b. She ended her code with a semicolon (`;`) instead of a colon (`:`).

c. She typed only `reg` instead of the whole word `registered`.

d. She forgot to enclose her code inside the `<character>` tag.

4. Benji has structured his document with DIV tags, but things just aren't displaying as he wants. He has defined major regions with DIV tags as follows:

- The masthead section is structured with
  `<div id="masthead"></div>`

- The navigation bar under the masthead is structured with
  `<div id="navbar"></div>`

- The content area is structured with
  `<div id="content"></div>`

- Additional navigation at the bottom of the page is structured with
  `<div id="navbar"></div>`

What has Benji done wrong?

a. He has used too many DIV tags.

b. His id attributes are not unique.

c. Masthead is not a valid value for his id attribute.

d. He has nested a DIV inside another DIV.

Skill Builders

Skill Builder 4.1 Create the Document Structure

In this exercise, you will create the XHTML document structure.

1. Start Notepad and save the blank file to your Lesson 04 folder as **sb_4_1.htm**.

2. Type the following to create the required structural tags:

```
<!DOCTYPE html PUBLIC "-//W3C//DTD XHTML 1.0 Transitional//EN" [Enter]
"http://www.w3.org/TR/xhtml1/DTD/xhtml1-transitional.dtd"> [Enter][Enter]
<html xmlns="http://www.w3.org/1999/xhtml"> [Enter][Enter]
<head> [Enter]
<meta http-equiv="Content-Type" content="text/html; charset=utf-8" /> [Enter]
<title>Skill Builder 4</title> [Enter]
</head> [Enter][Enter]
<body> [Enter][Enter]
</body> [Enter][Enter]
</html>
```

3. Click between the opening and closing body tags and type the following to create the regional structure:

```
<div id="masthead"> [Enter][Enter]
</div> [Enter][Enter][Enter]
<div id="navbar"> [Enter][Enter]
</div> [Enter][Enter][Enter]
<div id="content"> [Enter][Enter]
</div> [Enter][Enter][Enter]
<div id="footer"> [Enter][Enter]
</div> [Enter]
```

Your document should resemble the following figure.

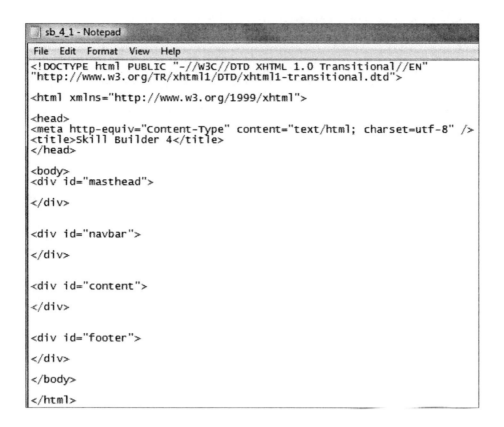

```
sb_4_1 - Notepad

File   Edit   Format   View   Help

<!DOCTYPE html PUBLIC "-//W3C//DTD XHTML 1.0 Transitional//EN"
"http://www.w3.org/TR/xhtml1/DTD/xhtml1-transitional.dtd">

<html xmlns="http://www.w3.org/1999/xhtml">

<head>
<meta http-equiv="Content-Type" content="text/html; charset=utf-8" />
<title>Skill Builder 4</title>
</head>

<body>
<div id="masthead">

</div>

<div id="navbar">

</div>

<div id="content">

</div>

<div id="footer">

</div>

</body>

</html>
```

4. Save your changes and minimize Notepad.

Test Your Code

5. Open your Lesson 04 folder and double-click the sb_4_1.htm file to preview it in your browser.

   You should see the page title in the web browser's title bar. No content should display in the main browser window. If necessary, go back and correct any errors before continuing with the next exercise.

The title bar should display the text from the `<title>` tag. ——

The main browser window should be blank. ——

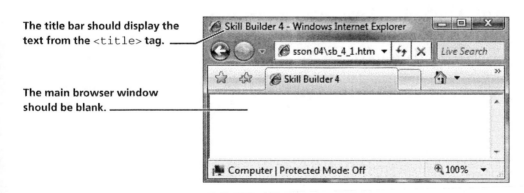

6. Close the browser and return to Notepad.

Skill Builder 4.2   Add Headings

In this exercise, you will add headings to your document.

Before You Begin: You must complete Skill Builder 4.1 before beginning this exercise.

1. Save a copy of the file to your Lesson 04 folder as **sb_4_2.htm**.

2. Follow these steps to create the page heading:

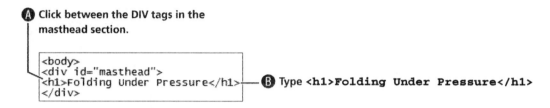

Ⓐ Click between the DIV tags in the masthead section.

```
<body>
<div id="masthead">
<h1>Folding Under Pressure</h1>
</div>
```

Ⓑ Type **<h1>Folding Under Pressure</h1>**

3. Click between the DIV tags in the content section and type the following:

   <h2>How To</h2> `Enter`

   Your code should resemble the following figure.

```
<div id="content">
<h2>How To</h2>

</div>
```

4. Save your changes and minimize Notepad.

Test Your Code

5. Open your Lesson 04 folder and double-click the sb_4_2.htm file to preview it in your browser.
   You should see the two headings in the main browser window. If necessary, go back and correct any errors before continuing with the next exercise.

The <h1> appears very large at the top of the page. ⎯⎯

The <h2> appears slightly smaller underneath it. ⎯⎯

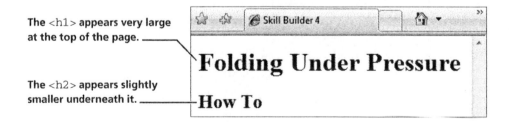

Folding Under Pressure

How To

6. Close the browser and return to Notepad.

Skill Builder 4.3   Add Paragraphs and Line Breaks

In this exercise, you will add paragraphs and line breaks to the document.

Before You Begin: You must complete Skill Builder 4.2 before beginning this exercise.

1. Save a copy of the file to your Lesson 04 folder as **sb_4_3.htm**.

Create Paragraphs

2. Click between the DIV tags in the navbar section and type the following to create the navigation bar:

   ```
   <p>Home - Gallery - How To - Resources - Contact</p>
   ```

3. Click in the space below the How To heading and type the following to create a paragraph:

   ```
   <p> Enter
   There are many types of paper crafts similar to origami. There are
   even variations of origami, including modular origami and kiragami.
   Enter
   </p> Enter Enter
   ```

4. Type the following to create a second paragraph in the Content section:

   ```
   <p> Enter
   The following hints will help you to fold traditional origami.
   Remember that traditional origami requires strict adherence to these
   rules. Enter
   </p>
   ```

   Your code should resemble the following figure. However, you lines may wrap differently.

   ```
   <div id="content">
   <h2>How To</h2>
   <p>
   There are many types of paper crafts similar to origami. There are even
   variations of origami, including modular origami and kiragami.
   </p>

   <p>
   The following hints will help you to fold traditional origami. Remember that
   traditional origami requires strict adherence to these rules.
   </p>
   </div>
   ```

Create Line Breaks

5. Follow these steps to create a line break in the Content section's second paragraph:

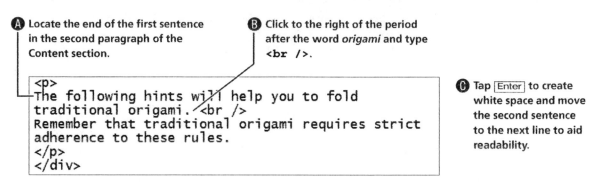

Ⓐ Locate the end of the first sentence in the second paragraph of the Content section.

Ⓑ Click to the right of the period after the word *origami* and type `<br />`.

```
<p>
The following hints will help you to fold
traditional origami.<br />
Remember that traditional origami requires strict
adherence to these rules.
</p>
</div>
```

Ⓒ Tap [Enter] to create white space and move the second sentence to the next line to aid readability.

6. Save your changes and minimize Notepad.

Test Your Code

7. Open your Lesson 04 folder and double-click the sb_4_3.htm file to preview it in your browser.

You should see the three paragraphs in the main browser window. Your lines may wrap differently from what is shown in the figure; however, the last sentence on the page should begin on its own line due to the line break. If necessary, go back and correct any errors before continuing with the next exercise.

The navigation bar paragraph appears under the page heading.

The first content paragraph appears under the subheading. Your lines may wrap differently.

The second paragraph contains a line break before the last sentence.

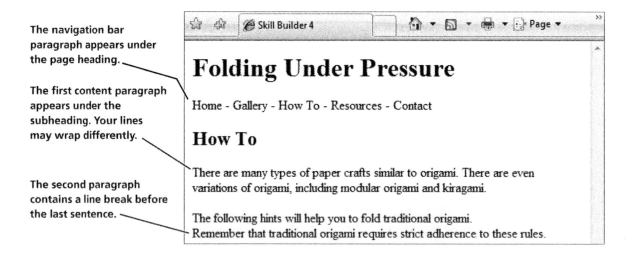

8. Close the browser and return to Notepad.

Skill Builder 4.4   Format Characters as Strong and Emphasized

In this exercise, you will create strong and emphasized text.

Before You Begin: You must complete Skill Builder 4.3 before beginning this exercise.

1. Save a copy of the file to your Lesson 04 folder as **sb_4_4.htm**.

Create Emphasized Text

2. Follow these steps to create emphasized text in the first paragraph of the Content section:

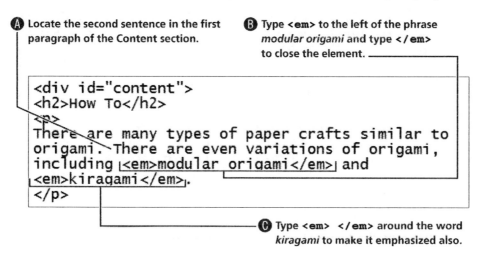

A Locate the second sentence in the first paragraph of the Content section.

B Type **** to the left of the phrase *modular origami* and type **** to close the element.

```
<div id="content">
<h2>How To</h2>
<p>
There are many types of paper crafts similar to
origami. There are even variations of origami,
including <em>modular origami</em> and
<em>kiragami</em>.
</p>
```

C Type **** **** around the word *kiragami* to make it emphasized also.

3. Make the last sentence in the second paragraph of the Content section emphasized.

```
<p>
The following hints will help you to fold
traditional origami. <br />
<em>Remember that traditional origami requires
strict adherence to these rules.</em>
</p>
</div>
```

4. Locate the word *strict* in the same sentence and make it strong.

```
<em>Remember that traditional origami requires
<strong>strict</strong> adherence to these
rules.</em>
```

5. Save your changes and minimize Notepad.

Test Your Code

6. Open your Lesson 04 folder and double-click the sb_4_4.htm file to preview it in your browser.

Your page should resemble the following figure. If it doesn't, go back and correct any errors.

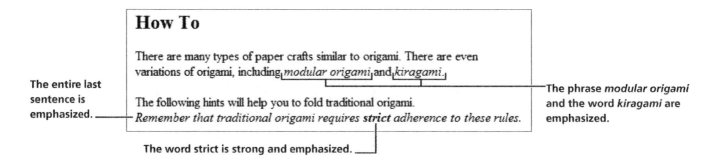

The entire last sentence is emphasized.

How To

There are many types of paper crafts similar to origami. There are even variations of origami, including *modular origami* and *kiragami*.

The following hints will help you to fold traditional origami. *Remember that traditional origami requires **strict** adherence to these rules.*

The phrase *modular origami* and the word *kiragami* are emphasized.

The word strict is strong and emphasized.

7. Close the browser and return to Notepad.

Skill Builder 4.5   Insert Special Characters

In this exercise, you will insert special characters using HTML character codes.

***Before You Begin:** You must complete Skill Builder 4.4 before beginning this exercise.*

1. Save a copy of the file to your Lesson 04 folder as **sb_4_5.htm**.

Insert Special Characters

2. Click between the Footer DIV tags and type the following:

Folding Under Pressure. All material © 2007. .

3. Follow these steps to insert special characters in the navigation bar:

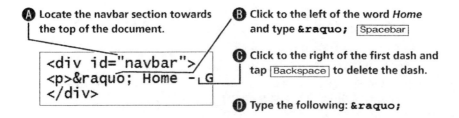

A Locate the navbar section towards the top of the document.

B Click to the left of the word *Home* and type **»** [Spacebar]

C Click to the right of the first dash and tap [Backspace] to delete the dash.

D Type the following: **»**

```
<div id="navbar">
<p>&raquo; Home - G
</div>
```

Technically, adding » in this case is being done for presentational reasons and, as such, should be avoided in XHTML 1.0 strict. A visual element could be defined via CSS instead. However, as we are using XHTML 1.0 transitional, we can get away with it!

4. Continue to replace all the dashes in the navigation bar with the » character. *Your code should resemble the following.*

```
<p>&raquo; Home &raquo; Gallery &raquo; How To &raquo; Resources
&raquo; Contact</p>
```

5. Save your changes and minimize Notepad.

Test Your Code

6. Open your Lesson 04 folder and double-click the sb_4_5.htm file to preview it in your browser.
Your page should resemble the following figure. If it doesn't, go back and correct any errors.

The navigation bar should feature the special character and not dashes. ————

The footer displays the copyright symbol. ————

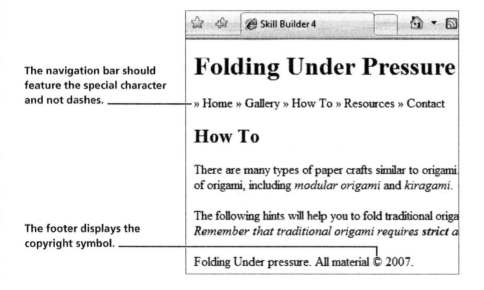

7. Close the browser and return to Notepad.

Skill Builder 4.6   Create a List and Sub-list

In this exercise, you will create a list and a sub-list.

Before You Begin: You must complete Skill Builder 4.5 before beginning this exercise.

1. Save a copy of the file to your Lesson 04 folder as **sb_4_6.htm**.

Create an Ordered List

2. Follow these steps to create an ordered list at the end of the Content section:

A Locate the end of the last paragraph in the Content section.

```
<p>
The following hints will help you to fold traditional
origami. <br />
<em>Remember that traditional origami requires
<strong>strict</strong> adherence to these rules.</em>
</p>

<ol>

</div>
```

B Click to the right of the closing `</p>` tag and tap [Enter] twice to create white space.

C Type **<ol>**, then tap [Enter] [Spacebar] [Spacebar] to start an ordered list.

3. Type **<li>Have patience</li>**, tap [Enter], and tap [Spacebar] twice to create the first list item.

4. Type **<li>Honor the tradition</li>**, tap [Enter], and tap [Spacebar] twice to create the second list item.

5. Type **<li>Have more patience</li>**, tap [Enter], and type **</ol>** to create the final list item and close the list.
   Your code should resemble the following figure.

```
<ol>
   <li>Have patience</li>
   <li>Honor the tradition</li>
   <li>Have more patience</li>
</ol>
</div>
```

Create a Sub-list

6. Follow these steps to start a nested unordered list:

Ⓐ Click to the right of the end of the word *tradition* in the second list item, before the closing </li> tag.

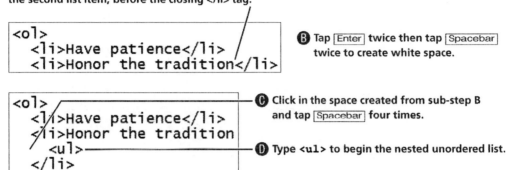

```
<ol>
   <li>Have patience</li>
   <li>Honor the tradition</li>
```

Ⓑ Tap ⌷Enter⌷ twice then tap ⌷Spacebar⌷ twice to create white space.

```
<ol>
   <li>Have patience</li>
   <li>Honor the tradition
      <ul>
   </li>
```

Ⓒ Click in the space created from sub-step B and tap ⌷Spacebar⌷ four times.

Ⓓ Type <ul> to begin the nested unordered list.

7. Tap ⌷Enter⌷ then tap ⌷Spacebar⌷ six times to create white space.

8. Type the first list item: **<li>Use square paper only</li>**

9. Tap ⌷Enter⌷ then tap ⌷Spacebar⌷ six times to create white space.

10. Type the second list item: **<li>Do not cut, rip, or tear the paper</li>**

11. Tap ⌷Enter⌷ then tap ⌷Spacebar⌷ six times to create white space.

12. Type the final list item: **<li>Do not use glue, tape, or any adhesive</li>**

13. Tap ⌷Enter⌷ then tap ⌷Spacebar⌷ four times to create white space.

14. Type the closing **</ul>** tag.
    Your code should resemble the following figure.

```
<ol>
   <li>Have patience</li>
   <li>Honor the tradition
      <ul>
         <li>Use square paper only</li>
         <li>Do not cut, rip, or tear the paper</li>
         <li>Do not use glue, tape, or any adhesive</li>
      </ul>
   </li>
   <li>Have more patience</li>
</ol>
</div>
```

15. Save your changes and minimize Notepad.

Test Your Code

16. Open your Lesson 04 folder and double-click the sb_4_6.htm file to preview it in your browser.

Your page should resemble the following figure. If it doesn't, go back and correct any errors.

The list displays after the second paragraph in the Content section.

The outer list uses numbers.

The nested list uses bullets.

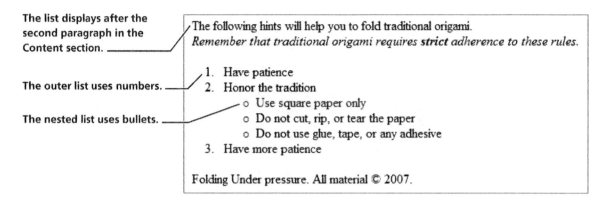

The following hints will help you to fold traditional origami.
*Remember that traditional origami requires **strict** adherence to these rules.*

1. Have patience
2. Honor the tradition
   - Use square paper only
   - Do not cut, rip, or tear the paper
   - Do not use glue, tape, or any adhesive
3. Have more patience

Folding Under pressure. All material © 2007.

17. Close the browser.

18. Close Notepad.

Assessments

Assessment 4.1   Create a Document Structure

In this exercise, you will create an XHTML document structure around existing content.

1. Open the as-4-1-text.txt file from your Lesson 04 folder in Notepad.
   The text file contains a lot of text and white space. You will need to turn this into a valid XHTML document.

2. Save a copy of the file to your Lesson 04 folder as **as_guitar1.htm**.

Create XHTML Structure

3. At the very top of the document, type the following tags:
   - DOCTYPE declaration for XHTML 1.0 transitional
   - Opening HTML tag with the xmlns attribute
   - Opening HEAD tag
   - Title tags with the title **Guitar Pioneers**
   - Meta tag to declare the character encoding as UTF-8
   - Closing HEAD tag
   - Opening BODY tag

4. At the very end of the document, after all the content, close the BODY and HTML tags.

5. Save your changes and preview the page in a web browser to verify that it displays as expected.
   The title should display in the browser's title bar and the content should display as one large block.

Create DIV Tags

6. Use DIV tags with unique IDs to identify the following sections:
   - Masthead containing the page heading
   - Introductory paragraph text at the top of the document
   - List of featured artists
   - Blues rock subheading and paragraph
   - Shred subheading and paragraph
   - Rock subheading and paragraph
   - The footer

7. Save your changes.

Test Your Code

8. Preview your page in a browser and fix any errors before continuing.

Assessment 4.2　　Add Headings, Paragraphs, and Special Characters

In this exercise, you will add headings, paragraphs, and special characters to the document.

Before You Begin: You must complete Assessment 4.1 before beginning this exercise.

Headings and Paragraphs

1. Save a copy of the file to your Lesson 04 folder as **as_guitar2.htm**.

2. In the masthead, turn the text *Guitar Greats* into a heading 1.
   Remember that headings cannot contain DIVs, but DIVs can contain headings.

3. Use <p> tags to create a paragraph out of the text following the Guitar Greats page heading.
   Remember that paragraphs cannot contain DIVs, but DIVs can contain paragraphs.

4. If necessary, scroll down to the three paragraphs for *Blues Rock*, *Shred*, and *Rock*.

5. Turn *Blues Rock* into a heading 2 and the text that follows into a paragraph.

6. Turn *Shred* into a heading 2 and the text that follows into a paragraph.

7. Turn *Rock* into a heading 2 and the text that follows into a paragraph.

Special Characters

8. If necessary, scroll down to the footer.

9. Replace the word *copyright* with the copyright symbol.

10. Replace the letter *u* in *Blouse* with an umlaut.

11. Save your changes.

Test Your Code

12. Preview your page in a browser and fix any errors before continuing.

The page heading is an `<h1>`.

The text following the heading is a paragraph.

The list is not yet formatted.

These three sections each contain an `<h2>` and a paragraph.

The copyright symbol and umlaut *u* display properly.

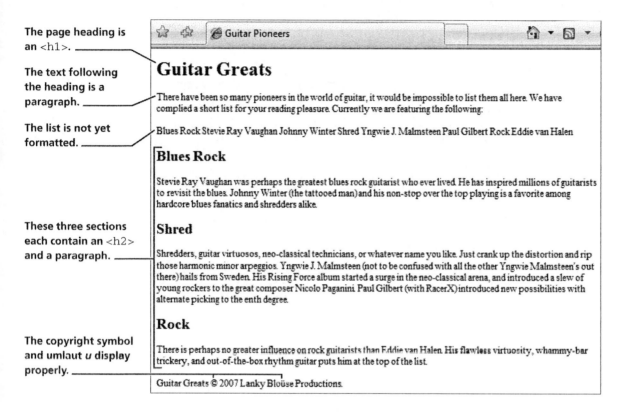

Guitar Greats

There have been so many pioneers in the world of guitar, it would be impossible to list them all here. We have complied a short list for your reading pleasure. Currently we are featuring the following:

Blues Rock Stevie Ray Vaughan Johnny Winter Shred Yngwie J. Malmsteen Paul Gilbert Rock Eddie van Halen

Blues Rock

Stevie Ray Vaughan was perhaps the greatest blues rock guitarist who ever lived. He has inspired millions of guitarists to revisit the blues. Johnny Winter (the tattooed man) and his non-stop over the top playing is a favorite among hardcore blues fanatics and shredders alike.

Shred

Shredders, guitar virtuosos, neo-classical technicians, or whatever name you like. Just crank up the distortion and rip those harmonic minor arpeggios. Yngwie J. Malmsteen (not to be confused with all the other Yngwie Malmsteen's out there) hails from Sweden. His Rising Force album started a surge in the neo-classical arena, and introduced a slew of young rockers to the great composer Nicolo Paganini. Paul Gilbert (with RacerX) introduced new possibilities with alternate picking to the enth degree.

Rock

There is perhaps no greater influence on rock guitarists than Eddie van Halen. His flawless virtuosity, whammy-bar trickery, and out-of-the-box rhythm guitar puts him at the top of the list.

Guitar Greats © 2007 Lanky Blöuse Productions.

Assessment 4.3   Format Characters

In this exercise, you will format characters as strong and emphasized.

Before You Begin: You must complete Assessment 4.2 before beginning this exercise.

Format Characters

1. Save a copy of the file to your Lesson 04 folder as **as_guitar3.htm**.

2. If necessary, scroll to the *Blues Rock* paragraph.

3. Make the names Stevie Ray Vaughan and Johnny Winter strong.

4. Make the text *tattooed man* emphasized.

5. If necessary, scroll to the *Shred* paragraph.

6. Make the names Yngwie J. Malmsteen and Paul Gilbert strong.

7. Make the name Nicolo Paganini emphasized.

8. If necessary, scroll to the *Rock* paragraph.

9. Make the name Eddie van Halen strong.

10. Make the entire footer both strong and emphasized.

11. Save your changes.

Test Your Code

12. Preview your page in a browser and fix any errors before continuing.

The guitarists' names are strong while *tattooed man* is emphasized.

Blues Rock

Stevie Ray Vaughan was perhaps the greatest blues rock guitarist who ever lived. He has inspired millions of guitarists to revisit the blues. **Johnny Winter** (the *tattooed man*) and his non-stop over the top playing is a favorite among hardcore blues fanatics and shredders alike.

The guitarists' names are strong while Paganini's name is emphasized.

Shred

Shredders, guitar virtuosos, neo-classical technicians, or whatever name you like. Just crank up the distortion and rip those harmonic minor arpeggios. **Yngwie J. Malmsteen** (not to be confused with all the other Yngwie Malmsteen's out there) hails from Sweden. His Rising Force album started a surge in the neo-classical arena, and introduced a slew of young rockers to the great composer *Nicolo Paganini*. **Paul Gilbert** (with RacerX) introduced new possibilities with alternate picking to the enth degree.

The name is strong.

Rock

There is perhaps no greater influence on rock guitarists than **Eddie van Halen**. His flawless virtuosity, whammy-bar trickery, and out-of-the-box rhythm guitar puts him at the top of the list.

The entire footer is both strong and emphasized.

Guitar Greats © 2007 Lanky Blouse Productions.

Assessment 4.4   Create Lists

In this exercise, you will create a nested list.

Before You Begin: You must complete Assessment 4.3 before beginning this exercise.

Create a List

1. Save a copy of the file to your Lesson 04 folder as **as_guitar4.htm**.

2. If necessary, scroll to the list of styles and guitarists towards the top of the document.

3. Follow these steps to create an ordered list:

   - Start the ordered list before *Blues Rock*.
   - Set the type attribute to `type="I"` to use Roman numerals.
   - Create the first list item around *Blues Rock*.
   - Create the second list item around *Shred*.
   - Create the third list item around *Rock*.
   - Close the ordered list after Eddie van Halen.

4. Create a nested unordered list of two items around the names Stevie Ray Vaughan and Johnny Winter. Set the type attribute of the unordered list to `type="square"` so it will display square bullets.

5. Create another nested unordered list of two items around the names Yngwie J. Malmsteen and Paul Gilbert. Set the bullet type to display squares.

6. Create a final nested unordered list of a single item around the name Eddie van Halen. Set the bullet type to display squares.

7. Save your changes.

Test Your Code

8. Preview your page in a browser and fix any errors before continuing.

9. Close your browser.

10. Close Notepad.

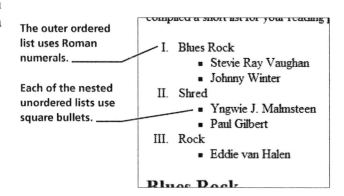

The outer ordered list uses Roman numerals. _____

Each of the nested unordered lists use square bullets. _____

Critical Thinking

Critical Thinking 4.1   Create a Document Structure

In this exercise, you will create an XHTML document complete with headings, paragraphs, lists, special characters, and character formatting.

1. Start Notepad and save the blank file to your Lesson 04 folder as **ct_4.htm**.

2. Type the XHTML structural tags necessary for a valid XHTML 1.0 transitional document. These include DOCTYPE, html, head, title, character encoding, and body.

3. Create body content based on the following criteria:

   - Choose any topic you like to serve as content. Write about your favorite travel destinations, favorite sports teams, favorite cartoon characters, etc.

   - Create an appropriate title within the title tags.

   - Create a heading 1 to serve as the page heading.

   - Create at least two subheadings.

   - Include at least three paragraphs of text.

   - Include a list with at least one nested list. You may use an ordered, unordered, or definition list for the outer or nested lists. Feel free to mix and match—and experiment with the type attribute.

   - Include at least two special characters created with HTML character codes. Use Appendix C, Working with Character Codes, or search online for HTML character codes.

   - Organize your body content with DIV tags that clearly define the various regions of your content. Be sure to use unique ids for your DIV tags.

   - Save your changes and test your page in at least two different browsers, such as Internet Explorer and Firefox. Does your page render exactly the same in the different browsers? Or are there subtle (or major) differences?

LESSON 5

Editing Images

In this lesson, you will learn the typical workflow sequence for acquiring and incorporating images into your web pages. You will learn about the various image file formats and where to legally acquire images for your site at no cost. Lastly, you will learn basic image editing techniques with Adobe Photoshop.

LESSON OBJECTIVES

After studying this lesson, you will be able to:

- Demonstrate website design workflow
- Describe the differences between JPEG, GIF, and PNG images and choose the best file format for a given image
- Download royalty-free images in the public domain for unrestricted use on your web pages
- Perform basic image editing functions with Adobe Photoshop

Case Study: Acquiring and Editing Images

Haylie knows that photographs of her folded works will be a large part of her site design. She brushes up on the differences between image file formats so she can optimize her photos for use on her website. She also wonders if there are free sources for images she can incorporate into her site. Her assistant Miguel is an expert with Adobe Photoshop, and Haylie knows that she can use his help in editing some photos and getting them ready for use on her pages.

A hand-drawn sketch can be provided to a graphic artist.

A graphic artist can create a computer file of the full design.

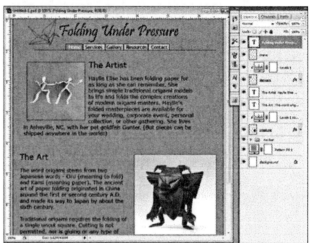

A web developer can extract portions of the graphic artist's file for use on the web page.

Selecting and Preparing Images

Being able to successfully (and legally) acquire, edit, and optimize images is a core skill any web developer must have. Even if your days are spent in front of a text editor typing line after line of code, some of those lines of code will reference images—and you will need to know the basics of image editing to be successful.

Design Considerations

As discussed in Lesson 1, Introducing Web Technologies, the user should be considered when designing a website's look and feel. If your client wants something they think looks good, but you know that the idea will hurt the usability or accessibility of the site, it is your responsibility as the developer to educate your client without being condescending. In the end, however, the customer is always right, and if your client insists, you will need to develop the site according to their specifications. Remember the basic guidelines, and remember that these guidelines are not hard and fast rules. They can be broken if you can clearly articulate your reasons for doing so.

- Keep images relevant to site content.

- Don't use too many images on a page or they may distract from the text.

- Use high-quality artwork (cheap clip art looks amateurish).

- Keep file sizes to a minimum so users on slower dial-up Internet connections have a positive experience.

Images and Graphics

In the world of web design, the terms *images* and *graphics* are used interchangeably. They both refer to electronic files, which can be photographs, scanned pictures, graphics drawn with computer software, or any other picture saved as a computer file.

Typical Workflow

A typical workflow in the design process of a web page can be outlined as follows:

1. Wire frame

2. Full comp

3. Graphics generation

4. Site integration

Wire Frame

As discussed in Lesson 1, Introducing Web Technologies, a *wire frame* is a block diagram showing the layout of page elements. The wire frame can be used by a graphic artist to guide the creation of a *comp*.

This wire frame was hand-drawn by a non-artist! Wire frames do not have to be works of art; they just need to convey the page layout and design elements.

Full Comp

A comp (short for "composite," as in a composite drawing or rendering) is a version of the web page normally created in a graphics program—but it can also be hand-drawn by an artist. "Full comp" refers to a comp that completely shows all page elements (text and graphics) and all colors. A full comp is often sent to the client for design approval before any web pages are developed. If you are comfortable with a program such as Adobe Photoshop or Adobe Fireworks you can create a comp yourself. Otherwise, this may be outsourced to a graphic artist.

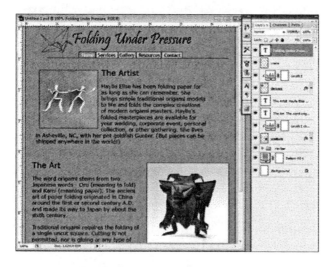

The previous wire frame was used as a guideline to create this full comp in Photoshop.

Graphics Generation

A comp created in a graphics program like Adobe Photoshop or Adobe Fireworks can be opened in one of those programs and parts of the comp extracted and saved as individual files for use on the web page. Similarly, the comp can act as a guideline if graphics are created from scratch. Again, if you are proficient in Photoshop or Fireworks you can do this work yourself. Otherwise, you will want to partner with or outsource to a graphic artist.

These four JPEGs were extracted from the original full comp to use on the web page.

Site Integration

Once you have all the individual graphics files, you can integrate them into your page with HTML tags. You will learn to do this in Lesson 6, Working with Images.

Image File Formats

There are many formats in which you can save graphics. These file formats are often referred to by their file extensions, such as .jpg, .gif, .png, .tif, .psd, .ai, .eps, etc. The good news is that only three of these are relevant for web pages: JPEG (.jpg), GIF (.gif), and PNG (.png).

Source Files

You normally begin with a *source file* and use it to generate the JPEG, GIF, or PNG to use on the web page. This is because the source file itself may not be a JPEG, GIF, or PNG. Additionally, the source file is often very large in file size (sometimes several megabytes); generating a web-friendly file can reduce the file size down to just a few kilobytes. Source files themselves can be JPEG, GIF, or PNG—but very often they are the native file format of the graphics program used to create them (.psd for Photoshop and .png for Fireworks).

Tagged Image File Format

A TIFF file (.tif) is often used as a source file. It is an image file format used mainly in the print world. Many digital cameras and scanners are capable of creating TIFFs. These files are much larger in file size than what would be suitable for the web, but their high quality makes them ideal source files.

Generated Files

In order to prepare your images for the web, you will need to create a *generated file* that is properly cropped, sized, and optimized. For example, you may snap a photo with your digital camera and transfer that photo to your computer as a JPEG. However, that original file may be too large to use on the web. You could then save a copy of the original source file with a section cropped out, resized smaller, and optimized for the web. Similarly, you may create a picture or a button from scratch with Photoshop. This .psd file would be your source file. You would then generate a copy in an appropriate format for the web.

It is a good idea to save all your source files in case you need to save alternate versions of the generated files. Creating a folder in the site root named "assets" or "original artwork" is a great place to store these source files.

Joint Photographic Experts Group

JPEG (pronounced "jay-peg") files usually use the .jpg file extension, though they sometimes use the file extension .jpeg. The difference between the .jpg and .jpeg file extension is similar to the difference between .htm and .html—nothing but a letter.

JPEG Compression

JPEG files use a *lossy* compression method to reduce file size. This means image data is literally discarded, resulting in blurred areas in the image. In other words, as you reduce the file size of a JPEG it becomes more and more blurry in parts. The blurry parts are called *artifacts*.

JPEGs support millions of colors, so they are a good choice for photographs or any images with gradients (one color blending into another).

JPEG at a high quality. Notice how crisp the edges are.

JPEG at a low quality. Notice the artifacts (blurry parts) around the edges. This will be even more apparent in Hands-On 5.1 when you see it in a browser window.

 Hands-On 5.1   Compare JPEG Compression

In this exercise, you will compare image quality to file size between JPEGs.

1. Open your Lesson 05 folder and double-click the file jpg_compression.htm.
   The web page opens in your default browser.

2. Follow the instructions on the screen to complete this exercise.

Graphics Interchange Format

GIF (pronounced with either a hard *G* as in "get" or a soft *G* as in "jet") images are limited to a color palette of 256 colors. They use a process called *dithering* to make images appear as if there are more colors present. As an example, let's take a two-color palette of yellow and blue. Only those two colors can be used. Now imagine the picture has yellow, blue, and green areas. If you interspersed a bunch of very small yellow dots with a bunch of very small blue dots, the human eye wouldn't be able to differentiate the yellow dots from the blue dots and would see only the green created by blending yellow with blue. This is the process of dithering: mixing colors in the palette to simulate colors outside of the palette.

GIF Compression

GIFs incorporate *lossless* compression. As file size is reduced, no image data is discarded (as with JPEG compression) so GIFs remain crisp and clean. However, the color palette is reduced. A 256-color GIF will have a much larger file size than the same GIF image saved with only 16 colors. But the quality of the 16-color GIF will suffer and begin to look splotchy.

A GIF with a full 256-color palette.

The same GIF reduced to only 16 colors. Notice that the edges are crisp but that you can see the individual dots throughout the picture.

GIF Animation

GIFs offer a couple of features not available to JPEGS: *animation* and *transparency*. Imagine a stack of index cards. Now imagine the top card has a picture of a plane. The second card has a picture of the plane moved a little to the right. The third card has the plane a little more to the right. This continues to the last card where the plane is all the way over to the right. As you flip through the cards, a crude animation plays and it appears as if the plane is flying. This is the concept of an animated GIF, but instead of index cards an animated GIF uses "frames."

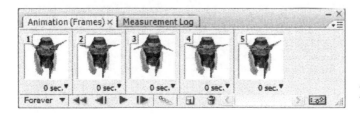

An animated GIF is created by several frames, each slightly different.

GIF Transparency

GIFs also support transparency. This means you can choose one color in the color palette to make transparent, or invisible. For example, imagine that same airplane on its white index card. Now imagine that the index card is invisible and all you see is the plane. Place that index card on a table and you wouldn't see the white index card; you would see only the plane as if it were stenciled on the table. The same idea applies to a GIF with a transparency. By making the color of the background transparent, you can allow the web-page background to show through and display your GIFs without a rectangular background.

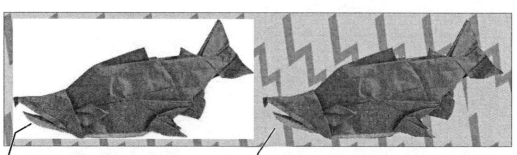

A JPEG does not support transparency, so a white box is shown around the image.

This GIF has the color white set to transparent, so the white box turns invisible and allows the web-page background to show through. This will be even more apparent in Hands-On 5.2 when you see it in a browser window.

 Hands-On 5.2   **Compare GIF Compression, Animation, and Transparency**

In this exercise, you will compare image quality of compressed GIFs. You will also see how animated and transparent GIFs behave in a browser.

1. Open your Lesson 05 folder and double-click the file gif_compression.htm.
   The web page opens in your default browser.

2. Follow the instructions on the screen to complete this exercise.

Portable Network Graphics

PNG (pronounced "ping") is the best of both worlds. It supports millions of colors like JPEGs and uses lossless compression like GIFs. It even supports *alpha transparency,* which allows for varying levels of transparency throughout the image (you will see this in action in the next exercise). However, PNG transparency is not supported in all browsers (specifically Internet Explorer 6 and lower) and very early browsers do not support PNG images at all. PNG was developed to improve upon and replace the GIF format.

It is important to note that the graphics program Fireworks uses PNG as its native file format. The version of PNG used by Fireworks is different from the version of PNG needed for web pages. This is not a problem because you can always use the original source PNG to generate a web-friendly PNG in Photoshop or Fireworks.

 NOTE!   *Remember that PNG transparency is not supported in all browsers. You will need to make sure that the images for your website are saved in the correct version of PNG.*

PNG-8 and PNG-24

Actually, there are several different versions of PNG. Each is normally denoted by a trailing integer. PNG-8 is similar to GIF in that it supports a 256-color palette. PNG-24 supports millions of colors. What's important to you as a web developer is the following:

- Photoshop allows you to save PNG-8 and PNG-24.

- Only PNG-24 supports alpha transparency.

- Early browsers don't support either PNG-8 or PNG-24 and may crash or fail to open the web page containing PNGs.

- Internet Explorer versions 4–6 don't support the alpha transparency in PNG-24.

 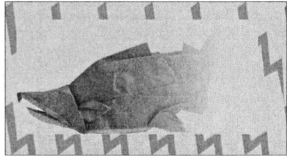

A PNG with alpha transparency allows the image to fade out as the page background shows through. This figure is from Firefox.

This is the same page displayed in Internet Explorer 6, which does not support PNG alpha transparency. Even though the fish fades, it is enclosed by a gray box and the page background does not show through.

 Hands-On 5.3   **Compare PNG Support in Various Browsers**

In this exercise, you will compare browser support of PNG files.

1. Open your Lesson 05 folder and double-click the file png_support.htm.
   The web page opens in your default browser.

2. Follow the instructions on the screen to complete this exercise.

The Difference Between Image File Formats

The decision about when to use a JPEG, a GIF, or a PNG depends largely on the image itself. The goal is to achieve the smallest file size with the highest quality. Unfortunately, these two elements are at direct opposites. As you increase the quality, you also increase file size. As you reduce the file size, you lose quality. It is important to strike a balance between acceptable quality and a file size suitable for users on slower dial-up Internet connections.

One main difference between the file formats suitable for the web is the way they compress files. The compression can be either *lossy* or *lossless*. Both of these methods have been discussed previously in this lesson.

IMAGE FILE FORMATS

File Format	Colors	Compression	Best Used For
JPG	Millions	Lossy	Photographs
GIF	256 maximum	Lossless	Line art, images with large areas of solid color, animation, transparency
PNG-8	256 maximum	Lossless	Substitute for non-animated GIFs; can crash very early browsers *This format should be avoided unless you can guarantee your users have supporting browsers.*
PNG-24	Millions	Lossless	Substitute for non-animated GIFs; can crash very early browsers Supports alpha transparency, which is not supported in all modern browsers *This format should be avoided unless you can guarantee your users have supporting browsers.*

 Hands-On 5.4   Compare Image File Formats

In this exercise, you will compare JPG, GIF, and PNG side by side.

1. Open your Lesson 05 folder and double-click the file compare_all.htm.
   The web page opens in your default browser.

2. Follow the instructions on the screen to complete this exercise.

Acquiring and Creating Images

Now that you know you need JPEGs or GIFs for your web pages, you must decide how to acquire your images. It boils down to four choices:

- Make your own with a graphics program like Photoshop or Fireworks.

- Outsource this work to a graphic artist.

- Purchase existing images from a legal source.

- Download royalty-free images from the public domain.

Image Editors

An image editor is software you use to either edit existing images or create them from scratch. While there are freeware programs you can use, the industry standard is Photoshop, developed by Adobe Systems Incorporated.

Commercial Editors

Adobe offers several image editors and computer-aided drawing programs including Photoshop, Fireworks, and Illustrator. Each program excels in certain areas; Photoshop is the most versatile.

- Fireworks excels at working with images for the web. If that is all you do, consider purchasing Fireworks.

- Illustrator excels at working with vector art, which means working with points, line segments, and curves. It is geared towards creating your own imagery from scratch. Many graphic artists use Illustrator.

- Photoshop is the most versatile in that it works well with web images, vector art, and photographs. Photoshop is used by web professionals, computer artists, and photographers alike. It has the richest feature set of the three programs mentioned here. As good as Photoshop is, remember that Fireworks and Illustrator are more targeted programs that outshine Photoshop in their respective areas.

Adobe offers several suites of programs, so you have the option of purchasing a suite that includes any combination of these three programs in addition to other professional-grade Adobe software.

Free Editors

There are alternatives to purchasing commercial software, which can be cost-prohibitive to fledgling developers. Free-image editors range from the basic Paint program included free with Windows to GIMP (GNU Image Manipulation Program), which rivals Photoshop in features but has a steep learning curve, even for professionals. A few free and easier-to-grasp image editors are listed in the following table.

QUICK REFERENCE: FREE IMAGE EDITORS

Editor	Developer	Basic Features
Paint	Microsoft	■ Installs with the Windows operating system ■ Basic drawing tools
IrfanView	Irfan Skiljan	■ Crop, rotate, and resize images ■ Convert between file formats
Picasa	Google	■ Organize and catalog images ■ Crop, rotate, fix red-eye, adjust color and contrast

Sources for Images

Rather than taking photographs yourself and learning about image composition and lighting or hiring a professional photographer, sometimes it is more efficient to purchase an image—or to find one for free (legally). The same holds true for artwork or other graphics. You can create your own or outsource this task, but sometimes it is more efficient and cost-effective to use graphics that already exist.

Royalty-Free

A *royalty-free image* is one you can use without paying usage fees. For example, the likenesses of many cartoon characters are trademarked and using their images may cost you thousands of dollars every time you use them. Royalty-free images fall into two categories: free and not free. If you purchase a royalty-free image from a service, you would be allowed to use that image as often as you like on any advertising material you like. (Restrictions may vary depending on the seller.) Commercial royalty-free images are available on CD/DVD collections or on a per-image basis from an online vendor. A few online sources are listed in the following table. If you don't want to pay for your images, you can acquire them from a service that offers royalty-free images in the public domain.

QUICK REFERENCE: COMMERCIAL SOURCES FOR ROYALTY-FREE IMAGES

Source	URL
Adobe Systems Inc.	adobe.com (search for "adobe stock photos")
Corbis Corporation	corbis.com
iStock International, Inc.	istockphoto.com
Shutterstock, Inc.	shutterstock.com

 NOTE! *If any of these links stop working, visit the website for this book, which maintains an up-to-date list of links.*

Free from the Public Domain

An image in the public domain has no legal restriction on its use. You can legally download it for free. As there are no legal restrictions, public domain implies royalty-free. There are many online sources which don't say their images are in the public domain, but instead say they are "free to use for personal or commercial purposes." This is basically the same thing. Most of these websites have a small "terms of service" link somewhere on their page which you *must* read to make sure you are not breaking any laws!

QUICK REFERENCE: SOURCES FOR PUBLIC DOMAIN OR "FREE FOR PERSONAL OR COMMERCIAL USE" IMAGES

Service	URL
PD Photo	pdphoto.org
Morgue File	morguefile.com
Image After	imageafter.com
Freerange Stock	freerangestock.com

 NOTE! *If any of these links stop working, visit the website for this book, which maintains an up-to-date list of links.*

 Hands-On 5.5   Find Images

In this exercise, you will use Internet Explorer 7 to find and download a royalty-free image in the public domain.

 NOTE! *The instructions in this lesson assume you are using Internet Explorer. If you are using a different browser, menu options may differ.*

Find an Image

1. Start your web browser and browse to **pdphoto.org**.

   At the time of this writing, a notice appears at the top of the homepage indicating that most, but not all, of the images on this site are in the public domain. It is up to you, the user, to verify that the images you select are in the public domain. Even if this notice no longer appears, it is a good practice to verify the legal use of any image before you download.

   > **If you want to use these images:** Go ahead. I've placed most of them in the public domain. **However** >>> While most of them are public domain, a few aren't. Be sure to read the license under each of the enlarged pictures. If you have any questions, please ask.
   >
   > **Keyword Search**   **Newest Photos**   **Today's Free Pic**

2. Click the Newest Photos link towards the top of the page.

3. Scroll through the page and click any thumbnail that interests you.
A new page loads with a larger version of the image.

4. Scroll to the bottom of the page and locate the Public Domain notice:

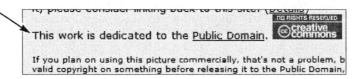

The Public Domain notice verifies that the image is available for you to use for free.

5. If the Public Domain notice is not present, use the browser's Back button and select a different image.

Save the Image

6. Right-click the large image and choose Save Picture As from the pop-up menu.

The Save As dialog box opens with the file name filled in.

7. Navigate to your Lesson 05 folder.

8. Type an appropriate filename for the file, if necessary, and click Save.
The image is saved to your Lesson 05 folder.

9. Close your browser.

Editing Tasks

Once you have acquired a variety of images (transferred from a digital camera or scanner, purchased, or downloaded) you may need to edit them before you can use them on your website. Basic editing tasks include changing the color mode, cropping, and resizing.

Adobe Photoshop CS3 is the industry standard graphics editor.

Changing the color mode and resizing the document can be accomplished with commands in the Image menu.

The Tools palette allows you to switch between various tools, such as painting, drawing, selection, and touch-up tools. This figure shows the Crop Tool selected.

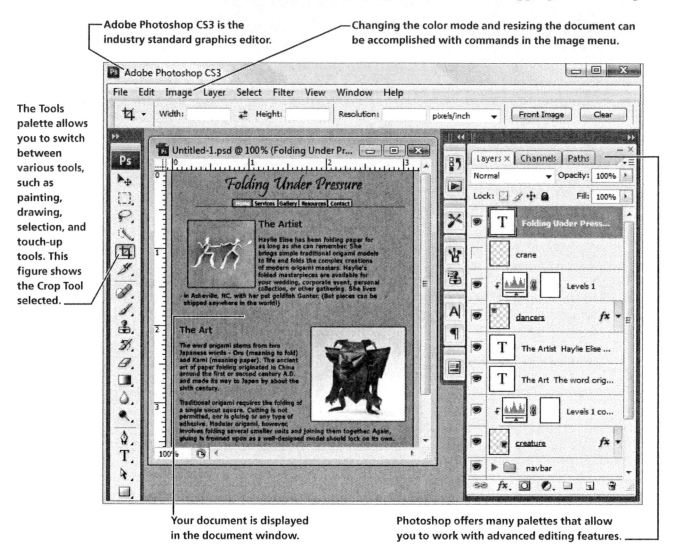

Your document is displayed in the document window.

Photoshop offers many palettes that allow you to work with advanced editing features.

Color Mode

An image's *color mode* defines how base colors are combined to create additional colors. For example, the RGB (Red Green Blue) color mode defines how the colors red, green, and blue combine to create the millions of other colors present in an image. The CMYK (Cyan Magenta Yellow Black) color mode defines how the colors cyan, magenta, yellow, and black combine to create other colors. CMYK is used primarily in the print world. The web world is limited to RGB. Any image you intend to use on your web pages *must* be RGB. A common frustration among new web developers is after verifying all your HTML code is correct and all files are present, images fail to display on the web page. This is often because the image was saved as CMYK (for print) when it should have been saved as RGB (for the web). The color mode can easily be changed from Photoshop (and other image editors).

⚠️ **NOTE!** *Make sure that all of the images you will be using on your website are saved as RGB!*

In this exercise, you will determine and change the color mode of an image.

Before You Begin: The next few exercises use Photoshop CS3, but previous versions of Photoshop will work also (though menu command text may differ slightly). Note that you must have Photoshop, not Photoshop Elements.

1. Launch Photoshop. It is most likely located in Start→All Programs→Adobe→Adobe Photoshop CS3, but you may need to check with your instructor.

2. Choose File→Open from the menu bar.

3. Browse to your Lesson 05 folder, select the file maekawa.tif, and click Open.

4. Locate the Zoom tool on the tool box (it looks like a magnifying glass) and double-click it.
   Double-clicking the Zoom tool zooms the image to 100 percent. The document title bar indicates that the zoom level is 100 percent. It also indicates the image is in the CMYK color mode, which is not usable for the web.

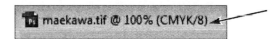

5. Choose Image→Mode→RGB Color from the menu bar.
   You may notice a slight shift in color as the image is converted to RGB. The document title bar indicates the new color mode.

6. Choose File→Save As from the menu bar.

7. If necessary, navigate to your Lesson 05 folder; follow these steps to save a copy of the file:

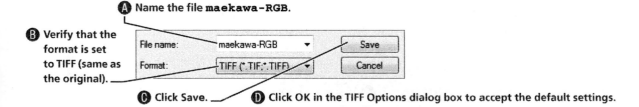

Ⓐ Name the file **maekawa-RGB**.

Ⓑ Verify that the format is set to TIFF (same as the original).

Ⓒ Click Save.

Ⓓ Click OK in the TIFF Options dialog box to accept the default settings.

The source file now uses the RGB color mode.

Cropping

Very often pictures from a digital camera or scanner, or even purchased or downloaded pictures, have more in the picture than you need. You can use Photoshop's crop tool to cut out the extraneous part of the picture.

If a full size image has more than you need...

...you can crop out the parts you don't want.

 ## Hands-On 5.7   Crop Images

In this exercise, you will crop out much of the border to tighten up the image.

1. Click once on the Tool Palette's Crop tool to select it.

2. Follow these steps to draw a preliminary crop area:

Ⓐ Point to the top-left section of the image.

Ⓑ Drag down and to the right to draw a crop area.

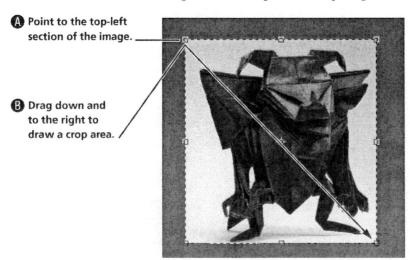

Don't worry if your crop area doesn't match the figure. You will adjust it in the next few steps.

3. Follow these steps to adjust your crop area:

Ⓐ **Point to the left-middle open square handle along the border of the dashed crop area until your cursor turns into a double-headed arrow.**

Ⓑ **Drag the handle left or right to adjust the left border, bringing the left border almost to the left wing of the origami creature.**

Ⓒ **Drag the middle handles of the top, right, and bottom borders to adjust the crop area as close to the origami creature as you can.**

Your final crop area should resemble the following figure.

4. Tap ⌈Enter⌉ to apply the crop.
Anything outside of the crop area is deleted.

5. Choose File→Save As from the menu bar.

6. Navigate to your Lesson 05 folder, if necessary.

7. Follow these steps to save a copy of the file:

Ⓐ **Name the file maekawa-cropped.**

Ⓑ **Verify that the format is set to TIFF (same as the original).**

| File name: | maekawa-cropped ▾ | Save |
| Format: | TIFF (*.TIF;*.TIFF) ▾ | Cancel |

Ⓒ **Click Save.** Ⓓ **Click OK in the TIFF Options dialog box to accept the default settings.**

Resizing

Files from a digital camera or scanner or downloaded from the web are often too large for a web page and need to be reduced in size. Some inexperienced web designers make the mistake of leaving the image in its large size, but adding some code to their HTML document to make the large image display at a smaller size. This is bad for two reasons:

■ The image quality is degraded and can look distorted.

■ The actual size of the file is still large, so users are forced to download a file much larger than they need.

If you need an image to display on a web page at a size smaller than the image actually is, you need to resize the image in a graphics-editing program and use the smaller copy of the image on your web page. If you need the image to display larger on the web page, you will need to acquire a larger version of the original file. Although image editors allow you to enlarge a picture, doing so results in extremely poor quality. Here's the general rule: You can safely reduce, but not enlarge, the dimensions of an image.

The Magic Size

There is no magic size! The size of an image is dictated by the design of the web page. However, widths between 75 pixels to about 250 pixels are standard for most images on the web. Of course, you may have images smaller or larger than that depending on your design.

TIP! *Remember to think about those with dial-up Internet access!*

Image Size Options

When resizing an image with Photoshop CS3, there are a few standard settings to keep in mind:

■ Resample

■ Constrain Proportions

■ Pixel Dimensions

NOTE! *These settings relate to terms and tasks in graphic design and, as such, are not discussed in detail in this XHTML book.*

The Image Size dialog box is used to resize an image in Photoshop.

The Pixel Dimensions section allows you to specify the new size of the document.

Constraining the proportions allows you to specify just the width or the height of the pixel dimensions. The other dimension will automatically scale to retain the width-to-height proportion.

The Resample options specify the method Photoshop uses to resize the image.

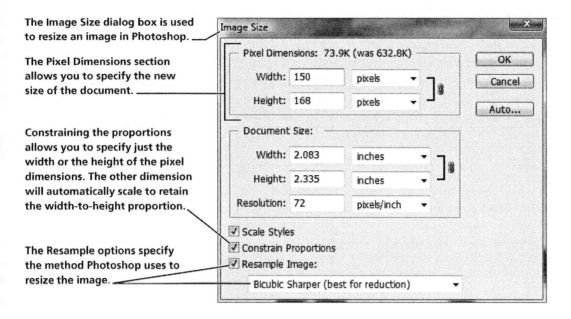

 Hands-On 5.8   Resize Images

In this exercise, you will resize an image.

1. Choose Image→Image Size from the menu bar and then follow these steps to resize the image:

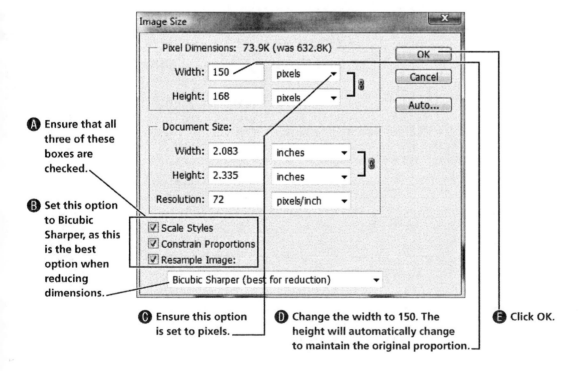

Ⓐ Ensure that all three of these boxes are checked.

Ⓑ Set this option to Bicubic Sharper, as this is the best option when reducing dimensions.

Ⓒ Ensure this option is set to pixels.

Ⓓ Change the width to 150. The height will automatically change to maintain the original proportion.

Ⓔ Click OK.

2. Choose File→Save As from the menu bar.

3. If necessary, navigate to your Lesson 05 folder and save the image as **maekawa-small**.

Optimizing Images

As you learned earlier in this lesson, some images are better saved as JPEGs while others do better as GIFs. Even once you decide on the file format, you still need to decide on the quality settings to balance the image quality with file size. This is the process of *image optimization*. The smaller the size the better, as the web page will load faster. It's difficult to say "all images should be under so many kilobytes" because size depends on how many images are on your page. An image at about 10 K is great—but not if you have 50 of them on the same page!

The Photoshop Save for Web & Devices Window

When generating files for the web, Photoshop offers the Save for Web & Devices dialog box (Save for Web in Photoshop CS2 and earlier), which is almost another software program in itself. This dialog window is used to compare different optimization settings so you can make an informed decision as to which is the best image file format (and which are the best settings) for a particular graphic.

The tabs allow you to switch between seeing just the original source file or just the optimized version, or to compare the original to one or three optimized versions.

The top-left quadrant displays the original source file while the remaining quadrants display different versions of the optimized graphic.

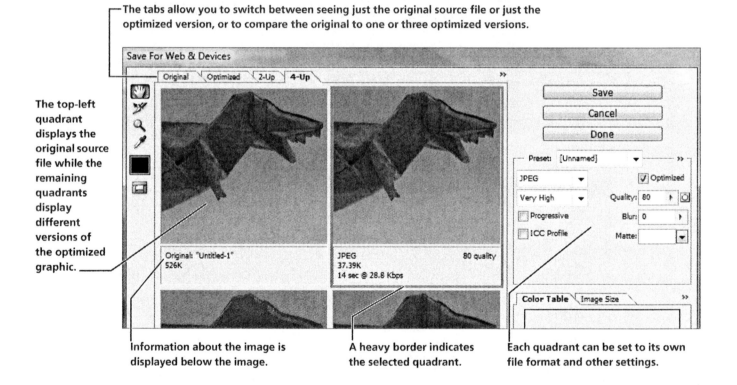

Information about the image is displayed below the image.

A heavy border indicates the selected quadrant.

Each quadrant can be set to its own file format and other settings.

Hands-On 5.9 **Optimize Images for the Web**

In this exercise, you will optimize an image for use on the web.

1. Choose File→Save for Web & Devices from the menu bar. (If you are using Photoshop CS2 or earlier, the option is simply Save for Web.)
   The Save For Web & Devices dialog box appears.

2. Click the 4-Up tab in the top-left corner of the dialog window to display the original image with three optimized versions.

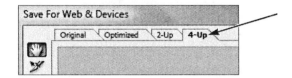

As the image is a photograph, a JPEG will probably yield better results than a GIF.

3. Click the image in the top-right quadrant to select it and to configure the optimization settings for it.
   A blue border appears around the quadrant to indicate it is selected.

4. Follow these steps to optimize the image in the top-right quadrant:

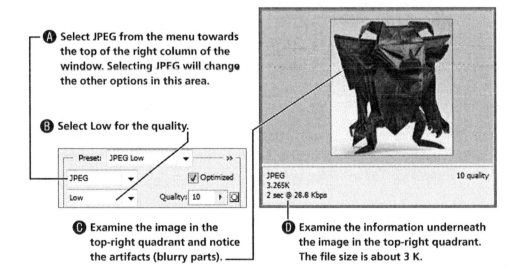

Ⓐ Select JPEG from the menu towards the top of the right column of the window. Selecting JPEG will change the other options in this area.

Ⓑ Select Low for the quality.

Ⓒ Examine the image in the top-right quadrant and notice the artifacts (blurry parts).

Ⓓ Examine the information underneath the image in the top-right quadrant. The file size is about 3 K.

Although the file size is small, the image quality is unacceptable.

5. Click the image in the bottom-left quadrant and then follow these steps to optimize it:

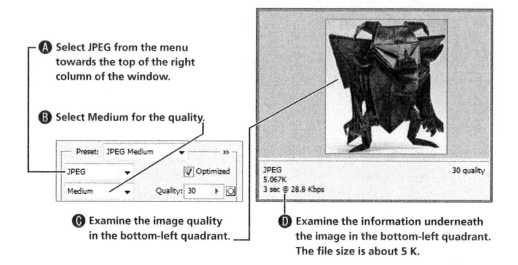

Ⓐ Select JPEG from the menu towards the top of the right column of the window.

Ⓑ Select Medium for the quality.

Ⓒ Examine the image quality in the bottom-left quadrant.

Ⓓ Examine the information underneath the image in the bottom-left quadrant. The file size is about 5 K.

The file size is larger than the previous setting, but now the image quality is acceptable. Let's optimize the last quadrant as a GIF just to compare.

6. Click the image in the bottom-right quadrant and then follow these steps to optimize it:

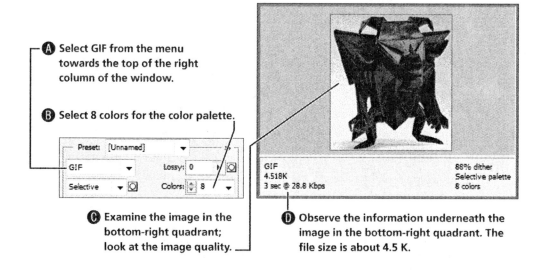

Ⓐ Select GIF from the menu towards the top of the right column of the window.

Ⓑ Select 8 colors for the color palette.

Ⓒ Examine the image in the bottom-right quadrant; look at the image quality.

Ⓓ Observe the information underneath the image in the bottom-right quadrant. The file size is about 4.5 K.

Although the file size is smaller than the medium JPEG, the image quality is not acceptable.

7. Click the image in the bottom-left quadrant to select it as it is the best one.
You could have changed the settings in any one of the quadrants to continue testing optimization settings until you found one you liked better. The key is to remember to select your desired quadrant so it displays a heavy border, indicating it has been selected.

8. Click Save at the top-right column of the window.

9. If necessary, navigate to your Lesson 05 folder.

10. Save the file as **maekawa-web**.

11. Close Photoshop; choose Don't Save if prompted to save any changes.

Concepts Review

True/False Questions

1. Based on a typical web design workflow, you must create a full comp before a wire frame can be developed.   TRUE   FALSE

2. A .tif file is an excellent choice to use on a web page.   TRUE   FALSE

3. All web graphics must use the RGB color mode.   TRUE   FALSE

4. JPEGs support alpha-transparency.   TRUE   FALSE

5. GIFs support animation.   TRUE   FALSE

6. JPEGs are usually best for photographs and GIFs are best for linc art.   TRUE   FALSE

7. The wide support of PNG has made it a popular image file format for the web.   TRUE   FALSE

8. You may legally copy an image from a website to use on your own as web images cannot be copyrighted.   TRUE   FALSE

9. Images in the public domain are very expensive, so unless your client has a large budgct, consider hiring a professional photographer instead.   TRUE   FALSE

10. JPEGs support millions of colors while GIFs are limited to a palette of 256 colors.   TRUE   FALSE

Multiple Choice Questions

1. Ernesto has transferred several photos from his digital camera to his hard drive for use on his website. He has opened the images in Photoshop to optimize them. Which file format would be the most appropriate for saving the optimized-generated files?

   a. .gif

   b. .jpg

   c. .png

   d. .tif

2. Hùong needs to create a short slideshow of product images, but she doesn't have the time to learn the advanced programming to make it work. Which file format will allow her to create a single image file that simulates a slide show?

   a. .gif

   b. .jpg

   c. .png

   d. .tif

3. Kwabena is searching online for images to use on his website. What keywords should he use in his search to find images he can legally use at no charge?

   a. Free images, no charge

   b. Clip art, photographs

   c. Royalty-free images, public domain

   d. Graphics, personal use

4. Brady has purchased a CD of print-quality images to use on her website. However, the images fail to display on her pages. She has checked her HTML code and is confident that it is correct. What could be wrong with the images?

   a. The images are photographs but she has saved them as GIFs instead of JPEGs.

   b. She has used the .jpeg file extension instead of .jpg.

   c. The images are not in the public domain.

   d. Because the CD contained images for print, they are in the CMYK color mode instead of RGB.

Skill Builders

Skill Builder 5.1   Find Images

On the Web

In this exercise, you will use the Morgue File website to find images you can legally use on your own website.

Before You Begin: *The Morgue File website may not be currently functioning in the state represented in this WebSim. The generic steps in this exercise will also work for similar sites.*

1. Start your web browser, browse to **www.labpub.com/learn/wdhtml**, and click the Skill Builder 5.1 Find Images link.

2. On the WebSim, launch Internet Explorer and browse to **www.morguefile.com**.
   Be careful as you type. It is morguefile.com, not morguefiles.com. There is no "s." These are very different sites.

3. Locate the Terms hyperlink along the right column on the homepage; click the link to read the terms and conditions.

4. Read through the license agreement, paying close attention to the License Grant and Use Restrictions sections.
   It may seem like a lot of legal mumbo jumbo, but this is no joke. You don't want to receive a nasty letter via certified mail informing you that you are being sued for copyright infringement!

5. Click the Archive hyperlink along the right column on the homepage to browse to the image repository.

6. Click the Animals link on the left side of the page to browse for animal photos.

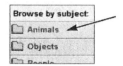

7. Click the Cats link to browse for cats.

8. Click the Cats Assorted link.

9. Click any of the thumbnails to view a larger version of the image.
You may need to wait a moment as the large image loads in the browser window.

10. Right-click the large image and choose Save Picture As from the popup menu.

11. If necessary, browse to your Lesson 05 folder.

12. Type an appropriate filename for the image and click Save.

13. Close Internet Explorer.

Skill Builder 5.2   Change the Color Mode

In this exercise, you will use Photoshop to edit an image.

Before You Begin: This exercise uses Photoshop CS3, but previous versions of Photoshop will also work (though the menu command text may differ). Note that you must have Photoshop, not Photoshop Elements.

Open an Image

1. Start Photoshop.

2. Choose File Open from the menu bar.

3. If necessary, navigate to your Lesson 05 folder.

4. Choose the sb-trex.tif file and click Open.

5. Locate the document title bar and read the information provided in it.

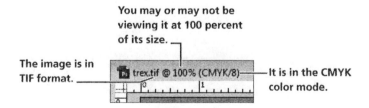

Change the Color Mode

6. Choose Image→Mode→RGB Color from the menu bar.

7. Verify that the document title bar indicates RGB and not CMYK.

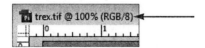

The image is now in the appropriate color mode for web graphics.

8. Use Ctrl+S to save the file, accepting any default settings Photoshop offers.

Skill Builder 5.3 Crop an Image

In this exercise, you will crop the image.

Before You Begin: *You must complete Skill Builder 5.2 before beginning this exercise.*

1. Select the Crop tool from the Tool palette.

2. Follow these steps to crop the head of the T-rex:

Ⓐ Point a little to the left and above the head. Then drag down and to the right to draw a preliminary crop area.

Ⓑ Point to the left-middle handle until your cursor turns into a double-headed arrow. Then drag left or right until the entire neck is included in the crop area.

Ⓒ Adjust the remaining three sides until your screen resembles the figure.

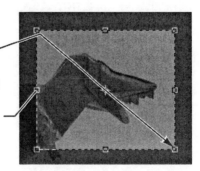

Ⓓ Tap Enter to perform the crop.

3. Use Ctrl+S to save the file, accepting any default settings Photoshop offers.

Skill Builder 5.4   **Resize an Image**

In this exercise, you will resize the image.

Before You Begin: You must complete Skill Builder 5.3 before beginning this exercise.

Zoom to 100 Percent

1. Double-click the Zoom tool toward the bottom of the Tool palette to zoom the document to 100 percent.

Resize the Image

2. Choose Image→Image Size from the menu bar.

3. Follow these steps to reduce the image size:

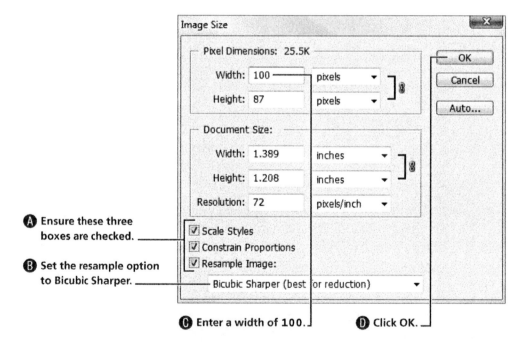

Ⓐ **Ensure these three boxes are checked.**

Ⓑ **Set the resample option to Bicubic Sharper.**

Ⓒ **Enter a width of 100.**

Ⓓ **Click OK.**

Do not save the image. You will optimize and save it in the next exercise.

Skill Builder 5.5 Optimize an Image

In this exercise, you will optimize the image.

Before You Begin: You must complete Skill Builder 5.4 before beginning this exercise.

Configure Optimization Settings

1. Choose File→Save For Web & Devices from the menu bar. (If you are using Photoshop CS2 or earlier, the option is simply Save for Web.)

2. Follow these steps to configure one set of optimization settings:

A Click the 4-Up tab to display the original in the top-left quadrant and three other quadrants to optimize.

B Click in the top right quadrant to select it.

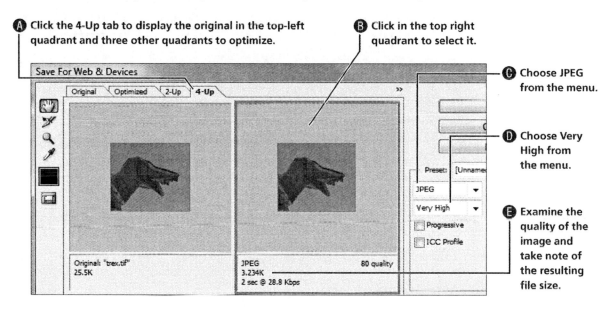

C Choose JPEG from the menu.

D Choose Very High from the menu.

E Examine the quality of the image and take note of the resulting file size.

3. Follow these steps to configure the next quadrant:

A Click the bottom-left quadrant to select it.

B Choose JPEG from the menu.

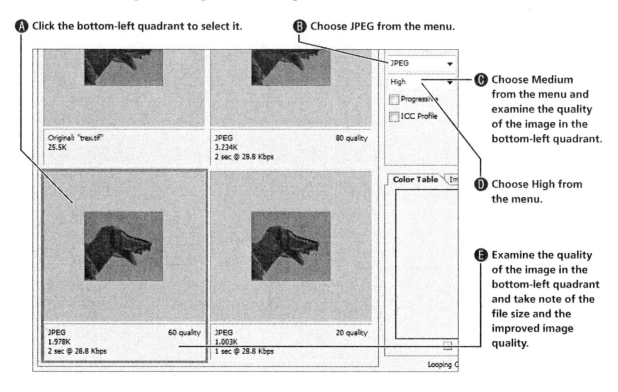

C Choose Medium from the menu and examine the quality of the image in the bottom-left quadrant.

D Choose High from the menu.

E Examine the quality of the image in the bottom-left quadrant and take note of the file size and the improved image quality.

4. Follow these steps to configure the final quadrant:

A Click the bottom-right quadrant to select it.

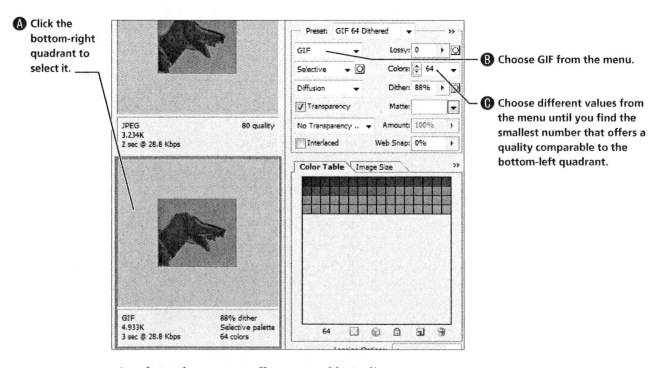

B Choose GIF from the menu.

C Choose different values from the menu until you find the smallest number that offers a quality comparable to the bottom-left quadrant.

Sixty-four colors seem to offer comparable quality.

Save the Optimized Image

5. Compare the quality of the three optimized quadrants to the original in the top-left corner and to each other.
   The bottom-left quadrant offers acceptable quality at the smallest file size.

6. Click the bottom-left quadrant to select it.
   The bottom-left quadrant displays a heavy border to indicate it is selected.

7. Click Save.

8. Navigate to the Lesson 05 folder if necessary.

9. Name the file **sb-trex_small** and click Save.

10. Exit Photoshop and choose No if prompted to save changes.

 **Assessments**

Assessment 5.1   Find Images

In this exercise, you will find an image in the public domain.

1. Launch Internet Explorer and browse to **www.morguefile.com**, **www.pdphoto.org**, or another site recommended by your instructor that offers images in the public domain.

2. Locate and read the terms and conditions on the website to ensure you will not be in violation of copyright law by using images from the site on your web pages.

3. Browse the available images on the site until you find one you like.

4. Save the image to your Lesson 05 folder as **as-publicdomain**.

5. In a word processing document, type the URL of the page from which you saved the image. You may want to copy and paste the URL from Internet Explorer's address bar.

6. Save the word processing document to your Lesson 05 folder as **as-PD Location**.

Assessment 5.2   Edit and Optimize an Image

In this exercise, you will edit an image.

Edit an Image

1. Start Photoshop and open the manswatter.tif image from your Lesson 05 folder.

2. Convert the image to the RGB color mode.

3. Crop the image to remove the swatter's handle and any extra space around the swatter end. *Your cropped image should resemble the following figure.*

4. Resize the image to 150 pixels wide. Be sure the height is resized proportionally.

5. Save the image to your Lesson 05 folder as **as-manswatter-edited**. It should be saved in the TIF format.

Optimize an Image

6. Use the Save for Web & Devices dialog window to optimize the image for the Web. Remember to achieve the highest quality with the smallest file size in a format appropriate for the Web.

7. Save the optimized image to your Lesson 05 folder as **as-manswatter-web**.

# Critical Thinking

Critical Thinking 5.1   Find Images

In this exercise, you will find alternate sources for images in the public domain.

You have learned about two sources for royalty-free Public Domain images: Morgue File and PD Photo.

Using your favorite search engine, find at least three other sources for high-quality images in the public domain.

In a word processing document saved to your Lesson 05 folder as **ct-PD Sources**, list the website URLs for the sources you found.

Critical Thinking 5.2   Find a Photoshop Alternative

In this exercise, you will find alternate image editors to Photoshop.

You have worked a little with Photoshop in this lesson and have read about other image editors, such as Fireworks.

Using your favorite search engine, find at least three other free image editors that allow you to crop and resize images.

Research the safety of the image editors you found to see if others report them as spyware.

In a word processing document saved to your Lesson 05 folder as **ct-Image Editors**, list the following about each of the image editors:

■ Program name

■ Software developer/company name

■ Website URL

■ Comments from other users about the safety of this product (causes system instability, installs spyware, etc.)

■ URLs of the websites containing the user comments

LESSON 6

Working with Images

In this lesson, you will learn the mechanics of adding images to your web pages. You will learn how to identify which images should be coded in your HTML and which should be defined in CSS. You will also learn how to visually format an image with HTML attributes. Lastly, you will learn how to add a page background.

LESSON OBJECTIVES

After studying this lesson, you will be able to:

- Identify essential and non-essential graphics
- Add images to a web page
- Visually format an image with HTML attributes
- Apply a background to a web page

Case Study: Adding Images

Haylie and Miguel have added quite a bit of text to the homepage, but Haylie knows the design needs spicing up. Thanks to the wire framing and full comp Miguel created earlier, they are well prepared to move forward with the development. Miguel has already created the images they need with Photoshop. Now it is time to add them to the page.

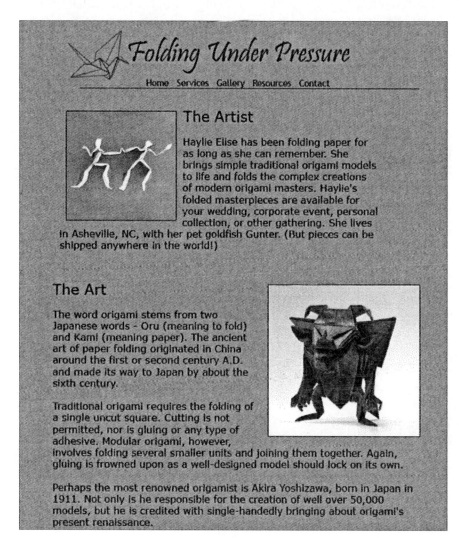

Images not only greatly enhance the visual presentation of a page, but they can be informative as well. The crane graphic in the masthead conveys the subject matter of the page.

Adding Images to a Page

Remember that XHTML deals with structure and CSS is used to achieve visual presentation. You might ask where images fit in. Images typically fall into one of two categories:

- **Essential**—*Essential graphics* are ones that provide information relative to your site's content, such as a company logo, staff photos, or product thumbnails.

- **Non-essential**—*Non-essential graphics* are those that add "eye-candy" (visual presentation) without offering information, such as background images or other visual enhancements. A user would still be able to use your site, purchase products, or access the information you are offering even if these graphics did not display.

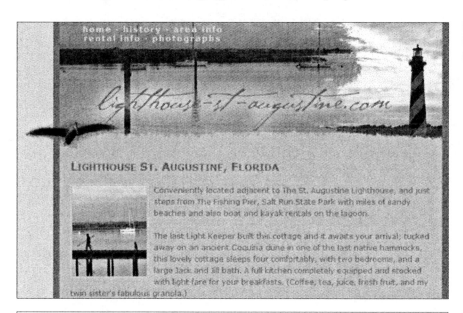

Non-essential graphics help to make the site more visually appealing.

When non-essential graphics are removed, such as when disabling CSS, the site content is still readable and accessible.

The basic rule for using images on your pages is that essential graphics should be coded directly into your XHTML code while non-essential graphics should be defined as background images in CSS. This way, non-visual browsers such as screen readers and search engines aren't slowed down by processing code for images they can't display.

Design Tips and Other Recommendations

As discussed in Lesson 1, Introducing Web Technologies, graphics should have relevance to your site content. Whether they are essential or non-essential, they should enhance the site design—not detract from it. Images should be reasonably sized, both in dimensions and file size. Try to keep essential images to no more than about 300 pixels wide. Any wider and they overwhelm the page content. As for file size, it depends on your target audience. Do your users have broadband Internet connections or dial-up? In general, try to keep images down to no more than about 30 kilobytes. Of course, this is a very loose recommendation and would not be ideal if your page had 20 of those images!

The Image Tag

You add images to your page using the <img> tag, which is a replacement tag (replaced at runtime by the image itself). As such, there is no opening or closing <img> tag. The <img> tag begins the replacement element and incorporates a closing statement all at once. Only two attributes are required in the <img> tag.

- **src**—Defines the URL or path to the image

- **alt**—Provides an alternate text description of the image for non-visual browsers

 TIP! *Use a null device, as in* alt=" ", *for non-essential graphics. This tells assistive devices like screen readers to ignore it.*

The <img> tag's src attribute defines the path to the image, which displays as in the previous two figures.

The alt attribute displays a text alternative to the image for non-visual browsers, search engines, and screen readers.

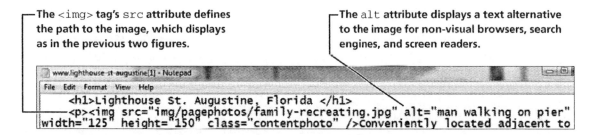

The Lynx browser, a text-only browser, displays the alt text instead of the image.

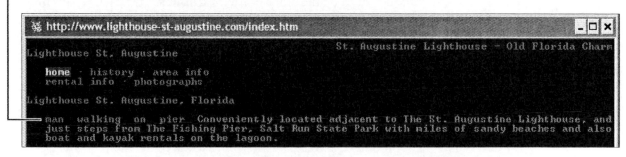

Visual browsers display the alternative text description if the image cannot be displayed.

Relative and Absolute Paths

Setting the `src` attribute properly requires an understanding of relative and absolute paths. "Specifying the path" means giving the browser directions for finding the image. All of your images must reside in your site root but can be stored in a subfolder. The path in the `src` attribute equates to directions on getting from the web page to the image—and these directions must be very specific. Imagine standing in your kitchen and asking your friend to get you the newspaper, which is in the living room. If your friend were a computer, "Get the newspaper" wouldn't be enough information. Your friend would be looking all over the kitchen for the newspaper and never find it. You'd have to give more specific directions, such as "Go to the living room, and then get the newspaper."

Relative paths provide very specific directions for referencing files.

Absolute Paths

An *absolute path* is one that starts from the site root, which is represented with a forward slash (`/`). A path such as `/images/global/photo.jpg` means the image photo.jpg resides in the folder named global, which is a subfolder of images, which resides in the site root. Giving the browser this path tells it to begin at the site root and then to follow the path to the image. An absolute path can also be specified by a full URL, such as `http://www.example.com/images/global/photo.jpg`. The benefit of using an absolute path is that it doesn't matter where in the site root the web page resides. For example, it can reside in the site root or in a subfolder named htmlfiles. The path to the image would always start from the site root. Absolute paths can be problematic if you change web servers or try to view the web page locally (directly from your hard drive), so most web developers use relative paths instead.

Relative Paths

A *relative path* is one that is relative to the web page's current location. For example, if the web page resides in the site root and the image resides in a subfolder of the site root named images, the relative path starts from the location of the web page. In this case the path would be `images/photo.jpg`. This translates to "Start from the web page's current location, then go into the images folder, then find photo.jpg." The benefit of relative paths is that you can easily change web servers and all of the paths will still work (provided the file locations inside the site root haven't changed). Relative paths also work well when the page is viewed locally from your hard drive. A problem with relative paths is that if you move a web page to a different folder within the site root, the path may be broken.

 TIP! *To specify moving backwards out of the current folder, use* `../` *as in* `src="../images/photo.jpg"`.

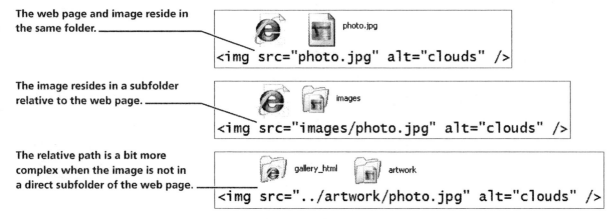

The web page and image reside in the same folder.

`<img src="photo.jpg" alt="clouds" />`

The image resides in a subfolder relative to the web page.

`<img src="images/photo.jpg" alt="clouds" />`

The relative path is a bit more complex when the image is not in a direct subfolder of the web page.

`<img src="../artwork/photo.jpg" alt="clouds" />`

If any of the images are moved, the relative path is no longer valid.

 ## Hands-On 6.1   Add Images to a Page

In this exercise, you will add images to a web page.

1. Open your Lesson 06 folder.

2. Open the fup_site_root folder.
   Notice that the homepage, named index.htm, resides directly inside the site root. There is also a folder named images *that contains the images you will use. There is nothing significant about this folder being named* images *other than that it clearly indicates its contents. It could just as easily have been named* media *or* pics.

3. Double-click the index.htm file to display it in your browser.

4. Start Notepad and choose File→Open.

5. Navigate to the fup_site_root folder inside your Lesson 06 folder, if necessary.
   You don't see the HTML pages because Notepad displays only files ending with the .txt file extension by default.

6. Change the Files of Type to All files.

7. Open the index.htm file.
   There is some additional code in this document you may not have seen before, such as the styles towards the top of the file. You will learn about these styles later in the book.

8. Follow these steps to add the first image:

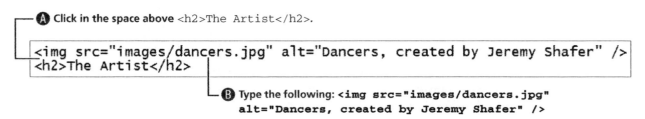

Ⓐ **Click in the space above** `<h2>The Artist</h2>`.

```
<img src="images/dancers.jpg" alt="Dancers, created by Jeremy Shafer" />
<h2>The Artist</h2>
```

Ⓑ Type the following: `<img src="images/dancers.jpg" alt="Dancers, created by Jeremy Shafer" />`

9. Save your changes and make your web browser the active window.

10. Tap F5 to refresh the page.
    The image of the dancers appears above The Artist. Remember that The Artist is a <h2>, which is a block-level element, so the image appears on its own line.

11. Make Notepad the active window.

12. If necessary, scroll down until the next subheading, The Art, is visible.

13. Using the steps outlined in step 8, add the second image, keeping the following in mind:
    - Click in the space above `<h2>The Art</h2>`.
    - Type this code: **`<img src="images/creature.jpg" alt="Devil, created by Jun Maekawa" />`**

14. Save your changes and make your web browser the active window.

15. Tap F5 to refresh the page.
    The second image displays on the page.

Using Optional Attributes

In addition to the required `src` and `alt` attributes, there are several other attributes supported by the `<img>` tag. Many of these are presentational, so while they are supported in XHTML 1.0 transitional, you should use CSS instead as you strive for XHTML 1.0 strict. You will learn more about CSS later in this book.

- **align**—Defines how the image aligns with text
- **border**—Defines the thickness in pixels of the image border
- **height**—Defines the height of the image
- **hspace**—Creates space on the left and right sides of the image to move it away from other page elements and give the image "breathing room"
- **vspace**—Creates space on the top and bottom of the image to move it away from other page elements and give the image "breathing room"
- **width**—Defines the width of the image

 TIP! *The order in which you add attributes to your tags does not matter. They are listed here alphabetically but can be added in any order.*

Align

The `align` attribute is used to position an image with text or other inline objects. Remember that inline elements can share the same horizontal space, much like typing them out on a typewriter. By default, the bottom of an image and the bottom of the text next to it sit on the same imaginary horizontal line. If an image is much taller than the text next to it, this can look bad as it creates a large block of "dead space" above the text. The align attribute shifts the text next to an image so the top of the text aligns with the top of the image, the bottom of the text aligns with the middle of the image, or the text wraps around the image as in the figures below. As this is presentational, the align attribute should be avoided if possible in favor of the CSS float property. It is allowed in XHTML 1.0 transitional, but forbidden in XHTML 1.0 strict.

The following table lists the valid values for the align attribute and their effects.

QUICK REFERENCE: ALIGN ATTRIBUTE VALUES

Value	Code	Description	Effect
Default or bottom	Attribute not coded, or `align="bottom"`	The bottom of the text aligns with the bottom of the image.	Paper airplanes have always fascinated young children. Here is one that fascinates adults too. Folded from a single uncut square, Robert Lang's Biplane is a bit different from the paper airplanes we folded as kids.
top	`align="top"`	The top of the text aligns with the top of the image.	Paper airplanes have always fascinated young children. Here is one that fascinates adults too. Folded from a single uncut square, Robert Lang's Biplane is a bit different from the paper airplanes we folded as kids.
middle	`align="middle"`	The bottom of the text aligns with the middle of the image.	Paper airplanes have always fascinated young children. Here is one that fascinates adults too. Folded from a single uncut square, Robert Lang's Biplane is a bit different from the paper airplanes we folded as kids.
left	`align="left"`	The text wraps around the image with the image on the left.	Paper airplanes have always fascinated young children. Here is one that fascinates adults too. Folded from a single uncut square, Robert Lang's Biplane is a bit different from the paper airplanes we folded as kids.
right	`align="right"`	The text wraps around the image with the image on the right.	Paper airplanes have always fascinated young children. Here is one that fascinates adults too. Folded from a single uncut square, Robert Lang's Biplane is a bit different from the paper airplanes we folded as kids.

In this exercise, you will use the align attribute to align images to text.

1. Switch to Notepad and locate the `<img>` tag for the dancers.jpg image.

2. Follow these steps to insert the align attribute:
   Your code may wrap differently than the code shown in the figure.

   Ⓐ Click after the closing quotation mark of the `alt` attribute.

   ```
   <img src="images/dancers.jpg" alt="Dancers, created by
   Jeremy Shafer" align="left" />
   ```

   Ⓑ Tap `Spacebar` and type `align="left"`.

3. Using the steps outlined in step 2, add **align="right"** to the second `<img>` tag.

4. Save your changes and make the web browser the active window.

5. Tap `F5` to refresh the page.
   The dancers image sits to the left of the text while the second image sits to the right.

Border

The `border` attribute is used to create a border around an image and is defined in pixels. For example, `border="3"` creates a 3-pixel border. You must specify an integer as the value of the border attribute. Sometimes a thin border helps an image stand out from the page. If no border attribute is present in the `<img>` tag, the border defaults to zero. However, a border of 1 pixel is automatically applied to images that are hyperlinks (you will learn about hyperlinks in Lesson 7, Working with Hyperlinks). You can remove that border by setting the border to zero. As the border is presentational, the border attribute should be avoided if possible in favor of the CSS border property. It is allowed in XHTML 1.0 transitional, but forbidden in XHTML 1.0 strict.

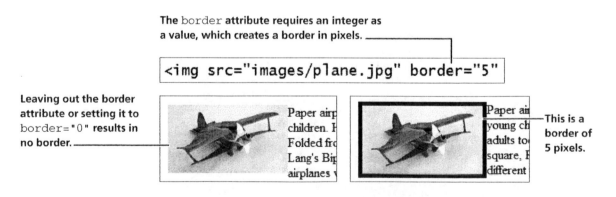

The `border` attribute requires an integer as a value, which creates a border in pixels.

```
<img src="images/plane.jpg" border="5"
```

Leaving out the border attribute or setting it to `border="0"` results in no border.

This is a border of 5 pixels.

Hands-On 6.3   Add an Image Border

In this exercise, you will add an image border.

1. Switch to Notepad and locate the `<img>` tag for the dancers.jpg image.

2. Follow these steps to add an image border:

⚠️ **NOTE!** *Your code may wrap differently from the code shown in the figure.*

Ⓐ Click after the closing quotation mark of the `align` attribute.

```
<img src="images/dancers.jpg" alt="Dancers, created by
Jeremy Shafer" align="left" border="1" />
```

Ⓑ Tap `Spacebar` and type **border="1"**.

3. Using the instuctions outlined in step 2, add **border="1"** to the second `<img>` tag.

4. Save your changes and make the web browser the active window.

5. Tap `F5` to refresh the page.
   Both images display a thin 1-pixel border.

Height and Width

The `height` and `width` attributes let the browser know the dimensions to display the image. The value for each attribute is usually an integer that specifies pixels. A percentage value, such as `height="90%"`, can also be specified, but this is not recommended because it is not supported by all browsers. These attributes can be dangerous if used incorrectly.

Making Images Larger

If your image is, for example, 50 pixels by 50 pixels but you want it larger, you can set the width and height to something like 400 pixels each. This has the effect of enlarging the image in the browser. However, this causes the image to become distorted and to lose quality. If you want an image to display larger than its actual dimensions, you should acquire a larger version of the image. Simply setting a larger width or height via HTML is not recommended.

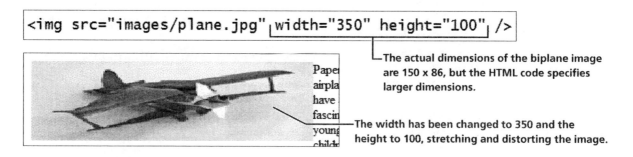

```
<img src="images/plane.jpg" width="350" height="100" />
```

The actual dimensions of the biplane image are 150 x 86, but the HTML code specifies larger dimensions.

The width has been changed to 350 and the height to 100, stretching and distorting the image.

Making Images Smaller

Similarly, if an image's actual dimensions are something like 200 pixels by 200 pixels and you want it displayed smaller, you may be tempted to assign a width and height of something smaller, such as 75 pixels. This results in the image being displayed at the smaller dimensions, but the image's file size hasn't changed. It would be better to reduce the image's dimensions in a graphics editing program (such as Photoshop) and benefit from the smaller file size displaying properly.

Structure, Not Presentation

Height and width may sound presentational, but they are not. They provide information to the browser to help speed rendering of the page. When the browser knows the dimensions, it can reserve that space while it reads through the rest of the code. Otherwise, it has to display things as best it can and then readjust displayed objects as the images are filled in. Both the height and width attributes are supported in XHTML 1.0 transitional and strict.

 Hands-On 6.4   **Specify the Width and Height**

In this exercise, you will specify the width and height of an image.

1. Switch to Notepad and locate the `<img>` tag for the dancers.jpg image.

2. Follow these steps to add the width and height attributes:

NOTE! *Your code may wrap differently from the code shown in the figure.*

Ⓐ **Click after the closing quotation mark of the** border **attribute.**

```
<img src="images/dancers.jpg" alt="Dancers, created by Jeremy
Shafer" align="left" border="1" width="300" height="300" />
```

Ⓑ Tap ⎵Spacebar⎵, **type** width="300", **tap** ⎵Spacebar⎵, **and type** height="300".

3. Save your changes and make the web browser the active window.

4. Tap F5 to refresh the page.
   The image of the dancers enlarges to 300 x 300 pixels. These dimensions are larger than the actual dimensions, so the image looks distorted and blurry. You will correct that in the next step.

5. Make Notepad the active window.

6. Locate the `<img>` tag for the dancers and change the width to **180** and the height to **120**.
   Your code should resemble the following.

```
<img src="images/dancers.jpg" alt="Dancers, created by Jeremy
Shafer" align="left" border="1" width="180" height-"120" />
```

7. Save your changes and make the web browser the active window.

8. Tap F5 to refresh the page.
   The dancers image displays at its actual size and is no longer blurry.

9. Using the instructions outlined in step 2, add width and height attributes to the second image. Both should be 252.
Your code should resemble the following.

```
<img src="images/creature.jpg" alt="Devil, created by Jun Maekawa"
align="left" border="1" width="252" height="252" />
```

10. Save your changes and make the web browser the active window.

11. Refresh the page.
Both images are displayed at their actual size.

Hspace and Vspace

Hspace creates space on the sides of an image to push it away from other page elements. This is useful for creating breathing room. The value must be an integer, which specifies pixels on each side. For example, hspace="5" creates 5 pixels of space on the left of the image and 5 pixels of space on the right of the image for a total of 10 pixels additional space across the page. Vspace works the same way, but creates space above and below an image. As the spacing is presentational, these attributes should be avoided if possible in favor of the CSS padding and margin properties. The attributes are allowed in XHTML 1.0 transitional but are forbidden in XHTML 1.0 strict.

With no spacing, the text is too close to the image.

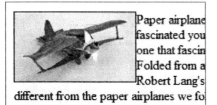

With hspace="10" and vspace="10", the text is easier to read.

 Hands-On 6.5 **Add Breathing Room**

In this exercise, you will add spacing to images in order to create breathing room.

1. Switch to Notepad and locate the `<img>` tag for the dancers.jpg image.

2. Follow these steps to add horizontal space:

⚠ **NOTE!** *Your code may wrap differently from the code shown in the figure.*

Ⓐ Click after the closing quotation mark of the height attribute.

```
<img src="images/dancers.jpg" alt="Dancers, created by
Jeremy Shafer" align="left" border="1" width="180"
height="120" hspace="50" />
```

Ⓑ Tap ⌷Spacebar⌷ and type **hspace="50"**.

3. Save your changes and make the web browser the active window.

4. Tap F5 to refresh the page.
The browser displays 50 pixels of space to the left of the dancers and 50 pixels of space to the right. This is too much. You will reduce this in the next step.

 NOTE! *It is very common when hand-coding to type some code, check how it displays in the browser, edit the code, check in the browser, and so on. Many of the attribute settings are determined through trial and error.*

5. Make Notepad the active window.

6. Change 50 to **10** as the hspace value so your code resembles the following.

```
<img src="images/dancers.jpg" alt="Dancers, created by Jeremy
Shafer" align="left" border="1" width="180" height="120"
hspace="10" />
```

7. Using the instructions outlined in step 2, add 10 pixels of hspace to the second image.

```
<img src="images/creature.jpg" alt="Devil, created by Jun Maekawa"
align="left" border="1" width="252" height="252" hspace="10" />
```

8. Save your changes and make the web browser the active window.

9. Tap F5 to refresh the page.
The browser displays 10 pixels of space on each side of the images, creating enough breathing room so the text doesn't look cramped.

Adding a Horizontal Ruled Line

A *horizontal rule* is a line created with HTML code rather than in a graphics editing program such as Photoshop. While it's not officially a graphic, it can be considered a graphical element. It is a block-level element, so it always resides on its own line. Horizontal rules are useful in creating a separation between sections of content, as in the following figure.

Paper airplanes have always fascinated young children. Here is one that fascinates adults too. Folded from a single uncut square, Robert Lang's Biplane is a bit different from the paper airplanes we folded as kids.

Eric Joisel's Rat merges cartoon pop culture with a sculpture's eye for lines. The roundness of the ears and curvature of the snout are not elements you typically see in folded paper.

A horizontal rule helps to cleanly separate areas of content.

The Horizontal Rule Tag and Its Attributes

A horizontal rule is created with an `<hr />` tag. It is a replacement tag that is replaced at runtime by a horizontal line. Several attributes can be added to the tag to affect its presentation. As these attributes are presentational, they are supported in XHTML 1.0 transitional, but forbidden in XHTML 1.0 strict.

- align
- noshade
- size
- width

Align

By default, horizontal rules span 100 percent of their container and center themselves. If you use the width attribute so the line is not 100 percent, you can then use the align attribute to move it to the left or right as in the following figures.

Origami Sculpture

Folding the creases is just a small part of origami. To make a model truly come alive, it must be sculpted and acressed into submission.

By default, a horizontal rule is centered. The width attribute has been applied to the line in this figure so it does not span the full width of the browser window.

Origami Sculpture

Folding the creases is just a small part of origami. To make a model truly come alive, it must be sculpted and acressed into submission.

Use the align attribute to align it left or right. In this example, the rule is aligned left.

Noshade

By default, horizontal rules display a slight 3-D bevel. You can use the noshade attribute to disable this effect.

Size

Size refers to the thickness or height of the ruled line. Be aware that different browsers display horizontal rules very differently, and while this is not noticeable at the smaller default sizes, it becomes clear when the size increases.

Origami Sculpture

Folding the creases is just a small part of origami.

A size of 20 in Internet Explorer 7

Origami Sculpture

Folding the creases is just a small part of origami.

The same page viewed in Firefox

Width

Horizontal rules take up 100 percent of the available space by default, but you can specify a static pixel width that never changes. You can also specify a percentage so the line widens and narrows with the browser window. This is often referred to as *liquid* because it can vary based on the width of the browser window.

Origami Sculpture

The code `<hr width="90" align="left"/>` creates a horizontal rule 90 pixels wide and left-aligned.

Origami Sculpture

Using a pixel value causes the line not to change when the browser window widens.

Origami Sculpture

The code `<hr width="75%" align="left"/>` creates a left-aligned horizontal rule that is always 75 percent of the available space.

Origami Sculpture

As the browser window widens, the horizontal rule expands to 75 percent of the width.

QUICK REFERENCE: HORIZONTAL RULE ATTRIBUTES

Attribute	Valid Values	Sample Code
align	left, center, right	`<hr align="left" />`
noshade	noshade; disables the 3-D shading	`<hr noshade="noshade" />`
size	an integer; defines a static thickness in pixels	`<hr size="5" />`
width	an integer; defines a static width in pixels	`<hr width="500" />`
	a percentage; defines a variable width in relation to the available space	`<hr width="75%" />`

 Hands-On 6.6   Add a Horizontal Rule

In this exercise, you will add and configure a horizontal rule.

1. Switch to Notepad and locate the paragraph for the navigation bar, starting with `<p>Home - Gallery - How To`.

2. Follow these steps to add and configure a horizontal rule:

Ⓐ Click after the closing paragraph tag and tap Enter to create a new line.

```
<p>Home - Gallery -  How To - Resources - Contact</p>
<hr width="85%" />
```

Ⓑ Type **<hr width="85%" />**.

3. Save your changes and make the web browser the active window.

4. Tap F5 to refresh the page.
The horizontal rule appears on its own line because it is a block-level element. It is centered by default and spans 85 percent of the available width.

Using Background Images

A background image is one that sits in the background of an element, such as a table, table cell, or the whole page itself. This lesson focuses on page backgrounds. Of course, background images are presentational, so the method outlined in the next section is fully supported by XHTML 1.0 transitional but not by XHTML 1.0 strict. Page backgrounds can be used to unify the design of a website or offer that little piece of eye candy that makes your design visually stimulating.

 TIP! *Don't overdo it. The background, as its name implies, should be in the background. It should not overpower or distract from the main content.*

This background is too distracting.

Even when it is faded out, it is still too much.

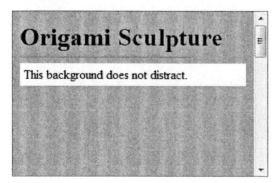

A more subtle background doesn't distract from the content.

Tiles

Backgrounds are typically small images that are *tiled*, as in the preceding figures. The image starts in the top-left corner, repeats across to the end of the line, then repeats across a second line, a third line, and so on until the entire page is filled. A well-designed tile won't look like it's tiled (it will be seamless). You can always identify a poorly designed tile because you can see the seams. Unfortunately, you can't tell the seams will be visible until you apply the background to your code and view it in a browser.

This poorly created tile...

This background does not tile well.

...looks like it's been tiled. You can see the seams where it is repeated.

This tile is much better...

This background tiles well.

...because it tiles to create a seamless background. However, it is still distracting. It is shown here to illustrate a seamless tile.

Adding Background Images

In XHTML 1.0 transitional, page backgrounds can be defined as an attribute of the <body> tag. XHTML 1.0 strict requires backgrounds to be defined in CSS, which you will learn in Lesson 11, Doing More with CSS.

 Hands-On 6.7   Add a Background Image

In this exercise, you will add a page background.

1. Switch to Notepad and locate the opening <body> tag.

2. Follow these steps to add a page background:

A Click after the word body.

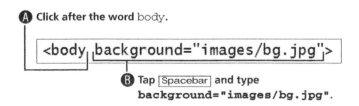

```
<body background="images/bg.jpg">
```

B Tap [Spacebar] and type
`background="images/bg.jpg"`.

3. Save your changes and make the web browser the active window.

4. Tap F5 to refresh the page.
   The background image displays.

5. Close your web browser.

6. Close Notepad.

QUICK REFERENCE: SUMMARY OF IMAGE TAGS AND ATTRIBUTES

Tag	Notes
Image `<img />`	■ Replacement tag ■ Requires both the `src` and `alt` attributes **Attributes for the `<img />` tag:** ■ src—Specifies the path to the image ■ alt—Specifies alternate text for browsers that do not display the image ■ align—Specifies how the image aligns to other inline elements such as text ■ border—Specifies the width of a border in pixels ■ height—Specifies the height at which to display the image ■ hspace—Specifies space in pixels to the left and right sides of the image ■ vspace—Specifies space in pixels to the top and bottom of the image ■ width—Specifies the width at which to display the image Both `src` and `alt` are required. Both `height` and `width` are recommended. All the others are supported in XHTML 1.0 transitional but are forbidden in XHTML 1.0 strict.
Horizontal rule `<hr />`	■ Replacement tag ■ No required attributes **Attribute for the `<hr />` tag:** ■ align—Specifies the position of the line in relation to the page ■ noshade—Removes the three-dimensional shading ■ size—Specifies the height of the line ■ width—Specifies the width of the line in pixels or a percentage All the attributes are supported in XHTML 1.0 transitional but are forbidden in XHTML 1.0 strict.
Body `<body></body>`	■ One of the main structural tags that defines an XHTML document **Attribute for the `<body>` tag:** ■ background—Specifies the path to the image to be used as a page background The `background` attribute is supported in XHTML 1.0 transitional but is forbidden in XHTML 1.0 strict.

Concepts Review

True/False Questions

1. All graphics are considered presentational and, as such, should not be included in your XHTML.

    TRUE   FALSE

2. Both the `src` and `alt` attributes are required for `<img>` tags in XHTML.

    TRUE   FALSE

3. Both the `width` and `height` attributes are required for `<img>` tags in XHTML.

    TRUE   FALSE

4. The `<img>` tag is a container tag and requires a closing `</img>` tag.

    TRUE   FALSE

5. To have your text wrap on the right side of an image, set the `<img>` tag's `align` attribute to "left."

    TRUE   FALSE

6. To add space to the left and right sides of your image, use the `vspace` attribute.

    TRUE   FALSE

7. Background images can be added to your page with an attribute of the `<body>` tag.

    TRUE   FALSE

8. Absolute paths always begin from the site root, unless they are specified by a full URL.

    TRUE   FALSE

9. The `<hr />` tag is useful for creating a visual separation between page sections.

    TRUE   FALSE

10. When specifying an integer value for an attribute, such as `border="4"` or `width="172"`, the number refers to pixels.

    TRUE   FALSE

Multiple Choice Questions

1. Adeline's site root is organized with folders as in the following figure. She wants to include the logo.gif graphic on her gallery.htm page. Which code snippet should she use?

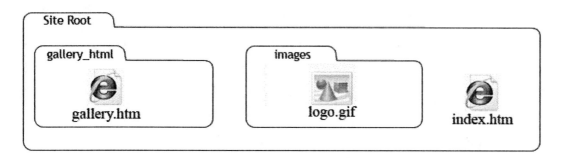

   a. `<img src="logo.gif" alt="company logo" />`

   b. `<img src="../images/logo.gif" />`

   c. `<img src="images/logo.gif" alt="company logo" />`

   d. `<img src="../images/logo.gif" alt="company logo" />`

2. Maliq is striving for XHTML 1.0 strict and knows he needs to move his non-essential graphics out of his XHTML code and into his CSS code. How should he handle the company logo and page background?

   a. Leave both graphics in his XHTML code as they are both essential.

   b. Move both graphics to his CSS code as they are both non-essential.

   c. Keep the company logo in the XHTML code and move the background image to CSS.

   d. Move the company logo to the CSS code and keep the background image in the XHTML.

3. Damika wants to insert a horizontal rule on her page. It should be centered and change in length as the browser window narrows and widens. It should span about three-quarters of the page. Which code snippet should she use?

   a. `<hr width="75%" />`

   b. `<hr width="75%" align="middle" />`

   c. `<hr width="300" align="center" />`

   d. `<hr width="300" />`

4. Laslo wishes to add some space to the sides of his images so the text isn't right up against them. How should he accomplish this?

   a. Click after the `<img>` tag and tap the spacebar several times to create space.

   b. Set the width attribute to about 10 pixels wider than the actual image dimensions.

   c. Set the hspace attribute to 10, as in `hspace="10"`.

   d. Set the hspace attribute to 10 pixels, as in `hspace="10px"`.

 # Skill Builders

Skill Builder 6.1   Add Images and a Horizontal Rule

In this exercise, you will add images and a horizontal rule to your page.

Replace the Background

1. Open your Lesson 06 folder, and then open the sb_images folder.

2. Double-click the index.htm file to view it in your web browser.
   The background is a little dark. You will replace it with a lighter background.

3. Start Notepad.

4. Choose File→Open from the menu bar.

5. Open the sb_images subfolder in your Lesson 06 folder.

6. Open the index.htm file.

7. Locate the opening <body> tag towards the top of the document.

8. Follow these steps to replace the page background:

   A Click after the bg, but before the .jpg file extension.

   ```
   <body background="images/bg_gold.jpg">
   ```

   B Type _gold.

9. Save your changes, switch to your web browser, and tap F5.
   The page background changes from a dark brown to a light gold. If it didn't, go back and fix your code before continuing.

Replace the Page Heading

10. Switch back to Notepad.

11. Locate the <h1> tag towards the top of the document. Then follow these steps to replace the text with an image:

   A Select the entire <h1> element and tap Backspace to delete it.

   ```
   <div id="masthead">
   <h1>Folding Under Pressure</h1>
   ```

   ```
   <div id="masthead">
   <img src="images/pagehead.gif" alt="Folding Under Pressure" />
   ```

   B Type <img src="images/pagehead.gif" alt="Folding Under Pressure" /> in its place.

12. Click to the left of the `<img>` tag you just typed and tap ⌷Enter⌷ to create a space above the `<img>` tag.

13. Type **`<img src="images/crane1.gif" alt="origami crane" />`** in the space you just created.

14. Click in the space below the pagehead.gif `<img>` tag and type the following:
    `<img src="images/crane2.gif" alt="origami crane" />`

15. Save your changes, switch to your web browser, and refresh the page.
    The top of your page should resemble the following figure. If it doesn't, go back and fix the errors in your code before continuing. Note that all three images are transparent GIFs so you can see the page background through the holes.

Add a Horizontal Rule

16. Switch back to Notepad and locate the footer at the bottom of the document.

17. Follow these steps to insert a horizontal rule:

Ⓐ Click to the left of the opening `<p>` tag in the footer.

```
<hr width="75%" align="left" />
<p>Folding Under Pressure &copy; 2007</p>
```

Ⓑ Type `<hr width="75%" align="left" />` and tap ⌷Enter⌷.

18. Save your changes, switch to your web browser, and refresh the page.
    The bottom of your page should resemble the following figure. If it doesn't, go back and fix the errors in your code before continuing.

Others pioneers at the forefront of this art include Robert Lang, John Montroll, Fumiaki Kawahata, Jun Maekawa, Issei Yoshino, Jeremy Shafer, Neil Elias, and Eric Joissel, just to name a few.

Folding Under Pressure © 2007

Skill Builder 6.2   Adjust Image Attributes

In this exercise, you will adjust several <img> *tag attributes.*

Before You Begin: *You must complete Skill Builder 6.1 before beginning this exercise.*

1. Notice the following aspects of the current design:

The image is too close to the horizontal rule.   The cranes are too close to the page heading graphic.

You will fix these issues in the next few steps.

2. Switch to Notepad.

3. Locate the code for the pagehead.gif <img> tag towards the top of the document.

4. Follow these steps to add some breathing room:

Ⓐ Click after the closing quote of the alt attribute.

```
<div id="masthead">
<img src="images/crane1.gif" alt="origami crane" />
<img src="images/pagehead.gif" alt="Folding Under Pressure" hspace="50" />
```

Ⓑ Tap ⌈Spacebar⌋ and type **hspace="50"**.

5. Save your changes, switch to your web browser, and refresh the page.
   Fifty pixels of space is added to both sides of the pagehead.gif graphic, pushing the cranes away. However, now they seem a little too far away. You will reduce the space in the next step.

6. Switch back to Notepad and locate the pagehead.gif <img> tag towards the top of the document.

7. Change the hspace="50" attribute to hspace="**10**".

8. Save your changes, switch to your web browser, and refresh the page.
   The space to each side of the pagehead.gif graphic has been reduced to 10 pixels each.

9. Switch back to Notepad and locate the code for the dancers.gif <img> tag.

10. Follow these steps to push the image away from the horizontal rule:

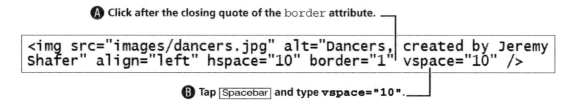

Ⓐ Click after the closing quote of the `border` attribute.

```
<img src="images/dancers.jpg" alt="Dancers, created by Jeremy
Shafer" align="left" hspace="10" border="1" vspace="10" />
```

Ⓑ Tap [Spacebar] and type **vspace="10"**.

11. Save your changes, switch to your web browser, and refresh the page.
The dancers image is pushed down 10 pixels. If there was text below the image, it may no longer wrap underneath as 10 pixels of space was also added below the image.

12. Close your web browser.

13. Close Notepad.

 **Assessments**

Assessment 6.1   Add Graphic Elements

In this exercise, you will add graphical elements to a web page.

Add a Page Background

1. Open your Lesson 06 folder and then open the as_guitar folder.
   Take note of the name of the subfolder storing the images.

2. Open the index.htm file in both your web browser and in Notepad.

3. Add the bg.jpg file as a page background.

Add Images

4. Delete the `<h1>Guitar Greats</h1>` text heading and replace it with the greats.gif graphic. Be sure to give it an appropriate `alt` attribute.

5. To the left of the `<h2>Blues Rock</h2>` subheading, insert the tone.jpg photo with an appropriate `alt` attribute.

6. To the left of the `<h2>Shred</h2>` subheading, insert the frets.jpg photo with an appropriate `alt` attribute.

7. Add the pickups.jpg photo to the left of the `<h2>Rock</h2>` subheading with an appropriate `alt` attribute.

Add Horizontal Rules

8. Add a horizontal rule under the greats.gif image.

9. Add another horizontal rule above the footer.

10. Be sure to save the changes to your index page and test the page, if possible, in more than one browser.

Assessment 6.2   Configure Image Attributes

In this exercise, you will tweak the appearance of the images with HTML attributes.

Before You Begin: *You must complete Assessment 6.1 before beginning this exercise.*

1. Add the appropriate attributes to each of the three images next to the subheadings to accomplish the following:
   - A three-pixel border
   - Aligned to the left of the text
   - Horizontal space of 10 pixels
   - Vertical space of 10 pixels
   - Specify the actual dimensions of 75 pixels wide x 56 pixels tall

2. Configure both of the horizontal rules to remain fluid at 85 percent of the browser window width. They should also be aligned to the left side of the page.

3. Be sure to save the changes to your index page and test the page, if possible, in more than one browser.

Critical Thinking

Critical Thinking 6.1   Create a Page with Images

In this exercise, you will create a web page with images.

1. Think of a topic for which you can create enough text for a single web page.

2. Using the skills you have acquired in this and earlier lessons, create a folder named **ct_mypage** in your Lesson 06 folder. In the ct_mypage folder, create a blank HTML file named **index.htm** and a subfolder with an appropriate name in which to store images.

3. Acquire images for your web page that are relevant to your content. You may use your own images or download royalty-free images in the public domain.

4. Your page should consist of the following elements:
   - All required XHTML tags
   - At least one `<h1>` element
   - At least two `<h2>` elements
   - All non-heading text should be contained within `<p>` tags
   - Structural `<div>` tags to define the masthead, content, and footer regions
   - At least three images with the required attributes and at least two optional attributes
   - At least one horizontal rule

LESSON 7

Working with Hyperlinks

In this lesson, you will connect pages to each other with hyperlinks. You will create text and image hyperlinks and link to web pages, email addresses, named anchors, and other documents and files. You will learn the theory behind image maps and you will learn about old-style formatting methods and why CSS is preferred to style your hyperlinks.

LESSON OBJECTIVES

After studying this lesson, you will be able to:

- Insert text and image hyperlinks
- Link to a specific location on a web page
- Work with image maps
- Link to documents and files other than web pages
- Style links with color

Case Study: Connecting Pages

Now that Miguel has added pictures to several of the pages, Haylie is ready to start connecting her pages. She creates a navigation bar of text links to aid the site's accessibility and ensures it displays consistently across all pages for usability. She also creates a photo gallery by linking small-image thumbnails to larger versions of the photos. Lastly, she creates in-page navigation with named anchors and links to a PDF file.

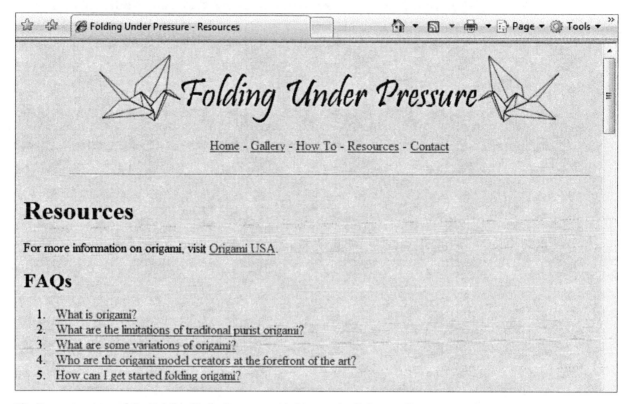

The Resources page of the Folding Under Pressure website contains links to other pages within the site, links to specific locations within the same page, and a link to a completely different website.

Working with Hyperlinks

Most websites have more information than can fit comfortably on a single page. The question is, what constitutes a single page? And what is considered comfortable? As users can simply scroll down, down, down through a single long page, there is no physical limitation as to the length of a web page. However, most usability guidelines state a single page should be no more than about two to three screens (no more than tapping the [PageDown] button three times). Any longer than that and the page content is overwhelming. Additionally, by breaking up content across several pages you can better organize your information with each page covering a specific topic or subtopic. You use *hyperlinks* to navigate from page to page.

Navigation Bars

A *navigation bar*, often called a *navbar*, is a collection of hyperlinks that are usually related to each other. For example, a site's main pages may include Home, Products, About Us, and Contact Us. A navigation bar for this scenario is shown in the following illustration.

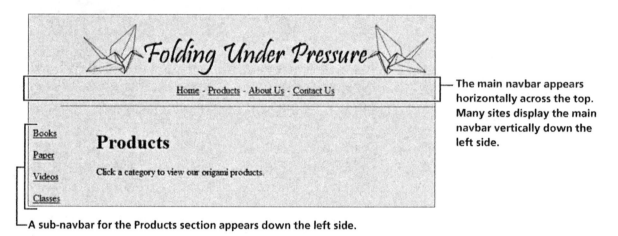

The main navbar appears horizontally across the top. Many sites display the main navbar vertically down the left side.

A sub-navbar for the Products section appears down the left side.

A web page may include several navbars. One may be in the masthead for main page navigation, another may be in a sidebar for sub-navigation, while another may be in the footer.

TIP! *The navbars should not jump around or change from page to page. A consistently placed navbar with the same links on every page helps users navigate your site and reduces the chances of users becoming lost or frustrated. The same holds true for the masthead in general—or any page elements that appear on all the pages.*

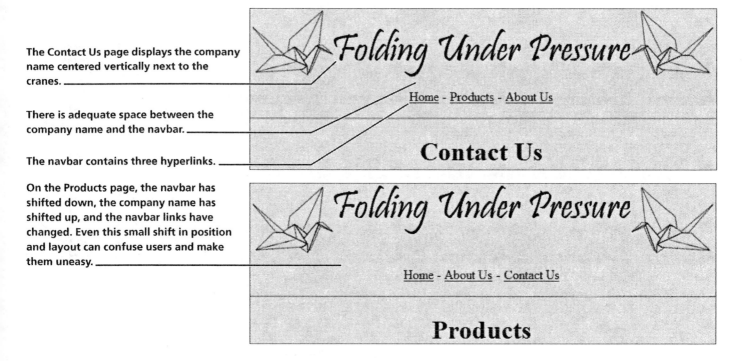

The Contact Us page displays the company name centered vertically next to the cranes.

There is adequate space between the company name and the navbar.

The navbar contains three hyperlinks.

On the Products page, the navbar has shifted down, the company name has shifted up, and the navbar links have changed. Even this small shift in position and layout can confuse users and make them uneasy.

Hyperlinking from Text

Hyperlinks can be created from text. There are two things to consider when creating text links:

- **Action**—What happens when the link is clicked

- **Link text**—What the text should read

For usability, the link text should indicate the action. For example, a hyperlink that reads "Click here" does not indicate what will happen when clicked and can be considered mystery meat navigation. "Download the file" or "Contact Us" are better choices for link text.

The link text "Click here" does not indicate what will happen when clicked. This is not user-friendly.

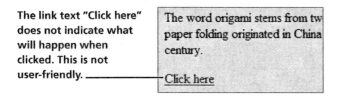

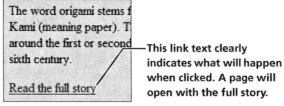

This link text clearly indicates what will happen when clicked. A page will open with the full story.

The Anchor Tag

The anchor tag is used to create hyperlinks; it requires a few attributes in XHTML to work, depending on the anchor's function. Note that officially there are no required attributes of the anchor tag (they are all optional) as the anchor tag can perform different functions. To create a clickable hyperlink, certain attributes are needed. To create a named anchor, or a bookmark, different attributes are needed. (You will learn about named anchors later in this lesson.) The anchor tag is a container tag, so it requires an associated closing `</a>` tag at the end. Anything enclosed by the `<a>` and `</a>` tags is clickable. Anchor tags cannot be nested inside each other, but can be nested inside a heading, paragraph, list item, or any other tag.

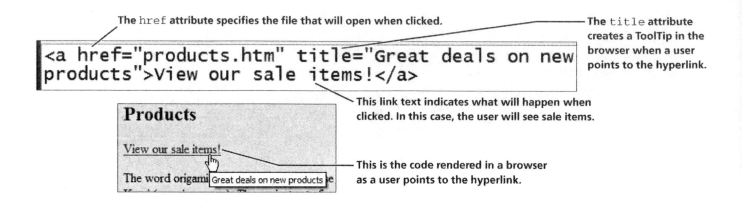

The `href` attribute specifies the file that will open when clicked.

The `title` attribute creates a ToolTip in the browser when a user points to the hyperlink.

```
<a href="products.htm" title="Great deals on new
products">View our sale items!</a>
```

This link text indicates what will happen when clicked. In this case, the user will see sale items.

Products

View our sale items!

The word origami [Great deals on new products]

This is the code rendered in a browser as a user points to the hyperlink.

 QUICK REFERENCE: ANCHOR TAG ATTRIBUTES FOR HYPERLINKS IN XHTML 1.0 TRANSITIONAL

Attribute	Function	Valid Values	Sample Code
href	Specifies the page or file to open when clicked	A relative or absolute path	`<a href="cart.htm">`
target (forbidden in XHTML 1.0 strict)	Specifies how the target file should open	_blank (the target opens in a new window)	`<a href="cart.htm" target="_blank">`
title	Specifies text that displays in a ToolTip when a user points to the link	Text	`<a href="cart.htm" title="view cart contents">`

 TIP! *Use the* `title` *attribute sparingly. Overuse can annoy visual users and blind readers.*

 Hands-On 7.1   Create Text Hyperlinks

In this exercise, you will create and test text hyperlinks.

Open the Index Page

1. Open your Lesson 07 folder and then open the fup_site_root folder.
   Notice that there are several web pages already created in the site root.

2. Double-click the index.htm file to view it in your browser.

3. Start Notepad and open the index.htm file from the fup_site_root folder in your Lesson 07 folder.

Create Text Hyperlinks

4. Scroll to the `<div id="masthead">` section. Then follow these steps to create a hyperlink:

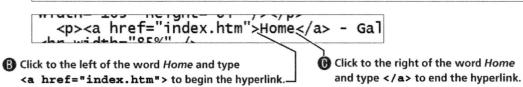

ⓐ Locate the paragraph containing the navigation bar.

```
<div id="masthead">
    <p><img src="images/crane1.gif" width="103" height="8
src="images/pagehead.gif" width="369" height="60" /><im
width="103" height="84" /></p>
    <p>Home - Gallery -  How To - Resources - Contact</p>
```

```
    <p><a href="index.htm">Home</a> - Gal
```

ⓑ Click to the left of the word *Home* and type
`<a href="index.htm">` to begin the hyperlink.

ⓒ Click to the right of the word *Home*
and type `</a>` to end the hyperlink.

You have created a link to the index page. Even though that is the current page, the navigation bar should be consistent across all pages in the site.

5. Click to the left of the word *Gallery* and type **`<a href="gallery.htm">`** to begin the Gallery hyperlink.

6. Click to the right of the word *Gallery* and type **`</a>`** to end the hyperlink.

7. Create hyperlinks for the remaining navigation bar elements.

This Text	Should Link to ...
How To	howto.htm
Resources	resources.htm
Contact	contact.htm

8. Save your changes.
Your code should look like the following example.

```
<p>a href="index.htm">Home</a> - <a href="gallery.htm">Gallery</a> -
<a href="howto.htm">How To</a> - <a href="resources.htm">Resources</a>
- <a href="contact.htm">Contact</a></p>
```

Test Hyperlinks

9. Switch to your web browser and tap <kbd>F5</kbd> to refresh the page.

10. Follow these steps to test the hyperlinks:

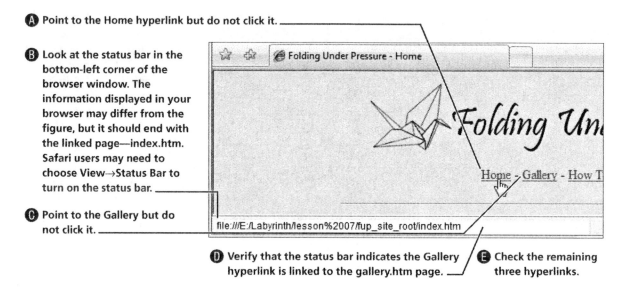

A Point to the Home hyperlink but do not click it.

B Look at the status bar in the bottom-left corner of the browser window. The information displayed in your browser may differ from the figure, but it should end with the linked page—index.htm. Safari users may need to choose View→Status Bar to turn on the status bar.

C Point to the Gallery but do not click it.

D Verify that the status bar indicates the Gallery hyperlink is linked to the gallery.htm page.

E Check the remaining three hyperlinks.

Folding Under Pressure - Home

folding Un

Home - Gallery - How T

file:///E:/Labyrinth/lesson%2007/fup_site_root/index.htm

11. Click the Gallery hyperlink.

12. The browser displays the Gallery page.
The text in the navigation bar on the Gallery page has not been turned into hyperlinks yet. You will have an opportunity to complete this task in the Skill Builder exercises at the end of this lesson.

13. Click the browser's Back button to return to the index page.

14. Continue to check the How To, Resources, and Contact hyperlinks, using the browser's Back button to return to the index page each time.

15. Close your web browser.

16. Close Notepad.
You will link the navigation bars on the other pages in the Skill Builder exercises at the end of this lesson.

Linking to External Pages

Hyperlinks on your pages can point to pages from other websites. As these files do not exist within your site, the links are called *external links*. The syntax of the anchor tag is the same, but the `href` attribute must specify an absolute path in the form of a full URL as in the following example.

```
<a href="http://www.google.com">Search with Google</a>
```

 Hands-On 7.2   **Link to External Pages**

In this exercise, you will create a hyperlink to an external page.

1. Start your web browser and open the resources.htm file from the fup_site_root folder in your Lesson 07 folder.

2. Start Notepad and open the same resources.htm file from the fup_site_root folder in your Lesson 07 folder.

3. Locate the following paragraph in the HTML code:

```
<p>
For more information on origami, visit Origami USA.
</p>
```

4. Follow these steps to create an external link:

Ⓐ **Click to the left of the word *Origami*.**

```
visit <a href="http://www.origami-usa.org" target="_blank">Origami USA</a>.
```

Ⓑ **Type `<a href="http://www.origami-usa.org" target="_blank">` to start the hyperlink.**

Ⓒ **Click after the letters *USA* and type `</a>` to end the hyperlink.**

Including the target attribute with the value `_blank` *forces the Origami USA website to open in a new browser window when the link is clicked.*

5. Save your changes and switch to your web browser.

6. Tap `F5` to refresh the page.

7. Click the Origami USA hyperlink.
Depending on your browser settings, the Origami USA website may open in a new window or a new tab.

Named Anchors

Sometimes you will have content on a long single page that can be organized into sections. For example, a page stating your privacy policy or frequently asked questions (FAQ) may fare better as a single long page rather than as several pages. To help users locate information on this page quickly, you can provide *named anchors*, commonly called *bookmarks*.

An Analogy

Imagine a long bulletin board (an old-fashioned cork bulletin board) with index cards thumb-tacked down its length, each with a different colored tack. If you wanted to direct someone to one of the index cards, you could say "Look for the green thumb tack" or "Look for the red thumb tack." This is the principle behind named anchors. The basic steps follow.

1. Identify each section of content with a named anchor, similar to a thumbtack marking a position on the page.

2. Create hyperlinks pointing to the named anchors.

3. When a user clicks a hyperlink, the page automatically scrolls to the specified named anchor.

Named Anchor Syntax

There are two anchors that must be coded in this case: the named anchor and the hyperlink. The named anchor (the thumbtack) consists of an empty `<a></a>` container with a single id attribute, as in `<a id="question1"></a>`. The hyperlink's href attribute must begin with the pound symbol followed by the name of the named anchor, as in `<a href="#question1"> Click here for question 1</a>`.

 TIP! *The value of the* id *attribute must begin with a letter or the underscore character and cannot contain any spaces. While a number may be part of the id's value, it cannot begin with a number.*

The `href` attribute references a named anchor on the same page. Notice it starts with the # symbol.

This code...

```
<h3>Question #1</h3>
<p>What guitar did AC/DC's Angus Young make famous?<br />
<a href="#q1">Read the answer</a></p>
```

...produces this in the browser.

> **Question #1**
>
> What guitar did AC/DC's Angus Young make famous?
> Read the answer

When this link is clicked...

> **Solution #1**
>
> The answer to question #1 is a Gibson SG.

...the browser window automatically scrolls to this section in the same page...

```
<a id="question1"></a>
<h3>Solution #1</h3>
The answer to question #1 is a Gibson SG.
```

...that was produced by this code. Notice that the `<a></a>` tags are empty and the id attribute does not begin with the # symbol. This is the named anchor.

Named Anchors on Another Page

By combining a regular hyperlink with a named anchor, it is possible to create a link to a named anchor on a different page. For example, consider an index.htm page with this code:

```
<a href="products.htm#new">New Products</a>
```

The `href` references a different page, products.htm, in addition to a named anchor. When clicked, the browser navigates to the products.htm page and automatically scrolls to the `new` named anchor.

 Hands-On 7.3 Link to Named Anchors

In this exercise, you will create links to named anchors.

Create a Named Anchor

1. Make Notepad active and locate the `<h3>What is origami?</h3>` block of code:

```
<h3>What is origami?</h3>
<p>
Simply put, origami is the
```

2. Follow these steps to create a named anchor:

Ⓐ **Click in the space above the** `<h3>` **tag.**

```
<a id="whatis"></a>
<h3>What is origami?</h3>
```

Ⓑ Type `<a id="whatis"></a>` to create the first named anchor.

The `<a>` tag uses the `id` attribute to uniquely identify the named anchor.

Create a Link to a Named Anchor

3. Scroll up and locate the ordered list in the FAQ section. Then follow these steps to create a link to the first named anchor:

Ⓐ **Click after the first opening** `<li>` **tag and type** `<a href="#whatis">`**.**

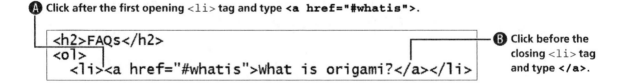

```
<h2>FAQs</h2>
<ol>
    <li><a href="#whatis">What is origami?</a></li>
```

Ⓑ **Click before the closing** `<li>` **tag and type** `</a>`**.**

The `<a>` tag uses the `href` attribute to link to the similarly named anchor. Note that the `href` begins with the # symbol.

Test the Link

4. Save your changes and switch to your web browser.

5. Tap [F5] to refresh the page.

6. Click the What Is Origami? hyperlink.
   The page automatically scrolls so the named anchor appears at the top of the browser window.

7. Close your web browser and Notepad.
   You will create the rest of the named anchors for the FAQ section in the Skill Builder exercises at the end of this lesson.

Creating Email Links

Providing a clickable link to an email address is a handy way for users to pre-address an email message. However, including an email link does not enable your web page to send email. When a user clicks an email link, their default email program opens with the recipient's address pre-filled. The user can then type their subject and message and click Send just as they would when composing any other email.

Email Link Syntax

Linking to an email address uses an anchor tag and is created almost exactly the same as with a regular hyperlink. The only difference is that the value of the `href` attribute must begin with `mailto:` followed by the email address, as in the following example.

```
<a href="mailto:admin@example.com">Send mail to the admin</a>
```

Because of the code, email links are often referred to as *mailto: links*. Again, the link text should indicate the action of the hyperlink.

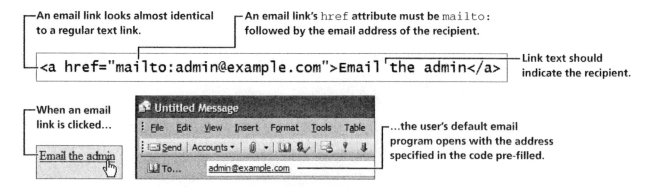

─An email link looks almost identical to a regular text link.

─An email link's `href` attribute must be `mailto:` followed by the email address of the recipient.

```
<a href="mailto:admin@example.com">Email the admin</a>
```

Link text should indicate the recipient.

─When an email link is clicked...

...the user's default email program opens with the address specified in the code pre-filled.

Email the admin

Untitled Message
File   Edit   View   Insert   Format   Tools   Table
Send | Accounts ▾ | 🔗 ▾ | 📖 &, | 🔗 ! ↓
To...   admin@example.com

Spam

Unfortunately, some very savvy computer programmers have written programs referred to as *spam harvesters* or *email harvesters*. These software programs visit millions of websites a day looking for email addresses in the HTML code. Any addresses it finds are added to their harvested database and the spam begins. The best thing you can do to protect your (and your client's) email addresses is to not include them in your HTML code. That can be tricky because the HTML code requires an email address for your `mailto:` links. There are several ways around this, but the methods are beyond the scope of this book. If you are motivated to hide email address on web pages from spam harvesters, check out the website for this book for a link to various methods of hiding and masking email addresses.

 Hands-On 7.4   Link to Email Addresses

In this exercise, you will create a link to an email address.

Create a mailto: Link

1. Start your web browser and open the contact.htm page from the fup_site_root folder in your Lesson 07 folder.

2. Start Notepad and open the same contact.htm page from the fup_site_root folder in your Lesson 07 folder.

3. Locate the `<h1>Contact</h1>` block of code.

```
<h1>Contact</h1>
<p>
Phone: 555-1212<br />
Email: Send email to Haylie
```

4. Follow these steps to create an email link:

Ⓐ Click before the word *Send* and type **`<a href="mailto:haylie@example.com">`** to start the hyperlink.

```
Email: <a href="mailto:haylie@example.com">Send email to Haylie</a>
```

Ⓑ Click after the name *Haylie* and type **`</a>`** to end the hyperlink.

5. Save your changes and switch to your web browser.

6. Tap [F5] to refresh the page.

Test the Link

Your computer must be configured to use an email program such as Outlook, Outlook Express, Windows Mail, or Mozilla Thunderbird. Check with your instructor before completing these steps.

7. Click the Send email to Haylie hyperlink.
   Your email program launches and a new blank message is created with the To: field pre-addressed.

8. Close the message window and choose No if prompted to save changes.

9. Close your email program if it is still open.

10. Close your web browser.

11. Close Notepad.

Styling Text Hyperlinks

A hyperlink on a web page that has not yet been clicked is said to be in the *link state*. By default, most browsers display hyperlinks in the link state in the color blue. Hyperlinks that have been clicked are in the *visited state*. Most browsers display visited links in purple. Hyperlinks that are currently being clicked are in the *active state*. There usually is no default color for active links; they are colored based on if they have been visited or not. These colors can be changed to match the color scheme of your web page.

The Old HTML Way

This old-style HTML way of styling links is included in this book as you are likely to work on a preexisting web page at some point that implements this method—and you will need to recognize it. However, the preferred method using CSS is discussed in Lesson 10, Using CSS to Style Text. XHTML 1.0 transitional supports coloring your hyperlinks via <body> tag attributes. This method is forbidden in XHTML 1.0 strict. The following table lists the <body> tag attributes used to style hyperlinks.

 QUICK REFERENCE: BODY TAG ATTRIBUTES TO COLOR HYPERLINKS

Attribute	Function	Sample Code
alink	Specifies the color of active links	`<body alink="gold">`
link	Specifies the color of non-visited links	`<body link="green">`
vlink	Specifies the color of visited links	`<body vlink="orange">`

A Sample

The following sample code colors the links green, the visited links orange, and the active links gold. Again, while this is valid in XHTML 1.0 transitional, CSS should be used instead. Remember that attributes can appear in any order.

```
<body link="green" vlink="orange" active="gold">
```

Hyperlinking from Images

Hyperlinks are not limited to text. Images can be made into hyperlinks just as easily. The decision to use text or image hyperlinks is up to the developer, but the current push is towards text links styled with CSS as that decreases the time it takes for a page to load and is also more accessible. That is not to say you should never use image hyperlinks. For example, an image gallery of small thumbnail images that, when clicked, open a window with the full size image is a perfect place for image hyperlinks.

Button Links

When an image becomes a hyperlink, it is often called a button. This is not the element referred to as a button as you will see later in Lesson 12, Creating HTML Forms. An image link is created by nesting an <img> tag inside <a></a> tags, like this:

```
<a href="products.htm"><img src="images/sale.gif" alt="Click for
current sale items" /></a>
```

Button Borders

When text is made into a hyperlink, it becomes underlined. When an image becomes a hyperlink, it receives a border in whatever color you specified for your links. Some browsers (like Apple Safari) do not display this border, but most other browsers do. This border is normally an undesirable side effect, but it is easy to get rid of. The method outlined in the following Hands-On exercise is supported in XHTML 1.0 transitional, but forbidden in XHTML 1.0 strict because it adds presentational markup to your HTML. You will learn a preferred method of removing the border in Lesson 10, Using CSS to Style Text.

 Hands-On 7.5   Create Image Hyperlinks

In this exercise, you will create hyperlinks from images.

Create an Image Hyperlink

1. Start your web browser and open the gallery.htm page from the fup_site_root folder in your Lesson 07 folder.

2. Start Notepad and open the same gallery.htm page from the fup_site_root folder in your Lesson 07 folder.

3. Locate the code for the first image thumbnail.

```
<img src="images/knife_small.jpg" alt=
```

4. Follow these steps to create a hyperlink from the image:

Ⓐ Click to the left of the <img> tag and type **<a href="gal_knife.htm">** to begin the hyperlink.

```
<p>
<a href="gal_knife.htm"><img src="images/knife_small.jpg"
alt="Swiss Army Knife, Jun Maekawa" hspace="5" /></a>
```

Ⓑ Click after the <img> tag and type **</a>** to end the hyperlink.

5. Using the steps outlined in the previous step, create image hyperlinks around the next two thumbnails.

This Image	Should Link to . . .
fluffy_small.jpg	gal_fluffy.htm
present_small.jpg	gal_present.htm

View the Hyperlinks

6. Save your changes and switch to your web browser.

7. Tap F5 to refresh the page.
The thumbnails have a blue border because they are image hyperlinks. (Depending on your browser, you may not see the borders.) This detracts from the page design. You will remove the borders in the next few steps.

Remove the Border

8. Switch to Notepad and locate the code for the first thumbnail, knife_small.jpg.

9. Follow these steps to remove the blue border:

A Click after the closing quote of the hspace attribute.

```
<a href="gal_knife.htm"><img src="images/knife_small.jpg" alt="Swiss Army
Knife, Jun Maekawa" hspace="5" border="0" /></a>
```

B Tap Spacebar and type **border="0"** to remove the border.

10. Using the steps outlined above, remove the border from the fluffy_small.jpg and present_small.jpg images.

Test the Hyperlinks

11. Save your changes and switch to your web browser.

12. Tap F5 to refresh the page.
The thumbnails no longer display a blue border.

13. Click the thumbnail on the left.
The gal_knife.htm page opens and displays the full-size image. The Back hyperlink is not yet functional. You will fix this in the Skill Builder exercises at the end of this lesson.

14. Click the browser's Back button to return to the main gallery page.

15. Test the other two thumbnails and verify they navigate to the proper pages.

16. Close your web browser and Notepad.

Creating Image Maps

Now that you can create a link from an image, how about creating multiple links from a single image? For example, consider an image of the United States where users click on their state to go to a state-specific page. The problem is, how can you define multiple hyperlinks from a single image? The answer is with image maps.

Shapes and Coordinates

Imagine a single large image (such as a map of the United States) printed on a piece of graph paper. By taking a pen and outlining the parts of the image you want clickable (maybe around each state), you are creating shapes. A *shape* defines an area on the image to be turned into a hyperlink. (Sometimes shapes are called *hotspots*.) Image maps support rectangular, circular, and polygonal shapes (any closed shape). Now imagine you just don't want to take the time to draw the entire shape, so instead you simply place dots on the graph paper to define the shape. If the dots were connected, the shape would be outlined. The dots are referred to as the *coordinates*. When creating an image map, you state both the shape and the coordinates in your code. The web browser connects the coordinate dots to create the final hotspot.

NOTE! *Hotspots exist invisibly. They do not display in the browser, yet they exist for users to click.*

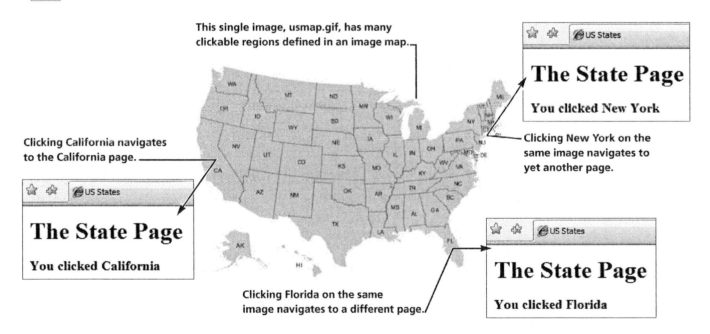

This single image, usmap.gif, has many clickable regions defined in an image map.

Clicking California navigates to the California page.

The State Page

You clicked California

Clicking New York on the same image navigates to yet another page.

The State Page

You clicked New York

Clicking Florida on the same image navigates to a different page.

The State Page

You clicked Florida

Image Map Syntax

Image maps require several tags and attributes working in tandem.

- The `<img>` tag requires a `usemap` attribute with a value that matches the `id` of the `<map>` tag. The `usemap` value must begin with the # symbol just as with a named anchor.

- The `<map>` tag requires an `id` attribute to uniquely identify it on the page.

- `<area>` tags are nested within the `<map></map>` tags and define the clickable regions of the image.

- `<area>` tags require `shape` and `coords` attributes to define a clickable region. They also require an `alt` attribute and should include an `href` attribute.

Syntax Example

The following <img> tag references an image map named *states*.

```
<img src="usmap.gif" alt="US States" usemap="#states" />
```

At another location in the document, the image map must be defined.

```
<map id="states">
<area shape="rect" coords="6,68,65,177" alt="California info" href="cal.htm" />
<area shape="rect" coords="274,203,345,261" alt="Florida info" href="fla.htm" />
</map>
```

 QUICK REFERENCE: TAGS AND ATTRIBUTES FOR IMAGE MAPS

Tag	Attribute	Notes
<img />	■ usemap—Specifies the map to use	You may have as many image maps on your page as you like as long as each image references a different image map.
<map></map>	■ id—Specifies a unique name for the map	The <map></map> tags contain the <area /> tags.
<area />	■ shape—Defines the shape of the area ■ (Valid values: rect, circle, poly) ■ coords—Defines a comma separated list of the coordinates that create the area ■ alt—Creates alternate text for non-visual browsers ■ href—Specifies the target file	The <area /> tag is a replacement tag. There is no closing tag.

Creating Image Maps

Basically, the coding of an image map is simple. The difficult part is figuring out what the shape and coords should be. In the old days, you would print out the image on graph paper, take out your slide ruler, and figure out the coordinates. Nowadays, there is software that creates this for you.

Some web-design software lets you draw "hotspots" on your image to define the areas. The HTML code is automatically generated for you.

It is not possible to create image maps with just Notepad (you can type the image map code, but Notepad cannot generate the code). Visit the website for this book for links to image-mapping software.

Linking to Files

Not all hyperlinks navigate to other web pages. Some hyperlinks allow users to download files or to play music. This is easily achieved by specifying the file in the `href` attribute rather than a web page.

Documents and Rich Media

It doesn't matter if you want to link to a Microsoft Word document, a PDF file, or even an audio MP3 or video MPG file. The same `<a>` tag is used for each. To aid usability, the `target` attribute may be used to specify that the linked file should open in a new browser window.

 TIP! *When linking to a document or media file, use* `target="_blank"` *to open the file in a new window. This makes for a nicer user experience as the original page is not lost when the linked document opens.*

Linking to a file, such as a PDF, an MP3, or an MPG, causes the computer's default software for that file type to launch. For example, clicking a link to a PDF file will launch Adobe Reader on most computers while clicking a link to an MP3 file is likely to open Windows Media Player or Apple iTunes, if installed. As a web developer, you have no control over which program opens as it is dependent upon each user's independent computer configuration. Additionally, some users may see a Download File dialog box asking them if they wish to save or open the file. Some users may not see this dialog box. Again, it depends on the computer configuration for each user and you, as the web developer, have no control over it.

```
<a href="diagrams/crane.pdf" alt="Crane diagrams">Crane
folding instructions (PDF 34k)</a>
```

The `href` attribute includes a relative path to the file to be downloaded.

When the hyperlink is clicked the user may be prompted to open or save the file.

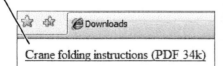

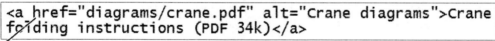
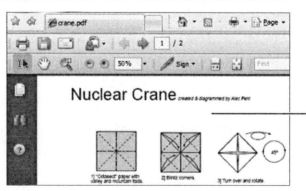

If the user chooses to open the file or if the computer is configured to open known file types automatically, the default program for the file type being downloaded opens. In this case, the PDF file was opened directly in the browser.

In this exercise, you will link to a PDF file.

Create the Link

1. Start your web browser and open the howto.htm page from the fup_site_root folder in your Lesson 07 folder.

2. Start Notepad and open the same howto.htm page from the fup_site_root folder in your Lesson 07 folder.

3. Locate the paragraph with the angel_thumb.gif image.

```
<p>
Click the image below to download folding diagrams for the Model
Of The Week.<br />
<img src="images/angel_thumb.gif" alt="Angel diagrams" vspace="5">
</p>
```

4. Follow these steps to link to the PDF file:

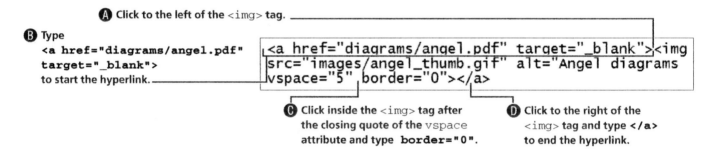

Ⓐ Click to the left of the `<img>` tag.

Ⓑ Type
`<a href="diagrams/angel.pdf"`
`target="_blank">`
to start the hyperlink.

```
<a href="diagrams/angel.pdf" target="_blank"><img
src="images/angel_thumb.gif" alt="Angel diagrams
vspace="5" border="0"></a>
```

Ⓒ Click inside the `<img>` tag after the closing quote of the `vspace` attribute and type `border="0"`.

Ⓓ Click to the right of the `<img>` tag and type `</a>` to end the hyperlink.

You have used a relative path to the PDF file. You have also used the `target` *attribute so the PDF opens in a new browser window. Lastly, you removed the border from the image so it does not display a blue border.*

Test the Link

You must have software to open a PDF, such as the free Adobe Reader, to complete the next steps.

5. Save your changes and switch to your web browser.

6. Tap F5 to refresh the page.

7. Click the thumbnail for the Angel diagrams.
The PDF opens in a new browser window.

8. Close the window displaying the diagrams.
The How To page is once again visible.

9. Close your web browser and Notepad.

 # Concepts Review

True/False Questions

1. A well-designed web page should not contain more than about three screens of content.   TRUE   FALSE

2. A web page is allowed to have only one navigation bar.   TRUE   FALSE

3. Hyperlinks can be created from text or images.   TRUE   FALSE

4. The `alt` attribute is required for all anchor tags.   TRUE   FALSE

5. The anchor tag's `target` attribute specifies the path to the page or file that should open when the link is clicked.   TRUE   FALSE

6. External links must specify an absolute path.   TRUE   FALSE

7. Named anchors can only link to bookmarks on the same page.   TRUE   FALSE

8. An email link allows users to send email directly from the web page.   TRUE   FALSE

9. The purpose of an image map is to allow a single image to have multiple hyperlinks.   TRUE   FALSE

10. Image maps are easily created with Notepad.   TRUE   FALSE

Multiple Choice Questions

1. Claudio is frustrated because the links on his website seem to change from blue to purple. What could be the problem?

   a. He specified the color purple for his links.

   b. He has an error in his HTML code so his colors are not properly recognized.

   c. There is no problem as this is the default behavior. Links are blue until they are clicked, at which time they turn purple.

   d. He is using Internet Explorer. The links will be different colors in different browsers.

2. Gloria is frustrated because all of the image thumbnails on her site have a blue border around them. How can she remove the borders?

   a. She should add `border="none"` to her `<img>` tags.

   b. She should add `border="0"` to her `<a>` tags.

   c. She should add `border="0"` to her `<img>` tags.

   d. She should change the border color to match her page background by adding `bordercolor="white"` to her `<img>` tags.

3. Emilio needs a link to an external site to open in a new browser window so his website doesn't disappear from a user's screen. How can he accomplish this?

   a. He should add `window="new"` to his `<a>` tag.

   b. He should add `target="blank"` to his `<a>` tag.

   c. He should add `target="new"` to his `<a>` tag.

   d. He should add `target="_blank"` to his `<a>` tag.

4. Mercedes has the following code block in her page:
   ```
   <a href="solutions">Click for solutions</a>
   ```
   Further down the page, she has this code block:
   ```
   <a id="solutions"></a>
   ```
   When the link text is clicked, the browser should automatically scroll down the page to the Solutions section, but it is not working. Why not?

   a. She is missing link text in the named anchor at the bottom of the page. It should be:
   ```
   <a id="solutions">Solutions</a>
   ```

   b. She forgot the # symbol in the hyperlink. It should be:
   ```
   <a href="#solutions">Click for solutions</a>
   ```

   c. She forgot the # symbol in the named anchor. It should be:
   ```
   <a id="#solutions"></a>
   ```

   d. She forgot the # symbol in both the hyperlink and named anchor. It should be:
   ```
   <a href="#solutions">Click for solutions</a>
   ```
   and `<a id="#solutions"></a>`

Skill Builders

Create Text Links

In this exercise, you will create navigation bars and text hyperlinks.

Before You Begin: *Note that this Skill Builder picks up where the Hands-On exercises left off. The work you did in the Hands-On exercises has been duplicated in the files you will use for the Skill Builders.*

Create a Navigation Bar

1. Start your web browser and open the gallery.htm page from the sb_fup_links folder in your Lesson 07 folder.

2. Start Notepad and open the same gallery.htm page from the sb_fup_links folder in your Lesson 07 folder.

3. Locate the paragraph containing the link text for the navigation bar towards the top of the document.

   ```
   <p>Home - Gallery -  How To - Resources - Contact</p>
   ```

4. Follow these steps to create a link back to the homepage:

   A Click to the left of the word *Home* and type **<a href="index.htm">**.

   ```
   <p><a href="index.htm">Home</a>
   ```

   B Click to the right of the word *Home* and type **</a>**.

   You have created the link back to the homepage.

5. Using the steps outlined in the previous step, create the remaining four hyperlinks in the navigation bar:

This Text	Should Link to . . .
Gallery	gallery.htm
How To	howto.htm
Resources	resources.htm
Contact	contact.htm

6. Save your changes.

Create Navigation Links on the Other Pages of the Website

7. Choose File→Open and then open the howto.htm page from the sb_fup_links subfolder in your Lesson 07 folder.

8. Using the instructions outlined in step 4, create all five of the navigation bar links; save your changes.

9. Create the same navigation bar links in the five remaining pages: resources.htm, contact.htm, gal_fluffy.htm, gal_knife.htm, and gal_present.htm. Be sure to save your changes.

Create Text Links

10. Open the gal_knife.htm file from the sb_sup_links folder and locate the paragraph for the Back to gallery text near the bottom of the document.

```
<p>Back to gallery</p>

  <hr align="left" width="85%" />
  <p>Folding Under Pressure &copy; 2007</p>
</div>
</body>
```

11. Click to the left of the word *Back* and type **<a href="gallery.htm">** to start the hyperlink.

12. Click to the right of the word *gallery* and type **</a>** to end the hyperlink.
Your code should resemble the following.

```
<p><a href="gallery.htm">Back to gallery</a></p>
```

13. Save your changes. Then open the gal_fluffy.htm file from the sb_fup_links folder.

14. Using the steps outlined in steps 10–12, create the Back to gallery text hyperlink in the gal_fluffy.htm page. Be sure to save your changes when you are through.

15. Create the Back to gallery text hyperlink in the gal_present.htm page. Be sure to save your changes when you are finished.

Test the Links

16. Switch to your web browser and test the three gallery thumbnails, using the Back to gallery hyperlink beneath the large photo to return to the gallery page each time.

17. Test the navigation links on each page.
You should be able to navigate to any page from any page using the navigation bar. Additionally, you should be able to navigate the gallery. If necessary, go back and fix any errors in your code before continuing.

Skill Builder 7.2   Link to Named Anchors

In this exercise, you will create named anchors.

Before You Begin: You must complete Skill Builder 7.1 before beginning this exercise.

Create Named Anchors

1. In your browser, open the resources.htm page from the sb_fup_links folder in your Lesson 07 folder.

2. Switch to Notepad and open the same resources.htm page from the sb_fup_links folder in your Lesson 07 folder.

3. Locate the `<h3>What are the limitations of traditional purist origami?</h3>` block of code towards the middle of the document.

4. Follow these steps to create a named anchor and hyperlink:

Ⓐ Click in the space above the `<h3>` tag and type **`<a id="limits"></a>`** to create the named anchor.

Ⓑ Scroll towards the top of the document and locate the code block for the ordered list.

Ⓒ Locate the second list item.

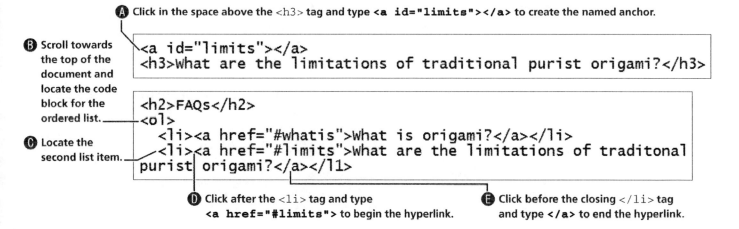

```
<a id="limits"></a>
<h3>What are the limitations of traditional purist origami?</h3>

<h2>FAQs</h2>
<ol>
   <li><a href="#whatis">What is origami?</a></li>
   <li><a href="#limits">What are the limitations of traditonal
purist origami?</a></li>
```

Ⓓ Click after the `<li>` tag and type **`<a href="#limits">`** to begin the hyperlink.

Ⓔ Click before the closing `</li>` tag and type **`</a>`** to end the hyperlink.

5. Scroll back down and locate the code block for `<h3>What are some variations of origami?</h3>`.

6. Using the instructions outlined in step 4, create a named anchor and associated hyperlink, keeping the following in mind:
   - The named anchor should be identified with **`id="vary"`** above the `<h3>` tag.
   - The third list item in the ordered list should link to the named anchor with **`href="#vary"`**.

7. Create a named anchor and the associated hyperlink in the ordered list for the remaining item as follows:
   - `<h3>How can I get started folding origami?</h3>` should be identified as **`id="started"`**.
   - The hyperlink should link to **`href="#started"`**.

Create a Back to Top Link

8. Scroll up to towards the top of the document and locate the opening <body> tag.

9. Click in the space below the opening <body> tag and type **<a id="top"></a>** to create a named anchor at the top of the page.

10. Scroll down to the *What is origami?* paragraph and follow these steps to create a Back to Top hyperlink:

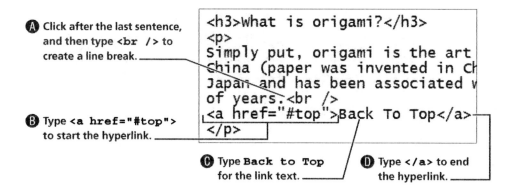

Ⓐ Click after the last sentence, and then type **
** to create a line break.

Ⓑ Type **<a href="#top">** to start the hyperlink.

```
<h3>What is origami?</h3>
<p>
Simply put, origami is the art
China (paper was invented in Ch
Japan and has been associated w
of years.<br />
<a href="#top">Back To Top</a>
</p>
```

Ⓒ Type **Back to Top** for the link text.

Ⓓ Type **</a>** to end the hyperlink.

11. Follow these steps to copy the Back to Top hyperlink so you can paste it to the other sections:

Ⓐ Drag to select all of the code you typed in the previous step.

```
Japan and has been associated w
of years.<br />
<a href="#top">Back To Top</a>
</p>
```

Ⓑ Choose Edit→Copy from the menu bar.

12. Follow these steps to paste the hyperlink to one of the other sections:

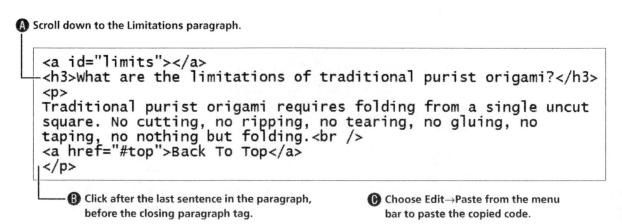

Ⓐ Scroll down to the Limitations paragraph.

```
<a id="limits"></a>
<h3>What are the limitations of traditional purist origami?</h3>
<p>
Traditional purist origami requires folding from a single uncut
square. No cutting, no ripping, no tearing, no gluing, no
taping, no nothing but folding.<br />
<a href="#top">Back To Top</a>
</p>
```

Ⓑ Click after the last sentence in the paragraph, before the closing paragraph tag.

Ⓒ Choose Edit→Paste from the menu bar to paste the copied code.

The same hyperlink now appears on the page twice.

13. Using the steps outlined in step 12, paste the Back to Top hyperlink after the last sentence, before the closing paragraph code, in the Variations and Get Started sections.

14. Save your changes.

Test the Links

15. Switch to your web browser and test the four FAQs links, using the Back to Top hyperlink beneath each section to return to the top of the web page each time.
    If necessary, go back and fix any errors in your code before continuing.

Skill Builder 7.3   Create Buttons to External Sites

In this exercise, you will create image hyperlinks to external websites that open in a new browser window or new tab (depending on the browser).

Before You Begin: You must complete Skill Builder 7.2 before beginning this exercise.

Create the Links

1. In your browser, open the index.htm page from the sb_fup_links folder in your Lesson 07 folder.

2. Switch to Notepad and open the same index.htm page from the sb_fup_links folder in your Lesson 07 folder.

3. Locate the code for the dancers.jpg image tag.

```
<img src="images/dancers.jpg" alt="Dancers, created by Jeremy
Shafer" hspace="10" vspace="10" border="1" align="left"/>
```

4. Follow these steps to create an external hyperlink that opens in a new browser window:

Ⓐ Click to the left of the `<img>` tag and type **`<a href="http://www.barf.cc" target="_blank">`**.

```
<a href="http://www.barf.cc" target="_blank"><img
src="images/dancers.jpg" alt="Dancers, created by Jeremy Shafer"
hspace="10" vspace="10" border="1" align="left"/></a>
```

Ⓑ Click to the right of the `<img>` tag and type **`</a>`** to end the hyperlink.

5. Locate the code for the creature.jpg image.

6. Using the steps outlined in step 4, create an image hyperlink to an external site, keeping the following in mind:

   ■ Link to **http://www.origami.gr.jp/index0.html**. You must specify the index0.html page name to link to the English language page.

   ■ Use **target="_blank"** to open the site in a new window.

7. Save your changes.

Test the Links

8. Switch to your web browser and test the two image links, closing the external site window after it opens to return back to the Folding Under Pressure window each time.

 NOTE! *Note there may be a border around each of the images. If you don't like the blue border changing to purple after the image is clicked, you may remove the border by setting the image's border attribute to zero.*

If necessary, go back and fix any errors in your code before continuing.

9. Close your browser and Notepad.

# Assessments

Assessment 7.1   Create Navigation Bars

In this exercise, you will create navigation bars.

1. Start your web browser and open the index.htm page from the as_3mw folder in your Lesson 07 folder.

2. Start Notepad and open the same index.htm page from the as_3mw folder in your Lesson 07 folder.

3. Locate the link for the navigation bar, `<p>Home :: Sound Bytes :: Links</p>`.

4. Create text links to the other pages in the site:

This Text	Should Link to ...
Home	index.htm
Sound Bytes	soundbytes.htm
Links	links.htm

5. Save your changes and create the navigation bar hyperlinks in the remaining two pages.

6. Switch to your browser and test the navigation bar hyperlinks on each page.
   If necessary, fix any errors in your code before continuing.

Assessment 7.2   Create External Links

In this exercise, you will create external hyperlinks.

Before You Begin: You must complete Assessment 7.1 before beginning this exercise.

1. In your browser, open the links.htm page from the as_3mw folder in your Lesson 07 folder.

2. Switch to Notepad and open the same links.htm page from the as_3mw folder in your Lesson 07 folder.

3. Locate the code for the unordered list.

4. Using the link text Gibson Guitars, create a hyperlink to www.gibson.com that opens in a new browser window.

5. Using the link text Fender Guitars, create a hyperlink to www.fender.com that opens in a new browser window.

6. Save your changes.

7. Switch to your browser and test both links.
   If necessary, fix any errors in your code before continuing.

Assessment 7.3   Create Named Anchors

In this exercise, you will create named anchors.

Before You Begin: You must complete Assessment 7.2 before beginning this exercise.

1. In your browser, open the soundbytes.htm page from the as_3mw folder in your Lesson 07 folder.

2. Switch to Notepad and open the same soundbytes.htm page from the as_3mw folder in your Lesson 07 folder.

3. Locate the code for `<h3>Currently Available</h3>`.

4. Create a named anchor above it with an appropriate id.

5. Locate the code for the sub-navigation bar starting with the link text *Current songs available online*.

6. Using the link text *Current songs available online*, create a link to the named anchor you created in step 4.

7. Create another named anchor above the `<h3>Available Soon</h3>` code.

8. Using the sub-navigation bar link text *Songs that will be available soon*, create a link to the named anchor you created in step 7.

9. Save your changes.

10. Switch to your browser and test both links.
    If necessary, fix any errors in your code before continuing.

Assessment 7.4   Link to Files

In this exercise, you will create links to media files.

Before You Begin: *You must complete Assessment 7.3 before beginning this exercise.*

1. Switch to Notepad and locate the code for the definition list following `<h3>`Currently Available`</h3>`.

2. For the song *Hypnotized*, link the text *Listen* to the hypnotized.mp3 file in the music folder within the site root.

3. For the song *I No, I No*, link the text *Listen* to the inoino.mp3 file in the music folder within the site root.

4. Save your changes.

5. Switch to your browser and test both links.
   The MP3 files should begin to play. You must have speakers turned on to hear the music. If necessary, fix any errors in your code before continuing.

6. Close your browser and Notepad.

Critical Thinking

Critical Thinking 7.1   Create a Three-page Website

In this exercise, you will create a three-page website.

1. Think of a topic for which you can create enough text for a three-page website.

2. Create a folder inside your Lesson 07 folder named **ct_mysite** that will act as your site root. Create two subfolders with the names **assets** and **images**.

3. Create a statement of purpose in a word processing document that explains what the site is about and what it will (and will not) accomplish. Save this as **ct-sop** to the assets folder in your ct_mysite folder.

4. Create a wire frame that outlines the basic block structure of the pages. If you create your wire frame with software, save the file to your assets folder as **ct-wireframe**.

5. Acquire any images you may need for your site and save the original source files to your assets folder.

6. If necessary, crop, resize, or optimize your images and save them in an appropriate format to the images folder.

7. Create your three pages to include the following elements:
   - Valid XHTML 1.0 transitional code
   - A masthead that indicates the name, title, or purpose of the website
   - A navigation bar that links to all three pages
   - Text or images in the main content area

8. One of your pages should contain a sub-navigation bar that links to named anchors on the same page.

Critical Thinking 7.2   Research Image Mapping Software

In this exercise, you will research image mapping software.

1. Start your web browser and browse to your favorite search engine.

2. Search for the phrase **image mapping software**.

3. Find at least three pieces of software that have not already been mentioned on the website for this book.

4. In a word processing document saved to your Lesson 07 folder as **ct-mapping**, answer the following about the software you found:
   - Name of the software
   - Software developer
   - URL to the software
   - Cost
   - Features
   - Is there a free trial available if the software is not completely free?

Unit 2

Beyond the Basics

In this unit, you will work with data and layout tables as you incorporate advanced table structures, merged cells, and nested tables. You will then add color to your pages via HTML attributes and CSS. As CSS is officially introduced, you will learn the fundamentals of typography as you style text. You will learn about the CSS box model as you incorporate margin and padding to add white space around page elements. You will also use the CSS float property as an alternative to presentational HTML code. You will complete your website design by adding a form to collect visitor feedback. Once your site is complete, you will learn about web-hosting companies and how to make your site available to the public using FTP. Finally, you will migrate a website created with outdated code to the current standards of valid XHTML 1.0 transitional and CSS.

LESSON 8

Working with Tables

In this lesson, you will learn about tables. You will differentiate between data tables and layout tables. You will format a table's display and format cell options. You will also learn about structural tags and attributes that operate behind the scenes. Lastly, you will learn about advanced table tasks, including merging cells and nesting tables.

LESSON OBJECTIVES
After studying this lesson, you will be able to:

- Create a table
- Format a table and its cells
- Create an accessible table structure
- Merge cells
- Nest tables
- Describe the difference between data tables and layout tables

Case Study: Using Tables

Thanks to Miguel, the images for the website have been created and added to most of the pages. Haylie feels the one thing missing from her site is a list of prices. She puts together a sales sheet and decides to display it as a table to make it easier to read.

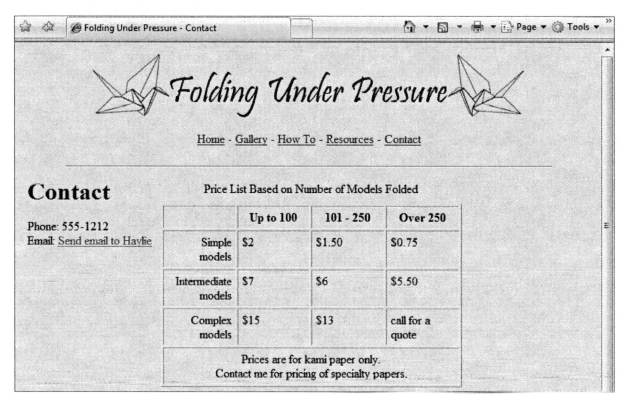

A table makes the price information easy to read. Another outer table with invisible borders helps to position the contact information and the price list on the page.

Outlining the Uses of Tables

Tables can be used in one of two ways on a web page: to display tabular data or to accomplish a certain layout. Either way, the same HTML tags are used. The terms *data table* and *layout table* refer to the way in which a table is used—not necessarily to the contents of the table.

Data Tables

Data tables are used to display content that makes sense living in a table, such as a calendar, a schedule, or another matrix. If the content were provided outside of a table, it may not make much sense or may be difficult to read.

This price information displayed as a long list is difficult to read.

The same information displayed in a table is much easier to read.

Basic Table Tags

There are many tags used to create table structures, but the basic building blocks include the following:

- Table `<table>`—Used to create the table container

- Table row `<tr>`—Used to create rows

- Table data `<td>`—Used to create cells within rows

All three of these tags are container tags, so they each have an associated closing tag.

Inserting a Table to Display Data

Perhaps the most difficult thing about creating tables with HTML is keeping your code readable. Many tags are needed to create even a simple table, and the tags must be properly nested and properly closed.

TIP! *Use white space when coding tables to make your HTML easier to read.*

The `<table>` tag begins and ends the table.

The `<tr>` tag defines each row.

The `<td>` tags define the cells.

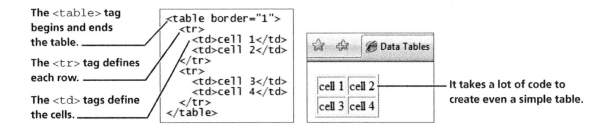

```
<table border="1">
    <tr>
        <td>cell 1</td>
        <td>cell 2</td>
    </tr>
    <tr>
        <td>cell 3</td>
        <td>cell 4</td>
    </tr>
</table>
```

It takes a lot of code to create even a simple table.

Empty Cells

Some browsers have difficulty displaying a table with empty cells because an empty cell can collapse in on itself. It is common practice to fill an otherwise empty cell with a single non-breaking space. Remember that HTML ignores white space, so you can't simply tap the Spacebar to create a space. Instead, the ` ` HTML character code is used to create a non-breaking space.

```
<td>This cell has content</td>
```
This cell contains content.

```
<td> </td>
```
This cell displays as empty. The ` ` character code creates a non-breaking space to keep the cell from collapsing.

QUICK REFERENCE: BASIC TABLE TAGS

Tag	Description
`<table></table>`	■ Defines the beginning and end of a table ■ Contains all the other nested table-related tags
`<tr></tr>`	■ Defines the beginning and end of a row
`<td></td>`	■ Defines the beginning and end of a cell ■ Use the HTML character code ` ` to keep otherwise empty cells from collapsing

Hands-On 8.1   Add a Table

In this exercise, you will add a table to display a price chart.

Type the Code

1. Open your Lesson 08 folder, then open the fup_site_root folder.

2. Double-click the contact.htm file to view it in your browser.

3. Start Notepad and open the contact.htm file from the fup_site_root folder in your Lesson 08 folder.

4. Locate the paragraph containing the email link.

```
<p>
Phone: 555-1212<br />
Email: <a href="mailto:haylie@example.com">
</p>
```

5. Click in the blank line after the closing paragraph tag and tap [Enter] twice to create white space below the paragraph.

6. Type **<table>** and tap [Enter] [Spacebar] [Spacebar] to start the table and create white space.

7. Type **<tr>**, tap [Enter], and tap [Spacebar] four times to start the first row and create white space.

8. Type the following to create the top row of cells:

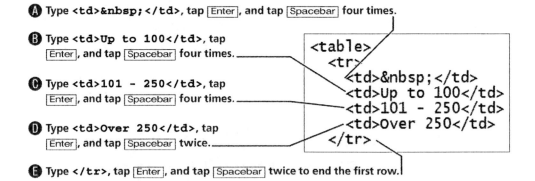

A Type **<td> </td>**, tap [Enter], and tap [Spacebar] four times.

B Type **<td>Up to 100</td>**, tap [Enter], and tap [Spacebar] four times.

C Type **<td>101 - 250</td>**, tap [Enter], and tap [Spacebar] four times.

D Type **<td>Over 250</td>**, tap [Enter], and tap [Spacebar] twice.

E Type **</tr>**, tap [Enter], and tap [Spacebar] twice to end the first row.

9. Type the second row as follows:

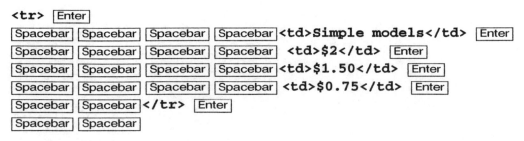

You may wish to review your code before you continue. There is no room for error!

10. Type the third row as follows, checking your code carefully:

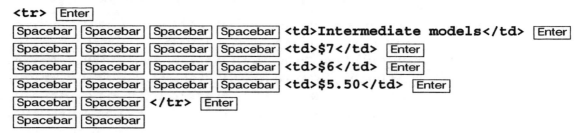

11. Type the final row and close the table as follows:

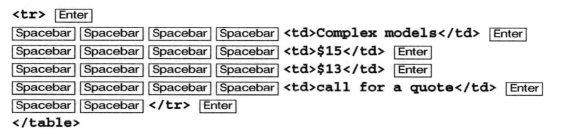

You may wish to review your code before you continue. There is no room for error!

12. Save your changes.

Preview in the Browser

13. Switch to your web browser and tap F5.
Your table should display as follows.

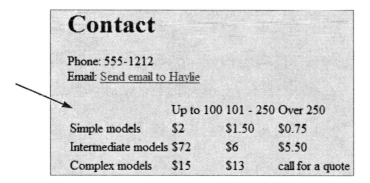

The content is too close together. You will fix that in the next exercise.

Formatting Tables and Cells with HTML

Tables and cells can be formatted with widths, heights, spacing, horizontal and vertical alignments, borders, and colors. This formatting is accomplished via attributes of the `<table>` and `<td>` tags. However, as most of this formatting is presentational and not structural, it should be handled with CSS. HTML formatting of tables is supported in XHTML 1.0 transitional but forbidden in XHTML 1.0 strict—just as is the formatting of text, lists, and other elements you have studied in this book. As a developer, you will have to make the decision to use HTML formatting, CSS formatting, or some combination of both. As you strive for stricter code, you will use CSS more than HTML formatting. In the transitional stage of learning about CSS (which you will begin in Lesson 9, Introducing CSS and Color), you may find it easier to use HTML formatting with your XHTML 1.0 transitional documents.

Formatting Tables

Formatting applied to the `<table>` tag affects the table container and has no effect on the contents. Valid `<table>` attributes include:

- Align
- Border
- Width

Align

The `align` attribute positions the table horizontally on the page. Valid values are `left`, `center`, and `right`. If this attribute is not set, the table will default to aligning left. Alignment is presentational (and forbidden in XHTML 1.0 strict), so you will eventually want to use CSS instead.

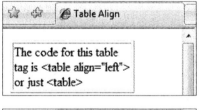
align="left" **positions the table on the left side of the screen. Leaving out the** align **attribute also aligns it left.**

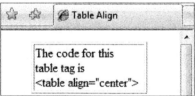
align="center" **centers the table in the browser window.**

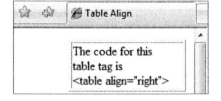
align="right" **positions the table on the right side of the browser window.**

 TIP! *Leave out the attribute completely if you wish to use the default value. Adding an attribute that has the same effect as leaving out the attribute only bloats your code. For example, rather than use* align="left"*, leave it out because the default behavior is to align left anyway!*

Border

The `border` attribute creates a border around the outside of the table and around all of the cells. Its value is an integer, which translates to the thickness of the border in pixels. Borders can appear slightly differently in various browsers. If the border attribute is left off, the table defaults to having no border. Border is presentational, so you will eventually want to use CSS instead. Oddly enough, the border attribute is supported under XHTML 1.0 strict.

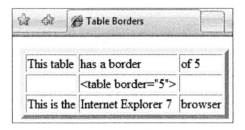

This is Internet Explorer 7. Notice the border is thicker around the outside of the table than it is around the cells. The right- and bottom-outside borders are darker, creating a 3D look.

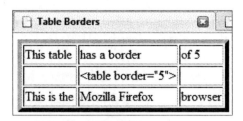

This is Mozilla Firefox. Notice the border is much darker than in Internet Explorer 7.

Width

The `width` attribute determines the width of the table. It can be entered in pixels or percents. If the `width` attribute is left off, the table will contract to be as small as it can to accommodate its contents. Width is structural, so using the attribute is valid even in XHTML 1.0 strict.

Pixel Width

If an integer is used, the width will be defined in pixels. Text inside the table will wrap rather than push the table out wider. The exception is if you have an image or some other object in the table that cannot wrap like text. If your table width is set to 100 pixels, but you have a 200-pixel wide image in it, the table will expand to 200 pixels.

Percentage Width

Setting the table width to a percentage allows the table to become fluid, expanding and contracting to maintain its width relative to the width of the browser window.

When a table is set to a pixel width, the table remains the same width regardless of the size of the browser window.

When a table is set to a percentage width, it will expand and contract based on the width of the browser window. At a width of 75 percent, the table is always 75 percent of the width of the browser window.

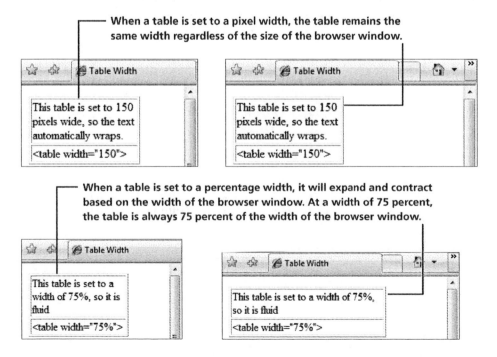

Height

The height attribute works just like the width attribute, except it defines the height of the table. You may see the height attribute on pages you are asked to update as many developers unknowingly use the height attribute. It is invalid code. Although some browsers support it, the height attribute is not part of any HTML specification. It should be avoided at all costs. If you wish to limit the height of a table, you can do so legally and validly with CSS.

 TIP! *Never use the* height *attribute on a table. It is invalid code for all versions of HTML and XHTML.*

 QUICK REFERENCE: TABLE FORMATTING ATTRIBUTES

Attribute	Usage	Description
align	■ Valid values: left, center, right ■ `<table align="center">`	Aligns a table horizontally within the browser window
border	■ Valid values: integers ■ `<table border="3">`	Creates a border around the outside of the table and the table cells
width	■ Valid values: integer, percentages ■ `<table width="300">` ■ `<table width="80%">`	Defines the width of the table in static pixels or a fluid percent

 ## Hands-On 8.2   Format a Table with HTML

In this exercise, you will format a table.

Assign the Width

You will define a static width so the table is always the same width.

1. Switch to Notepad and locate the code where the table starts.

```
<table>
  <tr>
    <td> </td>
```

2. Follow these steps to assign a table width:

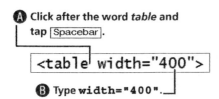

Ⓐ Click after the word *table* and tap [Spacebar].

```
<table width="400">
```

Ⓑ Type `width="400"`.

Assign the Alignment

3. Follow these steps to center the table on the page:

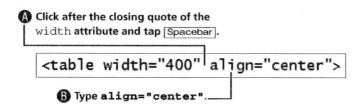

Assign a Border

4. Follow these steps to create a border:

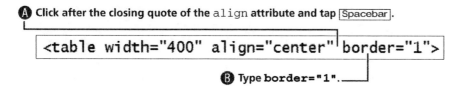

5. Save your changes.

Preview the Page

6. Switch to your browser and tap F5.
Your table should look like the following.

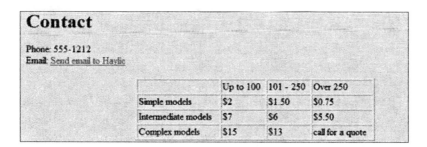

The contents inside the table still need to be formatted. You will do that in the next exercise.

Formatting Cells

Cell formatting can be accomplished by adding attributes to either the `<table>` tag or individual `<td>` tags. When added to the `<table>` tag, every cell in the table is affected. When added to an individual `<td>` tag, only that cell is affected.

Attributes added to the `<td>` tags include:

- Align
- Valign
- Nowrap
- Width
- Height

Attributes added to the `<table>` tag include:

- Cellpadding
- Cellspacing

Align

The `align` attribute in individual `<td>` tags is completely different from the `align` attribute in the `<table>` tag. When used in a `<td>` tag, the contents inside the cell are horizontally aligned. If this attribute is left off, cell contents default to left align. Align is valid even in XHTML 1.0 strict, but using CSS is still preferred.

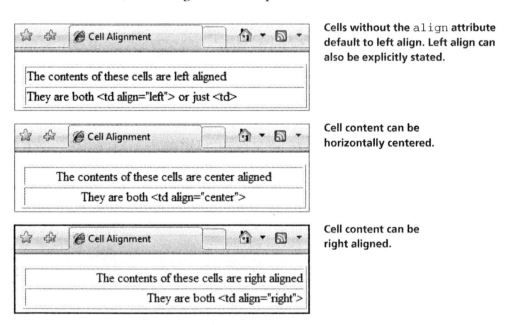

Cells without the `align` attribute default to left align. Left align can also be explicitly stated.

Cell content can be horizontally centered.

Cell content can be right aligned.

Valign

Valign positions content vertically within a cell. The default is middle, but other valid values include top and bottom. Valign is valid even in XHTML 1.0 strict, but using CSS is still preferred.

By default, cell content is vertically aligned in the middle of a cell.

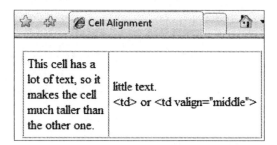

Vertically aligning content to the top can make it easier to read.

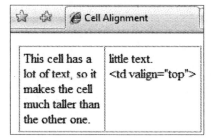

Content can also be vertically aligned to the bottom.

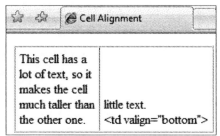

Nowrap

When text reaches the right edge of a cell, it automatically wraps to another line. This behavior can be overridden by using the nowrap attribute. This forces the cell contents to never wrap. Nowrap is valid XHTML 1.0 transitional and is forbidden in XHTML 1.0 strict.

 TIP! *Be careful using the* nowrap *attribute as it could cause your table to expand wider than the browser window.*

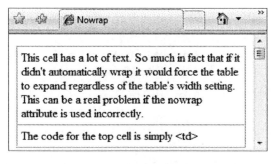

By default, text automatically wraps when it reaches the right edge of a cell.

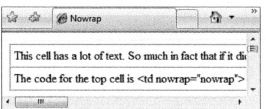

The nowrap **attribute has been set on the top cell, causing the text inside to no longer wrap. Notice how a bottom scrollbar now appears.**

Width

Cell width works the same way as table width. It is applied to individual cells and can be an integer (for a static pixel width) or a percent (for a fluid percentage width). When set to a percent, the cell is a percentage of the table width. For example, in the following code...

```
<table width="500"><tr><td width="50%">
```

...the table is 500 pixels wide and the cell is 50 percent of that, or 250 pixels wide. Why not just make the cell 250 pixels wide then? By using a percentage for the cell, the width of the table can be changed and the cell automatically adjusts to 50 percent of it. Cell width is forbidden in XHTML 1.0 strict. CSS should be used instead.

Mixing and Matching Pixels and Percents

Unfortunately, cell widths do not always behave as expected. Take the following code, for example:

```
<table>
  <tr>
    <td width="100">Static 100 pixel wide cell</td>
    <td width="50%">Fluid 50% wide cell</td>
  </tr>
</table>
```

You may think that the left cell will always be 100 pixels wide and only the right cell will automatically adjust as the browser window expands. In fact, both cells will change their width in this case. The reason for this requires some serious mathematical thinking. The right cell is set to 50 percent of the table width, which means the other 50 percent must be made up by the left cell. But the left cell is set to only 100 pixels. That's the problem—100 pixels plus 50 percent probably won't equal the full table width (unless the table is 200 pixels wide). To avoid problems such as this, use only pixels or only percentages in your cell widths. Try to avoid mixing and matching.

Height

Heights on cells are valid HTML (but forbidden in XHTML 1.0 strict) and can be defined in pixels or percentages, but percentages can behave unexpectedly in some browsers. Even though you can use a percentage height, it is best to avoid it and use pixels instead. Actually, the height attribute should be avoided altogether as it tends to cause many developers more trouble than it's worth. Cell height is forbidden in XHTML 1.0 strict. CSS should be used instead.

Cellpadding

Cellpadding, which is added to the `<table>` tag, adds white space to the inside of cells (inside cell borders), creating breathing room between the cell border and the content. Values are entered as integers and are treated as pixels. Cellpadding is valid even in XHTML 1.0 strict, but CSS is still preferred. If this attribute is left out, the default varies from browser to browser. If you want no padding at all, you must explicitly set `cellpadding="0"`.

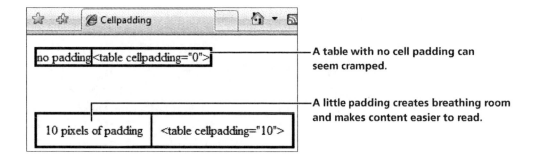

A table with no cell padding can seem cramped.

A little padding creates breathing room and makes content easier to read.

Cellspacing

`Cellspacing`, which is added to the `<table>` tag, adds white space to the outside of cells, creating breathing room between the individual cells themselves. Values are entered as integers and are treated as pixels. `Cellpadding` is valid even in XHTML 1.0 strict, but CSS is still preferred. If this attribute is left out, the default varies from browser to browser. If you want no padding at all, you must explicitly set `cellspacing="0"`.

`Cellspacing` adds space around the outside of table cells. But with no `cellpadding`, the content is still cramped.

This table uses both `cellpadding` and `cellspacing`.

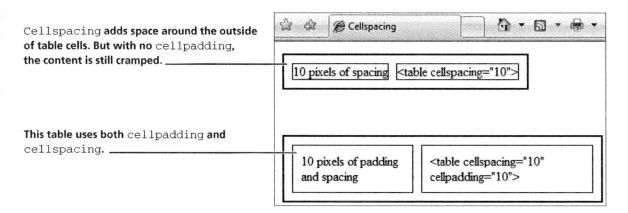

QUICK REFERENCE: ATTRIBUTES THAT AFFECT CELLS

Attribute	Usage	Description
align	Valid values: left, center, right `<td align="center">`	■ Use in `<td>` ■ Horizontally aligns cell contents
valign	Valid values: top, middle, bottom `<td valign="top">`	■ Use in `<td>` ■ Vertically aligns cell contents
nowrap	`<td nowrap="nowrap">`	■ Use in `<td>` ■ Prohibits text from wrapping in a table cell

width	Valid values: integers, percentages
	 `<td width="300">`
	 `<td width="78%">`
		■ Use in `<td>`
		 ■ Specifies the width of a cell

QUICK REFERENCE: ATTRIBUTES THAT AFFECT CELLS (CONTINUED)

Attribute	Usage	Description

height	Valid values: integers, percentages
	`<td height="160">`
	`<td height="100%">`
		■ Use in `<td>`
		■ Specifies the height of a cell
		■ Should be used sparingly, if at all

cellpadding	Value must be an integer `<table cellpadding="10">`	■ Use in `<table>` ■ Specifies spacing in pixels around the inside of each cell in a table
cellspacing	Value must be an integer `<table cellspacing="10">`	■ Use in `<table>` ■ Specifies spacing in pixels around the outside of each cell in a table

 Hands-On 8.3 **Format Table Cells with HTML**

In this exercise, you will format table cells.

Assign Cell Widths

You will make each column the same width by using percentage widths. Since there are four columns, each column will have a width of 25 percent.

1. Switch to Notepad and locate the code for the first row in the table.

```
<table width="400" align="center" border="1">
  <tr>
    <td> </td>
```

2. Follow these steps to assign widths to the cells so each column is the same width:

Ⓐ Click after the "`td`" (but before the closing >) in the first table cell and tap Spacebar.

Ⓑ Type `width="25%"`.

```
    <td width="25%"> </td>
    <td width="25%">Up to 100</td>
    <td width="25%">101 - 250</td>
    <td width="25%">Over 250</td>
  </tr>
```

Ⓒ Add `width="25%"` to the other cells in the top row.

3. Save your changes.

4. Switch to your browser and tap F5.
Each column's width is 25 percent of the table. Some rows are taller than others and the content looks too spread out.

Align Cell Content

5. Return to Notepad and follow these steps to align the content in the left column:

Ⓐ Locate the code for the *Simple models* cell in the second row.

```
<tr>
   <td align="right">Simple models</td>
```

Ⓑ Add the `align="right"` attribute to the `<td>` tag, making sure to include a space between the tag name and the attribute.

6. Using this same method, add **align="right"** to the *Intermediate models* and *Complex models* cells.

```
<tr>
   <td align="right">Intermediate models</td>
   <td>$72</td>
   <td>$6</td>
   <td>$5.50</td>
</tr>
<tr>
   <td align="right">Complex models</td>
```

7. Save your changes.

8. Switch to your browser and tap [F5].
The text in the left column is right aligned.

Vertically Align Cell Content

9. Return to Notepad and follow these steps to vertically align the prices in the second row:

Ⓐ Locate the row for *Simple models*.

Ⓑ Add **valign="top"** to the $2 cell, making sure to leave a space between the tag name and the attribute.

```
<td align="right">Simple models</td>
<td valign="top">$2</td>
<td valign="top">$1.50</td>
<td valign="top">$0.75</td>
```

Ⓒ Add **valign="top"** to the remaining cells in this row.

10. Using the same method, add **valign="top"** to the remaining six price cells.

```
   <td align="right">Intermediate models</td>
   <td valign="top">$7</td>
   <td valign="top">$6</td>
   <td valign="top">$5.50</td>
</tr>
<tr>
   <td align="right">Complex models</td>
   <td valign="top">$15</td>
   <td valign="top">$13</td>
   <td valign="top">call for a quote</td>
```

11. Save your changes.

12. Switch to your browser and tap ⎡F5⎤.
Each price cell is top aligned.

Add Padding

13. Return to Notepad and follow these steps to add padding to all cells:

A Locate the code for the start of the table.

```
<table width="400" align="center" border="1", cellpadding="5">
```

B Click after the closing quote of the border attribute and tap ⎡Spacebar⎤. **C** Type **cellpadding="5"**.

14. Save your changes.

15. Switch to your browser and tap ⎡F5⎤.
The cells each have five pixels of padding around the cell contents.

Advanced Table Structures

While the `<table>`, `<tr>`, and `<td>` tags are all you really need to create tables, there are a few other tags and attributes that help define the table structure. These are:

- The table header tag `<th>`

- The `scope` attribute

- The `<caption>` tag

- The `summary` attribute

Th and Scope

When looking at data in a table, such as in a spreadsheet, there are typically column headers and sometimes row headers. These headers act as labels for the columns and rows so readers know what data is being displayed. You can identify your HTML table columns and rows as headers by using the `<th>` tag instead of the `<td>` tag. You use the `scope` attribute to define if the cell is a column header or a row header. The `<th>` tag can use all the attributes of a regular `<td>` tag.

Built-in Formatting

The `<th>` tag comes with its own built-in formatting. Text inside a `<th>` is automatically bolded and centered. Of course, this visual style can be altered with CSS.

	Up to 100	101 - 250	Over 250
Simple models	$2	$1.50	$0.75

The top row consists of `<th>` tags instead of `<td>` tags. The `<th>` tag structurally identifies the cell as a header and visually bolds and centers the text.

Caption

The `<caption>` tag is a container tag that can act as a title or a caption for the table. Structurally, it helps define the table contents. Visually, it can be positioned above or below the table with the `align` attribute.

Aligning a Caption

Captions are positioned above or below the table. Oddly, HTML allows you to specify the horizontal alignment only if placed at the top, not at the bottom. If the align attribute is left out, the caption defaults to being centered above the table.

- The `align="top"` attribute centers the caption above the table.

- The `align="left"` attribute positions the caption above the table, left aligned.

- The `align="right"` attribute positions the caption above the table, right aligned.

- The `align="bottom"` attribute centers the caption below the table.

Summary

A table summary, like a summary for anything else, provides a brief description about the table contents. It is not displayed in the browser window but is read by search engines, screen readers, and other assistive devices. It is good to add this attribute to your tables to aid accessibility.

QUICK REFERENCE: ADVANCED TABLE STRUCTURES

Attribute/Tag	Usage	Description
`<th></th>`	`<th>Column 1</th>` `<th>Row 6</th>`	■ Defines a cell as a header cell ■ Visually makes text bold and centered
`scope`	`<th scope="row">` `<th scope="col">`	■ Defines a header as a column header or a row header
`<caption> </caption>`	`<caption>Current price list</caption>`	■ Creates a caption for the table, which can be used as a title for the table
`align`	`<caption align="bottom">Current price list</caption>`	■ Positions the caption above or below the table ■ Forbidden in XHTML 1.0 strict ■ Valid values: top, right, bottom, left
`summary`	`<table summary="Cost of items per unit sold">`	■ Creates a short text summary, or description, of the table contents

Hands-On 8.4   Add Advanced Table Structures

In this exercise, you will modify an existing table to include advanced table structures.

Add Column Headers

1. Switch to Notepad, locate the code for the beginning of the table, and follow these steps to create column headers:

A Change the second `<td>` tag into a `<th>` tag by changing the letter "d" to **h**.

B Change the closing tag to `</th>`.

```
<table width="400" align="center" border="1" c
   <tr>
      <td width="25%"> </td>
      <th scope="col" width="25%">Up to 100</th>
      <th scope="col" width="25%">101 - 250</th>
      <th scope="col" width="25%">Over 250</th>
   </tr>
```

C Add `scope="col"` to identify the second cell as a header for a column.

D Change the next two cells in this top row to column headers.

2. Save your changes.

3. Switch to your browser and tap [F5].
   The text across the top row becomes bold and centered.

Add Row Headers

4. Switch to Notepad, locate the second row, and follow these steps to create a row header:

A Change the opening and closing `<td>` tags to `<th>` tags.

```
<tr>
   <th scope="row" align="right" >Simple models</th>
```

B Add `scope="row"`.

5. Using a procedure similar to that outlined in step 4, change the first cell in each of the remaining two rows into headers with the scope of row.

6. Switch to your browser and tap [F5].
   The text down the first column becomes bold.

Add a Caption

7. Switch back to Notepad and again locate the code for the beginning of the table.

8. Follow these steps to create a table caption:

Ⓐ Click after the opening `<table>` tag and tap Enter.

```
<table width="400" align="center" border="1" cellpadding="5">
<caption>Price List Based on Number of Models Folded</caption>
```

Ⓑ Type the following: **<caption>Price List Based on Number of Models Folded</caption>**

9. Save your changes.

10. Switch to your browser and tap F5.
The caption appears in its default location centered above the table because you did not use the align *attribute on the* <caption> *tag.*

Add a Summary

11. Locate the opening table tag.

12. Follow these steps to add a table summary:

Ⓐ Click after the closing quote of the `cellpadding` attribute and tap Spacebar.

```
<table width="400" align="center" border="1"
cellpadding="5" summary="This table lists the
per unit price of folded models">
```

Ⓑ Type the following: **summary="This table lists the per unit price of folded models"**

13. Save your changes.

14. Switch to your browser and tap F5.
There is no visible change as the summary does not display in the browser window.

Merging Cells

At times you need a cell to span several rows or columns. This can be useful when including content in the table that needs to display the full width of the table, such as the disclaimer at the bottom of the table in the following figure.

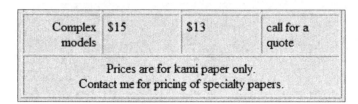

The bottom cell spans across four columns.

Colspan and Rowspan

The colspan attribute of the <td> tag is used to specify how many columns a cell should span. Similarly, the rowspan attribute specifies how many rows a cell should span.

```
<table>
  <tr>
    <td>This is cell 1</td>
    <td>This is cell 2</td>
    <td>This is cell 3</td>
  </tr>
  <tr>
    <td>This is cell 4</td>
    <td colspan="2">This cell spans 2 columns</td>
  </tr>
</table>
```

This code uses the colspan attribute to span a cell across two columns. Notice that the top row contains three <td> tags for the three cells while the bottom row contains only two <td> tags.

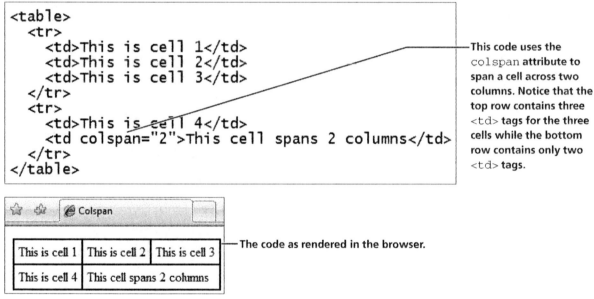

The code as rendered in the browser.

In the second row, the first cell is implied. The <td> tag refers to the second cell in this row.

```
<table >
  <tr>
    <td rowspan="2">This cell spans 2 rows</td>
    <td>row 1 second cell</td>
  </tr>
  <tr>
    <td>row 2 second cell</td>
  </tr>
</table>
```

This code uses the rowspan attribute to span a cell across two rows. Notice that the top row contains two <td> tags for the two cells. The first cell expands down to the second row.

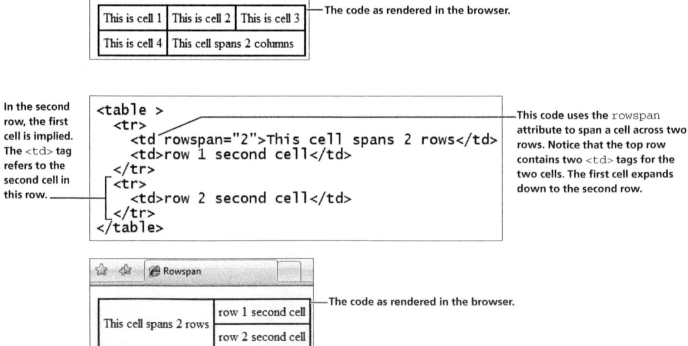

The code as rendered in the browser.

Hands-On 8.5   Merge Cells

In this exercise, you will create a large merged cell at the bottom of the table.

1. Switch to Notepad and locate the closing `</table>` tag towards the bottom of the document.

2. Follow these steps to start a new row for the merged cell:

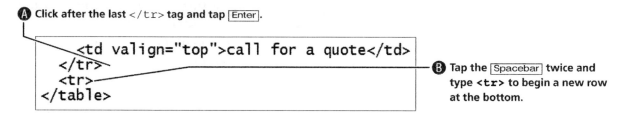

Ⓐ Click after the last `</tr>` tag and tap Enter.

```
        <td valign="top">call for a quote</td>
     </tr>
     <tr>
</table>
```

Ⓑ Tap the Spacebar twice and type `<tr>` to begin a new row at the bottom.

3. Tap Enter, then tap the Spacebar four times to create white space.

4. Type the following to create the merged cell:

   `<td colspan="4" align="center">Prices are for kami paper only.`
   `<br />` Enter
   `Contact me for pricing of specialty papers.</td>` Enter
   Spacebar Spacebar `</tr>`

   Your code should resemble the figure.

```
    <tr>
       <td colspan="4" align="center">Prices are for
kami paper only.<br />
Contact me for pricing of specialty papers.</td>
    </tr>
</table>
```

5. Save your changes.

6. Switch to your browser and tap F5.
   A new row with a single cell spanning four columns displays at the bottom of the table. The text is centered in the bottom cell.

Using Layout Tables

When a table is used to accomplish positioning of page elements, it is referred to as a *layout table*. The tags and attributes are no different from the tables you have studied in this lesson already. The only difference between a data table and a layout table is how the table is used.

Limiting Page Width

One common use of layout tables is to limit the width of a web page by creating a one-cell *wrapper table* that contains the entire <body> content. Users can set their screens to a specific *resolution*. Resolution is the number of pixels that the monitor can display; it differs from computer to computer based on the settings a user has configured. The most basic resolution setting on a modern computer is 800 pixels across by 600 pixels down (written 800 x 600). While many users have higher resolutions, enough people still use 800 x 600 to warrant your web pages accommodating them. For this reason, you should limit your page width to no more than 760 pixels. Limiting your page width to 760 pixels ensures that users will not have to scroll sideways to view all of your page content. A width of 760 pixels allows for the extra width taken up by the browser scrollbar and borders.

Readability

Another benefit of limiting the width of your page is related to readability. Long lines of text are difficult to read. By the time a user scans one line of text, their eyes must go all the way back to the left side of the page and find the next line. When the lines are very long this becomes difficult. Usability experts say no line of text should be more than about two alphabets—meaning 52 characters. Limiting your page width to 760 pixels wide helps maintain readable lines.

Centering Content

Another common use of layout tables is to center content in the browser window. When a wrapper table is used to limit the page contents to a certain width, such as 760 pixels, the table can be center aligned with the `align` attribute you learned about earlier in this lesson.

Nested Tables

When using layout tables, it is often necessary to nest one table inside another. There is no limit imposed by HTML as to how many tables can be nested, but the more nested tables you have, the longer it takes a web browser to draw the page. It is common practice to add borders to tables as you write the code. This makes it easy to see where the cells are when previewed in the browser, which can help tremendously when working with the complexities of nested tables. After the desired layout is accomplished, the borders can easily be removed.

TIP! *Nest tables no more than about three deep, otherwise browser performance can suffer.*

An outer table with one row and two columns acts as the parent container.

Regular heading and paragraph content lives in the left cell.

A nested table lives in the right cell.

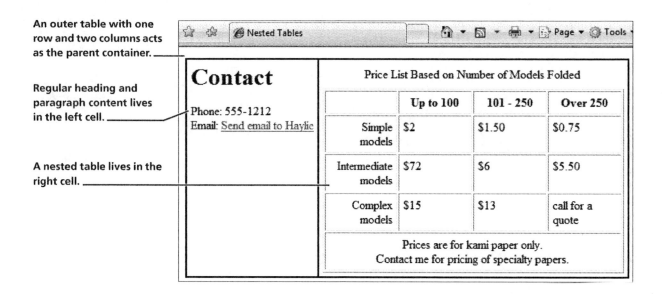

	Up to 100	101 - 250	Over 250
Simple models	$2	$1.50	$0.75
Intermediate models	$72	$6	$5.50
Complex models	$15	$13	call for a quote

Prices are for kami paper only.
Contact me for pricing of specialty papers.

 Hands-On 8.6   Create Nested Layout Tables

In this exercise, you will use nested layout tables to position page elements.

Create Nested Tables

1. Switch to Notepad and locate the `<h1>Contact</h1>` code block.

2. Click in the blank line above the `<h1>` and tap `Enter` four times to create white space.

3. Tap [↑] three times to position your cursor two lines below the closing `</div>` tag for the masthead.

4. Type the following to create the outer table structure for your nested tables:

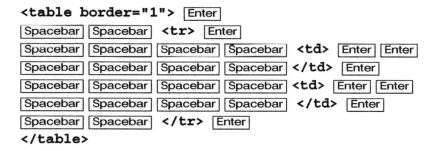

Your code should resemble the following figure.

```
<table border="1">
  <tr>
    <td>

    </td>
    <td>

    </td>
  </tr>
</table>
```

5. Scroll down, if necessary, and select the entire `<h1>Contact</h1>` code block down to the closing `</p>` tag below it.

```
<h1>Contact</h1>
<p>
Phone: 555-1212<br />
Email: <a href="mailto:haylie@example.com">Send
email to Haylie</a>
</p>
```

6. Choose Edit→Cut from the menu bar.

7. Scroll up, if necessary, and locate the code for your new table.

8. Follow these steps to paste the cut content into a table cell:

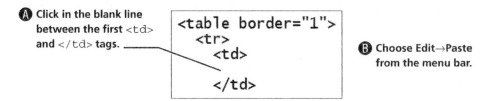

Ⓐ Click in the blank line between the first `<td>` and `</td>` tags.

```
<table border="1">
    <tr>
        <td>

        </td>
```

Ⓑ Choose Edit→Paste from the menu bar.

9. Scroll down, if necessary, and locate the opening `<table>` tag for the price table.

10. Click to the left of the opening table tag.

```
<table width="400"
```

11. Scroll down and locate the closing `</table>` tag. Be careful to click the scrollbar only and not in the Notepad window or you will lose the spot where you clicked.

12. Press ⃞Shift, click to the right of the closing `</table>` tag, and release ⃞Shift.
The entire table code block is selected.

13. Choose Edit→Cut from the menu bar.

14. Scroll up, if necessary, and locate the code for the new table.

15. Follow these steps to paste the cut table into the parent table:

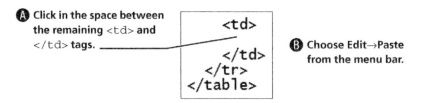

Ⓐ Click in the space between the remaining `<td>` and `</td>` tags.

```
        <td>

        </td>
    </tr>
</table>
```

Ⓑ Choose Edit→Paste from the menu bar.

16. Save your changes.

17. Switch to your browser and tap ⃞F5.
The contact information is vertically centered in the left cell because no `valign` was set. The outer table displays a border.

Format the Outer Table

18. Switch back to Notepad.

19. Locate the opening `<table>` tag for the outer table.

20. Follow these steps to format the outer table:

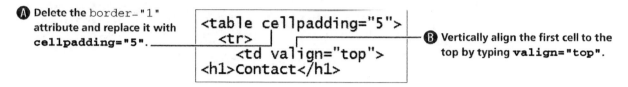

Ⓐ Delete the `border_"1"` attribute and replace it with `cellpadding="5"`.

```
<table cellpadding="5">
    <tr>
        <td valign="top">
<h1>Contact</h1>
```

Ⓑ Vertically align the first cell to the top by typing `valign="top"`.

21. Save your changes.

22. Switch to your browser and tap ⌨F5⌨.
The contact information moves to the top of the cell and the borders around the outer table are gone.

23. Close your browser and Notepad.

Image Slicing

An advanced application of layout tables revolves around *image slicing*. Image slicing is the act of cutting up a large image in a graphics-editing program and then piecing the slices back together inside HTML table cells like a puzzle. This usually involves merging cells across rows and columns. Image slicing is performed when the design of a web page deems it necessary and is the responsibility of the graphic artist designing the site or the web developer creating the code.

A design from a graphic artist includes some elements that will be created by HTML text (headings and paragraphs), such as the central portion of this design.

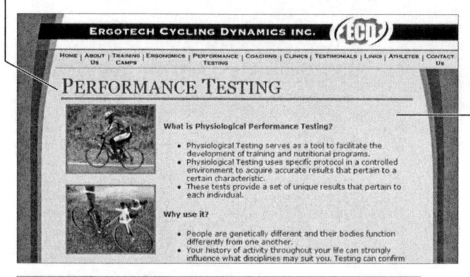

When the `cellspacing`, `cellpadding`, **and** `border` **are removed from the outer table, the slices fit together seamlessly to create the design.**

The left, top, and right sides can be sliced into individual JPEGs or GIFs.

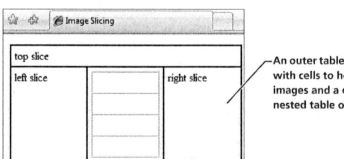

An outer table can be created with cells to hold the sliced images and a cell to hold a nested table of content.

Graphic Editors' HTML Output

Most graphics-editing programs have an option that will automatically create an HTML table, or an entire HTML page, for a sliced image. While tempting, this is usually a bad idea. Graphics-editing programs are, well, graphics-editing programs! They are not web-coding programs! They are notorious for creating bloated and often invalid code. You are better off practicing your coding of nested tables and merged cells, slicing the large image, and creating your own table by hand to piece it back together.

Concepts Review

True/False Questions

1. Data tables and layout tables require the use of completely different HTML tags. **TRUE   FALSE**

2. Empty table cells can collapse in on themselves, so every cell should contain some-thing—even if it's a non-breaking space. **TRUE   FALSE**

3. Tables can be aligned to the top, right, bottom, and left of the browser window. **TRUE   FALSE**

4. Table borders display differently in different browsers. **TRUE   FALSE**

5. There is officially no such thing as the `height` attribute for a table, though many developers mistakenly use it anyway. **TRUE   FALSE**

6. `Cellspacing` adds space to the inside of table cells. **TRUE   FALSE**

7. `Cellspacing` and `cellpadding` can be applied differently to various cells in a table. **TRUE   FALSE**

8. A table caption can display above, below, or to the left or right of a table. **TRUE   FALSE**

9. A table summary always displays immediately below the table. **TRUE   FALSE**

10. Cells can only be merged across multiple columns, not down multiple rows. **TRUE   FALSE**

Multiple Choice Questions

1. Deepak is frustrated because the little bit of text in his left cell continues to drift down as he types more text in the right cell. What is the problem and how can he fix it?

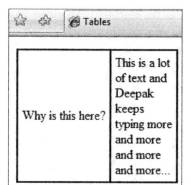

   a. He has set the left cell's align attribute to `align="center"`. He should change it to `align="top"`.

   b. He has used a `<th>` tag for the left cell instead of a `<td>` tag. He should change it back to a `<td>` tag.

   c. The left cell is spanning too many columns. He should remove the spanned cell and use a nested table.

   d. This is the default behavior of a cell when the `valign` attribute has not been used. He should add `valign="top"` to the left cell.

2. Khalida wishes to make her table accessible to assistive devices. What table structures can she implement to aid accessibility?

   a. `<caption>` and `<summary>` tags

   b. `caption` and `summary` attributes

   c. `<caption>` tag and `summary` attribute

   d. `<summary>` tag and `caption` attribute

3. Hugo is puzzled because the text in his cell displays on one long line and causes the table to be wider than the browser window, making a horizontal scrollbar appear at the bottom of the browser. What is the problem?

   a. He has the `nowrap="nowrap"` attribute in his cell.

   b. He failed to use line breaks (`<br />`).

   c. He failed to set the `align` attribute to `align="wrap"`.

   d. He has misused the `colspan` attribute.

4. Lena wants her table border to be a thickness relative to the browser window width. As the window widens, the border should become thicker. As the window narrows, the border should become thinner. How can she accomplish this?

   a. Set the table's `border` attribute to `border="10%"`.

   b. Set the table's `border` attribute to `border="fluid"`.

   c. Set the table's `border` attribute to `border="10p"`.

   d. This is not possible with HTML; borders must be specified in static pixel widths.

Skill Builders

Skill Builder 8.1   Add a Table

In this exercise, you will add an empty table to an existing page. You will then move existing content into the table cells.

Create a Table

1. Start your web browser and open the gallery.htm page from the sb_fup_tables folder from your Lesson 08 folder.

2. Start Notepad and open the same gallery.htm page from the sb_fup_tables folder from your Lesson 08 folder.

3. Locate the code for `<h1>Gallery</h1>`.

4. Click in the space below `<h1>Gallery</h1>` and tap Enter to create white space.

5. Type the following to create a 1 × 3 table:

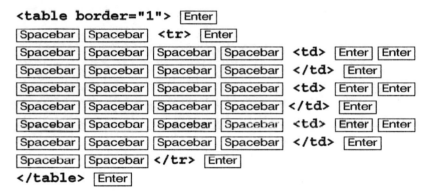

Move Existing Content

6. Select the first anchor tag (for the knife_small.jpg image hyperlink) below the table.

```
<a href="gal_knife.htm"><img src="images/knife_small.jpg" alt="Swiss
Army Knife, Jun Maekawa" hspace="5" border="0" /></a>
```

7. Choose Edit→Cut from the menu bar.

8. Follow these steps to paste the cut content into the first cell:

A Click in the space between the first `<td>` and `</td>` tags.

```
<table border="1">
    <tr>
        <td>

        </td>
```

B Choose Edit→Paste from the menu bar.

9. Select the next hyperlink for the fluffy_small.jpg image:

```
<a href="gal_fluffy.htm"><img src="images/fluffy_small.jpg"
alt="Fluffy, Marc Kirschembaum" hspace="5" border="0" /></a>
```

10. Choose Edit→Cut from the menu bar.

11. Click in the space between the next empty `<td></td>` tags.

12. Choose Edit→Paste from the menu bar.

13. Select the last hyperlink for the present_small.jpg image.

14. Cut and paste it in the last table cell.

15. Save your changes.

16. Switch to your browser and tap F5.
The images appear inside table cells.

Skill Builder 8.2   Add a Row

In this exercise, you will add a new row to the bottom of the table and fill the cells with new content.

Before You Begin: You must complete Skill Builder 8.1 before beginning this exercise.

1. Switch to Notepad and locate the bottom of the table.

2. Follow these steps to start a new row after the existing row:

3. Type the following to complete the first cell in the new row:

   \<tr\> [Enter]
   [Spacebar] [Spacebar] [Spacebar] [Spacebar] **\<td\>Swiss Army Knife by Jun Maekawa\</td\>**

4. Tap [Enter], then tap [Spacebar] four times.

5. Type the following to complete the second cell:

   \<td\>Fluffy by Marc Kirschenbaum\</td\>

6. Tap [Enter], then tap [Spacebar] four times.

7. Type the following to complete the final cell and close the row:

   \<td\>Present Box by Jeremy Shafer\</td\> [Enter]
   [Spacebar] [Spacebar] **\</tr\>**

8. Save your changes.

9. Switch to your browser and tap [F5].
   A new row appears at the bottom of the table with descriptions of the thumbnails.

Skill Builder 8.3   Format the Table and Cells

In this exercise, you will add padding, alignments, and cell widths. You will also remove the table border.

Before You Begin: You must complete Skill Builder 8.2 before beginning this exercise.

Add Padding

1. Switch to Notepad and locate the opening `<table>` tag, then follow these steps to add cellpadding and remove the table border:

Ⓐ **Select the entire** `border` **attribute/value and tap** `Backspace` **to delete it.**

`<table border="1">`

Ⓑ **Type** `cellpadding="10"` **to add 10 pixels of padding around the inside of every cell.**

Make Equal Width Columns

As there are three columns, each column can be defined as 33 percent wide. While that adds up to only 99 percent, the missing 1 percent is so small it won't be noticed.

2. Locate the first `<td>` tag and follow these steps to specify a cell width:

Ⓐ **Click after the letter "d" inside the tag and tap** `Spacebar`.

```
    <td width="33%">
<a href="gal_knife.htm">
```

Ⓑ **Type** `width="33%"`.

3. Locate the second `<td>` tag and add **`width="33%"`** to it.

```
    <td width="33%">
<a href="gal_fluffy.htm">
```

4. Add **`width="33%"`** to the third `<td>` tag.

```
    <td width="33%">
<a href="gal_present.htm">
```

Align Cell Content

5. Locate the first `<td>` tag again and follow these steps to center align the cell content:

A Click after the closing quote of the `width` **attribute and tap** `Spacebar`.

B Type `align="center"`.

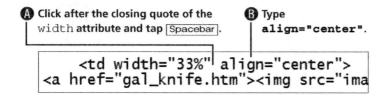

```
            <td width="33%" align="center">
<a href="gal_knife.htm"><img src="ima
```

6. Using the method outlined in step 5, add **align="center"** to the next two `<td>` tags (the ones with `width="33%"`).

7. Locate the code for the bottom row.

8. Add **align="center"** to the three `<td>` tags in the bottom row.

```
<tr>
  <td align="center">Swiss Army k
  <td align="center">Fluffy by Ma
  <td align="center">Present Box
```

9. Save your changes.

10. Switch to your browser and tap `F5`.
    The cell content is equally spaced and the thumbnails are centered over their descriptions.

Skill Builder 8.4   Add Advanced Table Structures and Merge Cells

In this exercise, you will add a table caption, merged cell, and table summary.

Before You Begin: You must complete Skill Builder 8.3 before beginning this exercise.

Add a Caption

First you will add a caption to serve as a title for the table.

1. Switch to Notepad and locate the opening `<table>` tag.

2. Click after the opening `<table>` tag and tap ⌷Enter⌷.

3. Type the following: **<caption>Recent Work for the Ramble-Bakshy Wedding</caption>**

Add a Merged Cell

You will now add a merged cell across the top of the table to provide instructions for users. As there are three columns in the table, the cell will use `colspan="3"`.

4. Click after the closing `</caption>` tag and tap ⌷Enter⌷ ⌷Spacebar⌷ ⌷Spacebar⌷ to create white space.

5. Type **<tr>**, tap ⌷Enter⌷, and tap ⌷Spacebar⌷ four times to start a new top row.

6. Type **<td colspan="3" align="center">** to begin the new cell.

7. Tap ⌷Enter⌷, type **Click a thumbnail to view the full size photo**, tap ⌷Enter⌷, and tap ⌷Spacebar⌷ twice to create emphasized cell content.

8. Type the following to close the cell and the row:

   </td> ⌷Enter⌷
   ⌷Spacebar⌋ ⌷Spacebar⌋ **</tr>**

Add a Summary

You will now add a table summary to aid search engine optimization and assistive devices such as screen readers.

9. Locate the opening `<table>` tag, click after the closing quote of the `cellpadding` attribute, and tap ⌷Spacebar⌋.

10. Type the following: **summary="This table displays thumbnail images of recent work. When a thumbnail is clicked, a new page displays the full size image."**

11. Save your changes.

12. Switch to your browser and tap ⌷F5⌋.
    The table caption appears at the top of the table and the content in the merged cell is centered and italic.

13. Close your browser.

14. Close Notepad.

Skill Builder 8.5   Center Page Content and Limit Page Width

In this exercise, you will limit the page width to 760 pixels while centering the content.

Explore the Unlimited Page Width

First you will explore how page content shifts when the browser window is resized.

1. Start Notepad and open the index.htm file from the sb_fup_tables folder in your Lesson 08 folder.

2. Start your web browser and open the same index.htm file from the sb_fup_tables folder in your Lesson 08 folder.

3. Locate the sizing buttons in the top-right corner of the browser window and take note of the middle button.
   If the middle button displays two squares, the window is maximized and cannot be resized by dragging.

   If the middle button displays a single square, your window is in windowed mode and can be resized by dragging.

4. If necessary, click the middle resize button to enter maximized mode (the middle button should display two squares).
   The content spans the entire width of the screen. This may be difficult to read at higher resolutions or on wide-screen monitors.

5. Click the middle resize button to enter windowed mode (the middle button should display a single square).

6. Point to the right edge of the browser window until your cursor becomes a double-headed arrow, then drag the window border to the left.
   As you narrow the browser window, the text shifts to wrap to the narrower window.

7. Click the middle resize button to enter maximized mode (the middle button should display two squares).

Limit the Page Width and Center the Content

8. Switch to Notepad and locate the opening <body> tag towards the top of the document.

9. Follow these steps to begin wrapping the body content:

Ⓐ Click in the space below the opening <body> tag.

```
<body background="images/bg.jpg">
<table width="760" align="center">
```

Ⓑ Type **<table width="760" align="center">**.

Ⓒ Tap [Enter] [Spacebar] [Spacebar] to create white space.

10. Type the following to create a top row for the masthead:

`<tr>` `Enter`
`Spacebar` `Spacebar` `Spacebar` `Spacebar` **`<td align="center">`**

11. Locate the closing `</div>` tag for the masthead and follow these steps to end the first row and begin the second row:

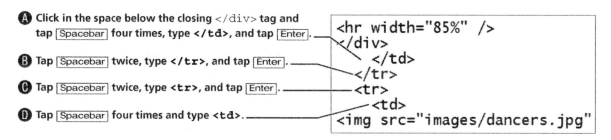

A Click in the space below the closing `</div>` tag and tap `Spacebar` four times, type **`</td>`**, and tap `Enter`.

B Tap `Spacebar` twice, type **`</tr>`**, and tap `Enter`.

C Tap `Spacebar` twice, type **`<tr>`**, and tap `Enter`.

D Tap `Spacebar` four times and type **`<td>`**.

```
<hr width="85%" />
</div>
    </td>
   </tr>
  <tr>
    <td>
<img src="images/dancers.jpg"
```

12. Locate the closing `</body>` tag at the bottom of the document.

13. Click in the space above the closing `</body>` tag and tap `Spacebar` four times.

14. Type the following to end the second row and the table:

`</td>` `Enter`
`Spacebar` `Spacebar` **`</tr>`** `Enter`
`</table>`

15. Save your changes.

16. Switch to your web browser and tap `F5`.
The content narrows to 760 pixels wide and is centered on the page. The masthead is centered in the top cell.

17. Click the middle resize button to enter windowed mode.

18. Drag the right border of the browser window to the left, then to the right.
As the window narrows, the text does not shift because the wrapper table is a static 760 pixels wide. As the browser window widens, the entire table shifts to maintain its centered position in the window.

19. Close your browser and Notepad.

Assessments

Assessment 8.1   Add a Layout Table

In this exercise, you will add a layout table with merged cells to limit page width and center content in the browser window.

Create a Wrapper Table

1. Open the index.htm page in the as_music_quiz folder in your Lesson 08 folder in both your web browser and Notepad.

2. In Notepad, type the following in the body section to create a wrapper table with a merged cell. Use [Enter] and [Spacebar] where appropriate to create white space:

```
<table border="1" width="760" align="center">
  <tr>
    <td colspan="2">
    <h1>Music Quiz</h1>
    </td>
  </tr>
  <tr>
    <td>
    <img src="images/guitarist.jpg" alt="guitarist" width="249"
height="472"/>
    </td>
    <td> </td>
  </tr>
</table>
```

3. Save your changes and preview the page in your browser.
   Your page should resemble the following figure.

Assessment 8.2   Add a Nested Table

In this exercise, you will add a nested table with a caption and a summary.

Before You Begin: You must complete Assessment 8.1 before beginning this exercise.

1. Switch to Notepad and delete the code for the non-breaking space (   ) in the empty cell.

2. Type the following in the empty cell to start a nested table with a summary and caption, remembering to use white space where appropriate:

```
<table width="75%" border="1" summary="This table contains the
first question in our daily music quiz.">
<caption>Today's Theme: Power Trios</caption>
```

The width of 75 percent will limit the table to 75 percent of the width of its container cell.

3. Type the following to create the first row. Use white space where appropriate:

```
<tr>
   <td><strong>What Canadian power trio recorded the classic 80s hits
Limelight and Tom Sawyer?</strong></td>
</tr>
```

4. Type the following to create the second row and end the table:

```
    <tr>
      <td>
      <ol>
        <li>Triumph</li>
        <li>Zebra</li>
        <li>Rush</li>
        <li>The Police</li>
      </ol>
      </td>
    </tr>
</table>
```

5. Save your changes and preview the page in your browser.
   The content still needs to be aligned; you will do that in the next exercise. Your page should resemble the following figure.

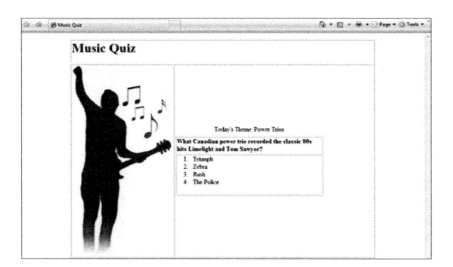

Assessment 8.3   Format Tables and Cells

In this exercise, you will format a table and cells with alignments. You will also remove the borders.

Before You Begin: You must complete Assessment 8.2 before beginning this exercise.

Remove the Borders

1. Switch to Notepad and locate the first opening `<table>` tag (for the wrapper table) and delete the `border="1"` attribute. Be sure to maintain a space between the tag name and the `width` attribute.

```
<table width="760" align="center">
```

2. Locate the second opening `<table>` tag (for the nested table) and delete the `border="1"` attribute. Be sure to maintain a space between the tag name and the `width` attribute.

Align Content

3. Locate the cell containing the `<h1>Music Quiz</h1>` and horizontally align the cell contents.

```
<td colspan="2" align="center">
<h1>Music Quiz</h1>
```

4. Locate the cell containing the nested table and vertically top-align the cell contents.

```
    <td valign="top">
<table width="75%" summary="
```

5. Horizontally align the nested table inside its container cell.

```
    <td valign="top">
<table align="center" width="75%" summary="
```

6. Save your changes and preview the page in your browser.
Your page should resemble the following figure.

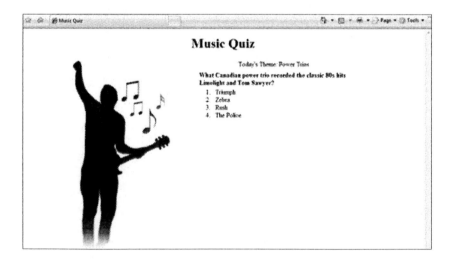

7. Resize the browser window by dragging the side border to narrow and widen it.
The text does not shift and the content remains centered because the wrapper table is a static pixel width.

8. Close your browser and Notepad.

Critical Thinking

Critical Thinking 8.1   Create a Table-based Layout

In this exercise, you will create a web page from a wire frame. Before you begin, open the ct_yarn folder in the Lesson 08 folder. Open the index.htm page in both your web browser and in Notepad. Notepad should be the active window.

Refer to the following wire frame. You will re-create the layout with a wrapper table and a nested table.

Wrapper table specifications:

- The table width should be 760 pixels wide.

- The table should be centered in the browser window.

- The top cell should be merged to span two columns and the content should be horizontally centered. Content should be a `<h1>`.

- The bottom cells should be top aligned.

- The bottom-left cell should display the lady.jpg image. Be sure you are aware of the folder and filenames in the site root so you can properly reference the image in your `<img>` tag. Don't forget the `alt` attribute!

- The bottom-right cell should contain a short line of paragraph text of your choice followed by a nested table.

Nested table specifications:

- Create a 2 × 2 table.

- The table should not have a width specified so it contracts to as narrow as can be to accommodate its contents.

- The table should include a summary describing the table contents.

- The caption centered above the table should read *Choose a category*.

- Each cell should contain one of the remaining images from within the site root folder. Be sure you are aware of the folder and file names in the site root so you can properly reference the images in your `<img>` tags.

- Each image must contain an appropriate `alt` attribute.

- Each image should be labeled as *Yarn*, *Sweaters*, *Hats*, or *Gloves*.

- Images should be hyperlinked with a "dummy" link as follows:
  `<a href="#">...img tag here...</a>`
  This code will create a hyperlink that is clickable but doesn't go anywhere.

- Be sure to remove the border from around the hyperlinked images.

- Add padding to the table as you feel is appropriate.

Make sure to complete the `<title>` tag so your page has an appropriate title.

Your final page may resemble the following figure.

LESSON 9

Introducing CSS and Color

In this lesson, you will learn the basics of color on the web. You will learn how to reference colors with hexadecimal color codes and named colors. You will also learn the basics of CSS, including the anatomy of CSS code, types of selectors, and the various ways to add CSS code to the pages.

LESSON OBJECTIVES

After studying this lesson, you will be able to:

- Identify best practices when designing with color
- Use named colors and hexadecimal color codes
- Add inline, embedded, and external styles
- Use type, class, and id selectors
- Use grouped, descendant, and pseudo-class selectors

Case Study: Formatting with Color and CSS

With Miguel's graphics in place and Haylie's attention to valid code, the Folding Under Pressure site is coming together. The team begins to format the pages with color. Knowing that ease of maintenance is something Haylie wants to incorporate from the start, she begins formatting her pages with an external stylesheet.

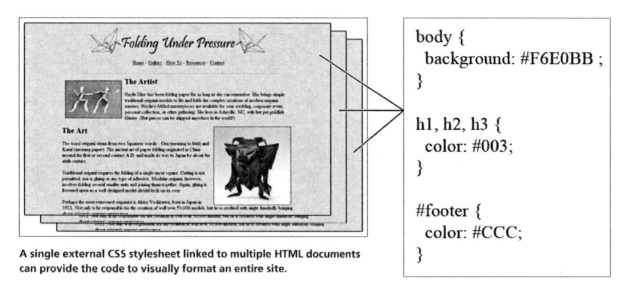

A single external CSS stylesheet linked to multiple HTML documents can provide the code to visually format an entire site.

```
body {
    background: #F6E0BB ;
}

h1, h2, h3 {
    color: #003;
}

#footer {
    color: #CCC;
}
```

Designing Tip: Be Aware of Your Colors

The web is a visual medium. As such, color plays an important part in a site's appeal. However, you must be aware of several things when working with color on a web page.

- Too many colors can be distracting and detract from your design.

- Some color combinations don't work well.

- Some colors are impossible for colorblind users to discern.

Less Is More

Too many colors on a page can be distracting. As with most subjective artistic works, there is no absolute. There is no magic number or rule that states, "Never have more than X colors on a web page." Just don't overdo it. Generally, most well-received designs tend to stick to about three main colors, with the main body text being a consistent color throughout.

Color Combinations

Strive for high contrast between foreground and background colors. Dark text on a dark background is difficult to read, just as light text on a light background is difficult to read. Black text on a white background is the easiest to read, albeit a little boring. Some combinations, such as bright red and blue, strain the eyes and look three-dimensional when used together. Red text on a blue background (or vice versa) is usually a bad idea. If you must use red and blue, try for darker or less saturated shades.

Colorblindness

There are several types of colorblindness. The most common type affects the ability to discern greens and reds, which in turn affects your decisions as a designer for an accessible site. For example, if you chose to use red text on a green background, most people would be able to separate the colors and see red on green. A colorblind person may not be able to discern these colors and instead may see light brown on light brown—very little contrast. See the web page for this book for links on more information about colorblindness and web design.

Named Colors

Colors can be specified in your HTML code several ways. The most intuitive is with the use of named colors. The following is an example of setting the page background to red using a named color.

 See the web page for this book for an online reference chart of named colors.

```
<body bgcolor="red">
```

 TIP! Named colors can vary from browser to browser. It is best to use another method of specifying colors, such as hexadecimal color codes.

Hexadecimal Color Codes

Colors are more often indicated in HTML code by their hexadecimal values than with a named color. In the decimal numbering system you use every day, the digits 0–9 (10 digits) are used to represent a value with 0 being the least value and 9 being the greatest. In the hexadecimal numbering system, the digits 0–9 and letters A–F (16 characters) are used to represent a value with 0 being the least value and F being the greatest.

QUICK REFERENCE: DECIMAL TO HEXADECIMAL CONVERSION				
Decimal	**Hexadecimal**		**Decimal**	**Hexadecimal**
0	0		8	8
1	1		9	9
2	2		10	A
3	3		11	B
4	4		12	C
5	5		13	D
6	6		14	E
7	7		15	F

Hex-6

Color codes can be indicated by hex-6, or a six character hexadecimal number. A hexadecimal color code must be in the format #RRGGBB, where RR indicates the amount of red, GG indicates the amount of green, and BB indicates the amount of blue. For example, to specify the color red you would need all the red you can get—no green and no blue. Remember that in hexadecimal notation 0 is the least and F is the greatest. So, all red, no green, and no blue would be #FF0000. The color code for pure blue would be #0000FF. Note that in these examples, the values appear in pairs. This is not required. The color code #F096CB is perfectly valid because it uses six characters and the digits 0–9 or the letters A–F. (However, you probably won't know what color it actually is unless you use it in your code and view it in a browser to test it!) The following is an example of setting the page background to red using hex-6.

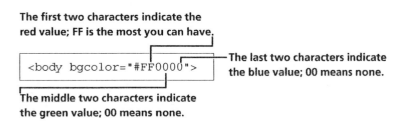

NOTE! *Hexadecimal color codes must begin with the pound (#) symbol.*

Determining the Color Code for a Desired Color

Nobody has memorized what color every combination of hex-6 code produces. To learn the hexadecimal code for your desired color, either consult a color chart (like the one on the web page for this book) or use a graphics-editing program that tells you the color code of a selected color. There are a few basic color codes every developer should have memorized. These are outlined in the following table.

QUICK REFERENCE: BASIC HEXADECIMAL COLOR CODES	
Code	**Color**
#000000	black
#FFFFFF	white
#FF0000	red
#00FF00	green
#0000FF	blue

Hex-3

Hex-3 is a shorthand method of writing your code if, and only if, your hex-6 appears in pairs. For example, #FFCC33 is written as a pair of Fs, a pair of Cs, and pair of 3s. This can be written in hex-3 shorthand as #FC3. Under hex-3, it is implied that each character is simply repeated. So, #DDCC44 can be written in hex-3 as #DC4. However, #DCDCFF cannot be written as hex-3 because neither the red nor the green values are in pairs. (Red is written as DC—not a pair. Green is also written as DC—not a pair.) Hex-3 is not supported in HTML attributes. The following code, while valid hex-3 code for the color red, is invalid because it is in an HTML attribute and would probably render as a black background instead of red.

```
<body bgcolor="#F00">
```

Hex-3 notation can be used with CSS, which you will see later in this lesson.

Web-safe Colors

In the early days of computing, computer monitors were only capable of displaying 256 colors, and 216 of these colors became known as the web-safe palette. (These 216 colors are consistent between Mac and PC, whereas the other 40 colors vary.) Early web designers limited themselves to these 216 colors so their designs would display consistently across all computer systems. A web-safe color can be identified by the following criteria:

■ RGB values appear in pairs, such as #FFCC33 or #669900.

■ Only the values 0, 3, 6, 9, C, and F are used.

Today, computer monitors are capable of displaying millions of colors, so the web-safe palette is not something to which you need to limit yourself. Feel free to use color codes such as #B0B8BB or #12AB68. (You just won't be able to specify them as hex-3 if they don't appear in pairs.)

Some of working with color is trial and error. Many times you need to type in a few characters, save and preview your page, and see what color you specified! See the web page for this book for an online reference chart of the 216 web-safe colors.

Hands-On 9.1   Use Color Codes

In this exercise, you will use HTML named colors and color codes with HTML attributes.

1. Start your web browser and open the contact.htm page from the fup_css folder in your Lesson 09 folder.
   Notice that the page background is white (though it might be gray depending on your web browser). The page background image has been removed from this page.

2. Start Notepad and open the same contact.htm page from the fup_css folder in your Lesson 09 folder; locate the opening <body> tag.

3. Follow these steps to turn the page background blue:

Ⓐ Click after the word body but inside the tag and tap [Spacebar].

`<body bgcolor="blue">`

Ⓑ Type **bgcolor="blue"**.

4. Save your changes, switch to your browser, and tap [F5].
   The page background is blue, making the hyperlinks difficult to see.

5. Switch back to Notepad and follow these steps to change the color of the hyperlinks:

Ⓐ Click after the closing quote of the bgcolor attribute and tap [Spacebar].

`<body bgcolor="blue" link="#FF0000" vlink="#00FF00">`

Ⓑ Type **link="#FF0000"** to color the links red.

Ⓒ Tap [Spacebar] and type **vlink="#00FF00"** to color the visited links green.

6. Save your changes, switch to your browser, and tap [F5].
   The red links on the blue background are hard on the eyes.

7. Click the Home hyperlink in the top navigation bar.

8. Click the Contact hyperlink to return to the Contact page.
   The Home hyperlink is now a visited link, so it turns green. It, too, is hard on the eyes. These bright colors do not work well together.

9. Switch back to Notepad and follow these steps to adjust the colors:

Ⓐ Change the bgcolor color code to **#F6E0BB** to specify a light brown.

`<body bgcolor="#F6E0BB" link="#000066" vlink="#660000">`

Ⓑ Change the link color code to **#000066** to specify a dark blue.

Ⓒ Change the vlink color code to **#660000** to specify a dark red.

10. Save your changes, switch to your browser, and tap [F5].
    These colors provide enough contrast to aid readability and do not hurt the eyes.

Defining CSS

CSS, or Cascading Style Sheets, provides a method to visually format your web pages. When used in conjunction with HTML, CSS can decrease page load times for users while making your site easier to maintain and update. CSS, like HTML, comes with its own set of syntax and rules, which you will learn throughout this lesson.

Benefits of CSS

CSS offers many benefits to both web developers and users of sites that incorporate CSS. Most benefits can be associated with one of the following categories:

- Streamlined HTML code
- Ease of site maintenance

Streamlined HTML Code

When all presentational code is moved out of an HTML file and into a CSS file, the file size of the HTML page reduces dramatically. This is known as "reducing code bloat." Reduced code bloat results in less bandwidth needed for users to download the HTML page. This places less stress on the web server and results in faster page loads for visitors.

Ease of Site Maintenance

CSS can be used to format an entire page or every page in a site by sharing a CSS file among all site pages. This means that if a client wants to change the page background color from red to blue on all pages in a site, the web developer can make a single change in a single CSS file to accomplish this task. Compared to changing every `<body bgcolor="red">` tag to `<body bgcolor="blue">` in hundreds of HTML files, CSS is much more efficient.

Applying CSS

CSS can be applied to your pages three different ways:

- Inline styles
- Embedded styles
- External stylesheets

Inline Styles

Inline styles are applied directly to an HTML tag with the `style` attribute. Inline styles are difficult to maintain as they are buried in the HTML code itself and cannot be shared with other elements on the HTML page. For these reasons, it is recommended to not use inline styles. However, you may inherit a website that uses inline styles, so you should know how to deal with them when you see them.

Hands-On 9.2   Apply Inline Styles

In this exercise, you will apply and remove inline styles.

Add Inline Styles

1. Switch to Notepad, locate the opening <body> tag, and delete all of the attributes so the tag looks like this: <body>.
   You have removed the presentational HTML code. You will now replace some of it with CSS.

2. Follow these steps to create an inline style:

A Click after the word *body* but inside the tag and tap [Spacebar].

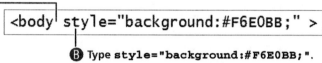

```
<body style="background:#F6E0BB;" >
```

B Type `style="background:#F6E0BB;"`.

Remember that in hexadecimal notation, only the digits 0–9 and the letters A–F are used. There is no letter zero. Also, remember that HTML and CSS code are very unforgiving. You must type the code exactly as written! Pay close attention to the colon (:) and semicolon (;).

3. Scroll down to the <h1>Contact</h1> block of code and follow these steps to color the text:

A Click in the opening <h1> tag after the number 1, tap the [Spacebar], and type `style="color:#600;"`.

```
<h1 style="color:#600;">Contact</h1>
<p style="color:#603030;">
```

B Click in the following <p> tag after the letter "p," tap the [Spacebar], and type `style="color:#603030;"`.

You have used the shortcut hex-3 color code #600 rather than typing #660000.

4. Save your changes, switch to your browser, and tap [F5].
   The Contact heading and the following paragraph turn a shade of dark red. The email link does not change color because it is a hyperlink and not regular paragraph text.

Remove Inline Styles

5. Switch back to Notepad and locate the opening <body> tag.

6. Delete the style attribute so the tag looks like this: <body>.

7. Locate the <h1> and <p> tags you modified in step 3 and remove their style attributes so the tags look like <h1> and <p>.

8. Save your changes, switch to your browser, and tap [F5].
   The page background color and text coloring disappear because you have removed the inline styles.

9. Close your web browser and Notepad.

Using Embedded Styles

Embedded styles are written at the top of an HTML page in the <head> section. These styles are applied throughout the entire page as opposed to an inline style that affects only a specific element. A block of embedded CSS begins and ends with <style></style> tags, as in the following example.

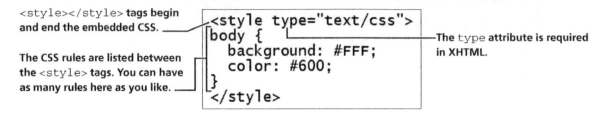

<style></style> **tags begin and end the embedded CSS.**

The CSS rules are listed between the <style> **tags. You can have as many rules here as you like.**

```
<style type="text/css">
body {
    background: #FFF;
    color: #600;
}
</style>
```

The type **attribute is required in XHTML.**

CSS Anatomy

A line of CSS code contains a *selector*, *property*, and *value*. These pieces combine to create *declarations* and *rules*. The anatomy of a CSS rule is as follows.

Declaration

Selector —— h1 { color:#6CC3CC; padding: 5px; } —Rule

Property   Value

In short, CSS code works like this:

1. The selector determines what element receives the formatting, such as a paragraph, a hyperlink, or something else. The selector is followed by an open curly brace, which contains the declarations.

2. A property is paired with a value, which formats some characteristic of the selected element. A property-value pair must be separated by a colon.

3. Property-value pairs are called declarations. Each declaration must end with a semicolon. You may have as many declarations as you like. The last declaration must be followed by a closing curly brace.

4. The entire block consisting of selector, braces, and declarations is called a rule.

QUICK REFERENCE: CSS ANATOMY

Anatomy	Function / Notes
Selector	■ Targets the HTML element or elements to receive the formatting
Property	■ A characteristic of the targeted element that can be formatted, such as the color, size, or border
Value	■ Associated with a property and defines how the property is formatted
Declaration	■ Property-value pairs are called declarations ■ Declarations must end with a semicolon ■ A declaration block begins and ends with curly braces
Rule	■ The selector and declaration(s) combine to create a rule ■ Rules can have as many declarations as you like

CSS Rules

CSS rules may be written across a single line or on different lines. Either way is valid, but using separate lines makes it easier to read.

```
h1 {background: #FFF; color: #600; padding: 10px;}
```

```
h1 {
    background: #FFF;
    color: #600;
    padding: 10px;
}
```

These identical rules contain three declarations. Writing a rule across a single line (top) or with declarations on separate lines (bottom) is a personal preference.

Selectors

The trick to applying CSS to certain elements throughout a page is understanding selectors. Selectors determine what element on the page receives the formatting. There are three main types of selectors:

■ Type selector

■ Class selector

■ Id selector

Type Selectors

Type selectors are used to target specific HTML tags. For example, to make every <p> tag display red text, you use the p type selector. Type selectors initiate a one-step process. Create the CSS rule and you are done. The formatting is applied to any tag on the page matching the type selector.

This CSS rule uses the type selector p to target all <p> tags.

```
<style type="text/css">
p {
  border-width: 1px;
  border-style: solid;
  border-color: #000000;
}
</style>
```

The HTML code contains no additional tags or attributes.

```
<p>This is a paragraph.</p>
<p>This is another paragraph.</p>
```

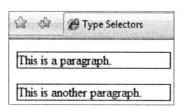

In the browser, all <p> tags receive the formatting defined in the CSS rule; in this case, a thin border.

 Hands-On 9.3 **Use Type Selectors**

In this exercise, you will use type selectors to target specific tags for CSS formatting.

1. Start Notepad and open the resources.htm page from the fup_css folder in your Lesson 09 folder.

2. Scroll through the document and notice there are several <h3> and <p> tags scattered throughout.

3. Start your web browser and open the same resources.htm page from the fup_css folder in your Lesson 09 folder.
   Notice that all of the text (except the hyperlinks) is black.

4. Switch back to Notepad, locate the closing </head> tag towards the top of the document, and follow these steps to create a container for the embedded CSS styles:

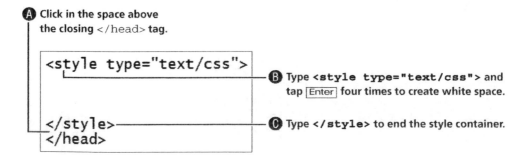

Ⓐ Click in the space above the closing </head> tag.

```
<style type="text/css">



</style>
</head>
```

Ⓑ Type **<style type="text/css">** and tap Enter four times to create white space.

Ⓒ Type **</style>** to end the style container.

5. Follow these steps to format all the <h3> and <p> elements, tapping the `Enter` key and `Spacebar` as necessary:

🅐 Click in the space below the opening <style> tag and type **h3** `{` `Enter` `Spacebar` `Spacebar` **color: #CC6600;** `Enter` `}` `Enter`. Use the `Enter` and `Spacebar` keys as shown.

🅑 Type the following to create a rule for the paragraphs: **p** `{` `Enter` `Spacebar` `Spacebar` **color: #660000;** `Enter` `}` `Enter`. Use the `Enter` and `Spacebar` keys as shown.

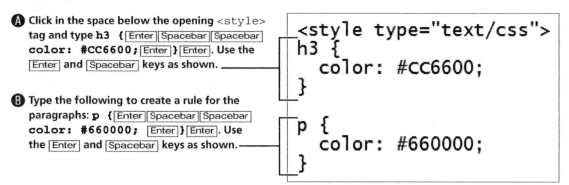

```
<style type="text/css">
h3 {
    color: #CC6600;
}

p {
    color: #660000;
}
```

You could have used hex-3 color codes here. The codes #C60 *and* #600 *would have worked just as well.*

6. Save your changes, switch to your browser, and tap `F5`.
All of the <h3> elements are burnt orange while all of the paragraph elements are a dark red. While these colors may not be optimal for the site, they illustrate how CSS type selectors are used.

Class Selectors

Class selectors are used to target more specific elements within a page. For example, if you want a single special paragraph to be colored differently from all of the other paragraphs, you could use a class selector to identify it. Classes can be used multiple times on the same page. Using a class selector is a two-step process:

1. Identify the HTML element with a `class` attribute.

2. Create a CSS rule that targets that class.

This paragraph is identified with the classname "special".

```
<p>This is a paragraph.</p>
<p class="special">This is a special paragraph!</p>
<p>This is another normal paragraph. </p>
```

```
p {
    color: #ABAABA;
}

.special {
    color: #000000;
    font-size: 200%;
    font-weight: bold;
}
```

All regular paragraphs are colored light gray.

This CSS rule uses a class selector to identify the class "special". A darker color of black is specified in addition to a few other properties.

This is a paragraph.

This is a special paragraph!

This is another normal paragraph.

When rendered in the browser, only the "special" paragraph receives the formatting. The other paragraphs receive the light gray coloring from the p type selector rule and nothing else.

These rules must be followed when using class selectors:

- An HTML tag uses the `class` attribute with a value of the classname. This value does not begin with a dot.
  Example: `<h1 class="pageHeading">`

- A CSS rule uses the same classname, but must begin with a dot.
  Example: `.pageHeading {color:#630;}`

CSS Hooks and the <span> Tag

Sometimes you don't want to apply a CSS rule to an entire paragraph or heading block, but only to a select word or phrase. To accomplish this, you need to create *CSS hooks* in your HTML code. CSS hooks are places to hang your CSS and can be accomplished with the `<span>` tag.

Only the second paragraph uses the class "special".

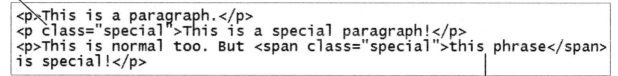

```
<p>This is a paragraph.</p>
<p class="special">This is a special paragraph!</p>
<p>This is normal too. But <span class="special">this phrase</span>
is special!</p>
```

The words *this phrase* are contained in a `<span>` tag that also uses the "special" class.

Anything using the "special" class receives the formatting.

Semantic Classnames

There is nothing magic about the classname "special". Only a few rules apply when choosing classnames:

- A classname should describe the function of the element—not the formatting.

- Classnames must begin with a letter, though numbers can be used within the name.

- Spaces cannot be used in classnames.

The classname "redText" describes the visual formatting. This is bad. If your client asks you to change the red text to green, the classname "redText" no longer accurately describes the class and could be very confusing when updating the site. Instead, a classname such as "special", "teaser", or "highlight" more accurately describes the meaning of the CSS rule and the function of the affected content. When the names describe the function rather than the visual formatting, it is known as *semantic naming*.

!TIP! *Make sure there is no space between the dot and the rest of the classname in your CSS rule.*

Hands-On 9.4   **Use Class Selectors and the <span> Tag**

In this exercise, you will use the <span> tag and class selectors.

Add <span> Tags

1. Switch to Notepad, locate the section beginning with the named anchor
`<a id="limits">`, and find the paragraph immediately following.

2. Follow these steps to add a `<span>` tag with a CSS hook:

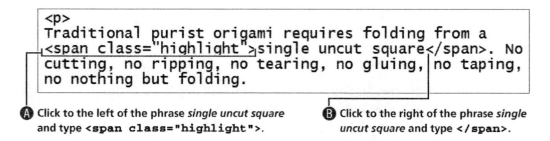

```
<p>
Traditional purist origami requires folding from a
<span class="highlight">single uncut square</span>. No
cutting, no ripping, no tearing, no gluing, no taping,
no nothing but folding.
```

A Click to the left of the phrase *single uncut square* and type **<span class="highlight">**.

B Click to the right of the phrase *single uncut square* and type **</span>**.

3. Locate the end of the next paragraph in the section beginning with the named anchor `<a id="vary">` and follow these steps to add another `<span>` tag:

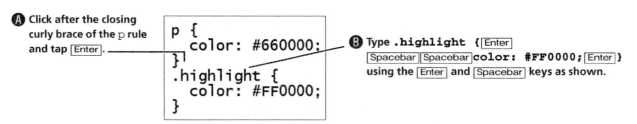

```
figures like this in the purist tradition of using an
<span class="highlight">uncut square</span>).
</p>
```

A Click to the left of the phrase *uncut square* and type **<span class="highlight">**.

B Click to the right of the phrase *uncut square* and type **</span>**.

Add CSS Rule with a Class Selector

4. Scroll towards the top of the document, locate the last CSS rule, and follow these steps to add a new rule:

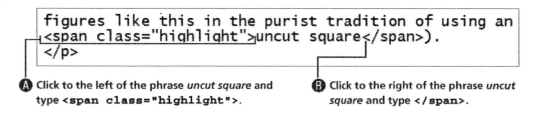

A Click after the closing curly brace of the p rule and tap Enter.

```
p {
    color: #660000;
}
.highlight {
    color: #FF0000;
}
```

B Type **.highlight** {[Enter] [Spacebar][Spacebar]**color: #FF0000;**[Enter]} using the [Enter] and [Spacebar] keys as shown.

5. Save your changes, switch to your browser, and tap [F5].
The second and third FAQ answers display the spanned phrases in red because the highlight class has been applied to them.

Id Selectors

An id selector is similar to a class selector in that it is used to target a specific element on the page. However, an id must be unique on the page (while a class can be used multiple times). For this reason, ids are more often used to identify structural regions that appear once per page, such as the masthead or footer. The steps to using id selectors are similar to those for using classes:

1. First, identify the HTML element with an `id` attribute.

2. Then, create a CSS rule that targets that id.

The following rules must be followed when using id selectors:

- An HTML tag uses the `id` attribute with a unique value on the page. Example: `<div id="maincontent">`

- A CSS rule uses the same id but must begin with a pound symbol. Example: `#maincontent {color:#630;}`

Just as with classes, an id must begin with a letter and cannot contain spaces.

 TIP! *Make sure there is no space between the pound symbol and the rest of the id name in your CSS rule. So,* `# maincontent` *will not work, but* `#maincontent` *will.*

 Hands-On 9.5   Use Id Selectors

In this exercise, you will use id selectors.

1. Switch to Notepad, scroll to the bottom of the document, and locate the paragraph containing the copyright.
   You will identify this paragraph as the footer.

2. Follow these steps to add an `id` attribute:

A Click inside the paragraph tag to the right of the p and tap Spacebar.

```
<p id="footer">Folding Under Pressure &copy; 2007</p>
```

B Type `id="footer"` to uniquely identify the paragraph.

3. Scroll towards the top of the document and locate the last CSS rule (the `.highlight` class).

4. Follow these steps to create a rule with an id selector:

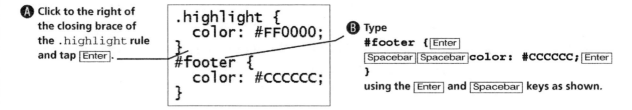

A Click to the right of the closing brace of the .highlight rule and tap Enter.

```
.highlight {
    color: #FF0000;
}
#footer {
    color: #CCCCCC;
}
```

B Type
#footer { Enter
Spacebar Spacebar color: #CCCCCC; Enter
}
using the Enter and Spacebar keys as shown.

5. Save your changes, switch to your browser, and tap F5.

6. Scroll to the bottom of the web page to view the footer paragraph.
The footer paragraph is gray because the #footer rule has been applied to it.

Grouped Selectors

Types, classes, and ids can be combined into group selectors, allowing you to apply a single group of declarations to several page elements. For example, if you wanted all the <h1> headings red, you could write this:

```
h1 { color: #FF0000; }
```

If you want all the <h2> and <h3> headings to also be red, you could write this:

```
h2 { color: #FF0000; }
h3 { color: #FF0000; }
```

Your CSS is getting a little bloated because the same color declaration is being repeated. Instead, you can group the selectors together into a single rule using commas to separate them, like this:

```
h1, h2, h3 { color: #FF0000; }
```

This means, "Apply the color red to all <h1>, all <h2>, and all <h3> elements."

Grouped selectors can include types, classes, and ids. The following is also valid.

```
p, #footer, .highlight { color: #FF0000; }
```

That makes all paragraphs, the unique element with id="footer", and any element with class="highlight" red.

TIP! *Grouped selectors must be separated by commas.*

Hands-On 9.6 **Use Grouped Selectors**

In this exercise, you will use grouped selectors to color all headings the same.

1. Switch to Notepad, scroll towards the top of the document, and locate the first CSS rule for the <h3> elements.

2. Follow these steps to edit the existing rule:

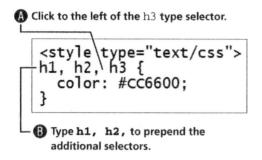

Ⓐ Click to the left of the h3 type selector.

```
<style type="text/css">
h1, h2, h3 {
    color: #CC6600;
}
```

Ⓑ Type **h1, h2,** to prepend the additional selectors.

3. Save your changes, switch to your browser, and tap F5.
The <h1> page heading (Resources), the <h2> section heading (FAQs), and each <h3> question are all the same color because they are all part of the same rule.

Bloated Code

Many developers new to CSS tend to bloat their code by using excessive classes (known as *classitis*) or excessive <div> tags (known as *divitis*). For example, imagine a client wanted each paragraph containing a question in the following page to be red.

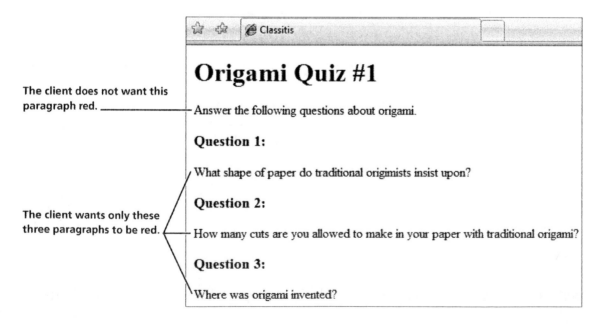

The client does not want this paragraph red.

The client wants only these three paragraphs to be red.

One option would be to use classes in each of the three paragraphs.

No class is
added to this
paragraph.

The same class
is used in
these three
paragraphs.

```
<h1>Origami Quiz #1</h1>
<p>Answer the following questions about origami.</p>

<h3>Question 1:</h3>
<p class="origamiQuestion">What shape of paper do traditional
origimists insist upon?</p>

<h3>Question 2:</h3>
<p class="origamiQuestion">How many cuts are you allowed to make in
your paper with traditional origami?</p>

<h3>Question 3:</h3>
<p class="origamiQuestion">Where was origami invented?</p>
```

Then, by creating this rule...

```
.origamiQuestion {color: #FF0000; }
```

...all of the questions would become red. However, this is an excessive use of classes. A better solution is to enclose all the questions in a `<div>` tag and use an id.

A single `<div>` tag with `id="origamiQuestions"` contains all the question paragraphs.

The paragraph
tags do not
contain any
attributes. No
class. No
id.

```
<div id="origamiQuestions">
<h3>Question 1:</h3>
<p>What shape of paper do traditional origimists insist upon?</p>

<h3>Question 2:</h3>
<p>How many cuts are you allowed to make in your paper with
traditional origami?</p>

<h3>Question 3:</h3>
<p>Where was origami invented?</p>
</div>
```

The CSS rule would be written with an id selector like this:

```
#origamiQuestions { color: #FF0000; }
```

The only problem with this is that all the text inside the `<div>` tag—the paragraphs and the `<h3>` headings—becomes red. The client wants only the paragraphs red, not the `<h3>` headings. The rest of the solution lies with descendant selectors.

Descendant Selectors

A descendant selector targets an element that is nested inside another element. For example, this code...

```
p a { color: #0000FF; }
```

...targets only anchor tags (hyperlinks) inside of paragraphs. Descendant selectors are similar to grouped selectors in that multiple selectors are included in the CSS rule. However, descendant selectors are separated by spaces whereas grouped selectors are separated by commas. These two rules are completely different:

```
p a { color: #0000FF; }
p, a { color: #0000FF; }
```

The first rule uses descendant selectors and translates to "Make all anchors **nested inside** paragraphs blue." The second rule translates to "Make all paragraphs **and** all anchors blue."

 Hands-On 9.7   Use Descendant Selectors

In this exercise, you will use descendant selectors to target elements nested inside other elements.

Create a CSS Hook

1. Switch to Notepad and locate the closing `</ol>` tag and the `<hr />` tag that follows it.

2. Follow these steps to insert a structural `<div>` tag:

Ⓐ Click in the blank line below the `<hr />` tag and tap [Enter].

Ⓑ Type `<div id="faqAnswers">` to begin the division.

```
</ol>
<hr />

<div id="faqAnswers">
<a id="whatis"></a>
```

3. Scroll down to the last answer just before the final `<hr />` tag and footer and follow these steps to close the division:

Ⓐ Click to the left of the `<hr />` tag.

Ⓑ Type `</div>` and tap [Enter] twice to close the division and create white space.

```
</p>
</div>

<hr />
<p id="footer">Folding Under Pressure &copy; 2007</p>
```

Create the CSS Rule

4. Scroll towards the top of the document and locate the last CSS rule for the #footer.

5. Follow these steps to use descendant selectors:

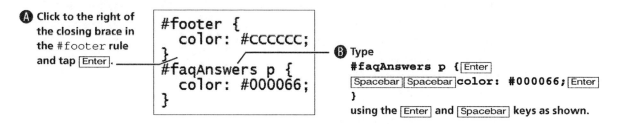

A Click to the right of the closing brace in the #footer rule and tap Enter.

```
#footer {
    color: #CCCCCC;
}
#faqAnswers p {
    color: #000066;
}
```

B Type

`#faqAnswers p {`Enter
Spacebar Spacebar`color: #000066;`Enter
`}`

using the Enter and Spacebar keys as shown.

You have targeted all the paragraphs inside the #faqAnswers element.

6. Save your changes, switch to your browser, and tap F5.
The top paragraph under the page heading Resources has not changed, but all the paragraphs in the #faqAnswers sections have turned blue.

Pseudo-class Selectors

Pseudo-classes are special selectors that can be used to style hyperlinks. The syntax for the selector consists of the anchor type selector followed by a colon and finally the hyperlink state, for example, a:link or a:visited. There are four link states you can style with CSS, and they must be listed in the following specific order or they will not work.

■ **Link**—The normal state a hyperlink is in when the page is first viewed

■ **Visited**—A link after it has been clicked

■ **Hover**—A link as a user is pointing to it with their mouse

■ **Active**—A link that is actively being clicked

TIP! *The simple mnemonic, "CSS is a LoVe HAte relationship" will help you remember LVHA: link, visited, hover, active.*

A typical block of code to style links may look like this:

```
a:link { color: #000066; }
a:visited { color: #000066; }
a:hover { color: #660000; }
a:active { color: #660000; }
```

Very often, the link and visited states are the same colors, while the hover and active states are the same colors. Of course, this is just personal preference. If that is the case for your links, you can use grouped selectors to reduce code bloat as long as you remember LoVe HAte:

```
a:link, a:visited { color: #000066; }
a:hover, a:active { color: #660000; }
```

In this exercise, you will use pseudo-classes to style hyperlinks.

1. Switch to Notepad and locate the last CSS rule towards the top of the document (the #faqAnswers rule).

2. Click after the closing curly brace in the #faqAnswers rule and tap `Enter`.

3. Type the following to style the hyperlinks with color using the `Enter` key as necessary to create line breaks:

```
a:link, a:visited {
  color: #000066;
}
a:hover, a:active {
  color: #CC0000;
}
```

4. Save your changes, switch to your browser, and tap `F5`.

5. Point to a few links to see the hover state color.
   All the links on the page are dark blue. When you point to a link, it turns red.

Using External Stylesheets

The problem with embedded styles is that the styles can only be used by the page in which they are embedded. You still have to re-create all of your styles in the other HTML pages. And if a client wants a change, every page's embedded styles need to be edited. This is clearly not efficient. The best way to work with styles is with external style sheets. The workflow is as follows:

1. Create your HTML pages with structural XHTML using <div> tags, class attributes, and id attributes to identify page elements.

2. Create a single CSS file containing all of your CSS rules and nothing else. This file must be saved with the .css file extension.

3. Link each HTML page to the shared CSS file.

By using a single linked CSS file, a change to a CSS rule affects every HTML page linked to it. This makes it possible to update the visual appearance of hundreds of pages at once by editing a single CSS rule.

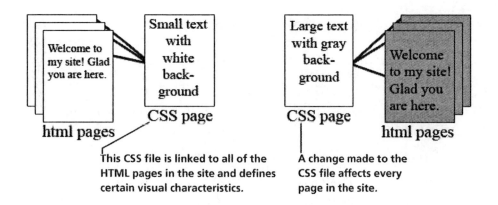

This CSS file is linked to all of the HTML pages in the site and defines certain visual characteristics.

A change made to the CSS file affects every page in the site.

Linking to an External Stylesheet

Linking to a CSS file from an HTML file requires a single line of code.

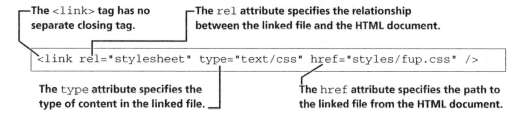

The `<link>` tag has no separate closing tag.

The `rel` attribute specifies the relationship between the linked file and the HTML document.

```
<link rel="stylesheet" type="text/css" href="styles/fup.css" />
```

The `type` attribute specifies the type of content in the linked file.

The `href` attribute specifies the path to the linked file from the HTML document.

If your HTML page already uses embedded styles, the steps to migrate to an external stylesheet are as follows:

1. Select and cut the embedded styles inside the `<style>` tag.

2. Create a new document, paste the cut styles, and save the document with the .css file extension.

3. Return to the HTML document and delete the now empty `<style></style>` tags.

4. Use the `<link>` tag to link to the new stylesheet.

5. Add the `<link>` tag to the other pages in your site.

Hands-On 9.9   Use External Stylesheets

In this exercise, you will create and link to an external stylesheet.

Cut the Styles from the HTML Document

1. Switch to Notepad and locate the first CSS rule. It should start with the `h1, h2, h3` grouped selectors.

2. Click to the left of the grouped selectors.

3. Scroll down, if necessary, and locate the last CSS rule. It should start with the `a:hover, a:active` grouped pseudo-classes.

4. Use Shift +click to the right of the closing curly brace of this last CSS rule.
   The entire block of CSS rules is selected.

5. Choose Edit→Cut from the menu bar. Your `<style>` block should look like the following figure.

```
<style type="text/css">

</style>
```

6. Save your changes and choose File→New from the menu bar.
   The current document closes and a new blank Notepad document appears.

Create the External CSS Document

7. Choose Edit→Paste from the menu bar.
   The styles you cut earlier are pasted into the blank document.

8. Choose File→Save As from the menu bar.

9. Navigate to your Lesson 09 folder, then into the fup_css folder, then into the styles folder.

10. Type **fup.css** as the filename and click Save.

Link to the CSS File

11. Choose File→Open from the menu bar.

12. Navigate to your Lesson 09 folder, then into the fup_css folder.
    Notepad doesn't display any HTML files in the Open dialog because the filter is set to Text Documents (.txt).*

13. Set the file type filter to show all files and open the resources.htm file.

14. Select the `<style></style>` tags and tap Backspace to delete them.

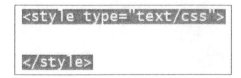

15. Save your changes, switch to your browser, and tap ⌷F5⌷.
    All of the color formatting disappears because you have removed the styles.

16. With your cursor still above the closing </head> tag, type the following:

    ```
    <link rel="stylesheet" type="text/css" href="styles/fup.css" />
    ```

17. Save your changes, switch to your browser, and tap ⌷F5⌷.
    All of the color formatting reappears because you have linked to the external stylesheet.

Attach the Stylesheet to Additional Pages

18. Switch to Notepad and open the howto.htm page.

19. Click above the closing </head> tag and type the following:

    ```
    <link rel="stylesheet" type="text/css" href="styles/fup.css" />
    ```

20. Save your changes.

21. Using instructions similar to steps 18–20, add the **<link rel="stylesheet" type="text/css" href="styles/fup.css" />** code to the following pages:
    - contact.htm
    - gal_fluffy.htm
    - gal_knife.htm
    - gal_present.htm
    - gallery.htm

    You will link the CSS document to the index page later in a Skill Builder.

Editing a Stylesheet

One of the benefits of using an external stylesheet is the ease of site maintenance. A single change to the stylesheet can affect every page that uses it.

 Hands-On 9.10   **Edit an External Stylesheet**

In this exercise, you will edit the external stylesheet and see how it affects all pages in the site that uses it.

1. If necessary, open the gallery.htm page in your browser; click through several hyperlinks and navigate through the site.
   Notice how all of the headings are burnt orange and all the paragraph text is blue or dark red. Also, no text in table cells is formatted. This is true of every page except the index page. The index page is the only page that is not linked to the external CSS file.

2. Switch to Notepad and choose File→Open from the menu bar.

3. Navigate to your Lesson 09 folder, then into the fup_css folder, then into the styles folder.
   Notepad doesn't display your CSS file in the Open dialog because the filter is set to Text Documents (.txt).*

4. Set the file type filter to show all files and open the fup.css file.
   The current document closes and the CSS file opens in Notepad.

5. Follow these steps to edit the colors:

```
h1, h2, h3 {
    color: #000033;
}

p {
    color: #333333;
}

.highlight {
    color: #660000;
}
```

Ⓐ Change the color of the headings to **#000033** (dark blue). You can also use the hex-3 code #003.

Ⓑ Change the color of the paragraphs to **#333333** (dark gray). You can also use the hex-3 code #333.

Ⓒ Change to color of the .highlight to **#660000** (dark red). You can also use the hex-3 code #600.

6. Change the color of the #footer rule to **#999999** (a slightly darker gray than the original color).

7. Change the color of the #faqAnswers p rule to **#333333** to match the regular paragraphs.

8. Add the following new rule at the bottom of the stylesheet:

   body {
     background: #F6E0BB;
   }

9. Save your changes, switch to your browser, and tap F5.

10. Navigate to a few of the pages and notice that the text color has changed for the headings, paragraph text, and .highlight on all pages (except the index page). Also, the page background is now a light brown instead of white.

11. Close your browser and Notepad.

# Concepts Review

True/False Questions

1. For a high level of accessibility, you should use red text on a green background or vice versa.   TRUE   FALSE

2. The more color your web page has, the more exciting and engaging it will be for visitors.   TRUE   FALSE

3. HTML can refer to colors by a color name or a binary color code.   TRUE   FALSE

4. You should limit your colors to the 216 color web-safe palette so your page displays consistently among different modern computer monitors.   TRUE   FALSE

5. Using CSS rather than presentational HTML markup can speed up the load time of your page.   TRUE   FALSE

6. Using CSS rather than presentational HTML markup can make your website easier to edit and maintain.   TRUE   FALSE

7. CSS can be applied inline, embedded, or via an external stylesheet.   TRUE   FALSE

8. A CSS rule targets HTML elements with selectors.   TRUE   FALSE

9. A CSS rule can contain as many declarations as you want, provided they are separated by semicolons.   TRUE   FALSE

10. Grouped selectors can reduce the code bloat of your CSS.   TRUE   FALSE

Multiple Choice Questions

1. Lauren wants just the paragraphs inside her `<div class="highlight"></div>` tags to be red. She has the following CSS rule in her code: `.highlight, p {color: red; }`.
   Every paragraph in her page is red instead of just the paragraphs in the `<div class="highlight"></div>` tags. What is the problem?
   a. She has the selectors backwards. It should be `p, .highlight`.
   b. She has used grouped selectors instead of descendant selectors. She needs to remove the comma so the selector is `.highlight p`.
   c. She forgot the dot in front of the `<div>` tag's classname. It should be `<div class=".highlight">`.
   d. There should not be a dot in front of the `highlight` selector in the CSS rule. It should be `highlight, p`.

2. Pasha has edited his `<body>` tag to set the page background blue. His code is as follows: `<body bgcolor="#00F">`. However, his page background is black instead! What is the problem?
   a. He has the wrong hexadecimal color code. The hexadecimal code he used, `#00F`, specifies black.
   b. His hexadecimal color code should not start with the pound symbol. His code should simply be `<body bgcolor="00F">`.
   c. It is invalid to use hexadecimal color codes in HTML tags. He must use a named color.
   d. It is invalid to use hex-3 color codes in HTML attributes (except the `style` attribute). He must specify the full hex-6 as `<body bgcolor="#0000FF">`.

3. What is one major difference between class selectors and id selectors?
   a. The same class may be used multiple times on the same page while an id must be unique and can be used only once on a page.
   b. The same id may be used multiple times on the same page while a class must be unique and can be used only once on a page.
   c. There is no difference. "Class" and "id" are different names for the same thing.
   d. Classes may only be used with embedded styles while ids may only be used with external stylesheets.

4. Zoe wishes to apply the same set of CSS declarations to several HTML elements. What type of selectors should she use?
   a. Descendant selectors
   b. Grouped selectors
   c. Pseudo-class selectors
   d. Deprecated selectors

Skill Builders

Create HTML Hooks

In this exercise, you will create <span> tags and add classes and ids to create hooks on which to attach CSS.

Use <span> Tags

You will wrap Haylie's name with a <span> tag so you can later emphasize it with CSS.

1. Start Notepad and open the index.htm page from the sb_color folder in your Lesson 09 folder.

2. Locate the first <p> tag after the <h2>The Artist</h2> tags and follow these steps to create a span:

Ⓐ **Click to the left of the name** Haylie Elise **and type** **<span class="highlight">** **to begin the span.**

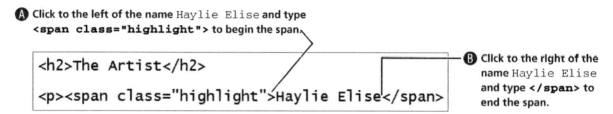

```
<h2>The Artist</h2>

<p><span class="highlight">Haylie Elise</span>
```

Ⓑ **Click to the right of the name** Haylie Elise **and type </span> to end the span.**

Although highlight *is used only once on this page, you are using it as a class instead of an id because it may be used more than once on another page.*

Use Ids

3. Scroll to the bottom of the document and locate the last paragraph with the copyright information.

4. Follow these steps to uniquely identify the footer:

Ⓐ **Click inside the opening** <p> **tag after the letter "p."**

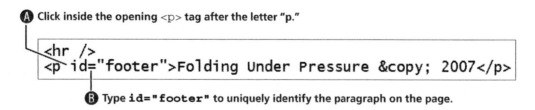

```
<hr />
<p id="footer">Folding Under Pressure &copy; 2007</p>
```

Ⓑ **Type** id="footer" **to uniquely identify the paragraph on the page.**

5. Save your changes.

6. Start your web browser and open the same index.htm page from the sb_color folder in your Lesson 09 folder.
Nothing changes in the browser. You have added CSS hooks but have not added any CSS to the page yet. The other pages in the site already have the footer identified.

Skill Builder 9.2   Create an External Stylesheet

In this exercise, you will create an external stylesheet with a few base styles.

Before You Begin: You must complete Skill Builder 9.1 before beginning this exercise.

Create an External Stylesheet

1. Switch to Notepad and choose File→New from the menu bar.
   The index.htm page closes and a new blank document appears.

2. Type the following to create basic styles (you may want to use additional white space between each rule to aid readability):

```
body {
  background: #F6E0BB;
}
h1, h2, h3 {
  color: #006;
}
.highlight {
  color: #600;
}
#footer {
  color: #999;
}
a:link, a:visited {
  color: #00C;
}
a:hover, a:active {
  color: #C00;
}
```

3. Choose File→Save As.

4. Navigate to your Lesson 09 folder, then into the sb_color folder, then into the styles folder.

5. Name your file **fup_base_styles.css** and click Save.

Skill Builder 9.3   Link to and Edit an External Stylesheet

In this exercise, you will link your external stylesheet to all pages in your site. You will then edit the external stylesheet to see how one change can affect an entire site.

Link to an External Stylesheet

1. Choose File→Open from Notepad's menu bar and open the index.htm file from the sb_color folder in your Lesson 09 folder.

2. Click in the space above the closing `</head>` tag and type the following to link to the external stylesheet:

   `<link href="styles/fup_base_styles.css" rel="stylesheet"`
   `type="text/css" />`

   You have specified a relative link from the index page to the stylesheet.

3. Save your changes, switch to your browser, and tap F5.
   The homepage displays the new colors for the page background, headings, hyperlinks, highlighted text, and footer. If it didn't, go back and make sure the value specified in your href *attribute of the* `<link />` *tag correctly points to the stylesheet you created in Skill Builder 9.2.*

4. Switch back to Notepad.

5. Select the entire `<link />` tag and choose Edit→Copy from the menu bar.

```
<meta http-equiv="Content-Type" content="text/html;charset=utf-8" />
<link rel="stylesheet" type="text/css" href="styles/fup_base_styles.css" />
</head>
```

6. Choose File→Open and open the contact.htm page from the sb_color folder inside your Lesson 09 folder.

7. Click in the space above the closing `</head>` tag and choose Edit→Paste from the menu bar.
   The `<link>` *tag is pasted into the contact page.*

8. Save your changes.

9. Using instructions similar to steps 5–7, paste the `<link />` tag into the following pages:
   - gal_fluffy.htm
   - gal_knife.htm
   - gal_present.htm
   - gallery.htm
   - howto.htm
   - resources.htm

10. Switch to your browser and tap F5.

11. Navigate the site and ensure all pages display the same colors from the linked external CSS file.

Edit the Stylesheet

12. Switch to Notepad and open the fup_base_styles.css file from the styles folder.

13. Change the color of the grouped heading rule to **#543B11** so the rule looks like this:

```
h1, h2, h3 {
   color: #543B11;
}
```

14. Save your changes, switch to your browser, and tap [F5].

15. Navigate the site and ensure that all pages display the new brown color for the headings.

16. Close your web browser and Notepad.

 # Assessments

Assessment 9.1   Create CSS Hooks and Link to an External Stylesheet

In this exercise, you will create CSS hooks and structure your pages for CSS. You will link to a yet-to-be-created external stylesheet.

Ready the Index Page

1. Start Notepad and open the index.htm page from the as_riffworld folder in your Lesson 09 folder.

2. Remove all the attributes from the opening `<body>` tag so the tag is simply `<body>`.

3. Click in the space above the closing `</head>` tag and type **`<link href="styles/baseriff.css" rel="stylesheet" type="text/css" />`** to create a link to an external stylesheet.
   You will create the actual stylesheet in the next activity.

4. Type **`id="footer"`** in the last `<p>` tag in the document to uniquely identify the page footer. Be sure to leave a space between the tag name and the attribute.

5. Enclose the page heading and the two paragraphs following in a **`<div>`** tag with an **`id`** of **`masthead`**.

```
<body>

<div id="masthead">
<h1>Riff World</h1>
<p>Are your fingers ready?</p>
<p><a href="index.htm">Home</a> | <a href="poprock.htm">80's Pop
Rock</a> | <a href="hardrock.htm">Hard Rock</a></p>
</div>
```

Ready the Hardrock Page

6. Open the hardrock.htm file from the sb_riffworld folder in your Lesson 09 folder in Notepad.

7. Click in the space above the closing `</head>` tag and type **`<link href="styles/baseriff.css" rel="stylesheet" type="text/css" />`** to create a link to an external stylesheet.

8. Using instructions similar to steps 4 and 5, use an `id` attribute to identify the footer and a `<div>` tag to identify the masthead.

9. Create another **`<div>`** tag with **`id="riffs"`** that contains the `<a id="smoke"></a>` named anchor down to the `back to top` paragraph below the "Crazy Train" riff.

10. Use <span> tags and class attributes with the values band and song to identify the band names and song names in the "Smoke on the Water" paragraph.

   ■ **<span class="band">**Deep Purple's**</span>**

   ■ **<span class="song">**Smoke on the Water**</span>**

   ■ **<span class="band">**Frank Zappa**</span>**

11. Use <span> tags and class attributes with the values band and song to identify the band names and song names in the "Crazy Train" paragraph.

   ■ **<span class="band">**Ozzy Osbourne's**</span>**

   ■ **<span class="song">**Crazy Train**</span>**

   ■ **<span class="band">**Randy Rhoads**</span>**

12. Save your changes.

Ready the Poprock Page

13. Open the poprock.htm file from the sb_riffworld folder in your Lesson 09 folder in Notepad.

14. Click in the space above the closing </head> tag and type **<link href="styles/baseriff.css" rel="stylesheet" type="text/css" />** to create a link to an external stylesheet.

15. Using instructions similar to steps 4 and 5, use an id attribute to identify the footer and a <div> tag to identify the masthead.

16. Create another **<div>** tag with **id="riffs"** that contains the <a id="jenny"></a> named anchor down to the back to top paragraph below the "Jessie's Girl" riff.

17. Use <span> tags and class attributes with the values band and song to identify the band names and song names in the "967-5309 (Jenny)" paragraph.

   ■ **<span class="band">**Tommy Tutone's**</span>**

   ■ **<span class="song">**967-5309 (Jenny)**</span>**

   ■ FYI - **<span class="band">**Tommy Tutone**</span>** is the …

18. Use <span> tags and class attributes with the values band and song to identify the band names and song names in the "Jessie's Girl" paragraph.

   ■ **<span class="band">**Rick Springfield's**</span>**

   ■ **<span class="song">**Jessie's Girl**</span>**

   ■ **<span class="band">**Sammy Hagar's**</span>**

   ■ **<span class="song">**I've Done Everything For You**</span>**

19. Save your changes.

20. Start your web browser and open the index.htm file from the as_riffworld folder in your Lesson 09 folder.

21. Use the navigation bar on the web page to navigate all three pages.
If any pages display improperly, go back and fix them before continuing. If there are any errors, they should be obvious—like HTML code itself displaying in the browser window.

Assessment 9.2   Create Type, Class, and Id Selector Rules

In this exercise, you will create CSS rules with type, class, and id selectors.

Before You Begin: *You must complete Assessment 9.1 before beginning this exercise.*

1. Switch to Notepad and choose File→New from the menu bar.
The current page closes and a new blank document appears.

2. Type the following rule to explicitly set the page background to white. Use white space where appropriate:

```
body {
   background: #FFF;
}
```

3. Create the following rule for the id footer to color it gray:

```
#footer {
   color: #777;
}
```

4. Create the following rule for the band and song classes to color them dark red:

```
.band {
   color: #600;
}
.song {
   color: #600;
}
```

You will vary these rules in later lessons.

5. Save the file as **baseriff.css** to the styles folder inside the as_riffworld folder.

Assessment 9.3　Create Advanced Selector Rules

In this exercise, you will create CSS rules with advanced selectors.

Group Selectors

1. Create a new rule in the baseriff.css document that groups the h1, h2, h3, and h4 type selectors and colors them #606. Remember to use commas to separate the grouped selectors.

Group Pseudo-classes

2. Create a new rule that groups the a:link and a:visited pseudo-class selectors and colors them #660.

3. Create a new rule that groups the a:hover and a:active pseudo-class selectors and colors them #609.

Create Descendant Selectors

4. Create the following new rule that targets only paragraphs inside the #masthead and makes them #606:

```
#masthead p {
   color: #606;
}
```

Group Descendant Pseudo-classes

5. Create the following new rule that groups the a:link and a:visited pseudo-classes inside the #masthead and colors them #006:

```
#masthead a:link, #masthead a:visited {
   color: #006;
}
```

6. Create a new rule that groups the a:hover and a:active pseudo-classes inside the #masthead and colors them #900.

7. Save your changes, switch to your browser, and tap [F5].

8. Navigate the pages in the site.
   The colors display as specified in the external stylesheet. Only the paragraph in the masthead is purple. All other paragraphs are black. The links in the masthead are colored differently than the links on the rest of the page. The footer is gray.

9. Close your web browser and Notepad.

Critical Thinking

Critical Thinking 9.1   Ready a Document for CSS

In this exercise, you will remove presentational code from an HTML document and get it ready for CSS. You will be working with the files inside the ct_balloons folder within your Lesson 09 folder.

Starting with the index.htm page, complete the following actions:

- Remove all attributes from the `<body>` tag.

- Create a `<div>` container for the masthead that contains the two headings and the navigation bar at the top of the document.

- Use `<span>` tags with classes to identify several words or phrases of your choice. Specify at least two different classnames and use them several times on the page.

- Add a footer at the bottom of the page with a new `<p>` tag or create a new `<div>` tag. Make sure to use an `id` attribute to uniquely identify it.

- Create a link to a stylesheet in the styles folder. Choose any filename you like for the stylesheet, but remember it because you will have to create it in the next exercise.

- Save your changes, then repeat the above steps on the twists.htm page.

Critical Thinking 9.2   Create External CSS

In this exercise, you will create and code an external stylesheet.

Create a blank stylesheet saved to the styles folder. Be sure to use the filename you specified in Critical Thinking 9.1.

Create the following rules to specify colors with the following selectors:

- At least one type selector not in a group

- At least two class selectors not in a group

- At least one grouped selector

- At least one descendant selector that includes an id

- At least four pseudo-classes to color the hyperlinks; can be separate or grouped

Test your pages in the browser and ensure that the colors display as expected on both HTML pages.

Using CSS to Style Text

In this lesson, you will learn a few basics of typography. You will then use CSS to visually format many properties of text, including the typeface, size, variants, decorations, and alignment. You will then use shorthand to reduce CSS code bloat.

LESSON OBJECTIVES

After studying this lesson, you will be able to:

- Differentiate between a font and a typeface
- Identify standard typefaces
- Format many characteristics of text

Case Study: Formatting Text with CSS

Now that the content for the Folding Under Pressure site is in place, Haylie feels it is time to make it a little more visually appealing. Using an external stylesheet, Haylie easily formats all the text throughout the entire site with just a few CSS rules.

Masthead hyperlinks are set in small caps.

Serif fonts have been specified for the headings.

Main body text uses a sans-serif font.

Main body hyperlinks have the underline removed but display both an underline and an overline when pointed to.

The footer is smaller and italicized.

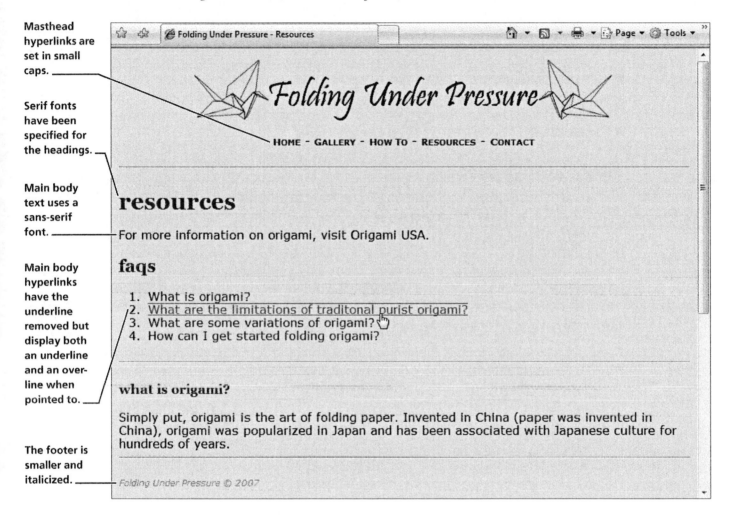

Designing Tip: Typography

The process of working with type, or text and lettering, is called *typography*. Huge volumes have been written on typography and it is a much deeper subject than many people realize. As a web developer, there are a few basic guidelines to working with type:

- Specify standard fonts.

- Large blocks of centered text look amateurish.

- Try to stick to no more than three different fonts per page.

- Page width should not exceed 52 characters.

- Sans-serif type is easier to read on the web.

Fonts and Typefaces

The terms *font* and *typeface* are often used interchangeably, though they are not really the same thing. A font is a subset of a typeface. A typeface normally refers to a family of fonts, such as the Arial family or the Helvetica family. These families may also be referred to as a *face*. The term "font" refers to a specific weight, width, and style of a typeface. For example, Arial, bold, and size 14 pixels is a font. Arial itself is a font family or typeface. CSS properties use the term font, so that is the term used in this book (even when technically it is a typeface).

Use Standard Font Families

There are a few fonts that every computer has, though these may differ between a MAC and a PC. Using standard fonts ensures that users will see your page as intended. If you choose to use a font that is on your computer but no one else's, your web page will not be displayed as expected on other computers. The web browser will substitute its default font, which may throw off your layout.

The Art

The word origami stems from two Japanese words and Kami (meaning paper). The ancient art of p China around the first or second century A.D. a by about the sixth century.

A non-standard font may look good on your computer...

The Art

The word origami stems from two Japanese words (meaning to fold) and Kami (meaning paper). The ancient art of paper folding originated in China arc the first or second century A.D. and made its way t Japan by about the sixth century.

...but if other users don't have that font installed, the pages display with the browser's default font, which may throw off your layout.

STANDARD FONTS

Font	Sample
Arial	This is the Arial font.
Helvetica	This is the Helvetica font.
Verdana	This is the Verdana font.
Times New Roman	This is the Times New Roman font.
Georgia	This is the Georgia font.
Courier New	This is the Courier New font.

Avoid Centered Text

When an entire web page displays centered text, the result is amateurish. Avoid centering large blocks of text.

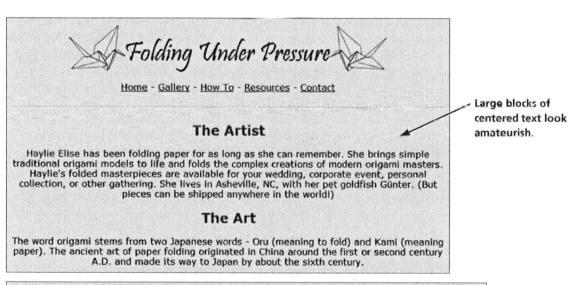

Large blocks of centered text look amateurish.

Use left-aligned text for the bulk of your content.

Less Is More

Stick to no more than three fonts throughout any single page. More than that distracts the reader's eye and makes text difficult to read.

The Artist

Haylie Elise has been folding paper for as long as she can remember. She brings simple traditional origami models to life and folds the complex creations of modern origami

---

Too many fonts on a page make a page difficult to read.

Limit Page Width

Long lines of text are difficult to read. When the reader's eyes reach the right end of a line, they must return to the left side of the next line. Having to travel a long distance makes this tracking difficult. Optimal page width should not exceed about 60 characters (usability studies typically recommend a range of 52–70 characters). For this reason, you may want to limit the width of your content by enclosing it in a table or `<div>` tag with a width specified.

Serif and Sans-serif

Serif fonts have extra non-structural enhancements appended to the letter shapes. They are non-structural because without them, it would still be clear what the letter is. Serif fonts tend to be easier to read in print. The opposite is true for text on the web. When reading text on a computer screen, text without the serifs, a sans-serif font, is easier to read. The exception is with large headings. For visual interest, it is nice to vary the font in headings to a serif font. But the bulk of page text should be sans-serif.

A serif font has "feet," like on the ends of the capital "S" or the bottom of the "-rif." ———— # Serif

A sans-serif font is composed of clean lines. ———— # Sans-serif

STANDARD SERIF AND SANS-SERIF FONTS	
Font	**Serif or Sans-serif**
Arial	Sans-serif
Helvetica	Sans-serif
Verdana	Sans-serif
Times	Serif
Georgia	Serif
Courier	Serif

 TIP! *The Verdana font was specifically designed for use on a computer so it is very easy to read.*

Reviewing Font Characteristics

CSS allows you to specify many characteristics of type, including the typeface, size, weight, style, and line height. You can even transform text to uppercase, lowercase, or small caps.

Font-family

The `font-family` property is used to specify the typeface. If applied to a type selector of `body`, it will make all the text on your page use the family specified. However, some older browsers do not fully honor font settings on the `body` selector because they fail to apply the formatting to text inside paragraphs or table cells. Instead, using a grouped selector such as `body, p, td` ensures the font will be properly applied across all modern browsers. Multiple typefaces can be specified in a comma-separated list. The browser will attempt to use the first font specified and, if it is not installed, it will attempt to use the next one in the list and so on.

Grouped type selectors ensure that the rule is applied across all browsers.

```
body, p, td {
    font-family: arial, helvetica, sans-serif;
}
```

A comma-separated list of typefaces provides the browser with alternatives if the first choice is not installed.

 NOTE! *Typefaces are not case-sensitive, but many developers prefer to capitalize them because they are proper nouns. You can capitalize or not—just stay consistent.*

 Hands-On 10.1 **Specify the Font Family**

In this exercise, you will specify the typeface to be used for several HTML elements.

1. Start your web browser and open the index.htm file from the fup_fonts folder inside your Lesson 10 folder.
   The font displayed is most likely a serif font (unless your web browser settings have been changed).

2. Start Notepad and choose File→Open from the menu bar.

3. Open your Lesson 10 folder, then open the fup_fonts folder, then open the styles folder.

4. Open the fupstyles.css file from the styles folder. (Remember to set the file type filter to All Files.)

5. Follow these steps to specify the default font for the page:

A Click after the closing brace of the body rule and tap Enter twice to create white space.

```
body {
    background: #F6E0BB;
}

body, p, td {
    font-family: verdana, arial, helvetica, sans-serif;
}
```

B Type the rule for the grouped body, p, td selectors as shown. Be sure to separate the selectors with commas. Use white space where appropriate.

You created a new rule rather than adding the declaration to the existing body rule because you do not want to specify a background color for the p and td selectors.

6. Follow these steps to specify a typeface for the headings:

A Click after the color declaration and tap Enter Spacebar Spacebar to create white space.

```
h1, h2, h3 {
    color: #543B11;
    font-family: georgia, times, serif;
}
```

B Type font-family: georgia, times, serif; to specify the typeface for the headings.

7. Save your changes, switch to your web browser, and tap F5.
The page font changes to Verdana (or Arial or Helvetica, depending on your computer). The page headings change to Georgia (or Times, or your default serif font).

8. Navigate to other pages within the site.
The fonts specified in the external stylesheet are applied to every page in the site.

Font-size

There are three main units of measure you will use when specifying font sizes:

- Pixels
- Percents
- Ems

Using pixels specifies an absolute size. Most browsers default to about 12 or 14 pixels. Using percentages allows you to increase or decrease a font proportionally compared to the default font size. Using ems is similar to using percentages in that it is proportional. An "em" is often thought of as the width of the letter "m" in the current font. Though this is not exactly correct, it's a fair approximation. One em is the same as 100 percent, 1.5 em is the same as 150 percent, and 0.75 em is the same as 75 percent.

Line-height

The `line-height` property determines the vertical spacing between lines of text. Many designers from the world of print liken this CSS property to leading (pronounced *led-ing*). The `line-height` property is often specified in percentages and should be increased to aid the readability of large blocks of small text.

The Artist

Haylie Elise has been folding paper for as long as she can remember. She brings simple traditional origami models to life and folds the complex creations of modern origami masters. Haylie's folded masterpieces are available for your wedding, corporate event, personal collection, or other gathering. She lives in Asheville, NC, with her pet goldfish Günter. (But pieces can be shipped anywhere in the world!)

Small text with the default line height is difficult to read.

The Artist

Haylie Elise has been folding paper for as long as she can remember. She brings simple traditional origami models

to life and folds the complex creations of modern origami masters. Haylie's folded masterpieces are available for

your wedding, corporate event, personal collection, or other gathering. She lives in Asheville, NC, with her pet

goldfish Günter. (But pieces can be shipped anywhere in the world!)

Small text with increased line height is easier to read.

 Hands-On 10.2   Specify the Font Size and Line Height

In this exercise, you will specify the font size and line height of text.

1. Switch to Notepad and open the index.htm file from the fup_fonts folder in your Lesson 10 folder.

2. Locate the opening `<body>` tag and look at the HTML code immediately following it.
   The crane images and navigation bar are enclosed in a single `<div>` tag with `id="masthead"`. *All pages in the site have this same* `<div>` *structure. This is important to remember throughout the exercises in this lesson.*

3. Scroll to the bottom of the document and locate the final `<p>` tag.
   The last paragraph in the document is identified with `id="footer"`. *All pages in this site have this same footer structure. This is important to remember throughout the exercises in this lesson.*

4. Choose File→Open and navigate to the styles folder inside the fup_fonts folder.

5. Remember to change the file type filter to all files, then open the fupstyles.css stylesheet.

6. Locate the `body`, `p`, `td` rule and follow these steps to initialize the font size for the entire page:

Ⓐ **Click to the right of the font-family declaration and tap**
[Enter] [Spacebar] [Spacebar] **to create white space.** ⎯⎯⎯⎯⎯⎯⎯

```
body, p, td {
    font-family: verdana, arial, helvetica, sans-serif;
    font-size: 100%;
}
```

└─ Ⓑ **Type font-size: 100%; to initialize the font size.**

7. Locate the `#footer` rule and add **font-size: 75%;** to the rule to adjust the font size.

```
#footer {
  color: #999;
  font-size: 75%;
}
```

8. Scroll to the bottom of the document and add the following rule to reduce the size of the hyperlinks in the `#masthead` only.

```
#masthead a {
  font-size:80%;
}
```

9. Save your changes, switch to your browser, and tap `F5`.

10. Browse to a few pages, including the Contact and Resources pages.
The size of most of the text does not change as you initialized it to 100 percent. However, the hyperlinks in the masthead and the text in the footer are smaller in proportion to the page font.

Font-weight

The `font-weight` property is used to make text bold. A few browsers support numerical values, but most ignore it. The values you are likely to use are:

- **bold**—Makes text bold

- **normal**—Makes text the "normal," non-bold weight

Font-style

The `font-style` property is used to make text italic. The two most often used values are:

- **italic**—Makes text italicized

- **normal**—Makes text non-italicized

Font-variant

The `font-variant` property can be used to create small caps. The two most often used values are:

- **small-caps**—Creates small caps

- **normal**—Makes text non-small caps

Text-transform

The `text-transform` property can be used to make text display in uppercase, lowercase, or capitalized. For example, if your HTML code has the text "i like oriGaMi," applying either of the text transform values will make the text display as "i like origami," "I LIKE ORIGAMI," or "I Like Origami."

Hands-On 10.3 Adjust Font Weight, Style, Variant, and Transformation

In this exercise, you will make text bold and italic, create small caps, and change the text case.

Make Text Bold and Small Cap

1. Switch to Notepad, locate the rule at the bottom of the stylesheet for `#masthead a`, and add the following two new declarations to the rule to make the hyperlinks in the masthead bold and small caps:

   font-weight: bold;
   font-variant: small-caps;

   ```
   #masthead a {
      font-size:80%;
      font-weight: bold;
      font-variant: small-caps;
   }
   ```

2. Locate the `.highlight` rule and add the **font-weight: bold;** declaration.

   ```
   .highlight {
      color: #600;
      font-weight: bold;
   }
   ```

3. Save your changes, switch to your browser, and tap F5.

4. Navigate to a few pages, including the homepage and the Resources page.
   The hyperlinks in the masthead are bold and use small caps. Anywhere the `.highlight` *class is used (such as on Haylie's name on the index page and two phrases on the Resources page) the text is bold.*

Make Text Italic

5. Switch back to Notepad, locate the `#footer` rule, and add the **font-style: italic;** declaration to italicize the footer text.

   ```
   #footer {
      color: #999;
      font-size: 75%;
      font-style: italic;
   }
   ```

6. Save your changes, switch to your browser, tap F5, and navigate to a few pages.
   The text in the footer is italicized.

Adjust the Case of Words

7. Switch back to Notepad, locate the `body`, `p`, `td` rule, and add the **text-transform: capitalize;** declaration.

```
body, p, td {
    font-family: verdana, arial, helvetica, sans-serif;
    font-size: 100%;
    text-transform: capitalize;
}
```

8. Locate the `h1`, `h2`, `h3` rule and add the **text-transform: uppercase;** declaration.

```
h1, h2, h3 {
    color: #543B11;
    font-family: georgia, times, serif;
    text-transform: uppercase;
}
```

9. Save your changes, switch to your browser, tap ⟦F5⟧, and navigate to the homepage if necessary.
   The main body text is capitalized, making it very difficult to read. The headings are displayed in uppercase. It may look more "artsy" if the page headings were in lowercase.

10. Switch back to Notepad and follow these steps to adjust your CSS:

    🅐 **Delete the entire** `text-transform: capitalize;` **declaration from the** `body`, `p`, `td` **rule.**

```
body, p, td {
    font-family: verdana, arial, helvetica, sans-serif;
    font-size: 100%;
    text-transform: capitalize;
}

h1, h2, h3 {
    color: #543B11;
    font-family: georgia, times, serif;
    text-transform: lowercase;
}
```

🅑 **In the** `h1`, `h2`, `h3` **rule, change** uppercase **to** **lowercase.**

11. Save your changes, switch to your browser, and tap ⟦F5⟧.
    The text no longer displays in all capital letters. The headings display in lowercase letters.

Text-align

The `text-align` property is used to align content horizontally in a container. Its use is similar to that of the `align` attribute you used previously in this book.

Vertical-align

The `vertical-align` property can be used to vertically align content within the cell similar to the `valign` attribute you learned earlier in this book.

 Hands-On 10.4 Align Content

In this exercise, you will horizontally and vertically align content.

Horizontally Center the Masthead Content

1. Switch to Notepad, scroll to the bottom of the document, and add the following new rule to center all the content in the masthead:

```
#masthead {
   text-align: center;
}
```

2. Save your changes, switch to your browser, tap [F5], and navigate a few pages, stopping on the Contact page.
   The masthead content is horizontally centered on all pages.

   The Contact page uses a table to place the contact information and the nested price list side by side. The contact information is vertically centered in the cell. Shifting it to the top of its cell will look better. Only the gallery page also uses a table.

Vertically Align the Contact Info

3. Switch back to Notepad.
   Knowing that all content in all existing table cells should be top aligned, you will create a rule that applies to all table cells.

4. Create the following new rule at the bottom of the stylesheet to vertically align all cell content:

```
td {
   vertical-align: top;
}
```

5. Save your changes, switch to your browser, tap [F5], and navigate a few pages, stopping on the contact page.
   The contact information is top aligned in its table cell.

Text-decoration

The `text-decoration` property is used to underline, overline, or strike out text. This property is most often used to style hyperlinks. Using `text-decoration` to underline text is a bad idea, as users will think your underlined text is a hyperlink. However, using `text-decoration` to remove the underline from a hyperlink can add visual appeal. Decorations include:

- underline
- overline
- line-through
- none

Multiple decorations may be added to a single declaration by separating the decorations with spaces, like this:

```
text-decoration: underline overline;
```

However, a declaration like this...

```
text-decoration: underline none;
```

...would not display as expected. How can text have both an underline and none?!

The rules...

```
p {
text-decoration: underline;
}

p {
text-decoration: overline;
}

p {
text-decoration: line-through;
}

p {
text-decoration: underline overline line-through;
}
```

...create this formatting.

Of course, you would never have CSS code that specified four different paragraph rules as in this figure. If you did, the last rule would override the three previous rules!

In this exercise, you will style hyperlinks by removing the underline from the link state and adding an underline and an overline on the hover state.

1. Switch to Notepad, locate the a:link, a:visited rule, and add the **text-decoration: none;** declaration to remove the underline from the hyperlinks.

```
a:link, a:visited {
  color: #00C;
  text-decoration: none;
}
```

2. Locate the a:hover, a:active rule and add the **text-decoration: underline overline;** declaration to add both an underline and an overline to the hover and active link states.

```
a:hover, a:active {
  color: #C00;
  text-decoration: underline overline;
}
```

3. Save your changes, switch to your browser, tap ⌷F5⌷, and point to the hyperlinks in the navigation bar.
   The small-caps formatting may make the overline look "broken," depending on your browser.

In Internet Explorer, the overline appears broken as a result of the small caps. _____

4. Navigate to the Resources page and point to the hyperlinks in the FAQ section.
   These hyperlinks look fine.

5. Switch back to Notepad and locate the #masthead a rule.
   You will remove all decorations from the hyperlinks in the masthead.

6. Add the **text-decoration: none;** declaration to the #masthead a rule.

```
#masthead a {
   font-size:80%;
   font-weight: bold;
   font-variant: small-caps;
   text-decoration: none;
}
```

7. Save your changes, switch to your browser, tap ⌷F5⌷, and point to the hyperlinks in the navigation bar.
   The hyperlinks in the navigation bar no longer display decorations on any of their link states. The other hyperlinks in the main body do display their decorations on the hover and active states.

Font Shorthand

Any property that begins with "font-" may be written with font shorthand so that multiple declarations may be combined into a single declaration. Combining declarations helps to reduce code bloat. For example, this large block of CSS code...

```
#footer {
   font-family: arial, helvetica, sans-serif;
   font-size: 80%;
   font-style: italic;
}
```

...can be written as follows:

```
#footer {
   font: italic 80% arial, Helvetica, sans-serif;
}
```

A few rules apply when using font shorthand.

- Only properties that begin with "font-" may be combined.

- The values are separated by spaces.

- The values may appear in any order except that size and family must occur last and in that specific order (size, then family).

The following code is **invalid**.

```
#footer { font: bold italic 75%; }
```

It is invalid because it does not list the size followed by the family at the end.

The following code is **invalid**.

```
#footer { font: 110% arial, Helvetica, sans-serif bold; }
```

It is invalid because "bold" is at the end. The declaration must end with the size followed by the family.

The following code is **invalid**.

```
#footer { font: lowercase 110% arial, Helvetica, sans-serif; }
```

It is invalid because "lowercase" is a value of the `text-transform` property, not a "font-" property.

The following code is **valid**.

```
#footer { font: small-caps bold italic 110% arial, Helvetica,
sans-serif; }
```

It is valid because all the values are "font-" values and the declaration ends with the size followed by the family.

Hands-On 10.6   Use Font Shorthand

In this exercise, you will reduce CSS code bloat by using font shorthand.

1. Switch to Notepad and locate the `body`, `p`, `td` rule at the top of the document.

2. Follow these steps to use font shorthand:

Ⓐ Delete "-family".　　　Ⓑ Type 100% before the list of families.

```
body, p, td {
    font-family: verdana, arial, helvetica, sans-serif;
    font-size: 100%;
}
```

Ⓒ Delete the entire `font-size` declaration.

Your code should look like the following illustration.

```
body, p, td {
    font: 100% verdana, arial, helvetica, sans-serif;
}
```

3. Save your changes, switch to your browser, and tap ⌨F5.
   Nothing should change in the browser because you simply combined declarations.

4. Close your browser and Notepad.

QUICK REFERENCE: SUMMARY OF CSS FONT PROPERTIES

Property	Useful Values	Function	Example
font-family	Comma-separated list of typefaces	Specifies the typeface	`font-family: georgia, times, serif;`

font-size	Pixels, percents, or ems	Specifies the size of the text	`font-size: 12px;`
			`font-size: 125%;`
			`font-size: 1.25em;`

line-height	Pixels, percents, or ems	Specifies the vertical space between lines of text	`line-height: 12px;`
			`line-height: 125%;`
			`line-height: 1.25em;`

font-weight	bold, normal	Specifies if text is bold or not	`font-weight: bold;` `font-weight: normal;`
font-style	italic, normal	Specifies if text is italicized or not	`font-weight: italic;` `font-weight: normal;`
font-variant	small-caps, normal	Specifies if text uses small-caps or not	`font-variant: smallcaps;`
text-transform	lowercase, uppercase, capitalize	Specifies the case of test	`text-transform: uppercase;`
text-align	left, right, center	Specifies the horizontal alignment of content inside a container	`text-align: center;`
vertical-align	bottom, middle, top	Specifies the vertical alignment of a table cell	`vertical-align: top;`
text-decoration	underline, overline, line-through, none	Specifies a decoration for the text	`text-decoration: line-through;`
font	Space-separated list of any of the other "font-" values	Shorthand for combining multiple declarations	`font: bold italic small caps 110% arial, sans-serif;`

Concepts Review

True/False Questions

1. The term "font" refers to an entire family of typefaces, such as Arial or Helvetica. TRUE FALSE

2. You should stick to standard fonts on your web pages so your text displays consistently on every computer. TRUE FALSE

3. Large sections of centered text look slick and professional. TRUE FALSE

4. Arial, Helvetica, and Verdana are standard serif fonts. TRUE FALSE

5. Sans-serif fonts are easier to read on a computer screen than serif fonts. TRUE FALSE

6. Increasing the line height can help make small text more legible. TRUE FALSE

7. CSS has the ability to turn your text into uppercase, lowercase, or capitalized no matter how it was actually typed. TRUE FALSE

8. It is impossible to remove the underline beneath hyperlinks. TRUE FALSE

9. Limiting your pages to no more than three fonts helps to maintain readability. TRUE FALSE

10. Font shorthand can be used to specify the size, family, and horizontal alignment of text. TRUE FALSE

Multiple Choice Questions

1. Sabra has specified a custom font that looks like handwriting to be used as her page headings. The page looks as she intended on her computer; however, when viewing the page on a friend's computer the page headings are in a generic serif font. What is the problem?

   a. Sabra specified a non-standard font that was installed on her computer but not on her friend's computer.

   b. Sabra is using Internet Explorer and her friend is using Firefox.

   c. Sabra misspelled the name of the font in her CSS rule.

   d. Fonts can be specified for paragraphs only, not headings.

2. Which font was specifically designed for use on a computer screen?

   a. Arial

   b. Georgia

   c. Helvetica

   d. Verdana

3. Which group of fonts contains only serif fonts?

   a. Arial, Helvetica, Verdana

   b. Times, Georgia, Courier

   c. Times, Georgia, Verdana

   d. Arial, Helvetica, serif

4. Lars wants to display all his `<h1>` elements in small caps. He has the following code in his external stylesheet: h1 { text-transform: small-caps; }. However, his headings do not appear in small caps! What is the problem?

   a. The value "small-caps" should not contain a hyphen.

   b. The value "small-caps" should be capitalized, as in "Small-caps".

   c. Lars used the wrong CSS property. Small-caps is specified with the text-variant property.

   d. Lars used the wrong CSS property. Small-caps is specified with the font-variant property.

Skill Builders

Skill Builder 10.1   Style the Gallery Page

In this exercise, you will style the gallery page.

Identify the Table

The gallery page uses a table to arrange the thumbnails. The contact page also uses tables. You will identify the gallery table so you can target it with CSS

1. Start Notepad and open the gallery.htm page from the sb_fonts folder in your Lesson 10 folder.

2. Locate the opening `<table>` tag and follow these steps to give it an id:

    Ⓐ **Click to the left of the** summary **attribute.**

    ```
    <h1>Gallery</h1>
    <table id="gallery_thumbnails" summary="This
    ```

    Ⓑ **Type** id="gallery_thumbnails" **and tap** [Spacebar].

    The gallery thumbnail table is now uniquely identified and can be differentiated from the other tables on the site.

3. Save your changes.

4. Choose File→Open and navigate to your Lesson 10 folder.

5. Open the sb_fonts folder, then open the styles folder.

6. Set the file type filter to all files and open the fupstyles.css stylesheet.

Style the Caption

7. Create the following new rule at the bottom of the document using a descendant selector to target the table caption on the gallery page and style the text:

    ```
    #gallery_thumbnails caption {
      font: bold 115% georgia, times, serif;
    }
    ```

Center the Cell Content

8. Create the following new rule targeting the table cells in the gallery table and center align the contents:

```
#gallery_thumbnails td {
  text-align: center;
}
```

9. Save your changes.

10. Start your web browser and open the gallery.htm page from the sb_fonts folder in your Lesson 10 folder.

    The table caption displays the new larger fonts. The thumbnails and descriptions become centered in the cells.

Skill Builder 10.2   Style the Contact Page

In this exercise, you will style the contact page.

***Before You Begin:** You must complete Skill Builder 10.1 before beginning this exercise.*

Identify the Table and Cells

The contact page uses a table to arrange pricing information. The gallery page also uses tables. You will identify the price table so you can target it with CSS.

1. Switch to Notepad and open the contact.htm page from the sb_fonts folder in your Lesson 10 folder.

2. Locate the second opening `<table>` tag (the one for the nested table) and follow these steps to give it an id:

   A Click before the `summary` attribute.

   ```
   <table id="prices" summary="This
   ```

   B Type `id="prices"` and tap [Spacebar].

   The nested price table is now uniquely identified and can be differentiated from the other tables on the site.

3. Locate the Simple models cell and follow these steps to identify it with a reusable class:

Ⓐ **Click inside the** `<td>` **tag after the tag name.**

```
<td class="price_category">Simple models</td>
```

Ⓑ **Tap** [Spacebar] **and type** `class="price_category"`.

The cell containing the text Simple models can now be targeted with CSS.

4. Using similar steps, add **`class="price_category"`** to the *Intermediate models* and *Complex models* cells.

5. Save your changes.

Style the Caption

6. Open the fupstyles.css stylesheet from the styles folder inside the sb_fonts folder.

7. Create the following new rule at the bottom of the document that makes the caption in the price table bold:

```
#prices caption {
  font-weight: bold;
}
```

8. Create the following new rule to center all cell content for the price table:

```
#prices td {
  text-align: center;
}
```

9. Create the following new rule to right align the row headers:

```
#prices .price_category {
  text-align: right;
}
```

10. Save your changes, switch to your browser, and navigate to the Contact page.
The table caption displays as bold. All price content is centered in the cells except for the row headers (with the price_category class), which are right aligned. If you do not see these changes, you may need to tap [F5] *to refresh the page.*

Skill Builder 10.3 Make Global Changes

In this exercise, you will make changes to the stylesheet that affect every page.

Before You Begin: *You must complete Skill Builder 10.2 before beginning this exercise.*

1. Switch to Notepad and locate the h1, h2, h3 rule towards the top of the stylesheet.

2. Delete the text-transformation declaration so the headings return to their original case.
   Your code should look like the following figure.

```
h1, h2, h3 {
   color: #543B11;
   font-family: georgia, times, serif;
}
```

3. Locate the #footer rule and follow these steps to change the alignment:

```
#footer {
   color: #999;
   font-size: 75%;
   font-style: italic;
   text-align: right;
}
```

Ⓐ Click after the font-style declaration and tap [Enter] [Spacebar] [Spacebar].

Ⓑ Type the following: **text-align: right;**

4. Save your changes, switch to your browser, and tap [F5]. Navigate to a few of the pages.
   The page headings are "back to normal" while the footer displays on the right side of the screen.

5. Close your browser and Notepad.

Assessments

Assessment 10.1   Set Font Characteristics

In this exercise, you will specify font characteristics shared by every page on the site.

1. Start Notepad and open the baseriffs.css stylesheet from the styles folder in the as_riffworld_fonts folder from your Lesson 10 folder.

2. Add a new rule under the existing `body` rule that uses the grouped selectors `body`, `p`, `td` to initialize the following font characteristics:
   - The default typeface should be Arial. If that font is not installed, use Helvetica. If that is not installed, use the default sans-serif font.
   - The size should be initialized to 100 percent.
   - Increase the line height to 150 percent.

3. Edit the existing rule with the grouped headings and specify the following fonts: Georgia, Times New Roman, serif.

4. Edit the `#footer` rule to format the following:
   - The text should be centered in the browser window.
   - The text should be 75 percent of the default size.
   - The text should be italic.

5. Edit the rule that formats the hyperlinks in the masthead so the navigation bar hyperlinks are:
   - Eighty-five percent the size of the default font
   - Bold
   - Uppercase

6. Make the `.band` class bold.

7. Make the `.song` class italic.

8. Create a new rule to center everything in the masthead.
   Be sure to save your changes!

9. Start your web browser and open the index.htm page from the as_riffworld_fonts folder in your Lesson 10 folder. Navigate the pages and verify your CSS formatting displays as expected.

10. Close your web browser and Notepad.

Critical Thinking

Critical Thinking 10.1   Format Text and Hyperlinks

In this exercise, you will create a stylesheet to format text and hyperlinks. You will be working with the files inside the ct_balloons_fonts folder inside your Lesson 10 folder. The HTML pages are already linked to a blank stylesheet in the styles folder.

Initialize the default typeface and font size for the entire site.

Use the following properties in your stylesheet to format the text and hyperlinks as you see fit. Feel free to specify colors also. You may wish to add some CSS hooks, such as <span> tags, <div> tags, or additional class or id attributes in existing HTML tags.

- font-family
- font-size
- font-weight
- font-style
- font-variant
- text-align
- text-transform
- text-decoration
- line-height
- font (shorthand)

Critical Thinking 10.2   Research Additional Formatting

In this exercise, you will research other text formatting possibilities. You will be working with the files inside the ct_balloons_fonts folder inside your Lesson 10 folder. You must complete Critical Thinking 10.1 before beginning this exercise.

Using your favorite search engine, research the CSS properties **word-spacing** and **letter-spacing**.

Add a few CSS declarations to the balloons stylesheet that use these new properties.

Test your page in multiple browsers to see if these properties are universally supported.

Doing More with CSS

In this lesson, you will learn how to position an image with CSS rather than with the HTML `align` attribute. Then you will explore the box model to learn about borders, widths, and space. You will restrict the page width and center the content in the browser window. Also, you will use background images as more than just a page background. Finally, you will explore the CSS Zen Garden for inspiration.

LESSON OBJECTIVES

After studying this lesson, you will be able to:

- Float an image
- Describe the box model
- Limit page width and center content in the browser window
- Effectively use borders, padding, and margins
- Add backgrounds to HTML elements

Case Study: Formatting with Advanced CSS Properties

With Haylie's expertise in XHTML and CSS coding and Miguel's artistic eye, they begin to put the final touches on the site. Under Miguel's direction, Haylie adds backgrounds, borders, and space to page elements all with CSS—ensuring the separation of structure from presentation.

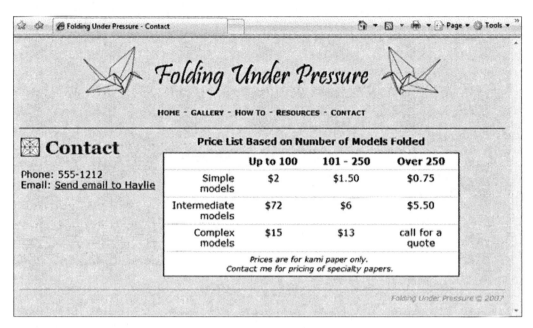

Using pure CSS, HTML horizontal ruled lines are replaced by borders, non-essential graphics are used as background images, and page elements are given the breathing room necessary for readability.

Floating

You have learned in previous lessons about the `align` attribute and how it can be used to reposition an element. For example, when used in a `<p>` or `<h1>` tag, `align` can center content in the browser window. When used in a table cell, the `align` attribute can position the cell content horizontally. In each of these cases, `align` can be replaced by the CSS `text-align` property you learned in Lesson 10, Using CSS to Style Text.

Floating an Image

When used on an `<img>` tag, `align` can change the location of the image relative to the text next to it, but `text-align` is not a valid alternative in this case. `Float` is a CSS alternative to the `align` attribute when positioning images relative to the content next to them.

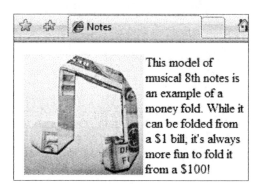

The image is positioned to the left of the text.

```
<img src="images/notes.jpg" align="left" />
```

The `align` attribute can position the image...

```
<style type="text/css">
img {
    float: left;
}
</style>
```

...or the CSS `float` property can position the image.

Advanced Floating

Just as `align` functions differently on different HTML elements, the CSS `float` property functions in a variety of ways. Floating an image is a useful and basic application of the `float` property. It can also be applied to other elements, such as DIVs and lists, but that requires a much deeper understanding of and experience with CSS.

In this exercise, you will float images.

Remove the HTML Presentational Code

1. Start your web browser and open the index.htm file from thc fup_advanced folder in your Lesson 11 folder.
   Notice that the images of the folded origami are positioned to the left and right of the text.

2. Start Notepad and open the same index.htm file from the fup_advanced folder in your Lesson 11 folder.
   Remember to set the file type filter to show all files.

3. Locate the code for the dancers.jpg image and follow these steps to remove the presentational code:

Ⓐ Select the four presentational attributes and their values (hspace, vspace, border, **and** align).   Ⓑ Tap [Backspace].

```
<img src="images/dancers.jpg" alt="Dancers,
created by Jeremy Shafer" hspace="10"
vspace="10" border="1" align="left" />
```

You are left with only the src *and* alt *attributes—both of which are required in XHTML.*

4. Locate the code for the creature.jpg image and using steps similar to those outlined above, remove the presentational code.
   Your final tag should look like the following figure.

```
<img src="images/creature.jpg" alt="Devil,
created by Jun Maekawa" />
```

5. Save your changes, switch to your browser, and tap [F5].
   The images display on their own lines above each heading. This is because the <h2> *tags come after the* <img> *tags in the HTML code and headings are block-level elements; they cannot share horizontal space with other elements such as images.*

Structure the Document to Target Homepage Images

As you will float these two images but not necessarily other images on other pages, you must identify these images with ids or classes. Since you may be floating several images on the same page, it is best to use a class.

6. Switch to Notepad, locate the code for the dancers.jpg image, and follow these steps to assign it a class:

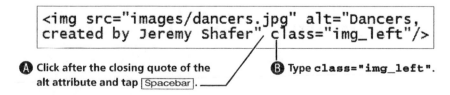

```
<img src="images/dancers.jpg" alt="Dancers,
created by Jeremy Shafer" class="img_left"/>
```

Ⓐ Click after the closing quote of the alt attribute and tap [Spacebar].   Ⓑ Type class="img_left".

Using a classname like img_left *indicates that this class should be applied to images that are floated left.*

7. Locate the code for the creature.jpg image and using steps similar to those outlined above, assign it a class of **img_right**.
Your final tag should look like the following figure.

```
<img src="images/creature.jpg" alt="Devil,
created by Jun Maekawa" class="img_right"/>
```

8. Save your changes, choose File→Open from the menu bar, and navigate to your Lesson 11 folder.

9. Open the fup_advanced folder, then open the styles folder.

10. Change the file type filter to show all files and open the fupstyles.css stylesheet.

Create the Styles

11. Scroll to the bottom of the stylesheet and add the following two styles. Use white space where appropriate (don't forget to begin each classname with a dot):

```
.img_left {
  float: left;
}
.img_right {
  float: right;
}
```

12. Save your changes, switch to your browser, and tap F5.
The images are repositioned to the left and right of the text because they have been floated. They are too close to the text now, but you will fix that later in this lesson with padding and margin.

Using the Box Model

At the core of more advanced CSS is the *box model*. The box model describes the various parts of an HTML element. These parts include the actual area for content, a border, and space around the content.

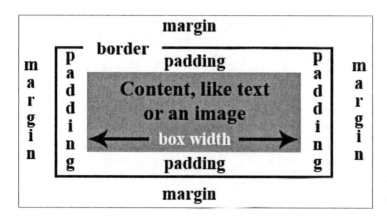

The box model describes the space around an HTML element.

 QUICK REFERENCE: BOX MODEL

Region or Property	Function and Notes
Content area	■ Where the content resides
Border	■ An optional border around the content area
Padding	■ Space between the inside of the border and the content area ■ Used to create space between content and the border ■ Can also be used to create space between the HTML element and other elements
Margin	■ Space around the outside of the border ■ Used to create space between the HTML element and other elements
Width	■ The width of the content area ■ The actual width consumed in the browser window is the box width (content area width) plus any padding, border, and margin

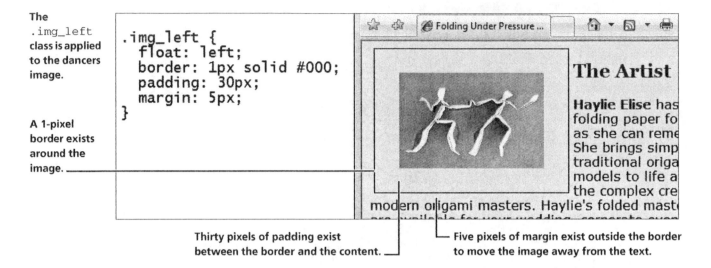

The .img_left class is applied to the dancers image.

A 1-pixel border exists around the image.

```
.img_left {
    float: left;
    border: 1px solid #000;
    padding: 30px;
    margin: 5px;
}
```

Thirty pixels of padding exist between the border and the content.

Five pixels of margin exist outside the border to move the image away from the text.

Broken Box Model in IE5

The W3C defined the box model so that the CSS `width` property specifies the width of the content area only. In other words, this code...

```
p {  width: 200px;  }
```

...makes the paragraph content area 200 pixels wide with the padding, border, and margin residing outside of those 200 pixels. This may cause your HTML element to consume more actual width on the page than you expect, as in the following example.

The CSS specifies a width of 200 pixels, but other box properties (border, padding, and margin) are specified as well.

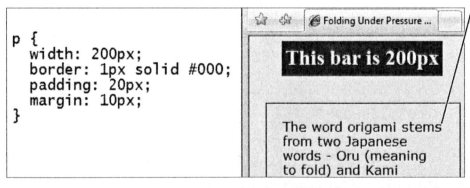

```
p {
    width: 200px;
    border: 1px solid #000;
    padding: 20px;
    margin: 10px;
}
```

The `width: 200px` declaration applies only to the content area—not the whole box. It is 200 pixels from the left edge of the content to the right edge of the content, as you can see when compared to the 200-pixel–wide image above it. The border extends beyond that.

The actual width consumed by a box is the content area + left padding + right padding + left border + right border + left margin + right margin. In this case, that's 200+20+20+1+1+10+10, or 262 pixels.

This may sound counterintuitive, but that's the way the standards are written. To make matters worse, the box model is broken in Internet Explorer 5 (and earlier) for Windows. In IE5, the `width` property actually includes the border, padding, and margin. This can lead to some real trouble! For example, if you know you need 200 pixels for your content, you may specify a width of 200 pixels (as per the standards) in addition to specifying padding and margin. In most browsers, that padding and margin would be added to the outside of the content area. In IE5, the border and padding eat into the content area, resulting in not enough room for your content.

There are a variety of CSS hacks to deal with this issue, but they are outside the scope of this book. A quick search on Google for "IE5 box model" will provide enough information to keep you reading well into the next century.

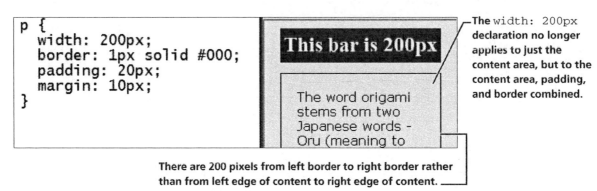

The same code now rendered in IE5 for Windows.

```
p {
    width: 200px;
    border: 1px solid #000;
    padding: 20px;
    margin: 10px;
}
```

This bar is 200px

The word origami stems from two Japanese words - Oru (meaning to

The width: 200px declaration no longer applies to just the content area, but to the content area, padding, and border combined.

There are 200 pixels from left border to right border rather than from left edge of content to right edge of content.

Width

The width property is useful on block-level elements such as headings, paragraphs, and divisions in addition to tables and table cells. With it, you can extend an element to 100 percent of the width of the browser window. Or you can limit the width to a percent or specific pixel width. One common use is to limit the width of your page overall by wrapping all of the body content into a single all-encompassing <div>, then limiting that <div> to a specific width.

The Magic Width

Although wide-screen monitors and high-screen resolutions have become increasingly popular, there are still many users with screens displaying only 800 pixels wide (resolutions of 800 x 600). For this reason, it is recommended that you limit the width of your pages to no more than 760 pixels wide. The additional 40 pixels allow for the scrollbars and borders of the browser window itself.

Hands-On 11.2   Limit the Content Width

In this exercise, you will limit the width of the page content.

Wrap the Content in a Division

1. Switch to Notepad and open the index.htm file from the fup_advanced folder in your Lesson 11 folder.

2. Locate the opening <body> tag towards the top of the document and follow these steps to begin a division that will contain all of the content:

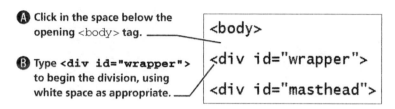

Ⓐ Click in the space below the opening <body> tag.

Ⓑ Type **<div id="wrapper">** to begin the division, using white space as appropriate.

```
<body>

<div id="wrapper">

<div id="masthead">
```

3. Scroll to the bottom of the document and locate the closing </body> tag and follow these steps to close the division:

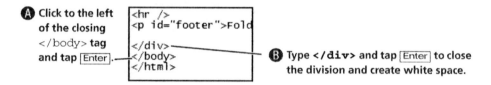

Ⓐ Click to the left of the closing </body> tag and tap Enter.

```
<hr />
<p id="footer">Fold

</div>
</body>
</html>
```

Ⓑ Type **</div>** and tap Enter to close the division and create white space.

4. Save your changes.

Create the Style

5. Choose File→Open from the menu bar and, if necessary, navigate to the styles folder inside the fup_advanced folder.

6. Change the file type filter to show all files and open the fupstyles.css stylesheet.

7. Scroll to the bottom of the document and add the following rule after the .img_right rule:

```
#wrapper {
  width: 760px;
  background: #FF0000;
}
```

You have limited the wrapper to 760 pixels wide. You have also added a temporary background color so you can see the width in action when you preview your page in the next step.

8. Save your change, switch to your browser, and tap F5.
Depending on the width of your browser window, the page content may shift as the wrapper division shrinks to 760 pixels wide. The red background fills the 760 pixel-wide wrapper so you can see it. You will remove the red background in the next step.

9. Switch back to Notepad and follow these steps to remove the red background:

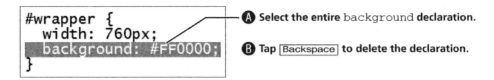

A Select the entire background declaration.

B Tap Backspace to delete the declaration.

10. Save your changes, switch to your browser, and tap F5.
The red background is removed but the content is still constrained to 760 pixels.

11. Navigate to the other pages in the site.
The other pages still span the full width of the browser window because they lack the #wrapper division. You will add the wrapper later in the Skill Builders.

Border

Borders themselves have three components: a style, a size, and a color. Not only are the border properties useful in creating borders, but you can use them to remove borders—such as the borders around images that are hyperlinks.

Border Properties

The following table summarizes the three border properties.

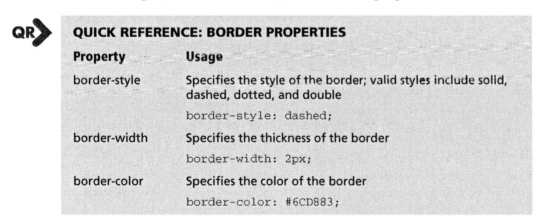

QR **QUICK REFERENCE: BORDER PROPERTIES**

Property	Usage
border-style	Specifies the style of the border; valid styles include solid, dashed, dotted, and double `border-style: dashed;`
border-width	Specifies the thickness of the border `border-width: 2px;`
border-color	Specifies the color of the border `border-color: #6CD883;`

If any of the border properties in the above table are used, the properties will apply to the top, right, bottom, and left borders of an element.

The border properties...

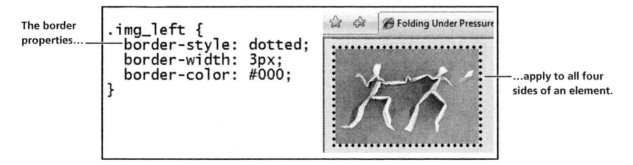

...apply to all four sides of an element.

You can target one side of the element by modifying the border property slightly, as in the following example.

Border properties may be modified...

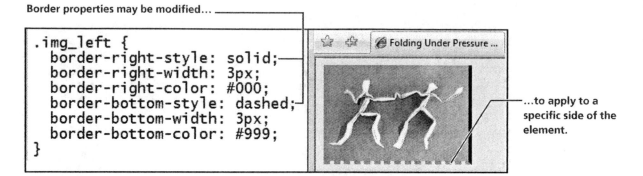

```
.img_left {
    border-right-style:  solid;
    border-right-width:  3px;
    border-right-color:  #000;
    border-bottom-style: dashed;
    border-bottom-width: 3px;
    border-bottom-color: #999;
}
```

...to apply to a specific side of the element.

Border Shorthand

Just as with font properties, the border properties can be combined into shorthand as the border property. It requires three values separated by spaces for the style, width, and color. These values can appear in any order.

The border shorthand specifies the width, style, and color in any order.

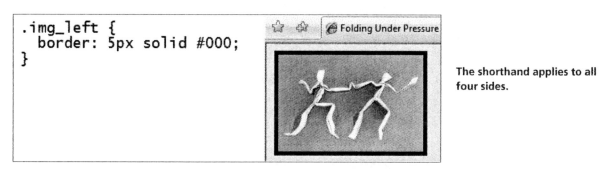

```
.img_left {
    border: 5px solid #000;
}
```

The shorthand applies to all four sides.

Removing Borders

Borders can be removed by setting the border shorthand to "none." This is helpful in removing the borders placed around images that are hyperlinked (and preferred to setting the <img> tag's border="0" attribute).

The border around a hyperlinked image can be removed via CSS.

```
a img {
    border: none;
}
```

By using descendant selectors, you can target only images nested inside anchor tags.

The same hyperlinked image with the border removed.

Border Collapse

Tables always have some cellspacing (space between cells). With HTML, you can use `cellspacing="0"` to get rid of it and have the table cells touch each other with no gap. You saw this first in Lesson 8, Working with Tables. You can use the `border-collapse` property on a table to remove the inherent cellspacing. This declaration is equivalent to the HTML attribute `cellspacing="0"`:

```
border-collapse: collapse;
```

Hands-On 11.3   Add and Remove a Border

In this exercise, you will add borders around some images and remove the border around others.

Add Borders

1. Switch to Notepad, scroll to the bottom of the stylesheet, and add the following new rule after the #wrapper rule:

```
img {
  border: 1px solid #000;
}
```

You have used border shorthand to create a thick black border around every image on the site.

2. Save your changes, switch to your browser, tap F5, and navigate to the homepage.
The homepage images of the dancers and the creature display a border that helps to define them on the page. Unfortunately, the three images in the masthead also display a border. You will fix this in the next section.

3. Navigate to the Gallery page.
The hyperlinked thumbnails display black borders.

4. Click any of the thumbnails to view the larger image.
The larger image displays the border.

5. Navigate to the How To page.
The folding diagram download image displays a border, which you don't want.

Remove Borders

6. Switch back to Notepad and add the following new rule at the bottom of the stylesheet:

```
a img {
  border: none;
}
```

This code removes the border from all images that are hyperlinks.

7. Add the following new rule to the bottom of the stylesheet to remove the borders from the images in the masthead by using a descendant selector to target them:

```
#masthead img {
  border: none;
}
```

8. Save your changes, switch to your browser, and tap F5.
The borders around the image in the masthead and the download image are gone.

9. Navigate to the Gallery page.
The borders around the thumbnails are gone because the thumbnails are hyperlinked (like the download image on the How To page). These thumbnails looked better with the border!

Add Back the Thumbnail Image Borders

10. Switch to Notepad.

Recall from previous work on this page that the thumbnails reside inside a table with id="gallery_thumbnails".

11. Type the following new rule at the bottom of the stylesheet. Use a descendant selector to target the images inside the gallery_thumbnail table.

```
#gallery_thumbnails img {
    border: 3px double #000;
}
```

12. Save your changes, switch to your browser, and tap F5 .

The thumbnails display a 3-pixel double-border: 1 pixel for the inner line, 1 pixel for the outer line, and 1 pixel between them.

Padding

Padding is applied inside a border and creates space between the border and the content. If no border is used, padding can create space between elements.

This image is too close to the heading and paragraph elements.

A little padding...

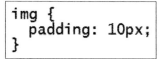

...creates space between elements.

If the border is added back, you can see the space is actually occurring inside the image's border.

Padding Shorthand

Padding, like other properties, can use shorthand or can target a specific side of an element. The following table summarizes the various options for specifying padding.

QUICK REFERENCE: PADDING PROPERTIES

Property	Usage
padding-top	Specifies the padding above the element
padding-right	Specifies the padding to the right of the element
padding-bottom	Specifies the padding below the element
padding-left	Specifies the padding to the left of the element
padding	Shorthand used to specify all four sides at once

Padding Shorthand Options

Padding shorthand can be specified several ways, with one, two, three, or four values.

QUICK REFERENCE: PADDING SHORTHAND

Example	Result
`padding: 10px;`	■ Ten pixels of padding are applied on all four sides of the element.
`padding: 1px 2px 4px 7px;`	■ The order is clockwise from top. ■ One pixel of top padding, two pixels of right padding, four pixels of bottom padding, and seven pixels of left padding
`padding: 3px 8px;`	■ The first value specifies the top/bottom padding. ■ The second value specifies the right/left padding.
`padding: 2px 5px 9px;`	■ The first value specifies top padding. ■ The second value specifies right and left padding. ■ The third value specifies bottom padding.

Margin

Margins are used to create space outside an element's border. In the following figure, the margin has created breathing room between the image's border and the text.

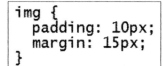

```
img {
    padding: 10px;
    margin: 15px;
}
```

...creates space outside the border, thereby separating the elements.

Margins can also use negative values (something padding cannot do). Negative margins can pull elements to a different location, which may be necessary for your layout.

Headings have space above and below by default, which can cause elements to not align as you like.

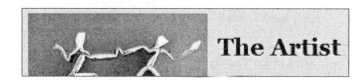

Setting the top margin to zero...

```
h2 {
    margin-top: 0;
}
```

...gets rid of the space above the element.

Setting a negative top margin...

```
h2 {
    margin-top: -10px;
}
```

...pulls an element up even further.

Margin Shorthand

The margin properties are stated just as the padding properties:

- margin-top
- margin-right
- margin-bottom
- margin-left

Additionally, the margin shorthand's values act the same as the padding shorthand with one, two, three, or four values. For example...

```
margin: 4px 7px 2px;
```

...applies 4 pixels of top margin, 7 pixels of left and right margin, and 2 pixels of bottom margin.

Auto Values

When the word "auto" is used as a value, it basically means, "Automatically figure out the available space and evenly distribute it." This can be used to center content in the browser window, as you will see in the next exercise.

 Hands-On 11.4   Control Padding and Margin

In this exercise, you will add padding and margin to elements. You will also center the content in the browser window.

Use Padding and Margin

1. Switch to Notepad and edit the existing #gallery_thumbnails img rule at the bottom of the document to add padding so the border moves away from the images slightly:

```
#gallery_thumbnails img {
    border: 3px double #000;
    padding: 2px;
}
```

2. Edit the existing img rule to create space outside the border of all the images:

```
img {
    border: 1px solid #000;
    margin: 0 10px;
}
```

You have specified a zero margin above and below all images and a 10-pixel margin on the left and right sides of all images.

3. Create a new rule at the bottom of the document to remove the top margins on all second-level headings:

```
h2 {
    margin-top: 0;
}
```

Note that when you specify zero as a value, you do not need to specify the unit of measure. 0px is the same as 0% or $0 or 0lbs. 0 is 0.

4. Edit the existing #wrapper rule to center the content in the browser window.

```
#wrapper {
    width: 760px;
    margin: 0 auto;
}
```

You have specified a zero top and bottom margin and specified the left and right margins are to be equally distributed. As the width of the wrapper is 760 pixels wide, the rest of the available width within the browser window will be split between the left and right margins of the wrapper.

5. Save your changes, switch to your browser, tap ⎡F5⎤, and navigate to the Gallery page.
The gallery thumbnails display a small amount of space between the border and the image because of the 2 pixels of padding. The images in the masthead are spaced out a little more because of the 10 pixels of left and right margins on all images.

6. Navigate to the homepage.
The dancers and creature images are pushed away from the text by their margins. The headings are moved up closer to the tops of the images because their top margins were removed. The homepage content is centered in the browser window because of the wrapper's auto margins.

Backgrounds

Backgrounds can be added to any element via CSS. You have already specified background colors in Lesson 9, Introducing CSS and Color. You can also use CSS to specify a background image, whether or not the background image repeats, and the position of the background. Backgrounds are not limited to whole pages either. You can add a background to a heading, a paragraph, or any other element.

 TIP! *Backgrounds display behind the content and through the padding of the box model. They do not display over a border or through the margin.*

Background Colors

Background colors are added with the `background-color` property. However, using the shorthand `background` property as you did in Lesson 9, Introducing CSS and Color is usually more convenient.

Background Images

Background images are added with the `background-image` property. The property's value looks a little odd, though.

```
background-image: url(../images/backgroundimage.jpg);
```

The `background-image` **property specifies the relative path to the image from the stylesheet, not from the HTML document.**

Repeating a Background

Background images can be repeated across the entire element, just horizontally, just vertically, or not at all. The default behavior is to repeat across the entire element.

A background image applied to a paragraph with no repeat declaration...

```
p {
   background-image: url(../images/creases.gif);
}
```

...repeats across the entire paragraph.

A background image set to repeat-x...

```
p {
   background-image: url(../images/creases.gif);
   background-repeat: repeat-x;
}
```

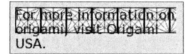

...repeats across a single horizontal line.

A background image set to repeat-y...

```
p {
   background-image: url(../images/creases.gif);
   background-repeat: repeat-y;
}
```

For more information on origami, visit Origami USA.

...repeats down a single vertical line.

A background image set to no-repeat...

```
p {
   background-image: url(../images/creases.gif);
   background-repeat: no-repeat;
}
```

For more information on origami, visit Origami USA.

...displays once without repeating.

Positioning a Background

Backgrounds don't have to start in the top-left corner and repeat from there. You can specify any position for the image to start. If it is set to repeat, it will radiate out from its starting position. When specifying the starting position, both a horizontal and vertical offset must be specified. The offsets may be specified as numerical values or keywords.

When no position is specified...

```
p {
    background-image: url(../images/bg_circle.gif);
}
```

...the background radiates out from the top-left corner.

Keywords can be used...

```
p {
    background-image: url(../images/bg_circle.gif);
    background-position: bottom right;
}
```

...to specify the starting position for the background image.

When numerical offsets are specified...

```
p {
    background-image: url(../images/bg_circle.gif);
    background-position: 50% 10px;
}
```

...the horizontal offset is first and the vertical offset is second.

In this case, the background image starts halfway across the element (50 percent) and 10 pixels down from the top.

Background Shorthand

When background shorthand is used, the values can appear in any order. The only requirement is that if the position is specified, both the horizontal and vertical offsets must be specified.

The following example is valid:

```
background: #060 url(images/bg.gif) no-repeat 50% top;
```

QUICK REFERENCE: BACKGROUND PROPERTIES

Property, Example, and Notes

```
background-color: #FF0000;
```
■ Specifies the background color of an element

```
background-image: url(images/bg.gif);
```
■ Specifies the path to the image, relative to the stylesheet

```
background-repeat: repeat-x;
```
■ Specifies how the image will repeat, if at all
■ Valid values include: `repeat`, `no-repeat`, `repeat-x`, `repeat-y`

```
background-position: left 25px;
```
■ Specifies where the background image starts
■ Requires two values to specify the horizontal and vertical offset
■ Values may include the keywords `top`, `bottom`, `left`, `right`, and `center` or may include numerical values
■ If a numerical value is used, the first value represents the horizontal offset and the second value represents the vertical offset

```
background: #FF0 url(../pics/clouds.jpg) no-repeat 50% 0;
```
■ Background shorthand lists the values, separated by spaces, in any order

---

 ## Hands-On 11.5   Add Backgrounds

In this exercise, you will add a page background.

Add a Page Background

1. Switch to Notepad, scroll to the top of the stylesheet, and follow these steps to edit the `body` rule:

A Click after the color code but before the semicolon and tap [Spacebar].

B Type `url(../images/bg.jpg)`.

```
body {
    background: #F6E0BB url(../images/bg.jpg);
}
```

The path to the image is relative to the stylesheet. The stylesheet must come out of the styles folder (../), then into the images folder (images/). Only then can it locate the image (bg.jpg).

Add a Heading Background

2. Scroll to the bottom of the page and add the following new rule to add a background to the page headings:

```
h1 {
    background: url(../images/bg_heading.gif);
}
```

3. Save your changes, switch to your browser, and tap F5.
   The homepage displays the page background—a slightly mottled texture.

4. Navigate to the Gallery page.
   The Gallery page also displays the page background. However, the background behind the h1 element should not repeat.

5. Switch back to Notepad and edit the h1 rule so the background no longer repeats:

```
h1 {
    background: url(../images/bg_heading.gif) no-repeat;
}
```

6. Save your changes, switch to your browser, and tap F5.
   The image no longer repeats, but it is overlapped by the text. Adding some left padding will shift the text over and leave the background where it is.

7. Switch back to Notepad and edit the h1 rule so the heading no longer overlaps the background image:

```
h1 {
    background: url(../images/bg_heading.gif) no-repeat;
    padding-left: 42px;
}
```

8. Save your changes, switch to your browser, and tap F5.
   The left padding has pushed the text over so it no longer overlaps the background image.

9. Switch back to Notepad and edit the h1 rule so the background image is vertically centered next to the text:

```
h1 {
    background: url(../images/bg_heading.gif) no-repeat 0 50%;
    padding-left: 42px;
}
```

   Remember that the first position value specifies the horizontal offset (0) and the second value specifies the vertical offset (50%). You could also have used left center.

10. Save your changes, switch to your browser, and tap F5.
    The image is vertically centered next to the heading.

11. Navigate to the other pages.
    All h1s display the background image.

12. Close Notepad but leave your web browser open.

Finding Inspiration

It takes a lot of practice before you become truly proficient with CSS, but the benefits are well worth the time and effort. At times, it can be frustrating when you are just starting out with CSS. It is helpful in those times to seek inspiration. Seeing what others have accomplished with CSS can be a great motivator. An inspirational site is the CSS Zen Garden.

CSS Zen Garden

The CSS Zen Garden site is not so much a website of information as a place for artists and CSS gurus to show off their skills and talents. The site consists of a single page of well-formed and valid XHTML. Visitors to the site can click hyperlinks to attach different CSS files to the XHTML document, resulting in completely different layouts and designs. When you consider that every hyperlink displays the same structural XHTML, the formatting possible with CSS becomes truly inspirational.

 Hands-On 11.6   Explore the CSS Zen Garden

In this exercise, you will explore the CSS Zen Garden website.

Before You Begin: If you are using Firefox, the Web Developer toolbar discussed in Lesson 3, Using Workspace Tools must be installed. If you are using Internet Explorer, the Web Accessibility Toolbar discussed in Lesson 3, Using Workspace Tools must be installed.

1. Use the address bar to browse to **www.csszengarden.com**.
   Read through some of the text to familiarize yourself with it so you can recognize it again later. Notice the subheadings for "The Road to Enlightenment," "So What Is This About?," "Participation," etc.

2. Follow the step for your web browser:

   Firefox and the Web Developer Toolbar:

   🅐 Click the CSS button on the Web Developer toolbar.

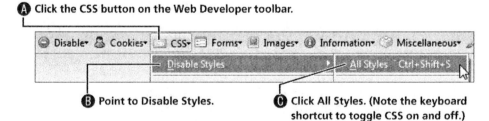

   🅑 Point to Disable Styles.   🅒 Click All Styles. (Note the keyboard shortcut to toggle CSS on and off.)

   Internet Explorer and the Web Accessibility Toolbar:

   🅐 Click the CSS button in the Web Accessibility Toolbar.

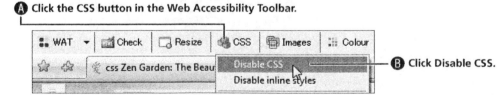

   🅑 Click Disable CSS.

The CSS is disabled and you are left viewing the raw structured XHTML.

3. Repeat step 2 to toggle the CSS back on.
   The visual formatting returns.

4. Click one of the hyperlinks in the Select a Design navigation bar to load a different CSS file.
   The layout of the page completely changes, but the text is the same. The sections for "The Road to Enlightenment," "So What Is This About?," "Participation," etc. still exist.

5. Repeat step 2 to toggle off the CSS.
   The same XHTML code and content exists beneath the CSS.

6. Repeat step 2 to toggle on the CSS.
   The visual formatting returns.

7. Continue to explore a few other links in the Select a Design navigation bar to view other CSS presentations. Continue to toggle the CSS on and off so you appreciate that each new "page" is really the same XHTML page with a different stylesheet attached.

8. Close your browser when you are finished exploring the site.

Property	Useful Values	Function	Example
float	left, right	Horizontally aligns an image	`float: left;`
width	pixels, percents	Specifies the width of an element	`width: 300px;` `width: 95%;`
border	pixels, none	Creates or removes a border	`border: 3px;` `border: none;`
border-collapse	collapse	Equivalent to setting the HTML attribute cellspacing="0" on a table	`border-collapse: collapse`
padding	pixels, em, none	Creates or removes space between the inside of a border and content	`padding: 10px;` `padding: 2px 0;`
margin	pixels, em, none	Creates or removes space outside of a border	`margin: 7px;` `margin: .5em 1px 1px`
background-color	hex-6, hex-3	Specifies a background color	`background-color: #FCC;`
background-image	Relative path to image	Specifies a background image	`background-image: url(../pics/bg.jpg);`
background-repeat	repeat, no-repeat, repeat-x, repeat-y	Specifies how the background image will repeat, if at all	`background-repeat: repeat-x;`
background-position	Horizontal offset followed by vertical offset, specified in keywords or numerical values	Specifies where the background will start	`background-position: left 3px;`
background	Any of the values from other background properties	Shorthand to combine all the background properties	`background: #CC6 url(photos/face.jpg) no-repeat 50% 50%;`

 **Concepts Review**

True/False Questions

1. The `float` property can be used instead of the `<img>` tag's `align` attribute.   TRUE   FALSE

2. The box model is broken in Firefox.   TRUE   FALSE

3. The box model defines the width of the box by the distance from the left border to the right border.   TRUE   FALSE

4. For a high level of usability, your web pages should not exceed 760 pixels in width.   TRUE   FALSE

5. A border always displays the same along all four sides of a box.   TRUE   FALSE

6. Margin controls the space between the inside of a border and the content.   TRUE   FALSE

7. Margins may specify a negative value, but padding cannot.   TRUE   FALSE

8. Margins may be used to center page content in the browser window.   TRUE   FALSE

9. Backgrounds can only be added to the body of a page.   TRUE   FALSE

10. Backgrounds always repeat horizontally down the entire page.   TRUE   FALSE

Multiple Choice Questions

1. Sidney has the `background-position: 50% 10px;` declaration in her CSS. Where will the background image start?

    a. In the horizontal center and 10 pixels down from the top

    b. In the horizontal center and 10 pixels up from the bottom

    c. Ten pixels over from the left and halfway down

    d. Ten pixels over from the right and halfway down

2. Which declaration will allow Nathaniel to center his page content in the browser window?

    a. `#wrapper { width: 100%; align: center;}`

    b. `#wrapper { width: 100%; align: auto;}`

    c. `#wrapper { width: 760px; margin: center;}`

    d. `#wrapper { width: 760px; margin: 10px auto;}`

3. Raina wants to remove the border from all hyperlinked images but not regular images, so she adds the following rule to her stylesheet: `img {border:none;}`. Will this accomplish what she wants?

    a. No, she must remove the borders from the anchors, not the images.

    b. No, this will remove the border from all images, not just hyperlinked images.

    c. No, it is not possible to remove the border from hyperlinked images.

    d. Yes, this accomplishes what she wants.

4. Oscar wants a border around all his images. He also wants 2 pixels of space between the border and the image. Which rule will accomplish this?

    a. `img { border: 1px solid #000; padding: 2px; }`

    b. `img { border: 1px solid #000; margin: 2px; }`

    c. `img { border: 1px solid #000 2px; }`

    d. `img { border: 1px solid #000; border-spacing: 2px; }`

Skill Builders

Skill Builder 11.1   Center Page Content

In this exercise, you will center the content in the rest of the pages.

Examine the CSS

1. Start Notepad and browse to your Lesson 11 folder, if necessary.

2. Open the sb_advanced folder, then open the styles folder.

3. Open the fupstyles.css stylesheet from the styles folder.
   Remember to set the file type filter to show all files.

4. Locate the `#wrapper` rule towards the top of the stylesheet.
   This rule constrains the width of the wrapper to 760 pixels wide and centers it in the browser window.

5. Choose File→Open from the menu bar.

6. Navigate to the Lesson 11 folder, if necessary.

7. Open the sb_advanced folder.

8. Change the file type filter to show all files, then open the gallery.htm file.

9. Follow these steps to begin wrapping the page content in the `#wrapper` division:

   Ⓐ Click in the space after the opening `<body>` tag.

   ```
   <body>
   <div id="wrapper">
   ```

   Ⓑ Type `<div id="wrapper">` to begin the division.

10. Scroll down to the bottom of the document, then follow these steps to close the wrapper:

    Ⓐ Click in the space above the closing `</body>` tag.

    ```
    </div>
    </body>
    </html>
    ```

    Ⓑ Type `</div>` to close the division.

11. Save your changes.

12. Using steps similar to steps 2–10, add the `#wrapper` division to the following pages:

    - contact.htm
    - gal_fluffy.htm
    - gal_knife.htm
    - gal_present.htm
    - howto.htm
    - resources.htm

13. Switch to your browser and tap `F5`.

14. Navigate all the pages in the site and verify that the content is centered on all pages. If it's not, fix the page in question before continuing.

Skill Builder 11.2 **Format the Masthead and Footer**

In this exercise, you will use borders, padding, and margins to format the masthead and footer.

Before You Begin: You must complete Skill Builder 11.1 before beginning this exercise.

Remove the Hrs

Horizontal-ruled lines create a visual separation between page elements. As they are presentational, they are best re-created with CSS. CSS borders can substitute for horizontal rules.

1. Switch to Notepad and open the index.htm file from the sb_advanced folder in your Lesson 11 folder.

2. Locate the first <hr /> tag on the page. (It appears after the masthead division.)

3. Delete the <hr /> tag completely.

4. Scroll to the bottom of the page and locate the next <hr /> tag, which is just above the footer paragraph.

5. Delete this second <hr /> tag completely.

6. Save your changes, switch to your browser, and tap F5.
   The horizontal lines beneath the masthead and above the footer are gone. You will re-create them in the next section.

7. Switch back to Notepad.

8. Using steps similar to steps 1–4, remove all the <hr /> tags from the following pages:
   - gallery.htm: Remove two <hr /> tags.
   - gal_knife.htm: Remove two <hr /> tags.
   - gal_fluffy.htm: Remove two <hr /> tags.
   - gal_present.htm: Remove two <hr /> tags.
   - howto.htm: Remove two <hr /> tags.
   - resources.htm: Remove three <hr /> tags.
   - contact.htm: Remove two <hr /> tags.

Create Horizontal Rules with Borders

9. Open the fupstyles.css stylesheet from the styles folder in the fup_advanced folder.

10. Edit the #masthead rule to add a border beneath the masthead:

```
#masthead {
  text-align: center;
  border-bottom: 2px solid #000;
  margin-bottom: 10px;
}
```

You have added a 2-pixel solid black bottom border. You have also added a 10-pixel margin beneath the border to push the rest of the page content away from it slightly.

11. Edit the #footer rule to add a border above the footer:

```
#footer {
  color: #999;
  font-size: 75%;
  font-style: italic;
  text-align: right;
  border-top: 1px solid #999;
  padding-top: 10px;
  margin-top: 15px;
}
```

You have added a 1-pixel top border in gray to match the color of the footer text. You have also created some space between the border and the footer text (padding) and between the border and the page content above it (margin).

12. Create the following new rule at the bottom of the stylesheet to create a line between the FAQ questions and answers (a \<div\> tag with id="faqAnswers" already exists on the resources page):

```
#faqAnswers {
  border-top: 1px dashed #999;
}
```

13. Save your changes, switch to your browser, and tap [F5].

14. Navigate every page in the site and note that the borders have created visual separations similar to that of a horizontal rule.
If you desired more or less space around a border, you could easily edit the CSS rule to add or remove padding or margin.

Skill Builder 11.3   Format the Price Table

In this exercise, you will use borders, padding, margins, and backgrounds to format the price table on the contact page.

Examine the Hooks

1. Switch to Notepad and open the contact.htm file from the sb_advanced folder in your Lesson 11 folder.

2. Locate the nested table and identify the CSS hooks:
   - The table has `id="prices"`.
   - The first row contains one regular cell (which is empty) and three table headers.
   - Several cells have `class="price_category"`.
   - The bottom merged cell has `class="price_footer"`.

Format the Table

3. Open the stylesheet and add the following new rule above the `#prices caption` rule so all table rules are kept in the same section of the stylesheet:

```
#prices {
  margin-left: 20px;
  background: #FFF;
  border: 1px solid #000;
  border-collapse: collapse;
}
```

   You have created 20 pixels of space between the left side of the table and the other contact information on the page. You have also given the table a white background with a thin black border.

4. Save your changes, switch to your browser, tap [F5], and navigate to the Contact page.
   The price table can use some visual separation between the rows.

5. Switch back to Notepad.

6. Edit the existing `#prices td` rule to affect the table headers also and to add a light line underline:

```
#prices td, #prices th {
  text-align: center;
  border-bottom: 1px solid #CCC;
}
```

7. Save your changes, switch to your browser, and tap [F5].
   The rows are now separated with lines, but the content is still a little cramped.

8. Switch back to Notepad.

9. Edit the existing `#prices td, #prices th` rule to add some breathing room:

```
#prices td, #prices th {
  text-align: center;
  border-bottom: 1px solid #CCC;
  padding: 5px;
}
```

10. Save your changes, switch to your browser, and tap [F5].
    The cell content is less cramped, but the caption is a bit too close to the table.

11. Switch back to Notepad.

12. Edit the existing `#prices caption` rule to add some breathing room:

```
#prices caption {
  font-weight: bold;
  padding-bottom: 10px
}
```

13. Save your changes, switch to your browser, and tap [F5].
    The table is pushed down slightly, creating breathing room for the caption. The price table footer text is too large in comparison to the rest of the table.

14. Switch back to Notepad.

15. Create a new rule after the `#prices .price_category` rule to adjust the font properties of the merged cell:

```
#prices .price_footer {
  font-size: 80%;
  font-style: italic;
}
```

16. Save your changes, switch to your browser, and tap [F5].
    The text in the merged cell looks better now. The table is almost complete. There is just something not quite right with it.

17. Switch back to Notepad.

18. Edit the existing #prices rule to add some thickness to the top border only:

```
#prices {
    margin-left: 20px;
    background: #FFF;
    border: 1px solid #000;
    border-collapse: collapse;
    border-top-width: 2px;
}
```

The declaration for the top border overrides the 1 pixel of thickness because it comes later in the rule than the regular border *property declaration.*

19. Save your changes, switch to your browser, and tap F5.
The extra weight at the top of the table completes the table formatting.

20. Close your web browser and Notepad.

Assessments

Assessment 11.1   Limit Page Width and Center Page Content

In this exercise, you will limit the width of the page to 760 pixels wide. You will also center the page in the browser window, and center content within the content area.

Examine the CSS Hooks

1. Start Notepad and open the index.htm file from the as_riffworld_advanced folder in your Lesson 11 folder.

2. Scroll through the homepage code and note the following structure:
   - #masthead contains the branding and navigation bar.
   - #main_photo contains the rock star image only.
   - #content contains the rest of the page content, including the footer.

3. Open the hardrock.htm page, scroll through the code, and note the following:
   - #masthead contains the branding and navigation bar.
   - #content contains the rest of the page content, including the footer.

4. Open the poprock.htm page, scroll through the page, and note the following:
   - #masthead contains the branding and navigation bar.
   - #content contains the rest of the page content, including the footer.

Limit Widths and Position Content

5. Open the baseriff.css stylesheet from the styles folder inside the as_riffworld_advanced folder.

6. Create a new rule for the #masthead that declares the following:
   - width should be specified as 760px.
   - margin should be set to 0 for the top and bottom and auto for the left and right.
   - text-align should be set to center.

7. Create a new rule for #content that declares the following:
   - width should be specified as 760px.
   - margin should be set to 0 for the top and bottom and auto for the left and right.

8. Create a new rule for the #main_photo that declares the following: text-align should be set to center.

9. Test the site in your browser.
The pages should resemble the following figures.

The masthead and photo are centered on the homepage. _____

The rest of the homepage content spans 760 pixels. _____

The mastheads on the poprock and hardrock pages are centered. _____

The rest of the content spans 760 pixels. _____

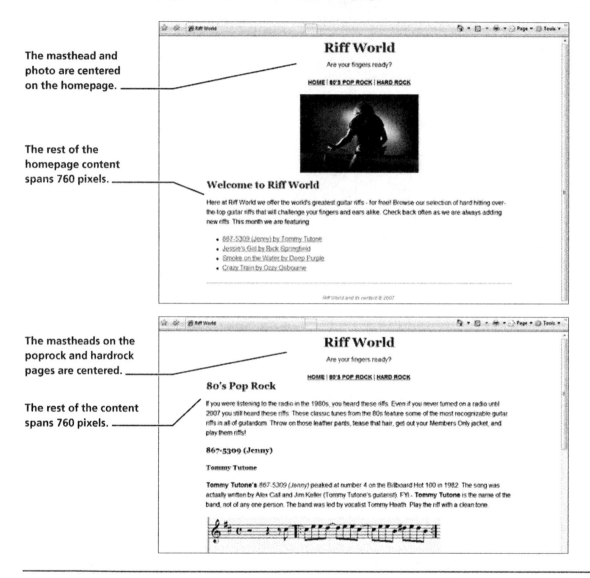

Assessment 11.2 **Add Backgrounds**

In this exercise, you will add backgrounds and adjust margins.

Before You Begin: You must complete Assessment 11.1 before beginning this exercise.

1. Switch to Notepad and change the existing page background color to **#C0C8CC**.

2. Edit the existing #main_photo rule to set the background color to **#000**.

3. Preview the homepage in your browser and note that the black background behind the rockstar photo doesn't extend to the edges of the browser window.

4. Edit the existing body rule to specify a top and bottom margin of 10 pixels and a left and right margin of 0, then preview the page in the browser and ensure that the black background extends to the edge of the browser window.

5. Add the bg_gtr.gif image (from the images folder) as a background to all h2 tags. Specify the following:

   ■ The image should appear next to all h2 elements.

   ■ The image should not repeat.

   ■ The image should appear to the left and vertically centered.

   ■ Appropriate padding should be added to the left of the h2 so the heading does not overlap the image.

   Remember: The path to the image is relative to the stylesheet!

6. Test the site in your browser.
   The pages should resemble the following figures.

The paragraph containing the homepage photo has a black background that extends to the edges of the browser window.

The h2s on every page display the background image.

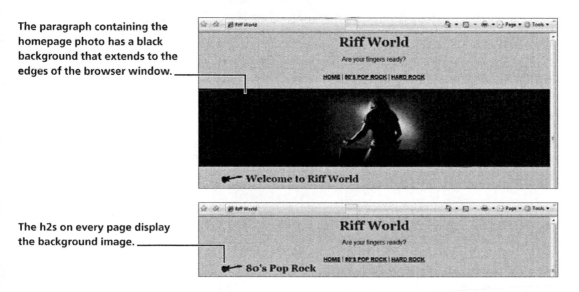

Assessment 11.3   Add Borders

In this exercise, you will add borders and adjust padding and margins.

Before You Begin: You must complete Assessment 11.2 before beginning this exercise.

1. Switch to Notepad and open the index.htm file from the as_riffworld_advanced folder in your Lesson 11 folder.

2. Remove the horizontal-ruled line from above the footer on all three HTML pages.

3. In the stylesheet, create a top border over the footer with the following criteria:
   - The border should be 1 pixel thick, solid, and colored #999.
   - Use appropriate padding and margin to create breathing room above and below the border.

4. Add a 2-pixel solid black border around all images inside the `#riffs` division.

5. Add a 1-pixel solid bottom border colored #777 to the masthead. Use appropriate padding and margin to create breathing room around it.

6. Remove the masthead border from only the homepage by following these steps:
   - Add **id="homepage"** to the `<body>` tag on the index page only.
   - Add the following rule with a descendant selector to the stylesheet to target the masthead on the homepage:

   ```
   #homepage #masthead {
     border: none;
   }
   ```

7. Add a top and bottom border to `#main_photo` that is solid, colored #333, and 5 pixels. (This will require two declarations: one for the top border and one for the bottom border.)

8. Test the site in your browser.
The pages should resemble the following figures.

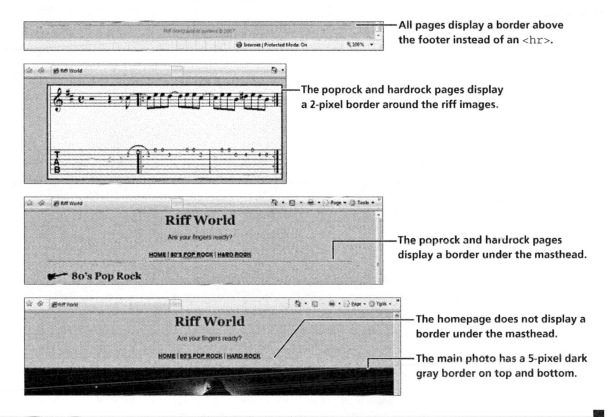

All pages display a border above the footer instead of an `<hr>`.

The poprock and hardrock pages display a 2-pixel border around the riff images.

The poprock and hardrock pages display a border under the masthead.

The homepage does not display a border under the masthead.

The main photo has a 5-pixel dark gray border on top and bottom.

Assessment 11.4 Adjust Margins

In this exercise, you will add borders and adjust padding and margins.

Before You Begin: You must complete Assessment 11.3 before beginning this exercise.

1. Switch to Notepad and remove the bottom margin from the h1 element.

2. Remove the top margin from the paragraph inside the masthead and make the text italic.

3. Save your changes and test the site in your browser.
The page should resemble the following figure.

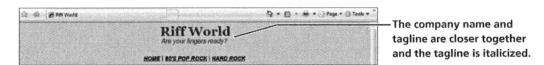

The company name and tagline are closer together and the tagline is italicized.

4. Close Notepad and your browser.

Critical Thinking

Critical Thinking 11.1   Format a Site with CSS

In this exercise, you will format the ct_balloons_advanced site. You will be working with the files inside the ct_balloons_advanced folder inside your Lesson 11 folder. The HTML pages are already linked to a basic stylesheet in the styles folder.

- Create new rules and edit existing rules so your site resembles the following figure. You may need to add DIV tags, ids, or classes to the existing HTML.

- Feel free to experiment with the colors.

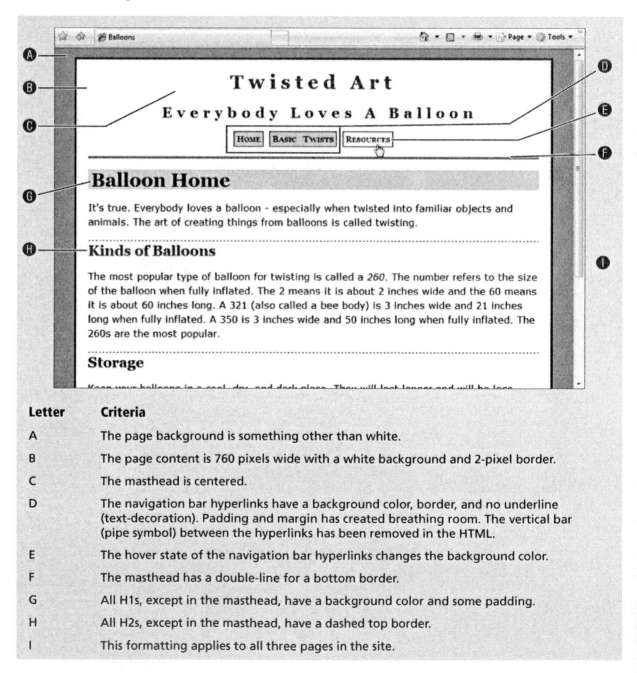

Letter	Criteria
A	The page background is something other than white.
B	The page content is 760 pixels wide with a white background and 2-pixel border.
C	The masthead is centered.
D	The navigation bar hyperlinks have a background color, border, and no underline (text-decoration). Padding and margin has created breathing room. The vertical bar (pipe symbol) between the hyperlinks has been removed in the HTML.
E	The hover state of the navigation bar hyperlinks changes the background color.
F	The masthead has a double-line for a bottom border.
G	All H1s, except in the masthead, have a background color and some padding.
H	All H2s, except in the masthead, have a dashed top border.
I	This formatting applies to all three pages in the site.

- Create a few rules to style the regular hyperlinks on the Resources page.

- Feel free to add color to the text, headings, and backgrounds.

- Experiment with padding and margin so all elements have enough breathing room.

- If you are comfortable with a graphics-editing program like Photoshop or Fireworks, create a few images to use as backgrounds and add them to your design.

Creating HTML Forms

In this lesson, you will learn how to create a form that visitors to your site can fill out to request information or provide feedback. You will add several form elements, including text fields, text areas, select menus, checkboxes, radio buttons, and submit and reset buttons. You will also learn what is involved in making a form truly functional by exploring a form handler script.

LESSON OBJECTIVES

After studying this lesson, you will be able to:

■ Add a form to a page

■ Visually format a form

■ Implement a form handler script

Case Study: Collecting Feedback with Forms

Now that the site's design is complete, Haylie wants a way for visitors to the site to request information. She likes the idea of providing a form on the contact page to allow visitors to send her messages directly from the website. Miguel is interested in collecting feedback about the site design and usability. They know they can use a single HTML form to satisfy their needs.

An HTML form provides many types of form controls to collect data.

Designing Forms

You use *forms* to collect feedback from site visitors, create online stores, and allow searches. With HTML, you can create boxes for users to type a single line of text, boxes where users can create multiple lines of text, drop-down menus, checkboxes, and other form elements. You may have as many forms on a page as you like, as long as each one is contained within its own set of <form> tags.

Forms may be very simple and contain only a few controls...

...or complex and offer many ways to enter data.

Form Workflow

Adding a form to a page involves more than simply typing the code. Just as with creating a new website, typing the code is one of the last things you do. First, you need to plan. The basic steps to adding a form to your site include the following:

1. Plan the form.

2. Type the HTML to create the form.

3. Format the form with CSS.

4. Make the form work.

Planning a Form

Planning a form involves making a list of what information you think you might want to collect from site visitors. Knowing how many pieces of information you want to collect helps with the layout of form elements. Knowing the types of information you want to collect dictates the types of form elements (text field, drop-down menu, etc.) you will need to use. In general, it is best to provide choices for users to select rather than allowing them to type freely. For a person's name or email address, they will need to be able to freely type. However, to indicate the state they live in or if they prefer to be contacted by phone or email, users can choose from options presented on the form. This helps to reduce errors in the data received from the form. In other words, a user may misspell their state when typing freely, but if choosing their state from a list, there is no chance for misspelling.

The Folding Under Pressure Form

The form you will create for the Folding Under Pressure website will collect the following information:

- Name
- Email address
- Address
- Type of event for origami art (wedding, corporate event, tradeshow, banquet, conference, etc.)
- How soon the origami is needed (immediately, within one month, within three months, within six months, etc.)
- How many pieces are needed (up to 20, up to 50, up to 100, more than 100)
- Preferred colors for paper (white, red, blue, green, yellow, purple, gray)
- Description of desired origami or other comments

 NOTE! *A figure of the final version of this form is shown on the Case Study: Collecting Feedback with Forms section on page 379 at the beginning of this lesson.*

Creating a Form

You create a form with a `<form>` tag, which is a container tag. The tags to create form elements are nested inside the form. A common practice is to first create an empty form, then nest a table inside the form to help with alignment of form elements, then finally create the form elements inside the table cells. HTML forms may include any of several attributes, as shown in the following table. You will learn about these attributes later in this lesson.

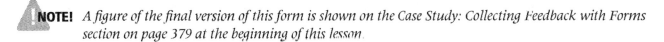

QUICK REFERENCE: FORM ATTRIBUTES

Attribute	Valid Values	Function
action	Path to the form handler	Points to the file that processes the form data once the user clicks the Submit button
method	post, get	Specifies how the form data is sent to the form handler
id	A unique name	Identifies the form with a name that is unique to the page

Hands-On 12.1   Add a Form and Table

In this exercise, you will add a form to a page. You will also create the table structure to hold the form elements.

Create a Form

1. Start Notepad and open the contact.htm page from the fup_forms folder inside your Lesson 12 folder.
    Remember to set the file type filter to All Files so you can see the HTML files in Notepad's Open dialog window.

2. Scroll to the bottom of the document and locate the code for the footer.

3. Follow these steps to create a blank form:

A Click in the blank line above the paragraph footer.   **B** Type **<form id="contact_form">**, tap Enter twice, and type **</form>**.

```
<form id="contact_form">

</form>

<p id="footer">Folding Under Pressure &copy; 2007</p>
```

C You may want to create additional white space above and below the form to make the code easier to read.

You have created an empty form. You will add additional attributes to the <form> *tag later in this lesson.*

Create a Table

You know from earlier in this lesson that there are eight pieces of information to collect on this form. Additionally, there will be a Submit button for users to click when they are finished entering their information. Therefore, you need nine rows in the table to hold all of the form elements.

4. Click in the space between the <form> and </form> tags and type the following to begin a 2 x 9 table, using white space where appropriate:

```
<table>
  <tr>
    <td></td>
    <td></td>
  </tr>
```

The start of the table includes the first row. Now you need to add eight more rows before indicating the end of the table.

5. Select the code for the row as shown below, copy it, and use Paste eight times to create a total of nine rows. Use white space where appropriate and be sure to tap [Enter] after the last row to create a space for the closing table tag.

```
<tr>
  <td></td>
  <td></td>
</tr>
```

6. Type **</table>** after the last row to close the table.

Adding Form Controls

A form control is something with which a user can interact, such as a text field or a checkbox. The decision to use one type of control instead of another is often a personal choice. Form controls can also be thought of as form elements, but technically a form element can create several types of form controls. For example, the "input" element (created by an <input> tag) can create text field, checkbox, and button controls depending on the value of the type attribute.

QUICK REFERENCE: HTML FORM CONTROLS

Control	Example	Best used for
text field	This is a textfield	Single lines of freely typed text, such as a name or email address
text area	This is a text area. It can accept multi-line input	Multi-line text, such as a street address or comments
select menu	Option 1 / Option 1 / Option 2 / Option 3	Allowing a single selection from a list
select menu	Option 1 / Option 2 / Option 3	A select menu can also be configured to allow multiple selections from a scrolling list
checkbox	☑ Option 1 / ☑ Option 2 / ☐ Option 3	Allowing multiple selections, similar to a scrolling select menu
radio buttons	○ Option 1 / ⊙ Option 2 / ○ Option 3	Allowing a single selection from a group
submit button	Submit Query	Allowing the user to send the form data when they are ready
reset button	Reset	Allowing the user to erase everything they have typed in the form and start over

Text Fields

Text fields are used to collect single lines of text, such as a name, email address, or city. The `<input>` tag (a replacement tag) creates a text field when the `type` attribute is set to "text".

The `<input>` tag creates a text field.

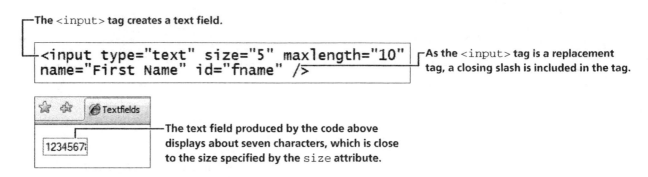

```
<input type="text" size="5" maxlength="10"
name="First Name" id="fname" />
```

As the `<input>` tag is a replacement tag, a closing slash is included in the tag.

The text field produced by the code above displays about seven characters, which is close to the size specified by the `size` attribute.

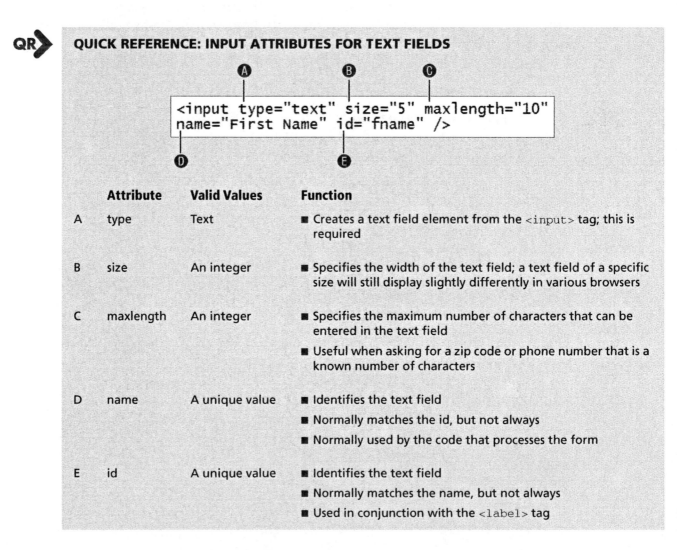

QUICK REFERENCE: INPUT ATTRIBUTES FOR TEXT FIELDS

```
<input type="text" size="5" maxlength="10"
name="First Name" id="fname" />
```

	Attribute	Valid Values	Function
A	type	Text	■ Creates a text field element from the `<input>` tag; this is required
B	size	An integer	■ Specifies the width of the text field; a text field of a specific size will still display slightly differently in various browsers
C	maxlength	An integer	■ Specifies the maximum number of characters that can be entered in the text field ■ Useful when asking for a zip code or phone number that is a known number of characters
D	name	A unique value	■ Identifies the text field ■ Normally matches the id, but not always ■ Normally used by the code that processes the form
E	id	A unique value	■ Identifies the text field ■ Normally matches the name, but not always ■ Used in conjunction with the `<label>` tag

Text Areas

Text areas are used to collect multi-line text, such as comments or questions users may type. Text areas are created with `<textarea></textarea>` tags. In XHTML, both the `rows` and `cols` attributes are required.

The `<textarea>` container tag creates a text area.

```
<textarea rows="5" cols="7" name="Comments"></textarea>
```

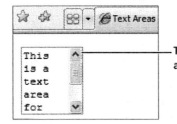

The text area created by the accompanying code is about five rows tall and seven characters wide.

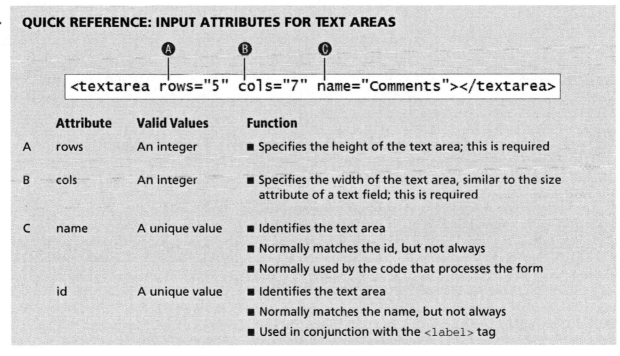

QUICK REFERENCE: INPUT ATTRIBUTES FOR TEXT AREAS

```
<textarea rows="5" cols="7" name="Comments"></textarea>
```

	Attribute	Valid Values	Function
A	rows	An integer	■ Specifies the height of the text area; this is required
B	cols	An integer	■ Specifies the width of the text area, similar to the size attribute of a text field; this is required
C	name	A unique value	■ Identifies the text area ■ Normally matches the id, but not always ■ Normally used by the code that processes the form
	id	A unique value	■ Identifies the text area ■ Normally matches the name, but not always ■ Used in conjunction with the `<label>` tag

Control Labels

Simply placing form elements such as text fields and text areas on your page doesn't make your form usable. Users won't know what to type in your text fields unless you label them.

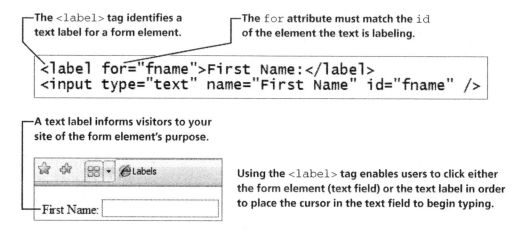

The `<label>` tag identifies a text label for a form element.

The `for` attribute must match the `id` of the element the text is labeling.

```
<label for="fname">First Name:</label>
<input type="text" name="First Name" id="fname" />
```

A text label informs visitors to your site of the form element's purpose.

First Name:

Using the `<label>` tag enables users to click either the form element (text field) or the text label in order to place the cursor in the text field to begin typing.

You gain additional usability and accessibility by identifying your text labels as actual structural labels by using the `<label>` tag. When a user clicks on a label, the associated form field becomes selected. When this happens, the form field is said to have *focus* and the user can enter data into the field.

 Hands-On 12.2   Add Text Fields and Text Areas

In this exercise, you will add text fields and text areas to the form.

1. Locate the first row of the table inside the form, then follow these steps to add a text field and label:

Ⓐ In the first cell, type **<label for="fullname">Name:</label>** to create a label for the text field.

```
<form id="contact_form">
<table>
    <tr>
       <td><label for="fullname">Name:</label></td>
       <td><input type="text" name="Name" id="fullname" /></td>
    </tr>
```

Ⓑ In the second cell, type **<input type="text" name="Name" id="fullname" />** to create the text field.

Notice that the id *attribute of the* <input> *tag matches the* for *attribute of the* <label> *tag.*

2. In the first cell of the second row, type **<label for="email">Email Address:</label>**.

3. In the second cell of the second row, type **<input type="text" name="Email Address" id="email" />**.
   Again, notice that the id *attribute of the* <input> *tag matches the* for *attribute of the* <label> *tag. The name attribute will be used by the program code that processes the form.*

4. Locate the third row of the table and follow these steps to add a text area:

A In the first cell of the third row, type `<label for="address">Address:</label>` to create the label.

```
<tr>
    <td><label for="address">Address:</label></td>
    <td><textarea cols="20" rows="4" name="Address"
id="address"></textarea></td>
  </tr>
```

B In the second cell of the third row, type `<textarea cols="20" rows="4" name="Address" id="address"></textarea>` to create the text area.

5. Locate the next to last row in the table (the eighth row).

6. In the first cell of the eighth row, type `<label for="comments">Description of desired origami or other comments:</label>`.

7. In the second cell of the eighth row, type `<textarea cols="20" rows="4" name="Comments" id="comments"></textarea>`.

8. Save your changes.

9. Start your web browser and open the contact.htm file from the fup_forms folder in your Lesson 12 folder.
Your form should resemble the following figure.

10. Click each text label and notice that your cursor moves to the associated text field or text area. (If it doesn't, your `<label>` tag `for` attributes doesn't match your `<input>` or `<textarea>` `id` attributes.)

Select Menus

Drop-down menus are created with `<select></select>` tags, so they are often called *select menus*. This type of menu is useful in offering users a list from which to choose. This helps to reduce errors and "bad data" caused by human mistakes. People are less likely to make a mistake when choosing from a list than they are by typing freely.

QUICK REFERENCE: SELECT ATTRIBUTES

Attribute	Valid Values	Function
name	A unique value	■ Identifies the menu ■ Normally matches the id, but not always ■ Normally used by the code that processes the form
id	A unique value	■ Identifies the menu ■ Normally matches the name, but not always ■ Used in conjunction with the `<label>` tag
size	An integer	■ Transforms the drop-down menu into a scrollable list; the value specifies how many items are shown
multiple	multiple	■ Applicable only when the size attribute is used; allows users to select multiple items by control-clicking

Menu Options

The `<select>` tag simply creates the container for the menu items. To create the actual menu items, you use `<option></option>` tags. The text between the `<option>` and `</option>` tags is what gets displayed in the menu.

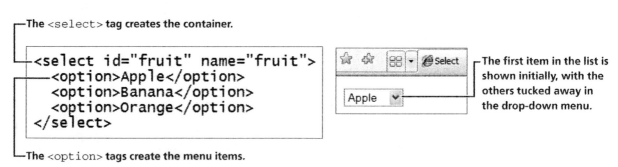

⌐The `<select>` tag creates the container.

```
<select id="fruit" name="fruit">
   <option>Apple</option>
   <option>Banana</option>
   <option>Orange</option>
</select>
```

The first item in the list is shown initially, with the others tucked away in the drop-down menu.

└The `<option>` tags create the menu items.

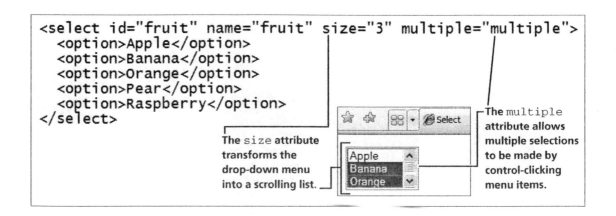

```
<select id="fruit" name="fruit" size="3" multiple="multiple">
   <option>Apple</option>
   <option>Banana</option>
   <option>Orange</option>
   <option>Pear</option>
   <option>Raspberry</option>
</select>
```

The `size` attribute transforms the drop-down menu into a scrolling list.

The `multiple` attribute allows multiple selections to be made by control-clicking menu items.

The Value Attribute

The optional `value` attribute, if present, is what is sent to the server and is helpful in presenting one thing to the user, but sending another thing to the server when the user completes the form. For example, if a user chose Apples from a menu generated by this code…

```
<select name="fruit" id="fruit">
<option>Apples</option>
<option>Bananas</option>
</select>
```

…then the word *Apples* would be sent to the server as the selection. However, if the user chose Apples from a menu generated by this code…

```
< select name="fruit" id="fruit">
<option value="app">Apples</option>
<option value="ban">Bananas</option>
</select>
```

…then the abbreviation *app* would be sent.

This is especially helpful in e-commerce applications where you want to present a friendly product name to users, but if selected, have the form process a product ID number instead.

Default Selections

By default, the first menu item after the opening `<select>` tag is displayed in the drop-down menu as items display in the order in which they appear in the HTML code. If you have a list of items but want an item other than the first one to display initially, use the `selected` attribute as in the following example.

The `selected` attribute specifies the menu item to display initially in the select menu.

```
<select id="fruit" name="fruit">
   <option>Apple</option>
   <option>Banana</option>
   <option selected="selected">Orange</option>
   <option>Pear</option>
   <option>Raspberry</option>
</select>
```

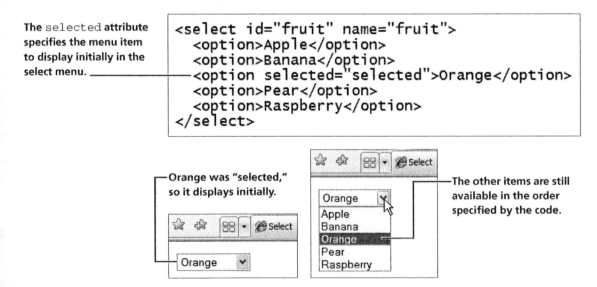

Orange was "selected," so it displays initially.

The other items are still available in the order specified by the code.

QUICK REFERENCE: OPTION ATTRIBUTES

Attribute	Valid Values	Function
value	Anything	Specifies the data to be sent to the form processor if the menu item is chosen
selected	selected	Specifies the menu item to display initially in the select menu

 Hands-On 12.3 Add Select Menus

In this exercise, you will add a drop-down menu to the form. You will also add a multi-select list.

Add a Drop-down Menu

1. Locate the fourth row in the table, after the Address row, and follow these steps to add a select menu:

Ⓐ In the first cell of the fourth row, type `<label for="eventtype">Type of Event:</label>` to create a label for the menu.

Ⓑ In the second cell of the fourth row, type Enter, then tap Spacebar a few times to add white space.

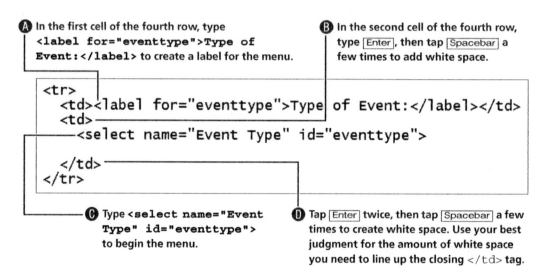

```
<tr>
   <td><label for="eventtype">Type of Event:</label></td>
   <td>
      <select name="Event Type" id="eventtype">

   </td>
</tr>
```

Ⓒ Type `<select name="Event Type" id="eventtype">` to begin the menu.

Ⓓ Tap Enter twice, then tap Spacebar a few times to create white space. Use your best judgment for the amount of white space you need to line up the closing `</td>` tag.

2. Click in the blank line below the opening `<select>` tag you created in the previous step and tap Spacebar until your cursor is two spaces past the start of the `<select>` tag.

3. Type the following to begin adding options to the menu (use white space as appropriate):

```
<option value="Banq">Banquet</option>
<option value="Corp evt">Corporate Event</option>
<option value="Trade">Trade Show</option>
```

4. Type the fourth option and set it as the default option so it displays initially in the menu:

```
<option value="Wed" selected="selected">Wedding</option>
```

5. Type the final option and close the tag:

```
<option value="other">Other</option>
</select>
```

Your final code should resemble the following figure.

```
<tr>
  <td><label for="eventtype">Type of Event:</label></td>
  <td>
    <select name="Event Type" id="eventtype">
      <option value="Banq">Banquet</option>
      <option value="Corp evt">Corporate Event</option>
      <option value="Trade">Trade Show</option>
      <option value="Wed" selected="selected">Wedding</option>
      <option value="other">Other</option>
    </select>
  </td>
</tr>
```

6. Save your changes, switch to your browser, and tap F5.
Your form should resemble the following figure. Notice that Wedding appears in the menu initially because it was set to "selected".

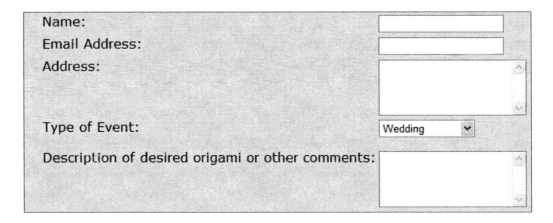

Add a Scrolling Menu

7. Switch back to Notepad and locate the opening `<select>` tag.

8. Add the `size` and `multiple` attribute to the `<select>` tag as follows:

`<select name="Event Type" id="eventtype" `**`size="3" multiple="multiple"`**`>`

9. Save your changes, switch to your browser, and tap F5.
Your select menu should resemble the figure at right. The drop-down menu has transformed into a scrolling list. Three items are shown because the `size` *attribute is set to "3".*

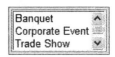

10. Scroll through the menu and notice that Wedding is pre-selected.

11. Scroll to the bottom of the menu and click Trade Show.
    Trade Show becomes selected and Wedding becomes deselected.

12. Press and hold the ⬚Ctrl⬚ key, click Other, and release the ⬚Ctrl⬚ key.
    Both Trade Show and Other become selected. Multiple selections are possible because the multiple *attribute is set to "multiple".*

13. Use ⬚Ctrl⬚-click on Other to deselect it.
    Using the ⬚Ctrl⬚-*click action on an item toggles it between selected and deselected.*

Revert to a Drop-down Menu

14. Switch back to Notepad and locate the opening `<select>` tag.

15. Remove both the `size` and `multiple` attributes so your code looks like this:

    `<select name="Event Type" id="eventtype">`

16. Save your changes, switch to your browser, and tap ⬚F5⬚.

17. Verify that the menu is once again a drop-down list. If it isn't, go back and fix your code. ■

Checkboxes

Checkboxes offer a way for users to make multiple selections, but with a slightly more intuitive interface than a scrolling multiple-select menu. Typically, a checked box indicates "yes" and an unchecked box indicates "no." You should stick to this convention rather than trying to confuse your visitors with checkboxes like the following.

| do not receive our newsletter. ☐ | **Not this way.** |

| receive our newsletter. ☐ | **This way.** |

Creating a Checkbox

You create checkboxes with the same `<input>` tag that creates text fields—but the `type` attribute is set to "checkbox". The `name` and `id` attributes are used the same way as with a text field. However, a checkbox requires a `value` attribute. It is this value that is sent to the server when the form is submitted.

The `type` **attribute must be set to "checkbox" to create a checkbox.**

```
<input type="checkbox" name="Newsletter" id="news"
value="Subscribe" />
```

If this box were to be checked, "Subscribe" would be sent as the form data.

Alternative to Multiple Checkboxes

You may have as many checkboxes as you wish in a form. However, if you have many, you may want to consider using a scrolling multiple-select menu instead to save space.

QUICK REFERENCE: INPUT ATTRIBUTES FOR CHECKBOXES

Attribute	Valid Values	Function
type	checkbox	■ Creates a checkbox; this is required
value	Anything	■ Is processed when the form is submitted
checked	checked	■ Displays the checkbox as initially checked
name	A unique value	■ Identifies the checkbox
		■ Normally matches the id, but not always
		■ Normally used by the code that processes the form
id	A unique value	■ Identifies the checkbox
		■ Normally matches the name, but not always
		■ Used in conjunction with the `<label>` tag

 ## Hands-On 12.4   Add Checkboxes

In this exercise, you will add checkboxes to the form.

1. Switch to Notepad and locate the seventh row of the table, above the Comments row.

2. Follow these steps to address usability issues with the form:

Ⓐ Click inside the first cell of the seventh row.

Ⓑ Type the following:
`Preferred paper colors:`

```
<tr>
    <td>Preferred paper colors:</td>
```

You are not using a `<label>` tag because each checkbox will need its own label.

3. Follow these steps to create white space:

Ⓐ Click in the next cell in the same row and tap Enter twice.

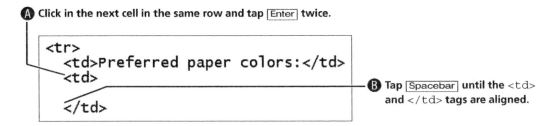

```
<tr>
    <td>Preferred paper colors:</td>
    <td>

    </td>
```

Ⓑ Tap Spacebar until the `<td>` and `</td>` tags are aligned.

4. Click in the space between the `<td>` and `</td>` tags and tap Spacebar until your cursor is indented two spaces beyond the `<td>` tag.

5. Type **`<input type="checkbox" name="Black Paper" id="paper_k" value="Black paper please" /> <label for="paper_k">Black</label><br />`** and tap Enter to create the first checkbox.

6. Tap Spacebar until your cursor is aligned with the beginning of the Black `<input>` tag.

7. Type **`<input type="checkbox" name="White Paper" id="paper_w" value="White paper please" /> <label for="paper_w">White</label><br />`** and tap Enter to create the second checkbox.

8. Tap Spacebar until your cursor is aligned with the beginning of the White `<input>` tag.

9. Type **`<input type="checkbox" name="Green Paper" id="paper_g" value="Green paper please" /> <label for="paper_g">Green</label>`** to create the last checkbox.
   Note that no line break is needed after this tag because it is the last checkbox.

10. Save your changes, switch to your browser, and tap F5.
    A section of your form should resemble the following figure. Each checkbox appears on its own line because of the `<br />` tags.

Type of Event:	Wedding ∨
Preferred paper colors:	☐ Black
	☐ White
	☐ Green

11. Click any of the labels: Black, White, or Green.
    Clicking a text label toggles the checkbox because the `<label>` tags are associated with the actual checkboxes.

Radio Buttons

Radio buttons are similar to checkboxes but are used when users are to make a single selection from a group of options. Like checkboxes and text fields, they are created with an `<input>` tag, but the `type` attribute is set to "radio". Following are the primary distinctions of radio buttons:

■ Radio buttons are said to be *mutually exclusive*, meaning one and only one may be chosen. (This is not the case with checkboxes.)

■ Radio buttons are aware of each other and know that only one of them can be selected based on their `name` attribute.

■ Buttons with the same name are considered part of the same radio button group, and radio buttons in the same group are mutually exclusive.

The "gender" group consists of two radio buttons separated by line breaks.

The common "age" name places these radio buttons into a single group.

```
<p>
<input type="radio" name="gender" id="male" value="m" /><br />
<input type="radio" name="gender" id="female" value="f" />
</p>
<p>
<input type="radio" name="age" id="age30" value="30 or younger" /><br />
<input type="radio" name="age" id="age50" value="Between 30 and 50" /><br />
<input type="radio" name="age" id="age51" value="Over 50" />
</p>
```

Only one button from each group can be selected.

The code lacks labels, so it is a mystery to users what the radio buttons are for.

Submitting Radio Button Values

Just like checkboxes, radio buttons require a `value` attribute, the value of which is sent to the server when the form is submitted. A specific button in a group can be pre-checked just like a checkbox with the `checked` attribute.

QR▸

QUICK REFERENCE: INPUT ATTRIBUTES FOR RADIO BUTTONS

Attribute	Valid Values	Function
type	radio	■ Creates a radio button; this is required
value	Anything	■ Is processed when the form is submitted
checked	checked	■ Displays the radio button as initially checked
name	A value unique to a group of radio buttons	■ Identifies a group of radio buttons ■ Normally used by the code that processes the form
id	A unique value	■ Identifies the individual radio button, not the group ■ Used in conjunction with the `<label>` tag

In this exercise, you will add radio buttons to the form.

Begin a Radio Button Section

1. Switch to Notepad and locate the fifth row of the table, after the row with the `<select>` menu.

2. Follow these steps to address usability issues with the form:

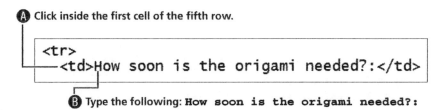

Ⓐ Click inside the first cell of the fifth row.

```
<tr>
    <td>How soon is the origami needed?:</td>
```

Ⓑ Type the following: `How soon is the origami needed?:`

You are not using a `<label>` tag because each radio button will need its own label.

3. Follow these steps to create white space:

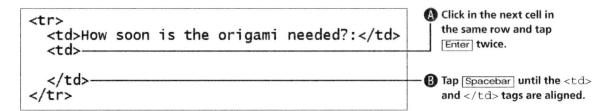

```
<tr>
    <td>How soon is the origami needed?:</td>
    <td>

    </td>
</tr>
```

Ⓐ Click in the next cell in the same row and tap `Enter` twice.

Ⓑ Tap `Spacebar` until the `<td>` and `</td>` tags are aligned.

4. Click in the space between the `<td>` and `</td>` tags and tap `Spacebar` until your cursor is indented two spaces beyond the `<td>` tag.

Create the Radio Buttons

Now that you've defined the table element, you are ready to add the radio buttons to the form.

5. Type **`<input type="radio" name="howsoon" id="month3" value="Within 3 months" checked="checked" /> <label for="month3">Within the next 3 months</label><br />`** `Enter` to create the first radio button in the "howsoon" group and have it checked initially.

6. Tap `Spacebar` until your cursor is aligned with the beginning of the Black `<input>` tag.

7. Type **`<input type="radio" name="howsoon" id="month6" value="Within 6 months" /> <label for="month6">Within the next 6 months</label><br />`** and tap `Enter` to create the second radio button in the "howsoon" group.

8. Tap `Spacebar` until your cursor is aligned with the beginning of the Black `<input>` tag.

9. Type **`<input type="radio" name="howsoon" id="monthX" value="More than 6 months" /> <label for="monthX">Later than 6 months</label>`** to create the last radio button in the "howsoon" group.
   Note that no line break is needed after this tag because it is the last radio button.

10. Save your changes, switch to your browser, and tap [F5].
    A section of your form should resemble the following figure. Each radio button appears on its own line because of the
 tags.

Type of Event:	Wedding ▾
How soon is the origami needed?:	⊙ Within the next 3 months ○ Within the next 6 months ○ Later than 6 months
Preferred paper colors:	☐ Black ☐ White ☐ Green

11. Click any of the radio buttons or text labels.
    Only one radio button in the group can be selected because they have the same name *attribute.*

Create a Second Radio Button Group

12. Locate the next row, then type the following in the first cell: **How many pieces are needed?:**

13. Type the following in the next cell of the same row to create a second radio button group, using [Enter] as shown:

```
<input type="radio" name="howmany" id="need50" value="Need up to 50 pieces"
checked="checked"/> <label for="need50">1-50 pieces</label><br /> [Enter]

<input type="radio" name="howmany" id="need100" value="Need up to 100 pieces"/>
<label for="need100">51-100 pieces</label><br /> [Enter]

<input type="radio" name="howmany" id="needX" value="Need more than 100 pieces"
/> <label for="needX">More than 100 pieces</label>
```

14. Save your changes, switch to your browser, and tap [F5].
    A section of your form should resemble the following figure.

Type of Event:	Wedding ▾
How soon is the origami needed?:	⊙ Within the next 3 months ○ Within the next 6 months ○ Later than 6 months
How many pieces are needed?:	⊙ 1-50 pieces ○ 51-100 pieces ○ More than 100 pieces

15. Click any of the radio buttons or text labels in the second group.
    The buttons in the second group do not interfere with the buttons in the first group because they have a different name *attribute.*

The Submit and Reset Buttons

Once a user has filled in a form, they need a way to send the data to the server. This is accomplished with a *submit* button. Alternatively, a user may need to erase everything they have typed and start over again—the job of a *reset* button. Both buttons are created with `<input>` tags and, once again, it is the `type` attribute that determines what kind of button is created.

Button Labels

By default, a submit button displays the phrase *Submit Query* while a reset button reads *Reset*. This can be changed with the `value` attribute.

QUICK REFERENCE: INPUT ATTRIBUTES FOR BUTTONS		
Attribute	**Valid Values**	**Function**
type	submit or reset	■ Determines if the button is a submit or reset button; this is required
value	Anything	■ This is displayed as text on the button face
name	A unique value	■ Identifies the button ■ Normally matches the id, but not always ■ Rarely needed with buttons
id	A unique value	■ Identifies the button ■ Normally matches the name, but not always ■ Rarely needed with buttons

 Hands-On 12.6   **Add Buttons**

In this exercise, you will add submit and reset buttons to the form.

1. Switch to Notepad, locate the last row in the table, and follow these steps to get the row ready for buttons:

Ⓐ Add `colspan="2"` to the first cell so it spans two columns.

```
<tr>
  <td colspan="2"></td>
  <td></td>
</tr>
```

Ⓑ Select the second cell and tap ⌨Backspace to delete it.

2. Follow these steps to create a Reset button:

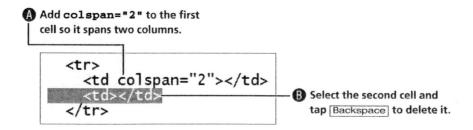

Ⓐ Click in the only cell in the last row.

Ⓑ Type `<input type="reset" value="Clear form" />` and tap ⌨Spacebar to create a reset button.

```
<tr>
  <td colspan="2"><input type="reset" value="Clear form" /></td>
</tr>
```

398 UNIT 2 Beyond the Basics   Lesson 12: Creating HTML Forms

3. Type **`<input type="submit" value="Request Information" />`** to create a submit button.

4. Your final code should look like this:

```
<td colspan="2"><input type="reset" value="Clear form" /> <input
type="submit" value="Request Information" /></td>
```

5. Save your changes, switch to your browser, and tap F5.

6. Fill out the form and click the Clear Form (reset) button.
   All of your data is erased and you may start over. Clicking the Request Information (submit) button would not send the form data because you have yet to implement a form processor. You will do that later in the next exercise.

Submitting Form Data

When a user clicks a submit button, the information they typed in the form (the form data) must be processed. This can include emailing the form data to someone, writing the information to a database, or automatically processing a credit card number and processing funds. It is the job of a *form handler* or *form processor* to do this work.

Form Handlers

A form handler can be nothing more than another HTML file that includes a bit of code from a more advanced programming language such as Javascript. It can also be a file that has nothing to do with HTML and is instead written in a completely different programming language like PHP, C++, or PERL. You link your form to a form handler by the form's `action` attribute. Form handlers usually end with a .cgi, .pl, .php, or .asp file extension—though this varies based on the programming language used to create the form handler.

NOTE! *Javascript, PHP, C++, and PERL are advanced programming languages often used on the web.*

Free Form Handlers

You don't need to be a programmer to use a form or a form handler—but you do need to read. There are many free form handlers available on the web, but you need to read the instructions included with the handler to know how to configure your form to work with a particular form handler.

NOTE! *See the web page for this book for links to free form handlers.*

Methods

In addition to specifying the `action` attribute within the `<form>` tag, you need to specify the `method` attribute. This determines how the form data is sent to the form handler. The options are "get" or "post"—and you must read the instructions for your form handler to know which one to use.

Get

The "get" method sends your data as a URL string. This means that everything you type into the form shows up in the web browser's address bar. This is bad for forms that collect personal information or credit card numbers because all data is clearly visible in the address bar. However, it is easy to bookmark a page and add it to your favorites. Search engines, like Google, use the "get" method. Next time you use a search engine, take a look at the address bar on the results page and you will probably see your search term right there in the browser's address bar.

Google uses a form handler in a folder named "search".

The text field on the search page has a `name` attribute with the value "q".

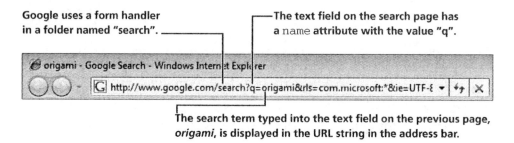

The search term typed into the text field on the previous page, *origami*, is displayed in the URL string in the address bar.

Post

The "post" method does not send your form data as a URL string so it is more secure than "get". However, it is not possible to bookmark a results page when the data is submitted via "post".

The Form Handler in This Book

The next exercise uses a simple form handler that comes with this book. In reality, it is pretty useless in any real-world situation because it simply displays the data the user submitted. Nothing is emailed, written to a database, or sent over the Internet. However, it gives you an idea of what a form handler is and what it does.

 Hands-On 12.7   Use a Form Handler and Test the Form

In this exercise, you will specify the form handler and test the form.

1. Switch to Notepad, locate the opening `<form>` tag, and add the following `action` attribute to point to the form handler included with this book:

   `<form id="contact_form" `**`action="process_form.htm"`**`>`

   The form still won't work until the `method` *attribute is set to "get" or "post". You must read the directions in the form handler to know which one to use.*

2. Save your changes and choose File→Open from the menu bar.

3. If necessary, navigate to your Lesson 12 folder; open the fup_forms folder.

4. Set the file type filter to All Files.

5. Select the process_form.htm file and click Open.
   The contact.htm page closes and Notepad displays the process_form.htm document.

6. Read the instructions at the top of the document so you know how to configure your form.
   The first instruction says to use the "get" method.

7. Choose File→Open from the menu bar.

8. Set the file type filter to All Files and open the contact.htm page.

9. Locate the opening <form> tag and add the method attribute as follows:

   ```
   <form id="contact_form" action="process_form.htm" method="get">
   ```

10. Save your changes, switch to your browser, and tap F5.

11. Fill in the form and click the Request Information button.
    The following actions take place:

    - *The browser locates the form handler specified in the form's action attribute and passes the data to it via the "get" method.*

    - *The results page displays the* name *attribute of each completed form field followed by the data you entered.*

    - *A more complex form handler may have automatically emailed this data or written it to a database.*

Formatting a Form

Like the rest of the code you have been learning, the form code is mainly structural. You need to use CSS to format the form for visual appeal. CSS properties can be applied to the table or cells containing the parts of the form, to the individual form elements, or to the form as a whole.

Tips for Formatting Forms

While everything you've learned about CSS and good formatting style applies to forms as well, the following guidelines warn again common pitfalls.

- Nesting a table inside a form is not required, but it helps in laying out form controls.

- Be careful when applying styles to the <input> tag. Many form elements are created with <input> tags, so styles applied via a type selector to *input* will affect text fields, radio buttons, checkboxes, and submit and reset buttons. For example, the following rule creates a thin border around text fields, radio buttons, checkboxes, and buttons: input { border: 1px solid #000; }

- To format just text fields and no other form control created with <input> tags, use the class attribute in your <input> tag and create CSS rules with class selectors. For example, you may add a class to your text fields like this: <input type="text" class="textfield" />. Then you may define a rule like this: .textfield { border: 1px solid #000; }.

In this exercise, you will use CSS to format the form.

Create CSS Hooks

1. Switch to Notepad, locate the opening <form> tag, and follow these steps to create a CSS hook for the text label for the first text field:

A Locate the first cell in the top row.   **B** Type **class="formlabel"** in the <td> tag to identify the cell as a label for a form element.

```
<form id="contact_form" action="process_form.htm" method="get">
<table>
   <tr>
      <td class="formlabel"><label for="fullname">Name:</label></td>
```

2. Type **class="formlabel"** seven more times—in the first cells of all but the last row.

3. Locate the cell in the last row (with the buttons) and type **id="formbuttons"** to identify the button cell.

```
<tr>
   <td colspan="2" id="formbuttons"><input type="reset"
```

4. Save your changes.

Create the CSS Code

5. Choose File→Open from the menu bar.

6. If necessary, navigate to the fup_forms folder inside your Lesson 12 folder.

7. Open the styles folder and set the file type filter to All Files.

8. Select the fupstyles.css file and click Open.

9. Scroll to the bottom of the document and add the following new rule:

```
form {
   width: 500px;
   margin: 20px auto;
   border: 1px solid #000;
   padding: 10px;
}
```

You have set the form's width to 500 pixels. You have given the form some breathing room by adding 20 pixels of margin above and below it while centering it in the browser window. You have also added a thin black border around the form and added 10 pixels of breathing room around the inside of the border with padding.

10. Create the following new rule after the form rule:

```
form td {
  padding: 5px;
  width: 50%
}
```

You have given all the cells inside the form 5 pixels of padding. You have also made the cells 50 percent the width of the form. As there are two columns, the cells should balance nicely.

11. Create the following new rule after the form td rule:

```
.formlabel {
  text-align: right;
}
```

You have aligned the text inside all cells with the class formlabel to the right.

12. Create the following new rule after the .formlabel rule:

```
#formbuttons {
  text-align: center;
}
```

You have centered the buttons in the form.

13. Create the following new rule to format the text inside text fields, buttons, and text areas:

```
input, textarea {
  font: bold 90% verdana, arial, helvetica, sans-serif;
  color: #C66;
}
```

14. Save your changes, switch to your browser, and tap [F5].
Your form should resemble the following figure. The form is formatted so it is easier to read and navigate.

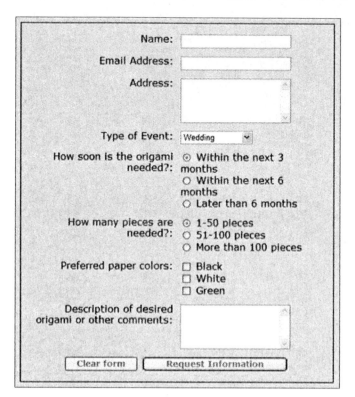

15. Close your web browser and Notepad.

Concepts Review

True/False Questions

1. A table can be nested inside a form to help with the positioning of form elements. **TRUE   FALSE**

2. You may have only one form per HTML document. **TRUE   FALSE**

3. All forms send their data via email. **TRUE   FALSE**

4. A checkbox and drop-down menu are examples of form controls. **TRUE   FALSE**

5. Text fields can accept only a single line of text. **TRUE   FALSE**

6. Text fields, checkboxes, radio buttons, submit and reset buttons, and text areas are all created with the same tag. **TRUE   FALSE**

7. Select menus can be displayed as a drop-down list or as a scrolling menu. **TRUE   FALSE**

8. Checkboxes are mutually exclusive. **TRUE   FALSE**

9. Only one radio button group can exist in a form. **TRUE   FALSE**

10. The "post" method is more secure than the "get" method. **TRUE   FALSE**

Multiple Choice Questions

1. Tarek has created a form, but the form elements are not aligned when previewed in a browser. How can he position the form elements to achieve his desired alignment?

   a. Tap the ⌐Spacebar⌐ several times before each form element until they align in the code. That will force them to align when previewed in the browser.

   b. Set the `align` attribute for each form element.

   c. Set the `align` attribute on the `<form>` tag.

   d. Create a table inside the form and place each of the form elements in a table cell and align the cell contents.

2. Faina has created a group of radio buttons where users can select "yes" or "no." However, users can check both buttons at the same time! What is the problem and how can she fix it?

   a. She has used radio buttons instead of checkboxes. She should change her code to use checkboxes.

   b. She has included the `multiple="multiple"` attribute/value in each of the `<input>` tags that created the radio buttons. She should simply delete the attribute.

   c. She failed to use the same value for the `name` attribute in each `<input>` tag that created the radio buttons. She should ensure that both `name` attributes have the same value.

   d. It is not possible to stop users from selecting multiple radio buttons in the same group. She should use a drop-down select menu instead.

3. Stanislav wants to change the text that is displayed on his submit button. It currently says *Submit Query*. Which block of code will make his button display the word *Send* instead?

   a. `<input type="submit" name="Send" />`

   b. `<input type="submit" value="Send" />`

   c. `<input type="submit" id="Send" />`

   d. `<input type="submit">Send</input>`

4. Emilia wants her form data submitted so nothing a user enters is visible in the address bar of the results page. Users will be submitting personal information and she wants to keep it as secure as possible. Which block of code should she use in her form?

   a. `<form action="processor.php" method="get">`

   b. `<form action="processor.cgi" method="post">`

   c. `<form action="processor.asp" method="secure">`

   d. `<form action="processor.htm" method="no-url">`

Skill Builders

Skill Builder 12.1 Add a Form

In this exercise, you will add a form to accommodate seven pieces of information.

Add a Form

1. Start Notepad and open the requests.htm page from the sb_riffworld_forms folder inside your Lesson 12 folder.
   Remember to set the file type filter to All Files so you can see the HTML files in Notepad's Open dialog window.

2. Locate the content section and follow these steps to add a form:

Ⓐ Click in the space below the paragraph tag.

```
<div id="content">
<h2>Requests</h2>
<p>Tell us what you want. We're listening!</p>

<form action="process_form.htm" method="get">

</form>
```

Ⓑ Type `<form action="process_form.htm" method="get">` and tap ⌷Enter⌷ twice.

Ⓒ Type `</form>`.

Add a Table

As there are seven pieces of information, you will create a table with eight rows to accommodate an extra row for submit/reset buttons.

3. Follow these steps to start the table:

Ⓐ Click in the blank line below the opening `<form>` tag.

Ⓑ Type `<table>` and tap ⌷Enter⌷ ⌷Spacebar⌷ ⌷Spacebar⌷.

Ⓒ Type `<tr>`, tap ⌷Enter⌷, and tap ⌷Spacebar⌷ four times.

Ⓓ Type `<td class="form-left-col"></td>`, tap ⌷Enter⌷, and tap ⌷Spacebar⌷ four times.

Ⓔ Type `<td></td>` and tap ⌷Enter⌷ ⌷Spacebar⌷ ⌷Spacebar⌷.

Ⓕ Type `</tr>` and tap ⌷Enter⌷ ⌷Spacebar⌷ ⌷Spacebar⌷.

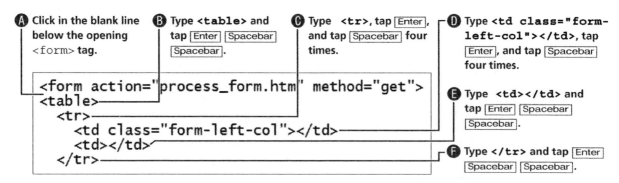

```
<form action="process_form.htm" method="get">
<table>
  <tr>
    <td class="form-left-col"></td>
    <td></td>
  </tr>
```

4. Type the following six more times for a total of seven rows (you may want to copy/paste):

```
<tr>
  <td class="form-left-col"></td>
  <td></td>
</tr>
```

5. Type the following to create a button row and close the table:

```
<tr>
  <td colspan="2" id="buttons"></td>
</tr>
</table>
```

6. Save your changes.

Skill Builder 12.2   Add Text Fields

In this exercise, you will add text fields to the form.

Before You Begin: You must complete Skill Builder 12.1 before beginning this exercise.

1. Locate the first table row and follow these steps to create a label:

A Click inside the first cell of the top row.

```
<table>
  <tr>
    <td class="form-left-col"><label for="name">Your Name:</label></td>
```

B Type `<label for="name">Your Name:</label>`.

2. Click inside the next cell in this row and type
`<input type="text" name="Name" id="name" />`.

3. Click inside the first cell of the next row and type
`<label for="email">E-mail Address:</label>`.

4. Click inside the next cell in the second row and type
`<input type="text" name="E-mail" id="email" />`.
The code for the entire second row should look like this:

```
<tr>
  <td class="form-left-col"><label for="email">E-mail Address:</label></td>
  <td><input type="text" name="E-mail" id="email" /></td>
</tr>
```

5. Save your changes, start your web browser, and open the requests.htm page from the sb_riffworld_forms folder in your Lesson 12 folder.

Both text fields display. Clicking in a text field or on the text label associated with a text field moves your cursor into the field ready to type.

Skill Builder 12.3 Add Radio Buttons

In this exercise, you will add two radio button groups.

Before You Begin: You must complete Skill Builder 12.2 before beginning this exercise.

Add the First Radio Button Group

1. Switch to Notepad, locate the third row of the table, and follow these steps to aid usability:

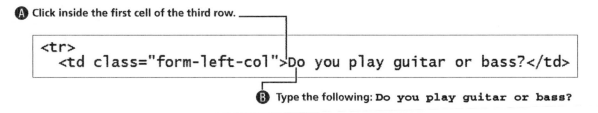

Ⓐ Click inside the first cell of the third row.

```
<tr>
    <td class="form-left-col">Do you play guitar or bass?</td>
```

Ⓑ Type the following: Do you play guitar or bass?

You did not use `<label>` *tags because each radio button requires its own label.*

2. Click inside the next cell in this row; tap [Enter] twice and [Spacebar] four times to create white space.

3. Click in the blank line you just created between the `<td>` and `</td>` tags and type the following to create the first radio button and its label, tapping [Enter] as shown:

```
<input type="radio" name="Instrument" id="gtr" value="guitar"
checked="checked" /> <label for="gtr">guitar</label><br /> [Enter]
```

4. Type the following to create the second radio button and its label, tapping [Enter] as shown:

```
<input type="radio" name="Instrument" id="bass" value="bass" />
<label for="bass">bass</label><br /> [Enter]
```

5. Type the following to create the last radio button and its label:

```
<input type="radio" name="Instrument" id="both" value="guitar and
bass" /> <label for="both">both</label>
```

Create the Second Group

6. Locate the fourth row of the table and follow these steps to aid usability:

Ⓐ Click inside the first cell of the fourth row.

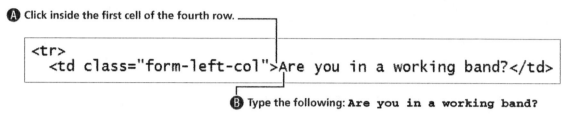

```
<tr>
    <td class="form-left-col">Are you in a working band?</td>
```

Ⓑ Type the following: **Are you in a working band?**

You did not use <label> tags because each radio button requires its own label.

7. Click inside the next cell in this row; tap ⌈Enter⌋ twice and ⌈Spacebar⌋ four times to create white space.

8. Click in the space you just created between the <td> and </td> tags and type the following to create the first radio button and its label, tapping ⌈Enter⌋ as shown:

```
<input type="radio" name="Working Band" id="yes" value="yes"
checked="checked"/> <label for="yes">yes</label><br />  ⌈Enter⌋
```

9. Type the following to create the last radio button and its label:

```
<input type="radio" name="Working Band" id="no" value="no" />
<label for="no">no</label>
```

10. Save your changes, switch to your browser, and tap ⌈F5⌋.
Both radio button groups display. Clicking a radio button or on the text label associated with one selects the button. The two groups are identified by their name *attributes.*

Skill Builder 12.4 **Add Checkboxes**

In this exercise, you will add checkboxes.

Before You Begin: You must complete Skill Builder 12.3 before beginning this exercise.

1. Switch to Notepad, locate the fifth row of the table, and follow these steps to aid usability:

Ⓐ Click inside the first cell of the fifth row.

```
<tr>
      <td class="form-left-col">Which styles of riffs would you<br />
like to see more of on our site?</td>
```

Ⓑ Type the following:
   Which styles of riffs would you <br /> like to see more of on our site?

You did not use <label> *tags because each checkbox requires its own label.*

2. Click inside the next cell in this row; tap ⎡Enter⎤ twice and ⎡Spacebar⎤ four times to create white space.

3. Click in the space you just created between the <td> and </td> tags and type the following to create the first checkbox and its label, tapping ⎡Enter⎤ as shown:

   **<input type="checkbox" name="Blues" id="blues" value="More blues" /><label for="blues">Blues</label>
** ⎡Enter⎤

4. Type the following to create the next checkbox and its label, tapping ⎡Enter⎤ as shown:

   **<input type="checkbox" name="Classical" id="class" value="More classical" /><label for="class">Classical</label>
** ⎡Enter⎤

5. Type the following to create the next checkbox and its label, tapping ⎡Enter⎤ as shown:

   **<input type="checkbox" name="Jazz" id="jazz" value="More jazz" /><label for="jazz">Jazz</label>
** ⎡Enter⎤

6. Type the following to create the last checkbox and its label:

   <input type="checkbox" name="Metal" id="metal" value="More metal" /><label for="metal">Heavy Metal</label>

7. Save your changes, switch to your browser, and tap ⎡F5⎤.
   The four checkboxes display. Clicking a checkbox or on the text label associated with one checks the box.

Skill Builder 12.5 Add a Select Menu

In this exercise, you will add a select menu.

Before You Begin: You must complete Skill Builder 12.4 before beginning this exercise.

1. Switch to Notepad, locate the sixth table row, and follow these steps to create a label:

Ⓐ Click inside the first cell of the sixth row.

```
<tr>
    <td class="form-left-col"><label for="fav">What is
your favorite brand?</label></td>
```

Ⓑ Type the following:
   `<label for="fav">What is your favorite brand?</label>`

2. Click inside the next cell in this row; tap Enter twice and Spacebar four times to create white space.

3. Click in the space you just created between the `<td>` and `</td>` tags and type the following to create the select menu, using white space as appropriate:

```
<select name="Favorite Brand" id="fav">
  <option>Carvin</option>
  <option>Charvel</option>
  <option>Dean</option>
  <option>Fender</option>
  <option>Gibson</option>
  <option>Ibanez</option>
  <option>Paul Reed Smith</option>
</select>
```

You did not use the `value` *attribute in the* `<option>` *tags. The text between the* `<option>` `</option>` *tags will be sent to the form handler as there is no* `value` *attribute.*

4. Save your changes, switch to your browser, and tap F5.
   The select menu displays with the first item initially displaying.

Skill Builder 12.6   Add a Text Area

In this exercise, you will add a text area.

Before You Begin: You must complete Skill Builder 12.5 before beginning this exercise.

1. Switch to Notepad, locate the seventh table row, and follow these steps to create a label:

Ⓐ Click inside the first cell of the seventh row.

```
<tr>
      <td class="form-left-col"><label
for="comments">Comments:</label></td>
```

Ⓑ Type the following:
```
<label for="comments">Comments:</label>
```

2. Click inside the next cell in this row; tap `Enter` twice and `Spacebar` four times to create white space.

3. Click in the space you just created between the `<td>` and `</td>` tags and type the following to create the text area:

```
<textarea cols="32" rows="7" name="Comments"
id="comments"></textarea>
```

4. Save your changes, switch to your browser, and tap `F5`.
   The text area displays at approximately 32 characters wide and 7 characters tall.

Skill Builder 12.7   Add Buttons

In this exercise, you will add reset and submit buttons.

Before You Begin: You must complete Skill Builder 12.6 before beginning this exercise.

1. Switch to Notepad, locate the last table row, and click in the single merged cell.
   Be sure to click between the `<td>` and `</td>` tags and not inside one of the tags.

2. Type the following to create the reset and submit buttons:

```
<input type="reset" value="Clear" /> <input type="submit"
value="Send Info" />
```

3. Save your changes, switch to your browser, and tap `F5`.
   With the addition of the buttons, the form is now fully functional.

4. Fill in the form and test the Clear and Send Info buttons.
   The Clear button should clear what you have filled in while the Send Info button should send the data to the form handler, which displays the results in your browser window.

Skill Builder 12.8   Format the Form

In this exercise, you will format the form with CSS.

Before You Begin: You must complete Skill Builder 12.7 before beginning this exercise.

1. Switch to Notepad and scroll through the form to familiarize yourself with the CSS hooks you created in Skill Builder 12.1.
   The cells on the left of the table all use class="form-left-col" *while the bottom row containing the buttons uses* id="buttons".

2. Choose File→Open from the menu bar.

3. If necessary, navigate to the sb_riffworld_forms folder in your Lesson 12 folder.

4. Open the styles folder.

5. Set the file type filter to All Files and open the baseriff.css stylesheet.

6. Scroll to the bottom of the stylesheet and type the following new rule to format the form:

```
form {
  border-top: 1px dashed #660;
  padding-top: 10px;
}
```

You have added a thin dashed border on the top of the form and have pushed the form content down away from the border by 10 pixels.

7. Save your changes, switch to your browser, and tap F5 to preview your formatting.

8. Switch to Notepad and type the following new rule after the form rule to format all of the table cells inside the form:

```
form td {
  vertical-align: top;
  width: 50%;
  padding: 5px;
}
```

You have made all the cells equal widths. You have also top aligned cell content and provided five pixels of breathing room throughout.

9. Save your changes, switch to your browser, and tap F5 to preview your formatting.

10. Switch to Notepad and type the following new rule after the form td rule to format the left column:

```
.form-left-col {
  text-align: right;
}
```

You have right aligned the content in the left column.

11. Save your changes, switch to your browser, and tap [F5] to preview your formatting.

12. Switch to Notepad and type the following new rule after the `.form-left-col` rule to format button row:

```
#buttons {
    text-align: center;
}
```

The form is complete.

13. Save your changes, switch to your browser, and tap [F5] to preview your formatting.

14. Close your browser and Notepad.

Assessments

Assessment 12.1   Create a Form

In this exercise, you will create a form. You will also create a table to hold the form elements.

Create a Form

1. Start Notepad and open the contact.htm file from the as_balloons_forms folder in your Lesson 12 folder.

2. Add a form element below the `<h1>Contact</h1>` line. Set the following attributes:
   - action="process_form.htm"
   - method="get"

Create a Table

3. Create a table inside the form that meets the following criteria:
   - The table should have seven rows and two columns.
   - The first cell in each of the first six rows should be identified with `class="contact-left"`.
   - The bottom row should contain a single merged cell identified with `id="buttons"`.

Assessment 12.2   Add a Text Field

In this exercise, you will add a text field.

Before You Begin: *You must complete Assessment 12.1 before beginning this exercise.*

1. Create a text field and a label to collect a user's name:
   - Use a `<label>` tag and a `for` attribute to create a label in the first cell of the first row.
   - Use an `<input>` tag with the `type`, `name`, and `id` attributes in the second cell of the first row.

   Your form should look like the following figure.

2. Preview your form in the browser and make sure the text field receives focus when you click on the text label.

Assessment 12.3   Add Radio Buttons

In this exercise, you will add radio buttons.

Before You Begin: You must complete Assessment 12.2 before beginning this exercise.

1. In the second row, create a radio button group to learn if the user twists or not, as in the following figure.

Are you currently a balloon twister?	⦿ Yes, I twist ◯ No, I do not twist

   - There should not be a `<label>` tag in the left cell as each radio button will need its own label.
   - The right cell should contain the radio buttons and labels separated by line breaks.
   - The first radio button should be checked by default.
   - Be sure to include a common `name` attribute to group the radio buttons; give each radio button a unique `id` and `value`.

2. Create a second group of radio buttons in the next row to learn if the user is a performer, as in the following figure.

Are you a professional performer?	⦿ Yes, I am a performer ◯ No, I am not a performer

   - The first radio button should be checked by default.
   - This second group of radio buttons should not interfere with the first group, so they will need a different value for the `name` attribute.

3. Preview the form in your browser and verify the radio button becomes selected when the text label is clicked. Also verify that the groups do not interfere with each other and that the buttons in each group are mutually exclusive.

Assessment 12.4   **Add Checkboxes**

In this exercise, you will add checkboxes.

Before You Begin: You must complete Assessment 12.3 before beginning this exercise.

1. In the fourth row, create three checkboxes to learn about the users' interests, as in the following figure.

- There should not be a `<label>` tag in the left cell as each checkbox will need its own label.
- The right cell should contain the checkboxes and labels separated by line breaks.
- Be sure to give a unique `name`, `id`, and `value` to each checkbox.

2. Preview the form in your browser and verify the checkboxes toggle when the text label is clicked.

Assessment 12.5   **Add a Select Menu**

In this exercise, you will add a select menu.

Before You Begin: You must complete Assessment 12.4 before beginning this exercise.

1. In the fifth row, create a drop-down menu to learn the type of balloon the user uses most often, as in the following figure.

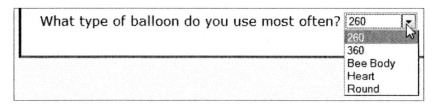

- The left cell should contain a `<label>` tag.
- Be sure to create a drop-down menu and not a scrolling list in the right cell.

2. Preview the form in your browser and verify that all five items appear in the menu when clicked.

Assessment 12.6 Add a Text Area

In this exercise, you will add a text area.

Before You Begin: *You must complete Assessment 12.5 before beginning this exercise.*

1. In the sixth row, create a text area to collect user comments, as in the following figure.

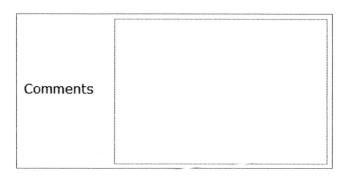

- The left cell should contain a `<label>` tag.
- The text area should be about 30 characters wide and 10 characters tall.

2. Preview your form in the browser and make sure the text area receives focus when you click on the text label.

Assessment 12.7 Add Buttons

In this exercise, you will add reset and submit buttons.

Before You Begin: *You must complete Assessment 12.6 before beginning this exercise.*

1. In the last row, create reset and submit buttons, as in the following figure.

- Both buttons should reside in the same merged cell in the bottom row.
- Use the `value` attribute to change the text on the buttons.

2. Preview your form in the browser and test both buttons. Make sure the form properly submits and you receive the correct form results. If you don't, go back and fix your code.

3. Switch back to Notepad and close the contact page but leave Notepad (and your browser) open for the next exercise.

Assessment 12.8   Format the Form

In this exercise, you will format the form.

Before You Begin: *You must complete Assessment 12.7 before beginning this exercise.*

1. In Notepad, open the balloons.css stylesheet from the styles folder in the as_balloons_form folder; scroll to the bottom of the page and create several new rules to format the form. *Remember that the CSS hooks in your form are* `class="contact-left"` *for the left column and* `id="buttons"` *for the button row.*

    Your final form may resemble the following figure, or you may get creative and do something completely different.

2. Test your form in your browser.

3. Close your browser and Notepad.

Critical Thinking

Critical Thinking 12.1   Create a Form

In this exercise, you will create and format a form.

1. Think about a questionnaire you can develop for some purpose: to learn about a friend's interests, how your child's day at school went, how shoppers feel about the new merchandise and store layout, etc.

2. On a sheet of paper, sketch a wire frame for your form. Include diagrams of the form fields showing if a question requires a text field, a radio button, or some other form element. If you create the wire frame with computer software, save the document to your ct_forms folder as **ct_form_wireframe**.

   ■ Include at least two text fields.

   ■ Include at least one text area.

   ■ Include at least one select menu.

   ■ Include at least one checkbox.

   ■ Include at least two radio button groups.

   ■ Include a submit button.

3. Create a new HTML file in the ct_forms folder in your Lesson 12 folder. Name the file **ct_contactform.htm**.

   ■ Be sure to include all the valid XHTML structures.

   ■ Add a page heading and a short paragraph describing the purpose of the form.

   ■ Create a form based on your wire frame.

   ■ Use the process_form.htm file in the ct_forms folder as the form handler.

4. Create a stylesheet named **ct_styles.css** and link it to your ct_contactform.htm document.

   ■ Store the stylesheet in an appropriate subfolder in the ct_forms folder.

   ■ Format the ct_contactform.htm page so the page and the form are visually appealing.

5. Test the form in your browser and verify the form results are correct.

Putting It on the Web

In this lesson, you will learn about making your website available to the public. You will learn about web servers and the companies that manage them, as well as the advertising jargon used by web-hosting companies. Also, you will be introduced to the domain name system and learn the process to register a domain name. Finally, you will learn to use FTP to transfer your local site files to a web server.

LESSON OBJECTIVES

After studying this lesson, you will be able to:

- Compare web-hosting plans
- Register a domain name
- Transfer site files using FTP

Case Study: Making a Site Available

Haylie and Miguel have put the finishing touches on their site and are now ready to go live! Haylie researches web-hosting plans to find a reputable web-hosting company that offers basic features at a fair price. Once she has registered her domain name and signed up for a web-hosting account, Miguel uses an FTP client to transfer the website files to their web server.

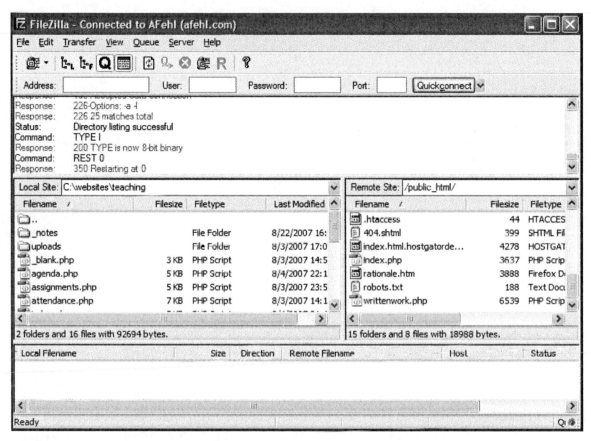

FileZilla, a free FTP client, can be used to transfer files between a local computer and a web server.

Hosting on the Web

Once you have built your website, you need to "put it on the web" so it can be viewed by the public. This entails copying your site files to a web server. Additionally, you must have a domain name so users know what to type in their browser's address bar to connect to your site. Web servers, domain names, and copying files are all covered in this lesson.

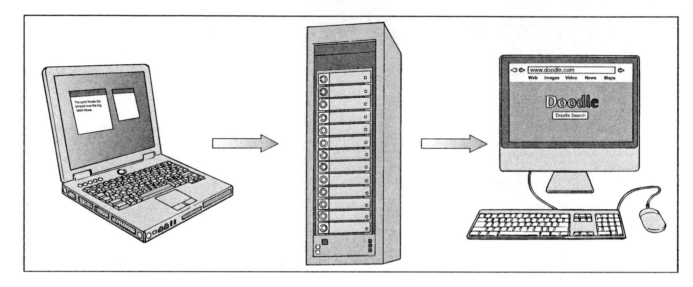

About Web Servers

For your site to be available to the public, it must reside on a computer capable of making websites publically available. A computer that can do that is called a *web server*. Any computer can be a web server, provided it has web server software installed. You may be thinking that if any computer can be a web server, why not just install the software to make your computer a web server? While you could, it would be a terrible idea! Configuring a web server is not an easy job—especially if you want it done in such a way that people can't hack into your site and change files on your computer or use your computer as a mindless drone to carry out viral attacks on the Internet. Maintaining a web server is best left to the professionals.

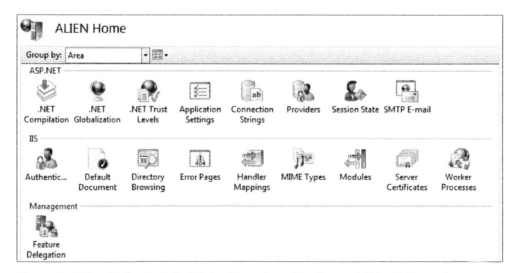

The main configuration screen for Microsoft's web server software, Internet Information Services, has many categories of settings. A wrong setting can lead to an insecure computer, making it a playground for hackers.

Web Server Software

While you are not likely to be installing or configuring web server software, it is beneficial to at least recognize the names so you can intelligently converse with the professionals who maintain web servers. The two most popular web server software packages are as follows.

- **Internet Information Services(IIS)**—Comes free with Windows (but Windows itself is not free) and runs only on Windows computers.

- **Apache HTTP Server (Apache)**—Free to download from apache.com and runs on Windows, Linux, and Macintosh operating systems. Apache has been the most widely used web server since 1996. As of July 2007, it holds about 53 percent of the market share with its closest competitor, IIS, at a distant 32 percent.

Choosing a Hosting Service

Companies that provide web servers to the public are known as *web hosts*. You can think of a web host as an Internet landlord. For a monthly or annual fee, you rent space on their web server's hard drive. A web-hosting company may have thousands of web server computers distributed throughout several cities or states.

Free Hosts

Many Internet service providers (such as AOL) provide free web space to their users. While this may be acceptable for personal homepages, it just doesn't suffice for a professional or commercial site. One reason is that you must use the Internet service provider's domain name followed by your username to connect to your site, for example, www.aol.com/myusername. Secondly, a free hosting plan may add advertising banners to your site. Lastly, a free hosting plan won't have anywhere near the quality or quantity of features included with a commercial plan.

Cost

You can find commercial hosting plans for anywhere from $1 per month to $500 per month, depending on features; however, plans around $10 per month are more than enough for most people. The cost is usually determined by the features of the hosting plan.

Service Plan Features

A Google search for "web hosting" returns almost 300 million hits, so how do you choose a good host? The best advice is to ask someone with more experience than you. Ask a friend who has a website if they are happy with their host. Ask other web developers who they use. Once you have identified one or two web-hosting companies, you will need to look at their websites to compare plans. Web hosts typically offer several hosting plans that vary by the included features. It is imperative that you understand their advertised features so you can make an informed decision. The following table lists just a few of the more common features and options offered by most web hosts.

COMMON WEB-HOSTING FEATURES AND OPTIONS		
Money-back guarantee	Tech support	Shared and dedicated hosting
Uptime guarantee	Scheduled backups	Windows and Linux plans
Storage space	Bandwidth	POP3 email accounts
Statistics	FTP accounts	Domain name registration

Money-back Guarantee

Don't sign up with a web host unless they offer a money-back guarantee. Most hosts offer a 30-day guarantee with a full refund and no cancellation fee. A reputable host knows that once you have signed up with them, their service will be good enough to keep you.

Tech Support

Don't sign up with a web host unless they offer "24/7/365" tech support (meaning 24 hours a day, 7 days a week, 365 days a year). Tech support should be available via email and toll-free phone. Test it before you buy it! Call tech support and see how long it takes them to answer. Email them and see how long it takes to get a response. Many web hosts have a great sales team who answers the phone after the first ring and responds to emails within the hour—but their tech support rarely responds or the phone system is broken. A "great deal" at $2.95 a month for hosting isn't such a great deal if you need tech support and the web host is unresponsive.

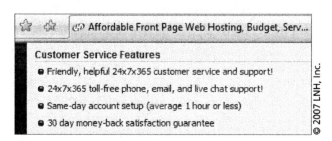

Host My Site (HostMySite.com), a popular web host, offers 24/7/365 tech support and a 30-day, money-back guarantee.

Shared and Dedicated Hosting

With a *dedicated hosting* plan, you get the entire web server computer to yourself. Your website is the only website on it and your site has full use of the computer's processor, RAM, and storage space. (Though some web hosts may allow you to have multiple sites on a dedicated server, the server is still dedicated to you and only you.) These plans typically cost a few hundred dollars a month and are overkill unless you have a huge website with a lot of traffic like Amazon or eBay. With a *shared hosting* plan, your website resides on a server along with hundreds and sometimes thousands of other websites. All the sites share the computer's resources (processor, RAM, etc.), but a good hosting company will make sure no one site is hogging everything. Shared hosting is the most common and a decent plan shouldn't cost more than about $10 per month.

Uptime Guarantee

Most web hosts offer an uptime guarantee of 99 percent, or very close to it. This means the server, and your site, will be online and accessible 99 percent of the time. There is almost nothing worse than your website going down because of a server crash. Don't sign up with a web host unless they offer an uptime guarantee between 97 and 99 percent.

Scheduled Backups

Computers crash; it's a fact of life. A web host should be backing up their servers, and therefore your site, on a regular basis (usually daily). Make sure this is included in your plan and that it happens automatically without you having to manually initiate a backup.

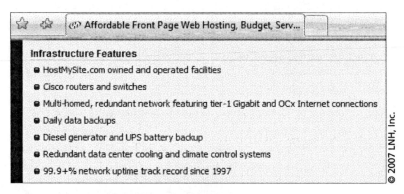

Host My Site offers daily backups and has had better than 99.9 percent uptime since 1997.

Windows and Linux Plans

Many hosts offer hosting plans on either a Windows or Linux server. Windows hosting is often a few dollars more expensive and is useful only if you use a Microsoft product, such as FrontPage or ExpressionWeb, to create your website. Linux plans tend to be less expensive and offer more features.

Storage Space

As HTML and CSS documents are plain text, the file sizes are fairly small. But add to that the other files in your site root, including images and other media files, and your site root may be as large as 10 MB. Most web hosts offer storage space hundreds of times as large—sometimes in the 50 GB range. This extra space can be useful for storing backups of your personal files—if the host allows this and if your personal files can be kept separate from the site root files.

Bandwidth

Bandwidth is sometimes referred to as *transfer rate*. It refers to the total amount of data that can be uploaded to and downloaded from your site. For example, imagine your plan comes with a monthly transfer rate of 500 GB. If someone visits your website, they need to download the HTML file, the CSS file, and any graphics—so maybe it takes 30 K to download an entire page. That 30 K counts towards your monthly bandwidth. If 100 users visited that same page, that would be 3,000 K (or about 3 MB). As more pages are viewed, more data is transferred and all of it counts towards your monthly limit. Files you upload to the server are also counted towards the limit. When the limit is reached, the web host may either cut off your site for the rest of the month or charge you for any additional bandwidth consumed.

POP3 Email Accounts

A POP3 email account allows you to create email addresses similar to your website address and to check that email with an email program like Outlook, Windows Mail, or MacMail. For example, if your website address is www.example.com, you could create email addresses such as support@example.com, sales@example.com, or bob@example.com.

Statistics

"Hit counters" placed at the bottom of a web page look amateurish. If you really want to know how many users have visited your site, make sure your plan comes with statistics. This is a feature that allows you to see how many visitors came to your site during which month, day, or hour, which pages were visited, which search engine users came from, and even which web browsers were used. A good statistics package is necessary for tracking search engine success.

A good statistics package, included free with many hosting plans, gives more useful information than a hit counter.

Total page visits throughout several days can be displayed as a line graph.

The most popular pages on the site are identified.

Track the search engines used to find your site.

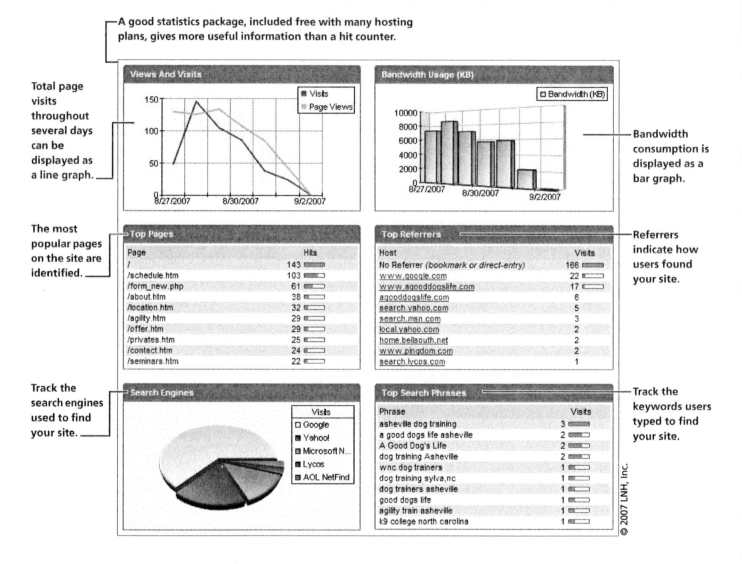

Bandwidth consumption is displayed as a bar graph.

Referrers indicate how users found your site.

Track the keywords users typed to find your site.

© 2007 LNH, Inc.

FTP Accounts

FTP (File Transfer Protocol), which is discussed in detail later in this lesson, is a way to transfer your site files from your local computer to the web server. To do this, you must have an FTP account on the server. Some web hosts allow only one FTP account. This can be a problem if you want to grant other people, like co-workers or third-party tech support, the ability to upload files or gain access to site files. For security and accountability, each user who uploads files should be doing so through their own account. If everyone is using the same FTP account, there is no way to know who did what or when.

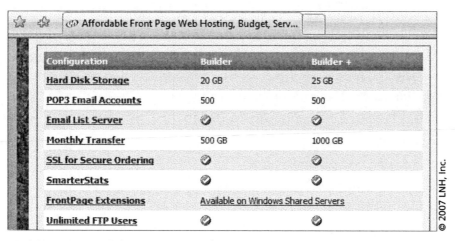

Configuration	Builder	Builder +
Hard Disk Storage	20 GB	25 GB
POP3 Email Accounts	500	500
Email List Server	✓	✓
Monthly Transfer	500 GB	1000 GB
SSL for Secure Ordering	✓	✓
SmarterStats	✓	✓
FrontPage Extensions	Available on Windows Shared Servers	
Unlimited FTP Users	✓	✓

A comparison between two Host My Site Linux plans.

Domain Name Registration

When you sign up for a web-hosting account, you'll need a domain name in order for users to connect to your website. For example, in http://www.labpub.com, "labpub.com" is the domain name. The details of domain names are covered in the next section, but first you should know a little bit about the registration process and how it relates to web hosts. Some web hosts offer free domain name registration with a hosting plan. While this sounds attractive, it is strongly recommend that you register the domain name on your own and have it ready before signing up with a web host. If your web host registers the domain name for you, it can be very difficult to switch to a different web host if you are unhappy with the current host. This is because of things like "name resolution" and "DNS propagation," which are covered in the next section along with registration. A plan that offers "free domain name registration" should not influence your decision to sign up with a host, as you should register and manage the domain name yourself.

Hands-On 13.1   Compare Web-hosting Plans

In this exercise, you will compare hosting plans.

1. Start your web browser and browse to **www.google.com**.

2. Type the phrase **web hosting** in the search box and click the Google Search button.

3. Click one of the links to visit any of the web-hosting companies found by Google.
   If the link you clicked is not for an actual web-hosting company, use the browser's Back button to return to the Google results page and try another link.

4. Start a word processing program such as Microsoft Word, WordPad, or TextEdit.

5. Create a blank word processing document and save it as **Web Hosts** to your Lesson 13 folder.

6. Answer the following questions in your Web Hosts document:

- What is the name of the web-hosting company and what is their web address (URL)?
- If the host offers different plans, choose one to read about. What is the name of the plan you selected?
- How much hard drive storage space is included?
- How many POP3 email accounts are included?
- Are site statistics available?
- Are multiple FTP accounts included?
- What is the monthly transfer limit (bandwidth)?
- What is the uptime guarantee?
- Is there a money-back guarantee? What are the guarantee details?
- What is their tech support policy? Toll-free phone? Email only? Live chat? 24/7/365?
- What is the cost of this plan?

7. Save the changes to your Web Hosts file, then close your word processor and your browser.

Working with Domain Names

A domain name uniquely identifies your website. Users type your domain name in their browser's address bar to connect to your site. A domain name is also used for "domain-name–based email" so you can have email addresses that match your web address.

Name Choices

Domain names should be easy to remember and easy to spell. Aside from that, there are different schools of thought as to what makes a successful domain name. One popular idea is to use a generic term that identifies your industry paired with a unique term that identifies your company. For example, a domain name like "hats.com" would be impossible to register nowadays as most generic terms have already been registered. A domain name like "BobSmith.com" may identify the company, but not what it sells. A domain name like "HatsByBobSmith.com" or "BobsHats.com" indicates that hats are sold there while identifying the company and promoting name recognition and branding. Of course, large corporations like Microsoft don't need to specify "MicrosoftComputerStuff.com," but for smaller businesses it is usually a good idea.

 TIP! *Domain names are not case-sensitive. Browsing to LabLearning.com or lablearning.com takes you to the same place.*

Top-level Domains

A top-level domain is the last part of a domain name, such as ".com" or ".net." Many website owners register multiple domain names with different top-level domains to stop competition from luring visitors away. For example, a company may register both labpub.com and labpub.net and associate both domain names with the same website. For smaller businesses, this is usually not necessary and not a justifiable expense. If you try to register a domain name like "hats.com" and you see it is already taken, it is a bad idea to register "hats.net." Most Internet users are more familiar with .com and even if your site is hats.net, they are likely to inadvertently type hats.com in their address bar. If the .com name you want is not available, it is better to come up with a completely different name so you can register it with a .com top-level domain.

Two Flavors

Top-level domains are categorized as "generic" or "country code." Top-level country codes include .us (for the United States), .ca (for Canada), .jp (for Japan), and about 143 more. There are about 22 generic top-level domains. The following table shows a few common top-level domains.

QUICK REFERENCE: COMMON GENERIC TOP-LEVEL DOMAINS

Domain	Notes
.com	Commercial—Any person can register a .com.
.net	Network—Any person can register a .net, but it is usually associated with websites relating to technology.
.org	Organization—Any person can register a .org, but it is usually associated with organizations.
.edu	Educational—Available only to qualifying educational institutions.
.mil	US military—Limited to the US military.
.gov	Governmental—Limited to government agencies.

NOTE! *Visit the website for this book for a link to a complete list of all current top-level domains.*

Domain Name Registrars

You register your domain name through an accredited registrar. (Registrars are accredited by ICANN, an organization you read about in Lesson 1, Introducing Web Technologies.) The cost to register and keep a domain is anywhere from $5 to $35 per year, depending on the registrar you use. Again, you should register your domain name with one company but host your website with another. The web-hosting company's tech support can give you instructions for associating your domain name with your website after everything is set up and registered. Some registrars allow you to set a preference that automatically charges your credit card every year to renew your domain name. This is a helpful option to turn on! Otherwise, you will need to remember to renew your registration manually. If your domain name registration is not renewed, users will no longer be able to type your domain name in their address bar to connect to your site.

Three popular domain name registrars are:

- Network Solutions (networksolutions.com or netsol.com)

- Go Daddy (godaddy.com)

- Register.com (register.com)

NOTE! *Visit the website for this book for a link to a list of accredited registrars.*

Whois

Whois is an Internet service that allows you to check the availability of a domain name. For example, you can check to see if hats.com is available before you attempt to register it with a registrar. Most web hosts and registrars have a form somewhere on their site that accesses whois information so you can easily check for availability.

The Host My Site site offers a whois lookup.

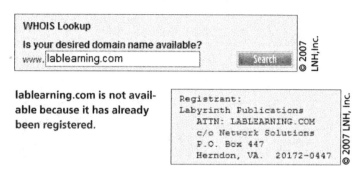

lablearning.com is not available because it has already been registered.

Domain Name Service

The real nuts and bolts behind how domain names work lies with the *domain name service*, or DNS. A complete technical analysis of this service is beyond the scope of this book—there are many websites that explain the system quite well—but the basics are covered here.

IP Addresses

The web servers managed by web-hosting companies are assigned *IP (Internet Protocol) addresses*, which uniquely identify them from other web servers on the Internet. Additionally, most websites themselves are assigned unique IP addresses by the web host. An example IP address looks like this: 84.40.26.37. (IP addresses are in the format xxx.xxx.xxx.xxx.) Every website has an IP address, and although users can connect to websites by typing the IP address in the browser's address bar, it would be difficult for users to remember them. Remembering a domain name is much easier. Also, if a website owner switched to a different web host, the IP address of the site would change, but the domain name would remain the same. If users memorized an IP address, then the site changed to a different server, the IP address would no longer work. Actually, any computer that is connected to the Internet has an IP address—even yours.

Name Resolution

The domain name service creates a mapping to associate a domain name with an IP address. When a user types "lablearning.com" in the browser's address bar, their computer locates a DNS server that has a mapping of all domain names to learn the associated IP address. The website is then located via the IP address. The process of looking up a domain name and finding the matching IP address is known as *name resolution* (resolving a domain name to an IP address). Resolution happens behind the scenes when you type a URL and tap Enter. When you register a domain name with a registrar, you can log in to your account on the registrar's website and associate your domain name with your web host's DNS server to create the resolution mapping. This is what makes it possible to easily switch to a different web host without too much trouble; you simply change the DNS server associated with your domain name to that of a different web host.

Propagation

Once you associate your domain name to a web host's DNS server, that mapping must be replicated to every other DNS server on the Internet. This process usually completes within 72 hours, which is why when you initially associate your domain name with a DNS server, it takes a few days until your URL works.

 Hands-On 13.2   Use the Whois Service

In this exercise, you will use the whois service to determine the availability of a domain name.

1. Start your web browser and browse to **www.internic.net**.
   InterNIC is a website operated by ICANN. It provides information about domain name registration to the general public.

2. Click the Whois hyperlink at the top of the page.

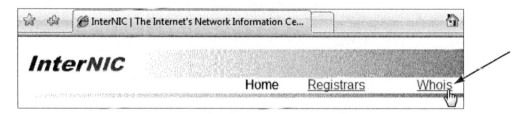

3. Follow these steps to search for a domain name:

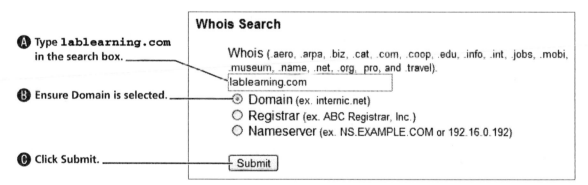

Ⓐ Type **lablearning.com** in the search box.

Ⓑ Ensure Domain is selected.

Ⓒ Click Submit.

Be patient as you wait for the results page to load.

4. Scroll through the results page and notice the following block of information:

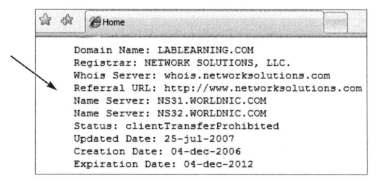

```
Domain Name: LABLEARNING.COM
Registrar: NETWORK SOLUTIONS, LLC.
Whois Server: whois.networksolutions.com
Referral URL: http://www.networksolutions.com
Name Server: NS31.WORLDNIC.COM
Name Server: NS32.WORLDNIC.COM
Status: clientTransferProhibited
Updated Date: 25-jul-2007
Creation Date: 04-dec-2006
Expiration Date: 04-dec-2012
```

The results page confirms that the lablearning.com domain is already registered and, therefore, is not available for you to register as your own.

5. Scroll back to the top of the page and, using steps similar to those in step 3, search for **i-dont-think-this-domain-is-registered.com**.

Unless someone has registered the domain since the publication of this book, the results page indicates the name is not currently registered—meaning you could register it if you wanted.

```
Whois Server Version 1.3

Domain names in the .com and .net domains can now be registered
with many different competing registrars. Go to http://www.internic.net
for detailed information.

No match for domain "I-DONT-THINK-THIS-DOMAIN-IS-REGISTERED.COM".
```

Making Your Site Available to the Public

Once you have registered a domain name, have signed up for a web-hosting account, and have configured your domain name's DNS through the registrar's website, you need to transfer your site files to the web server. You do this using an FTP program, which must be configured with the proper logon credentials. The web-hosting company should provide you with the following four pieces of information, probably in a "welcome" or "setup" email they sent once you signed up:

- FTP host
- Username
- Password
- Root folder

File Transfer Protocol

The file transfer protocol (FTP) is a method used to transfer files between computers across a network. While many web browsers incorporate this functionality, it is better to use a dedicated FTP program (an FTP client) as they offer more features and are written specifically for this purpose.

FTP Clients

At the time of this writing, an Internet search for *FTP client* returns close to 25 million results. Many of these programs cost only a few dollars, but the manufacturers typically offer a trial period for their software so you can "try before you buy." One free FTP client is FileZilla, written by Tim Kosse and available from Sourceforge.net.

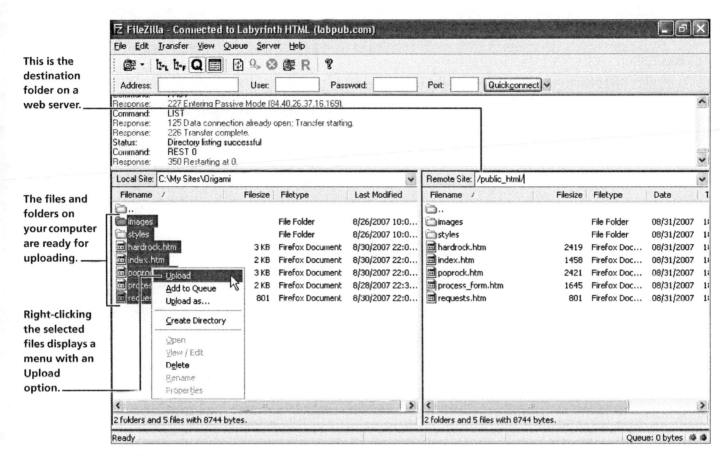

This is the destination folder on a web server.

The files and folders on your computer are ready for uploading.

Right-clicking the selected files displays a menu with an Upload option.

FileZilla, a free Windows FTP program

Working with an FTP Program

No matter which FTP client you use, they all work pretty much the same way. You enter the required information to connect to the web server, including the address of the web server (usually called the *host address* or the *FTP host*), your username, and your password. Once connected, files on your computer appear on one side of the screen and files on the web server appear on the other side. After browsing to the root folder on the server, you simply drag and drop files from one side to the other to transfer files between your computer and the web server.

QUICK REFERENCE: GENERIC STEPS FOR MOST FTP PROGRAMS

Step	Procedure
1	Get the logon information from your web host.
2	Start the FTP program.
3	Use the logon information provided by the web host to configure the FTP client. (Most FTP software includes dialog boxes that walk you through this process.)
4	Log on to the web server.
5	Navigate to the source and destination folders on your computer and the web server.
6	Use drag and drop or the Upload command in the FTP software to transfer the site files to the web server.
7	Test your site by entering its URL into the address bar of a web browser.

Hands-On 13.3   Upload Site Files

 In this exercise, you will use FTP to upload your files to a web server. As this is a web simulation, you won't actually be uploading any files, but the generic steps presented here are applicable to most FTP clients.

1. Start your web browser, browse to **www.labpub.com/learn/wdhtml**, and click the Hands-On 13.3 Upload Site Files link.

2. Chose Start→All Programs→FileZilla Client→FileZilla.

3. Follow these steps to enter the logon credentials:

A Type **ftp://lablearningstudent.joolo.com** for the host address.

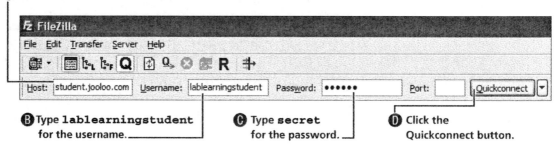

B Type **lablearningstudent** for the username.   **C** Type **secret** for the password.   **D** Click the Quickconnect button.

4. Click HTML Student Files in the left pane to drill down into the HTML Student Files folder:

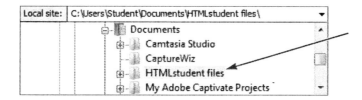

5. Click fup_forms in the left pane to drill down into the fup_forms folder.

6. Click images in the left pane to drill down into the images folder and display the contents in the pane below.
   You have navigated to the local folder containing the file you wish to upload.

7. Click the plus (+) sign in the right pane to expand the folder on the web server.

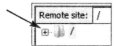

8. Click the images folder in the right pane to open it.
   You have navigated to the destination folder on the server.

9. Click the angel_thumb.gif file in the left pane.
   In the actual FileZilla program, you right-click a file to upload it. In this simulation, your left-click simulates a right-click action.

10. Choose Upload from the pop-up menu.
    The selected file, angel_thumb.gif, is uploaded to the images folder on the server.

11. Close all browser windows.

 **Concepts Review**

True/False Questions

1. Apache is the most widely used web server software today. TRUE FALSE

2. You should expect to pay about $60 a month for a web-hosting service plan. TRUE FALSE

3. A web host that advertises "99% Uptime" is referring to the hours throughout the day that tech support is available via telephone. TRUE FALSE

4. With a shared hosting plan, your website may reside on a server along with hundreds of other websites. TRUE FALSE

5. It is a good idea to have your web host register your domain name for you—especially as most offer to register it for free. TRUE FALSE

6. Any person can register a .com domain name, but only technical professionals can register a .net domain. TRUE FALSE

7. You can learn if a domain name is available by using the whois service. TRUE FALSE

8. You can connect to a website by typing its IP address in your browser's address bar. TRUE FALSE

9. A good web host will offer a free hit counter you can place at the bottom of all your pages to see how much traffic your site is getting. TRUE FALSE

10. When registering a domain name, be sure to verify your [Caps Lock] key is not on as domain names are case-sensitive. TRUE FALSE

Multiple Choice Questions

1. Rolf has subcontracted out some advanced web programming to another developer. He wants this developer to upload files to the web server using a separate username and password rather than sharing his administrative account. What feature should Rolf make sure is included with his web-hosting plan to accommodate this?

   a. 24/7/365 support

   b. Multiple POP3 accounts

   c. Multiple FTP accounts

   d. Hosted on a Windows server and not a Linux server

2. Of the following top-level domains, which can be registered by anyone?

   a. .edu

   b. .gov

   c. .mil

   d. .org

3. Which Internet service allows you to check the availability of a domain name?

   a. DNS

   b. IP addressing

   c. FTP

   d. Whois

4. Tara has configured her domain name registration account on her registrar's website so her domain name is associated with her website's DNS server. However, when she types her domain name into her browser's address bar, her site does not display. What is the most likely cause of the problem?

   a. Her computer does not have a valid IP address.

   b. Changes to DNS can take up to 72 hours to propagate. She needs to wait a few days and then try again.

   c. She uploaded her website files to the wrong web server.

   d. Her Windows browser is not compatible with the Linux web server.

Skill Builders

Skill Builder 13.1 Configure an FTP Client

On the Web *In this exercise, you will configure an FTP client with information provided by a web host. As this is a web simulation, you won't actually be configuring any software on your computer.*

1. Start your web browser, navigate to **www.labpub.com/learn/wdhtml**, and click the Skill Builder 13.1: Configure an FTP Client link.
   Yahoo! Mail is open on the Desktop.

2. Select the Welcome! message from the web host.

3. Take note of the host address, username, password, and site root.

4. Minimize the browser.

5. Choose Start→All Programs→FileZilla Client→FileZilla to launch the FTP client.

6. Click the Site Manager button at the far left end of the toolbar.

7. Click the New Site button.

8. Type **My New Site** to rename the site from the default offered by FileZilla.

9. In the Host box, type the host address from step 3.

10. In the Logontype area, select Normal.

11. In the User box, type the username from step 3.

12. In the Password box, type the password from step 3.

13. Click the Advanced tab at the top of the window.

14. Type the name of the remote site root from step 3 in the Default Remote Directory box, then click OK.

15. Click the small arrow next to the Site Manager button on the toolbar and choose My New Site to display a list of all saved sites.
    A connection to the server is established. The server automatically displays files in the remote site root because of the advanced setting you configured.

Assessments

Assessment 13.1   Check Domain Name Availability

In this exercise, you will check the availability of a domain name. You will then find an available domain name.

Check Domain Name Availability

1. Start your web browser and browse to **www.internic.net**.

2. Use the Whois service to check the availability of either microsoft.com or apple.com.

3. Start a word processor, create a new blank document, and save it as **as-Domains** to your Lesson 13 folder.

4. In your as-Domains document, state which domain you checked and list the following information reported by Whois:

   ■ Who is the registrar?

   ■ When was it registered (the creation date)?

   ■ When will it expire?

Find an Available Domain Name

5. Think of a domain name you would like to register for yourself. Come up with several in case your first choice is unavailable.

6. Use the Whois service on the InterNIC site to see if your first choice is available. If it's not, try your second choice, then your third choice, and so on until you find a domain name that is available.

7. Write your available domain name in your as-Domains document.

8. Save your changes, then close your web browser and word processor.

Assessment 13.2   Compare Web-hosting Service Plans

In this exercise, you will compare hosting plans between three different web hosts.

1. Start your web browser and use your favorite search engine to find three different web-hosting companies.

2. Select one plan from each of the three companies. The plans should be similar but do not have to match exactly. If there are no plans that are similar, find a different web-hosting company.

3. Start a word processor, create a new blank document, and save it as **as-Hosting** to your Lesson 13 folder.

4. In your as-Hosting document, answer the following questions about the first web-hosting company you chose:

   - What is the name of the web-hosting company?
   - What is the name of the hosting plan you selected from this company?
   - How much hard drive storage space comes with the account?
   - What is the monthly bandwidth transfer limit?
   - How many POP3 email accounts are included?
   - Are multiple FTP accounts included?
   - Is there an uptime guarantee, and if so, what is it?
   - What is the availability and the contact method for tech support?
   - What is the monthly or annual cost of the plan?
   - Is there a startup fee?

5. In your as-Hosting document, answer the same questions about the second web-hosting company you chose.

6. In your as-Hosting document, answer the same questions about the third web-hosting company you chose.

7. In your as-Hosting document, answer the following questions:

   - Between these three hosting companies/plans, which one would you be most likely to choose?
   - What makes the plan you selected more attractive to you than the others?

Critical Thinking

Critical Thinking 13.1 Research Name Resolution

In this exercise, you will research DNS to learn how name resolution works.

When a user types a domain name in their browser's address bar and taps Enter, the browser must learn the IP address associated with the domain name in order to connect to the website. This is accomplished through the process of name resolution.

- Using your favorite search engine, research the phrase *DNS name resolution* to learn how name resolution works.

- In a new word processing document, list the URLs you found in your search that were helpful in explaining the name resolution process.

- In the same word processing document, explain in your own words the name resolution process. In other words, what happens after a user types a domain name in their browser's address bar and taps Enter? Be sure to explain this in your own words.

- Save your document to your Lesson 13 folder as **ct-Name Resolution**.

LESSON 14

Migrating and Troubleshooting

In this lesson, you will review the importance of valid code. You will examine a document type declaration and learn how to validate your code. You will learn about deprecated tags and migrate an HTML page to XHTML. Lastly, you will find and fix errors in XHTML code.

LESSON OBJECTIVES

After studying this lesson, you will be able to:

- Identify common deprecated tags
- Validate a document
- Locate and fix code errors

Case Study: Validating Code

Haylie and Miguel have put a lot of time and energy into developing their website and finding a good web-hosting plan. Before they start advertising their website, Haylie validates the XHTML code to make sure everything is perfect. She uses the validation option in her browser add-on toolbar to streamline the process. Once she verifies the validity of her code, she and Miguel can rest easy knowing they have developed their website responsibly.

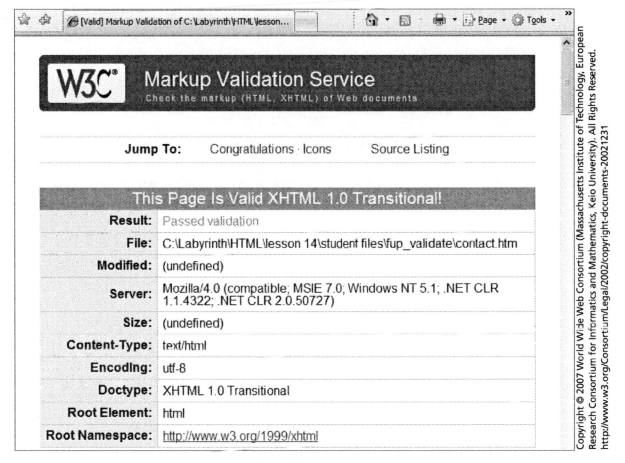

Free online validation tools help ensure your code is valid.

Validating XHTML

Writing valid code is important for many reasons:

- Your pages will display as expected in compliant browsers.

- Your pages will function in a wide variety of browsers.

- Your code will be easier to share with other developers should you need technical support or work with a team.

- Your code will not be bloated and your file sizes will be smaller, resulting in faster downloads and reduction of wasted bandwidth.

Remember that browsers render code differently. Even if your code validates, that is not a guarantee that your page will look exactly the same in all browsers.

Valid XHTML Defined

XHTML code is considered valid if it follows all of the rules and recommendations specified by the W3C. As there are different versions of HTML and XHTML, you must be familiar with the rules for the version you are using. You must also state which version you are using at the top of your page so the web browser knows how to interpret your code.

DOCTYPE Declaration Revisited

The DOCTYPE declaration you have been writing at the top of your XHTML pages throughout this book has been identifying the version of code you have been using—specifically XHTML 1.0 transitional. You have typed this DOCTYPE code several times, but may have never really looked at it.

```
<!DOCTYPE html PUBLIC "-//W3C//DTD XHTML 1.0 Transitional//EN"
"http://www.w3.org/TR/xhtml1/DTD/xhtml1-transitional.dtd">
```

This URL points to the actual document type declaration
(a DTD file) containing the rules for XHTML 1.0 transitional.

The DTD (document type declaration)
is specified as XHTML 1.0 transitional.

The actual document type declaration file can be viewed in Internet Explorer. You can determine which tags and attributes are required, optional, or forbidden by reading a document type declaration (DTD) document. You will do this in the first exercise.

HTML Comments

An HTML comment is a line of code that is not displayed in the browser but that may be helpful to the people working with the code. HTML comments can be used to identify page sections, identify the author of a specific block of code, or for any other reason where a comment may be helpful. HTML comments, when used in excess, can bloat your code so they should be used sparingly. A comment begins with <!-- and ends with -->.

```
<!-- Begin main navigation -->
```
HTML comments may span a single line...

```
<!--
Begin footer
includes footer navigation
-->
```
...or multiple lines.

 TIP! *Using more than two dashes at the start or end of the tag invalidates the code, as in* `<!---- This is invalid --->`. *To accomplish a similar visual, use a different character, as in* `<!--===== This is valid =====-->`.

 ## Hands-On 14.1   View a DTD

In this exercise, you will view a document type declaration document.

Before You Begin: You must use Internet Explorer for this exercise. Firefox will not work.

1. Start Internet Explorer and browse to the URL specified in the DOCTYPE declaration for XHTML 1.0 transitional:
   http://www.w3.org/TR/xhtml1/DTD/xhtml1-transitional.dtd
   The document is displayed in the browser window. Firefox would have asked you to save the file or select a program with which to view it. Internet Explorer can display the DTD natively.

2. Take a moment to read the information at the top of the DTD.

The DTD is for XHTML 1.0 transitional.

It is basically the same as HTML 4.

The namespace is what you have used as the `xmlns` attribute in your opening `<html>` tags.

A portion of the DOCTYPE tag is listed.

The standard was last revised August 1, 2002.

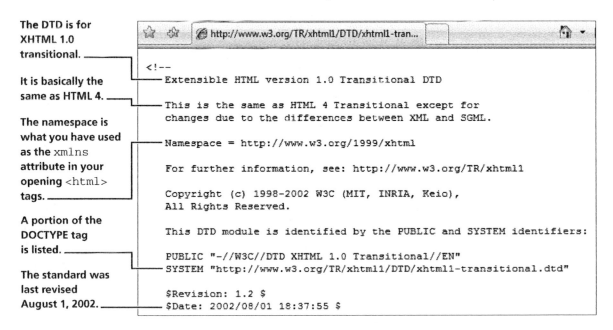

```
<!--
Extensible HTML version 1.0 Transitional DTD

This is the same as HTML 4 Transitional except for
changes due to the differences between XML and SGML.

Namespace = http://www.w3.org/1999/xhtml

For further information, see: http://www.w3.org/TR/xhtml1

Copyright (c) 1998-2002 W3C (MIT, INRIA, Keio),
All Rights Reserved.

This DTD module is identified by the PUBLIC and SYSTEM identifiers:

PUBLIC "-//W3C//DTD XHTML 1.0 Transitional//EN"
SYSTEM "http://www.w3.org/TR/xhtml1/DTD/xhtml1-transitional.dtd"

$Revision: 1.2 $
$Date: 2002/08/01 18:37:55 $
```

3. Notice that the next section begins with an HTML comment.

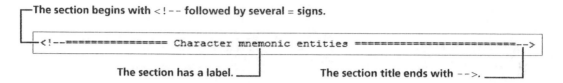

The section begins with `<!--` followed by several = signs.

```
<!--=============== Character mnemonic entities ========================-->
```

The section has a label. ___

The section title ends with `-->`. ___

4. Locate the start of the next section, titled *Imported Names*. *The content in this section is pretty technical.*

5. Locate the start of the next section, titled *Generic Attributes*:

The section begins with `<!--` followed by several = signs. ___

Generic attributes that are valid for most tags are listed. ___

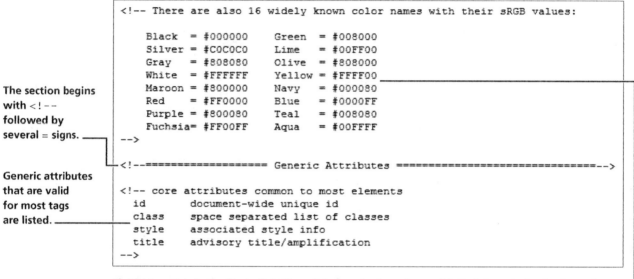

```
<!-- There are also 16 widely known color names with their sRGB values:

    Black   = #000000    Green  = #008000
    Silver  = #C0C0C0    Lime   = #00FF00
    Gray    = #808080    Olive  = #808000
    White   = #FFFFFF    Yellow = #FFFF00
    Maroon  = #800000    Navy   = #000080
    Red     = #FF0000    Blue   = #0000FF
    Purple  = #800080    Teal   = #008080
    Fuchsia = #FF00FF    Aqua   = #00FFFF
-->

<!--=================== Generic Attributes ==========================-->

<!-- core attributes common to most elements
    id          document-wide unique id
    class       space separated list of classes
    style       associated style info
    title       advisory title/amplification
-->
```

The first section in the figure lists the valid named colors along with their hexadecimal color code. ___

6. Tap `Ctrl`+`F` to open the Find dialog box.

7. Follow these steps to search for information about the `<img>` tag:

A Type **images** in the Find box.

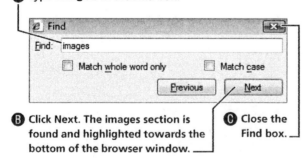

B Click Next. The images section is found and highlighted towards the bottom of the browser window. ___

C Close the Find box. ___

8. Scroll down a little to view the section about images.

Attributes that are valid to use with the `<img>` tag are listed here. Note that there are 12 valid attributes and that `align` and `border` are among them.

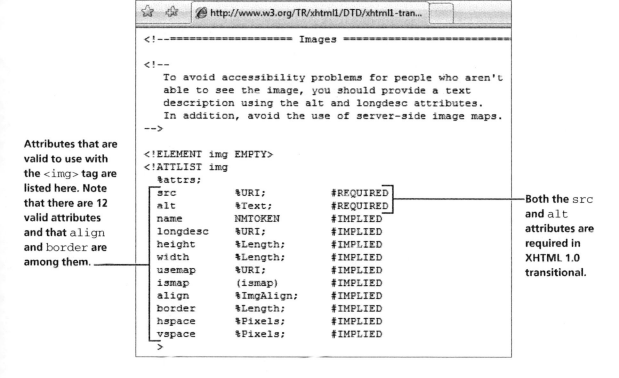

Both the `src` and `alt` attributes are required in XHTML 1.0 transitional.

9. View the DTD for XHTML 1.0 strict by editing the URL in the address bar as follows:

Ⓐ Click at the end of the URL. Make sure the URL does not highlight but that your cursor I-beam is flashing to the right of the URL.

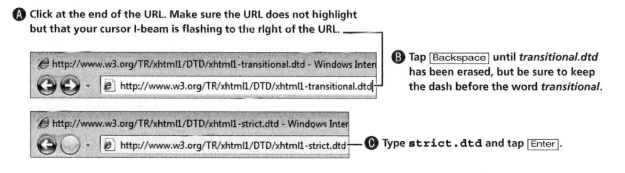

Ⓑ Tap `Backspace` until *transitional.dtd* has been erased, but be sure to keep the dash before the word *transitional*.

Ⓒ Type `strict.dtd` and tap `Enter`.

The DTD for XHTML 1.0 strict loads in the browser window.

10. Repeat steps 6 and 7 to find the section about images.

11. Scroll down to view the valid attributes for the <img> tag in XHTML 1.0 strict.

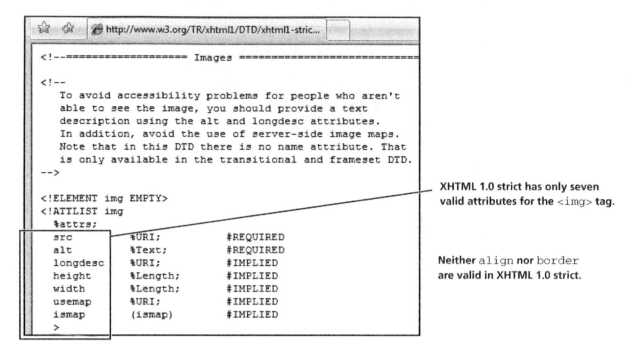

```
<!--================== Images ==========================

<!--
    To avoid accessibility problems for people who aren't
    able to see the image, you should provide a text
    description using the alt and longdesc attributes.
    In addition, avoid the use of server-side image maps.
    Note that in this DTD there is no name attribute. That
    is only available in the transitional and frameset DTD.
-->

<!ELEMENT img EMPTY>
<!ATTLIST img
  %attrs;
  src          %URI;        #REQUIRED
  alt          %Text;       #REQUIRED
  longdesc     %URI;        #IMPLIED
  height       %Length;     #IMPLIED
  width        %Length;     #IMPLIED
  usemap       %URI;        #IMPLIED
  ismap        (ismap)      #IMPLIED
  >
```

XHTML 1.0 strict has only seven valid attributes for the <img> tag.

Neither align nor border are valid in XHTML 1.0 strict.

12. Use the browser's Back button to return to the DTD for XHTML 1.0 transitional.

13. Feel free to scroll through the page and read more about what is required of valid XHTML 1.0 transitional code.

14. When you are finished, close Internet Explorer.

Online Validation Tools

Reading through a DTD to determine what is valid and what is not can be a painful and tedious process. Fortunately, there are free online tools that do this heavy lifting for you and simply report to you any invalid code. The W3C has a free online validation tool that allows you to validate the code on any website or in any local file, or by typing a block of code directly into their form.

Validating via a Toolbar Add-on

Browsing to a website to validate your code takes longer than it should. You need to browse to the site, wait for the page to load, navigate to the validation tool, wait for the page to load, type in the URL of the page you wish to validate or upload a local file to validate, and click a Check button, and only then do you finally get the results. Using a browser toolbar add-on such as the Web Developer toolbar for Firefox or the Web Accessibility Toolbar for Internet Explorer automates the process of connecting to the W3C validator and makes the validation process much quicker.

The Web Accessibility Toolbar for Internet Explorer offers a Check button with a drop-down menu that leads to the W3C validator.

Validate HTML will load the results in the same browser window. The New Window option loads the results in a new browser window so you don't lost your current page. The File Upload option allows you to upload a local file for validation.

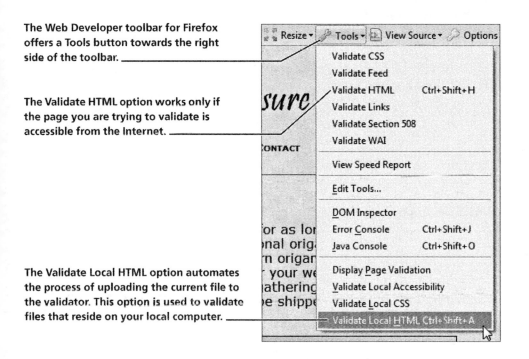

The Web Developer toolbar for Firefox offers a Tools button towards the right side of the toolbar.

The Validate HTML option works only if the page you are trying to validate is accessible from the Internet.

The Validate Local HTML option automates the process of uploading the current file to the validator. This option is used to validate files that reside on your local computer.

Hands-On 14.2 Validate Code

In this exercise, you will validate code using a toolbar.

1. Start your web browser, open the index.htm file from the validation folder in your Lesson 14 folder, and follow the instructions for your situation:

   ■ If you use Internet Explorer with the Web Accessibility Toolbar, complete steps 2–9.

   ■ If you use Firefox with the Web Developer toolbar, complete steps 10–15.

   ■ If neither of these situations applies to you, complete steps 16–24.

Internet Explorer and the Web Accessibility Toolbar

If you are using Internet Explorer and the Web Accessibility Toolbar complete steps 2–9 here.

2. Choose Check→W3C HTML Validator→Validate HTML [File Upload] from the Web Accessibility Toolbar.

   A new browser window opens and reports that the code is valid.

3. Close the browser window with the validation results to return to the browser window with the Folding Under Pressure homepage.

4. Tap ⌨Ctrl+⌨O to display the Open dialog box.

5. Click Browse.

6. Navigate to your Lesson 14 folder (not the fup_validate folder), if necessary; open the validation folder.

7. Select the trouble.htm page and click Open.
   The trouble.htm file is a copy of the previous index.htm file but with errors.

8. Repeat step 2 to validate the page.
   Validation fails because there are errors in the code. You will fix the errors later in this lesson.

   You will need to validate other pages later in this lesson, so make sure you know the steps to validate for your computer's configuration.

9. Close Internet Explorer.
   Skip the rest of this exercise and continue reading the Working with Deprecated Tags section on page 454.

Firefox and the Web Developer Toolbar

If you are using Firefox and the Web Developer toolbar, complete steps 10–15 here.

10. Choose Tools→Validate Local HTML from the Web Developer toolbar.

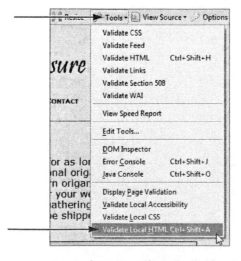

A new browser tab opens and reports that the code is valid.

11. Tap ⌈Ctrl⌉+⌈O⌉ to display the Open dialog box.

12. Navigate to your Lesson 14 folder (not the fup_validate folder), if necessary; open the validation folder.

13. Select the trouble.htm page and click Open.
    The trouble.htm file is a copy of the previous index.htm file but with errors.

14. Repeat step 10 to validate the page.
    Validation fails because there are errors in the code. You will fix the errors later in this lesson.

    You will need to validate other pages later in this lesson, so make sure you know the steps to validate for your computer's configuration.

15. Close Firefox.
    Skip the rest of this exercise and continue reading the Working with Deprecated Tags section on page 454.

Any Browser and No Toolbar

If you are not using the Web Accessibility Toolbar or the Web Developer toolbar, complete steps 15–23 here.

16. Type **www.w3.org** in the Address Bar and tap ⌈Enter⌉.

17. Scroll down the page and click the **HTML Validator** hyperlink in the navigation bar on the left side of the page.

18. Click the Validate by File Upload tab.

19. Click the Browse button.

20. Navigate to your Lesson 14 folder (not the fup_validate folder), if necessary; open the validation folder.

21. Select the index.htm page and click Open.

22. Click the Check button.
    Your page is validated and the code is valid.

23. Repeat steps 16–22, but select the trouble.htm page to validate this time.
    The trouble.htm file is a copy of the previous index.htm file but with errors.

    Validation fails because there are errors in the code. You will fix the errors later in this lesson.

    You will need to validate other pages later in this lesson, so make sure you know the steps to validate for your computer's configuration.

24. Close your browser.

Working with Deprecated Tags

Deprecated tags are those which still function but are being phased out and should be avoided. The intentional use of deprecated tags is not recommended. However, you may take over the maintenance of a website that uses deprecated code, so it is important to recognize it when you see it. There is nothing wrong with using deprecated tags—as long as they aren't deprecated. That may not make sense right away! A tag by itself cannot be deprecated. A tag can only be deprecated in a specific standard, such as being deprecated in XHTML 1.0 transitional or XHTML 1.0 strict. If a web page was coded using HTML 3.2, then <font> tags aren't deprecated. However, if a page's DOCTYPE declares XHTML 1.0 transitional, then the same <font> tag is deprecated and should be replaced with a CSS alternative.

Two Common Examples

Perhaps the two most often misused tags when coding XHTML are the <font> and <center> tags. These tags are deprecated as of HTML 4. Officially, they are deprecated in XHTML 1.0 transitional and forbidden in XHTML 1.0 strict. This means use of the tags will still validate in XHTML 1.0 transitional, but will cause validation to fail with XHTML 1.0 strict. The fact that they still validate in an XHTML 1.0 transitional page doesn't mean you should use them. As they are deprecated, you should replace them with CSS alternatives.

Formatting with the Font Tag

The <font> tag was used to modify the font of whatever text was contained within the tags. Three attributes were used:

- face—Specified the typeface
- color—Specified the color of the text
- size—Specified the size of text

This example would tell the browser to use the Arial or Helvetica font at a size of 4 in red:

```
<font face="arial,helvetica" size="4" color="#FF0000">This text is red</font>
```

Centering with the Center Tag

The <center> tag was used without attributes to center whatever the tags contained in the browser window. This code would center the heading and paragraph in the browser window:

```
<center><h1>Centered Text</h1><p>This is centered.</p></center>
```

Hands-On 14.3   Use the Font and Center Tags

In this exercise, you will use deprecated tags so you can identify them on pages you may be asked to update.

1. Start your web browser and open the deprecated.htm file from the validation folder in your Lesson 14 folder.
Notice that the text is aligned to the left of your browser window, all of the text is black, and the typeface is a default serif.

2. Start Notepad and open the same deprecated.htm file.

3. Locate the only heading tag in the code and follow these steps to format the text with deprecated tags:

A Click after the opening `<h1>` tag and type `<font color="#FF0000">`.

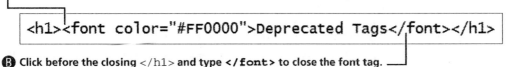

```
<h1><font color="#FF0000">Deprecated Tags</font></h1>
```

B Click before the closing `</h1>` and type `</font>` to close the font tag.

4. Save your changes, switch to your browser, and tap F5.
The heading text turns red.

5. Switch back to Notepad and follow these steps to continue formatting:

A Click after the word *the* following the opening `<p>` tag and type `<font size="+2" color="#00FF00">`.

```
<p>The <font size="+2" color="#00FF00">FONT and CENTER</font>
```

B Click after the word *CENTER* and type the closing `</font>` tag.

6. Save your changes, switch to your browser, and tap F5.
The phrase FONT and CENTER *turns green and the font size is increased.*

7. Switch back to Notepad and follow these steps to center the content:

A Click in the space after the opening `<body>` tag and type `<center>`.

```
<body>
<center>
```

```
</center>
</body>
```

B Click before the closing `</body>` tag and type `</center>`.

8. Save your changes, switch to your browser, and tap F5.
All page content is centered in the browser window.

9. Using the steps you followed in Hands-On 14.2, validate the page.
The page passes validation because the deprecated tags are still supported in XHTML 1.0 transitional.

10. If you validated via a browser toolbar add-on, close the validation results page. Otherwise, use the browser's Back button.
The deprecated.htm page should display in the browser window.

11. Follow these steps to change the DTD:

Ⓐ Change the word `Transitional` to **Strict**. Be sure to capitalize it.

```
<!DOCTYPE html PUBLIC "-//W3C//DTD XHTML 1.0 Transitional//EN"
"http://www.w3.org/TR/xhtml1/DTD/xhtml1-transitional.dtd">
```

Ⓑ Change the word `transitional` to **strict**. Be sure not to capitalize it.

Ⓒ Your code should look like this.

```
<!DOCTYPE html PUBLIC "-//W3C//DTD XHTML 1.0 Strict//EN"
"http://www.w3.org/TR/xhtml1/DTD/xhtml1-strict.dtd">
```

12. Save your changes, switch to your browser, and tap F5.
The page may still display as expected as many browsers are forgiving!

13. Using the steps you followed in Hands-On 14.2, validate the page.
The page fails validation because the deprecated tags are forbidden in XHTML 1.0 strict. The three deprecated tags have generated five validation errors.

You will replace deprecated code with valid XHTML in the next exercise.

14. Close your web browser and Notepad.

Migrating to XHTML and CSS

Migrating a page coded with older HTML to current XHTML/CSS standards can be a long and tedious process, but as discussed throughout this book, the benefits are many. Validation tools are helpful when rewriting code as there will probably be things you miss—and validation errors help you pinpoint these areas.

Cleaning Code

When updating a page from HTML to XHTML 1.0 transitional, there are several things to ensure:

■ There is a valid XHTML structure with a DOCTYPE declaration and `xmlns` attribute in the opening `<html>` tag.

■ There is a title element.

■ The character encoding is stated.

■ All tags and attributes are lowercase and all attributes have associated values enclosed in quotations.

■ All tags are closed and properly nested.

■ While not required for XHTML 1.0 transitional, it is a good idea to replace all presentational and deprecated tags and attributes with CSS if possible as you strive for XHTML 1.0 strict.

Hands-On 14.4   Migrate from HTML to XHTML/CSS

In this exercise, you will update an HTML page to valid XHTML.

Examine the Code

1. Start Notepad and open the migrate.htm file from the validation folder in your Lesson 14 folder.

2. Look through the code and note the following:
   - The DOCTYPE specifies HTML 4.01.
   - All tags and attributes are uppercase.
   - Values are not enclosed in quotes.
   - The <hr>, <br>, and <p> tags are not closed.
   - Deprecated <font> tags are used.
   - Presentational attributes such as align, border, and cellpadding are used.
   - Presentational tags such as <hr> and <b> are used.

3. Start your web browser, open the same migrate.htm file, and validate the page.
   The page passes validation because the code is valid HTML 4.01.

4. Close the validation page and ensure the migrate.htm page displays in the browser window.

Change the DOCTYPE

5. Switch to Notepad, select the entire DOCTYPE declaration as shown, and delete it.

```
<!DOCTYPE HTML PUBLIC "-//W3C//DTD HTML 4.01 Transitional//EN"
"http://www.w3.org/TR/html4/loose.dtd">
```

6. Type the following new DOCTYPE declaration at the top of the document:

   <!DOCTYPE html PUBLIC "-//W3C//DTD XHTML 1.0 Transitional//EN" Enter
   "http://www.w3.org/TR/xhtml1/DTD/xhtml1-transitional.dtd">

   You have replaced the HTML 4.01 transitional DOCTYPE declaration with an XHTML 1.0 transitional declaration.

7. Save your changes, switch to your browser, and tap F5.
   The page still displays as expected.

8. Validate the page.
   Validation fails with 59 errors because the code is not valid XHTML 1.0 transitional. There are probably fewer than 59 things to fix as a single code error may cause multiple validation errors.

9. Close the validation page and ensure the migrate.htm page displays in the browser window.

Remove Presentational Attributes

10. Switch to Notepad.

11. Locate the opening <BODY> tag and delete all the attributes/values so the tag looks like this: <BODY>.

12. Locate the opening <H1> tag and delete the `align` attribute/value so the tag looks like this: <H1>.

13. Locate the opening <TABLE> tag and delete all the attributes/values so the tag looks like this: <TABLE>.

14. Save your changes, switch to your browser, and tap [F5].
Most of the color formatting is removed.

15. Validate the page.
Validation fails with only 36 errors. Removing eight attributes cleared up 23 validation errors.

16. Close the validation page and ensure that the migrate.htm page displays in the browser window.

Remove Deprecated Tags

17. Switch to Notepad.

18. Locate the <FONT> tag and follow these steps to remove deprecated and presentational tags:

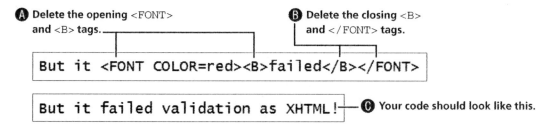

Ⓐ Delete the opening <FONT> and <B> tags.

Ⓑ Delete the closing <B> and </FONT> tags.

```
But it <FONT COLOR=red><B>failed</B></FONT>
```

```
But it failed validation as XHTML!
```

Ⓒ Your code should look like this.

19. Locate the <H1>Migrated Code</H1><HR> code block and delete the <HR> tag.

20. Save your changes, switch to your browser, and tap [F5].

21. Validate the page.
Validation fails with only 26 errors.

22. Close the validation page and ensure that the migrate.htm page displays in the browser window.

Fix the Remaining Tags

23. Switch to Notepad.

24. Follow these steps to add the required xmlns attribute to the `<html>` tag:

Ⓐ **Click after the letters** `html` **and tap** `Spacebar`.

```
<html xmlns="http://www.w3.org/1999/xhtml">
```

Ⓑ Type **xmlns="http://www.w3.org/1999/xhtml"**.

25. Type a closing slash (**/**) to properly close the `<meta>` tag.

```
<meta http-equiv="Content-Type" content="text/html;charset=utf-8" />
```

26. Delete the opening `<TABLE>`, `<TR>`, and `<TD>` tags.

27. Delete the closing `</TABLE>`, `</TR>`, and `</TD>` tags.

28. Change the opening `<HTML>` tag to lowercase. `<html>`

29. Continue changing the remaining opening and closing tags on the page to lowercase.

30. In the first paragraph, add a closing slash to the `<br>` tag so it looks like this: `<br />`.

31. Click after the second sentence and type **</p>** to close the first paragraph.

```
<p>This page started out as valid HTML.<br />
But it failed validation as XHTML!</p>
```

32. Type **</p>** in the appropriate place to close the second paragraph.

```
<p>That's okay. We'll migrate it to valid XHTML.</p>
```

33. Save your changes, switch to your browser, and tap `F5`.

34. Validate the page.
The page passes validation. You have migrated a page from HTML to XHTML! At this point, you could link to an external stylesheet to bring back the colors and alignment.

35. Close your web browser and Notepad.

Fixing Broken Code

Whether migrating a page from HTML to XHTML or starting out fresh with XHTML, everyone makes mistakes. The W3C validation tool you have been using is helpful when fixing validation errors, but as a single error in the code can cause many validation errors, it is sometimes difficult to find the exact location of the code error.

What to Look For

When a validation error is reported, the validation results page lists a line number in the code. The code error may be on that line or in some other place.

 Hands-On 14.5   Fix Code Errors

In this exercise, you will locate and fix code errors.

1. Start your web browser and open the resources.htm file from the fup_validate folder in your Lesson 14 folder.
   The page probably displays fine in the browser (depending on the browser you are using). Some browsers are forgiving and do their best to display the page as intended even when there is invalid code.

2. Validate the page.
   Fifteen errors are reported.

3. If necessary, scroll down the validation results page and look at the first error listed.

   ┌─The message indicates that there is an error with the opening <head> tag on line 7.

   ☆ ☆ 📄 [Invalid] Markup Validation of C:\Labyrinth\HTML\less...   🏠 ▾ 🗐 🖶 ▾ 📄 Page ▾ ◌

   ~~Validation Output: 15 Errors~~

   ⊘ *Line 7, Column 5:* **document type does not allow element "head" here** .

   <head>

4. Close the validation page and ensure that the resources.htm page displays in the browser window.

5. Switch to Notepad and locate the opening <head> tag.

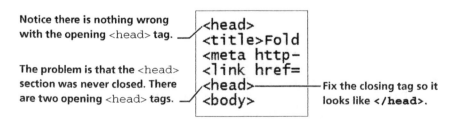

Notice there is nothing wrong with the opening <head> tag.

```
<head>
<title>Fold
<meta http-
<link href=
<head>
<body>
```

The problem is that the <head> section was never closed. There are two opening <head> tags.

Fix the closing tag so it looks like **</head>**.

6. Save your changes, switch to your browser, and tap [F5].

7. Validate the page.

Validation still fails, but with only six errors.

8. Study the first error listed.

The error indicates a problem with the closing `</li>` tag on line 24.

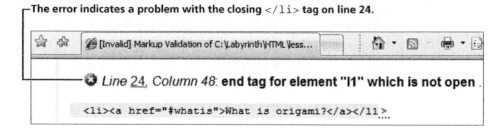

9. Close the validation page and ensure that the resources.htm page displays in the browser window.

10. Switch to Notepad and locate the first `<li>` tag.

This time, the validator identifies the actual line containing the error. The closing tag is not `</li>`, but instead `</l1>`. (The number 1 instead of the letter *i.*)

`<li><a href="#whatis">What is origami?</a></l1>`

Change the 1 to an **i** to fix the closing tag so it looks like this: `</li>`.

11. Save your changes, switch to your browser, and tap [F5].

12. Validate the page.

The page passes validation! Fixing two errors in the code cleared up 15 validation errors.

13. Close your browser and Notepad.

Working with CSS Hacks

All browsers are different. They may or may not render a page the same way, especially when CSS is involved. This is most often evident when using the CSS `float` property you first used in Lesson 11, Doing More with CSS. A CSS hack is additional code in the XHTML or the CSS that addresses these inconsistencies. A CSS hack should fix the display error in one browser without negatively affecting other browsers. While a hack shouldn't really be required in a perfect world, CSS hacks are a necessary evil for modern browsers.

A Simple Hack

Consider the following page—the same page with a floated image displayed in Internet Explorer 7 and Firefox.

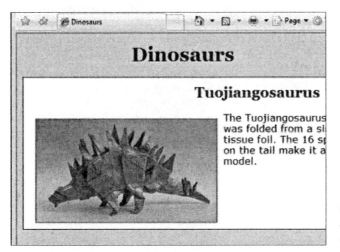

Internet Explorer displays the floated image alongside the text and inside the white container DIV.

In Firefox, the white container DIV knows to be as tall as the text but ignores the image.

A simple CSS hack, sometimes called the "clearfix" hack, is all that's needed to make Firefox behave. You will see this hack in action in the final Skill Builder in this lesson.

Concepts Review

True/False Questions

1. XHTML code is considered valid if it follows all the rules and recommendations specified by the W3C. TRUE FALSE

2. Add-on Web Developer toolbars can help streamline the process of validation. TRUE FALSE

3. Validation error codes always refer to the exact line of the error, making them easy to find and fix. TRUE FALSE

4. Deprecated tags are deprecated in all versions of HTML and XHTML. TRUE FALSE

5. Use of a deprecated tag always causes your page to fail validation. TRUE FALSE

6. By reading through an actual document type declaration document, you can learn what attributes are required or forbidden. TRUE FALSE

7. A page that validates will always look the same in all browsers. TRUE FALSE

8. A single error in your code can cause multiple validation errors. TRUE FALSE

9. Validating your code is a costly undertaking because validation software is very expensive. TRUE FALSE

10. Updating code from HTML to XHTML is a quick and easy process. TRUE FALSE

Multiple Choice Questions

1. Addam needs to validate his code. What is the URL he needs to type to get to an online validator?

   a. http://www.wc.org

   b. http://www.w3c.com

   c. http://www.w3.com

   d. http://www.w3.org

2. Margarete has the following DOCTYPE declaration at the top of her page, but the validator reports an error with it. In fact, this single error in her code causes 90 validation errors! What is the error?
   ```
   <!DOCTYPE html PUBLIC "-//w3C//DTD XHTML 1.0 Transitional//EN"
   "http://www.w3.org/TR/xhtml11/DTD/xhtml11-transitional.dtd">
   ```

   a. The word *Transitional* should not be capitalized in the first line.

   b. The word *transitional* should be capitalized in the second line.

   c. The domain name in the second line is wrong. It should be www.w3c.org.

   d. In the first line *w3c* should be uppercase, as in *W3C*.

3. Hari's code has passed validation. What benefits can he expect?

   a. Smaller file size and less code bloat

   b. A high rate of browser compatibility

   c. Identical display in all browsers

   d. A and B only

   e. A, B, and C

4. When is it recommended to use deprecated tags?

   a. In XHTML 1.0 strict

   b. In XHTML 1.0 transitional

   c. In HTML 3.2

   d. Using deprecated tags is never recommended

Skill Builders

Skill Builder 14.1   Validate Code

In this exercise, you will validate existing code.

1. Start your web browser and open the index.htm file from the sb_riffworld_validate folder in your Lesson 14 folder.

2. Notice the problems with the page.
   If you are using Internet Explorer, the text is much larger than expected throughout the page and the unordered list items run into each other. If you are using Firefox, the text in the masthead is much larger than expected.

3. Validate the page. If necessary, refer to Hands-On 14.2 for the steps.
   The page fails validation with 97 errors.

4. Close the validation results and return to the index.htm page from the Riff World site.

5. Use the navigation bar at the top of the page to browse to the 80's Pop Rock page.

6. Validate the page.
   The page passes XHTML 1.0 transitional validation.

7. Use the navigation bar at the top of the page to browse to the Hard Rock page.

8. Validate the page.
   The page passes XHTML 1.0 transitional validation.

9. Use the navigation bar at the top of the page to return to the homepage.

Skill Builder 14.2   Fix Invalid Code

In this exercise, you will fix invalid code.

Before You Begin: You must complete Skill Builder 14.1 before beginning this exercise.

1. Return to the index.htm page. Validate it and take note of the first Important Warning on the results page.

The validator is unable to determine the document type.

The validator does not understand your document type.

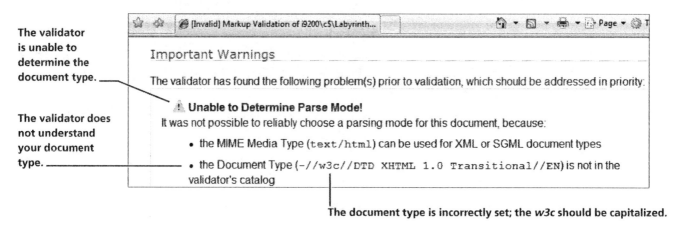

The document type is incorrectly set; the *w3c* should be capitalized.

2. Start Notepad, open the same index.htm file from the sb_riffworld_validate folder, and follow these steps to fix the document type declaration:

🅐 Select the w3c in the DOCTYPE declaration.

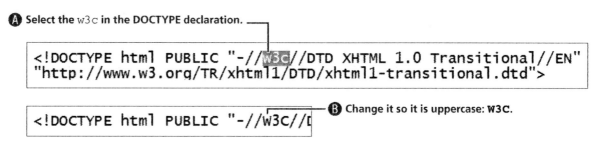

🅑 Change it so it is uppercase: **W3C**.

3. Save your changes, switch to your browser, and tap F5.

4. Validate the page again.
   Validation still fails, but with only 14 errors.

5. Scroll down to the first error.

The validator indicates an error at line 12 related to the h1 element.

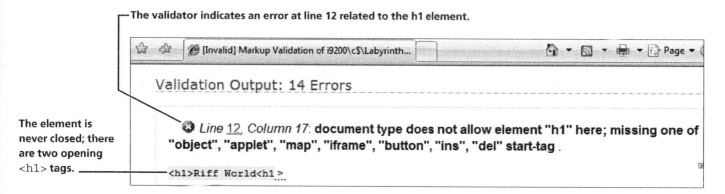

The element is never closed; there are two opening <h1> tags.

6. Close the validation results and return to the index.htm page.

7. Switch to Notepad and fix the element by typing a slash (**/**) to close the h1:

```
<h1>Riff World</h1>
```

8. Save your changes, switch to your browser, and tap F5.
The text displays at the intended size throughout the document.

9. Validate the page again.
Validation still fails, but with only six errors.

10. Scroll down to the first two errors.

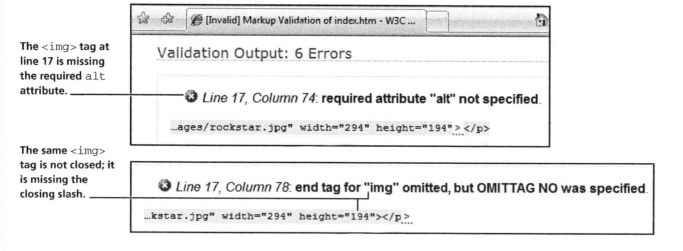

The <img> tag at line 17 is missing the required alt attribute.

The same <img> tag is not closed; it is missing the closing slash.

11. Close the validation results and return to the index.htm page.

12. Switch to Notepad, locate the image, and follow these steps to fix the tag:

Ⓐ Click after the height attribute/value and tap `Spacebar`.

```
<p id="main_photo"><img src="images/rockstar.jpg" width="294"
height="194" alt="rock star on stage" /></p>
```

Ⓑ Type `alt="rock star on stage"`, tap `Spacebar`, and
type **/** to insert the required attribute and the closing slash.

13. Save your changes, switch to your browser, and tap `F5`.
The text displays at the intended size throughout the document.

14. Validate the page again.
The page passes validation! Four errors in the code caused 97 validation errors.

15. Close your web browser and Notepad.

Skill Builder 14.3 Migrate from HTML to XHTML/CSS

In this exercise, you will migrate a page from HTML to XHTML/CSS.

Migrate to XHTML

1. Start your web browser and open the dinos.htm file from the sb_migrate folder in your Lesson 14 folder.
The layout is simple enough to be accomplished by floating the image. The table does not need borders around the individual cells, but the content may benefit from a single outline border.

2. Start Notepad and open the same dinos.htm page.

3. Follow these steps to delete the layout table:

Ⓐ Select the opening `<TABLE>`, `<TR>`, `<TD>`, and `<FONT>` tags.   **Ⓑ** Tap `Backspace` to delete them.

```
<BODY BGCOLOR=#CCCC99>
<CENTER><FONT SIZE="7" FACE="georgia">Dinosaurs</FONT></CENTER>
<TABLE WIDTH="760" ALIGN="center" CELLPADDING="10" CELLSPACING="0"
BGCOLOR=#FFFFFF BORDER=1>
   <TR>
      <TD COLSPAN="2" ALIGN=CENTER><FONT SIZE="4"
FACE="georgia">Tuojiangosaurus</FONT></TD>
```

```
<BODY BGCOLOR=#CCCC99>
<CENTER><FONT SIZE="7" FACE="
Tuojiangosaurus</FONT></TD>
   </TR>
   <TR>
      <TD VALIGN="top"><IMG HEI
```

Ⓒ Select the next few tags related to the font and table and delete them.

Ⓓ Continue deleting cell and font tags.

```
<BODY BGCOLOR=#CCCC99>
<CENTER><FONT SIZE="7" FACE="georgia">Dinosaurs</FONT></CEN
Tuojiangosaurus<IMG HEIGHT="170" SRC="images/dino.jpg" WIDT
BORDER=2></TD>
      <TD VALIGN="top"><FONT FACE="arial">The Tuojiangosaurus
Fumiaki Kawahata) was folded from a single uncut ten-inch s
```

```
<BODY BGCOLOR=#CCCC99>
<CENTER><FONT SIZE="7"
Tuojiangosaurus<IMG HEI
BORDER=2>The Tuojiango:
a single uncut ten-inch
and 4 spikes on the ta
model.</FONT></TD>
   </TR>
</TABLE>
</BODY>
</HTML>
```

Ⓔ Delete the last font and other tags associated with the table.

4. Remove the deprecated `BGCOLOR` attribute/value from the `<BODY>` tag:

```
<BODY BGCOLOR=#CCCC99>
<CENTER><FONT SIZE="7"
```

5. Follow these steps to remove the remaining deprecated tags:

Ⓐ Delete the opening <CENTER> and <FONT> tags.

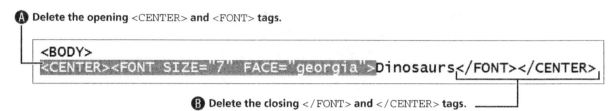

```
<BODY>
<CENTER><FONT SIZE="7" FACE="georgia">Dinosaurs</FONT></CENTER>
```

Ⓑ Delete the closing </FONT> and </CENTER> tags.

6. Delete the deprecated BORDER attribute/value from the <IMG> tag.

7. Change all remaining tags and attributes to lowercase:

- **<html>** and **</html>**
- **<head>** and **</head>**
- **<title>** and **</title>**
- **<body>** and **</body>**
- **<img>** and its attributes **height**, **src**, and **width**

8. Follow these steps to add XHTML body structure:

Ⓐ Type **<h1>** and **</h1>** tags around the page heading, tapping [Enter] as appropriate to create white space. **Ⓑ** Type **<h2>** and **</h2>** tags around the subheading, tapping [Enter] as appropriate to create white space.

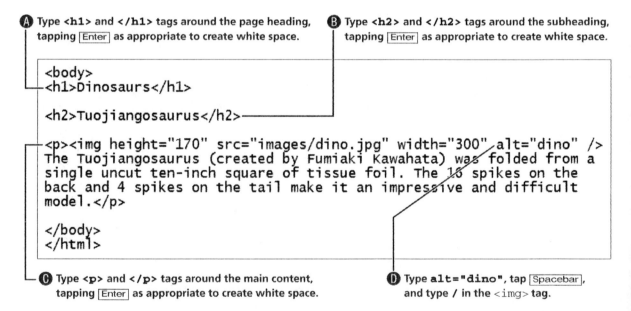

```
<body>
<h1>Dinosaurs</h1>

<h2>Tuojiangosaurus</h2>

<p><img height="170" src="images/dino.jpg" width="300" alt="dino" />
The Tuojiangosaurus (created by Fumiaki Kawahata) was folded from a
single uncut ten-inch square of tissue foil. The 15 spikes on the
back and 4 spikes on the tail make it an impressive and difficult
model.</p>

</body>
</html>
```

Ⓒ Type **<p>** and **</p>** tags around the main content, tapping [Enter] as appropriate to create white space. **Ⓓ** Type **alt="dino"**, tap [Spacebar], and type **/** in the <img> tag.

9. Follow these steps to create a CSS hook:

A Type `<div id="content">` above the `<h2>` subheading.

```
<div id="content">
<h2>Tuojiangosaurus</h2>
```

```
make it an impressive and difficult model.</p>
</div>
```

B Type `</div>` to close the division after the paragraph.

10. Follow these steps to finalize the document structure:

A Add the DOCTYPE declaration to the top of the document as shown here.

B Add the `xmlns` attribute to the `<html>` tag as shown here.

```
<!DOCTYPE html PUBLIC "-//W3C//DTD XHTML 1.0 Transitional//EN"
"http://www.w3.org/TR/xhtml1/DTD/xhtml1-transitional.dtd">

<html xmlns="http://www.w3.org/1999/xhtml">
<head>
<title>Dinosaurs</title>
<meta http-equiv="Content-Type" content="text/html;charset=utf-8" />
<link href="dinostyle.css" rel="stylesheet" type="text/css" />
</head>
```

C Add the character encoding after the `<title>` tag as shown here.

D Add a link to a stylesheet as shown here.

11. Save your changes, switch to your browser, and tap [F5].

12. Validate your page.
Validation passes! If yours failed, go back and fix any errors until it validates.

13. Close the validation results and return to the dinos.htm page.

Add the CSS

14. Switch to Notepad and choose File→New from the menu bar.
    The HTML document closes and a new blank document appears.

15. Choose File→Save As from the menu bar.

16. Navigate to the sb_migrate folder inside your Lesson 14 folder, if necessary.

17. Name the file **dinostyle.css** and click Save.

18. Add the following rule to color the page background and set the default font:

```
body {
  background: #CC9;
  font-family: verdana, arial, helvetica, sans-serif;
}
```

19. Add the following rule to format the page headings:

```
h1, h2 {
  font-family: georgia, times, serif;
  text-align: center;
}
```

20. Add the following rule to format the content container:

```
#content {
  width: 760px;
  background: #FFF;
  margin: 0 auto;
  padding: 10px;
  border: 1px solid #000;
}
```

21. Add the following rule to position the image:

```
#content img {
  float: left;
  margin-right: 10px;
  border: 2px solid #777;
}
```

22. Save your changes, switch to your browser, and tap F5.

The formatting is similar to the original. No XHTML code has changed, so the page still passes validation.

If you are using Internet Explorer, the page looks fine. However, if you are using Firefox, the image overlaps the white container as in the following figure. You will apply a CSS hack to fix this in the next exercise.

Skill Builder 14.4   Apply a CSS Hack

In this exercise, you will apply a CSS hack to fix a problem with Firefox.

Before You Begin: You must complete Skill Builder 14.3 before beginning this exercise. If you are using Firefox, the image appears partially outside of the white container.

1. Switch to Notepad and add the following rule to the bottom of the CSS file:

```
.clearfix {
  clear: both;
}
```

   You have created the CSS hack. Next you will create the element in the HTML document to attach the hack.

2. Save your changes and choose File→Open from the menu bar.

3. Navigate to the sb_migrate folder in your Lesson 14 folder, if necessary.

4. Set the file type filter to All Files.

5. Open the dinos.htm HTML file.

6. Locate the end of the paragraph and follow these steps to complete the hack:

   Ⓐ Click before the closing `</p>` tag.

   ```
   difficult model.<br class="clearfix" /></p>
   ```

   Ⓑ Type `<br class="clearfix" />`.

   You have added a line break tag that will have minimal effect on how the page displays. By adding `class="clearfix"`*, the* `.clearfix` *rule from the stylesheet will be applied to the line break.*

7. Save your changes, switch to your browser, and tap F5.
   The white container expands to contain the image.

8. Close your web browser and Notepad.

Assessments

Assessment 14.1 Validate and Fix Code

In this exercise, you will validate and fix code.

1. Start your web browser and open the index.htm page from the as_balloons_validate folder from your Lesson 14 folder.
    Code errors cause different behavior in different browsers. If you are using Firefox, the page may look fine. If you are using Internet Explorer 7, the page is probably completely blank!

2. Validate the page and note how many errors are reported.
    Remember that a single error in the code can cause multiple validation errors. Even if the validator reports 16 errors, that does not necessarily mean there are 16 errors in the code.

3. Locate the first error in the error report and notice that it refers to an invalid xmlns attribute.

4. Close the validation report and ensure that the index.htm page appears in the browser.

5. Start Notepad and open the same index.htm file from the as_balloons_validate folder.

6. Fix the xmlns attribute within the opening `<html>` tag.

7. Save your changes, switch to your browser, and tap F5.
    Firefox looks the same while Internet Explorer 7 still displays a blank page.

8. Validate the page.
    Two validation errors were fixed. There are only 14 errors left.

9. Read the first three errors in the error report.
    The first error refers to the TITLE element. The second error refers to the `<link>` tag not being allowed in its current location. The third error states clearly that the TITLE element is missing its closing tag.

10. Switch back to Notepad and locate the TITLE element.
    Since the TITLE is not closed, it appears as though the `<link>` tag is inside the title!

11. Fix the closing TITLE tag.

12. Save your changes, switch to your browser, and tap F5.
    If you are using Internet Explorer 7, it comes to life and displays the page content!

13. Validate the page.
    Many validation errors were fixed. There are only six errors left.

14. Read the first two errors in the error report.
The first error refers to a DIV tag where the value of the id *attribute is not enclosed in quotes. The second error clearly states that a closing paragraph tag is missing.*

15. Switch to Notepad and locate the `<div>` tag with the `id` of main_wrapper.

16. Type the quotation marks to fix the `<div>` tag.

17. Locate the paragraph with the missing closing tag and type the closing **`</p>`** tag.

18. Save your changes, switch to your browser, and tap F5.

19. Validate the page.
The page passes XHTML 1.0 transitional validation.

20. Close your web browser and Notepad.

Critical Thinking

Critical Thinking 14.1 Migrate and Validate Code

In this exercise, you will migrate code from HTML to XHTML/CSS. You will also validate your code. The migrate_me.htm file from the ct_migrate folder in your Lesson 14 folder should be open in both your web browser and Notepad. *Read through the following six bullets before you begin!*

- View the page in your browser to familiarize yourself with the layout, alignments, and color scheme.

- Migrate the code to valid XHTML 1.0 transitional.

- Add <div> tags or classes to create CSS hooks to help with the formatting.

- Link to a stylesheet with an appropriate name in the styles folder. Remember the name you use in your <link> tag as you will have to create a stylesheet with the same filename later.

- Create a stylesheet in the appropriate folder with all of the necessary CSS rules to match the original formatting as closely as possible.

- Remember that XHTML 1.0 transitional allows presentational code (such as the align and border attributes). However, as you strive to achieve XHTML 1.0 strict code, you should use CSS instead whenever possible.

Unit 3

Appendices

In this unit, you will learn how to use this book with various file storage media, such as a USB flash drive or hard drive. Additionally, reference tables for HTML character codes and HTML tags and attributes covered in the text are summarized.

Appendix A: Storing Your Exercise Files

Appendix B: Outlining Useful Development Resources

Appendix C: Working with Character Codes

Appendix D: Working with HTML/XHTML Tags and Attributes

APPENDIX A

Storing Your Exercise Files

This appendix contains an overview for using this book with various file storage media, such as a USB flash drive or hard drive. Detailed instructions for downloading and unzipping the exercise files used with this book appear in exercises for each type of media.

The following topics are addressed in this appendix:

Topic	Description	See Page
Downloading the Student Exercise Files	Retrieving the exercise files and copying them to your file storage location.	480
Using a USB Flash Drive	Storing your work on a USB flash memory drive.	481
Using the Documents Folder	Storing your work in the My Documents folder.	487
Using a Network Folder	Storing your work in a custom folder on a network.	489
Using a Floppy Disk with This Book	Using a floppy disk with this book is not recommended.	490

Downloading the Student Exercise Files

The files needed to complete certain Hands-On, Skill Builder, Assessment, and Critical Thinking exercises are available for download at the Labyrinth website. At the end of each media type topic is an exercise with instructions to copy the files to your computer and prepare them for use with this book.

Using a USB Flash Drive

NOTE!

Most students using this book store their files on a USB flash drive.

A USB flash drive stores your data on a flash memory chip. You simply plug it into a USB port on any computer and Windows immediately recognizes it as an additional disk drive. USB flash drives typically can store 256 megabytes (MB) or more. Large capacity USB flash drives can store 1 gigabyte (GB) or more. Flash drive versatility, capacity, and reliability have made them a popular replacement for the role once filled by the ancient (in computer terms) floppy disk.

Win XP

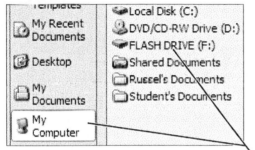

The Word 2007 Open dialog box displays a flash drive in the My Computer view in Windows XP.

Win Vista

The Word 2007 Open dialog box displays a flash drive in the Computer view in Windows Vista.

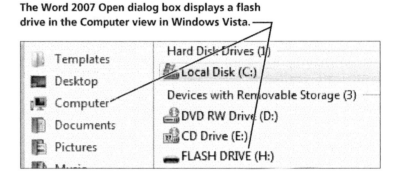

USB Flash Drive Letter

When you plug a USB flash drive into a Windows computer, Windows automatically assigns it the next available drive letter. Windows uses drive letters to identify each drive connected to the computer. For example, the primary part of the hard drive is always identified as the C drive. A CD/DVD drive is typically the D or E drive. Windows assigns a drive letter to your flash drive when you plug it in. The drive may receive a different drive letter on each computer you use it with.

Windows assigns a drive letter to your USB when you plug it in.

Windows lists a USB flash drive as a removable storage device.

TIP! *Your USB flash drive may receive a different drive letter on different computers. This does not affect any files stored on the drive.*

Hands-On A.1 Download and Unzip the Exercise Files— USB Flash Drive

Follow these steps to download a copy of the student files necessary for this book.

1. Launch Internet Explorer.

2. Enter **labpub.com/learn/wdhtml** in the browser's address bar and tap Enter.

3. Click the Student Exercise Files link below the Downloads heading.
   A prompt to run or save the student exercise files appears.

4. Click the Save button.
   Internet Explorer asks where you wish to save the downloaded file.

5. Carefully plug your USB flash drive into a USB port on the computer.

6. Click the Close ⌧ (Win XP) / ⌧ (Win Vista) button if a window appears asking what you want to do with the plugged-in flash drive.

7. Follow these steps for your version of Windows to choose the flash drive as the save destination:

Win XP

Ⓐ Click My Computer on the left side of the Save As window.

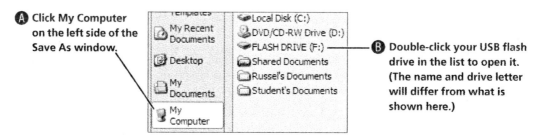

Ⓑ Double-click your USB flash drive in the list to open it. (The name and drive letter will differ from what is shown here.)

Win Vista

Ⓐ Click the Browse Folders button on the lower-left side of the dialog box if it does not display the computer option like the figure for steps B and C.

Browse Folders

Ⓑ Click Computer on the left side of the Save As window.

Ⓒ If necessary, scroll down the drive list until the flash drive is visible, and then double-click your USB flash drive in the list to open it. (The name and drive letter will differ from what is shown here.)

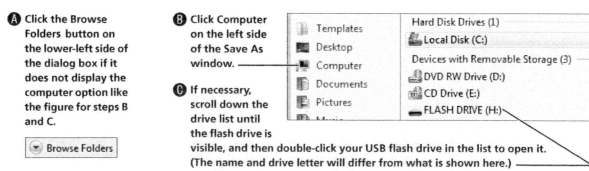

Now that you've shown Windows where to save the file, you are ready to download it.

The rest of the instructions for this exercise apply to both Win XP and Win Vista.

8. Click the Save button.

After a pause, the exercise file will begin downloading to your computer. Continue with the next step after the download is complete.

NOTE! *If you are downloading the files via a dial-up modem connection, it will take several minutes or more for the download to be completed.*

Unzip the Files

9. Click the Open Folder button on the Download Complete dialog box.

If the Download Complete dialog box closes after the download is completed, you will need to open a folder window to the USB flash drive you used in step 7:

- **Win XP:** Choose Start→My Computer. Double-click to open your USB flash drive.
- **Win Vista:** Choose Start→Computer. Double-click to open your USB flash drive.

10. Double-click the wdhtml_student_files icon, as shown at right.

wdhtml_student_files.exe

Windows may ask if you wish to run the software. This confirmation helps protect your computer from viruses. In this case, you know the file is safe.

11. Choose Run if Windows asks you if you are sure you want to run this software, otherwise continue with step 14.

A prompt appears, telling you where the student exercise files will be unzipped.

12. Click the Unzip button.

The self-extracting archive unzips all of the student exercise files for this book into the new folder. This should take less than one minute to complete.

13. Click OK to acknowledge the successful unzip process.

14. Click the Close button to close the self-extractor window.

All of the files necessary to use this book are now unzipped to your file storage location. They are located in a new folder named Web Page Design.

Since the zip file is no longer needed, you will delete it in the next step. (You can always download it again if you need fresh copies of the exercise files in the future.)

15. (Optional) Make sure that the wdhtml_student_files zip file is chosen, and then tap the Delete key on the keyboard. Click OK if you are asked to confirm the deletion.

Renaming Your Flash Drive

It may be easier to identify your flash drive on various computer systems if you give it a custom name. For example, you can use your first name, or a generic name such as Flash Drive or Pen Drive. The next exercise shows how you can rename your flash drive on most computer systems.

 NOTE! *Some Windows systems may not give you renaming privileges for drives. This depends on privileges associated with your login name.*

Hands-On A.2   Rename Your USB Flash Drive

You may find it convenient to rename your USB flash drive to make it easier to recognize when you save or open files.

 TIP! *Some Windows systems may not give you renaming privileges for drives.*

1. Plug the USB flash drive into an available USB port.

2. Click the Close | × | / | ×| button if a window appears asking what you want to do with the plugged-in flash drive.

3. Follow the step for your version of Windows:

   ■ **Win XP:** Choose Start→My Computer.

   ■ **Win Vista:** Choose Start→Computer.

4. Right-click your USB flash drive and choose Rename from the context menu.

 NOTE! *In the next step, Windows may display a prompt indicating that you cannot rename this flash drive. You have not done anything wrong! You can use the drive with its current name. You may also want to try renaming it later using a different login.*

   If you have renaming rights, Windows highlights the existing name.

5. Type **Flash Drive** (or any other custom name you wish to use) as the new drive name and tap [Enter], or click OK if you receive a prompt that you do not have sufficient rights to perform this operation.
   If you were unable to rename the flash drive, don't worry. Renaming the flash drive is a convenience for recognition and has no other effect.

Removing a Flash Drive Safely

Windows XP and Windows Vista allow you to remove a USB flash drive by simply unplugging the drive. However, this method requires you to make sure that no files are active on the drive when you unplug it. For example, if you unplug the drive while a file is being saved, there is a possibility that the file will be corrupted or lost altogether. Normally, if the light is not flashing on the USB flash drive, you can safely remove it. However, if you wish to be *absolutely certain* that the drive is ready for removal, you should use the following procedure.

If you are not sure a USB flash drive is ready to be unplugged, you can use the Safely Remove Hardware command to be certain.

WARNING! *Removing a USB flash drive while files on it are active could result in corruption of the entire drive and the loss of all files on it.*

QUICK REFERENCE: SAFELY REMOVE A USB FLASH DRIVE	
Task	**Procedure**
Remove the flash drive (standard method)	■ Close any program from which you opened files on the USB flash drive.
	■ Wait for the light on the drive to stop flashing.
	■ Gently unplug the flash drive from its USB port or cable.
Remove the flash drive (careful method)	■ Close any program from which you opened files on the USB flash drive.
	■ Click once on the Safely Remove Hardware 🖳 icon in the Notification Area on the Windows taskbar.
	■ Choose your USB flash drive from the pop-up list.
	■ Gently unplug the flash drive after Windows prompts that you can do so safely. Or, wait to unplug the drive if you see a prompt that the storage device cannot be stopped now.

Problem Ejecting USB Mass Storage Device

⚠ The device 'Generic volume' cannot be stopped right now. Try stopping the device again later.

OK

Hands-On A.3   Use the Safely Remove Hardware Command

In this exercise, you will use the Safely Remove Hardware command to make certain your USB flash drive is ready to be unplugged.

Before You Begin: Skip this exercise if you are not using a USB flash drive.

1. Make sure you have closed any open files on the USB flash drive.

> ⚠️ **NOTE!** *In the following step, the drive letter may differ from the one shown in the figures.*

2. Follow these steps to safely unplug the drive:

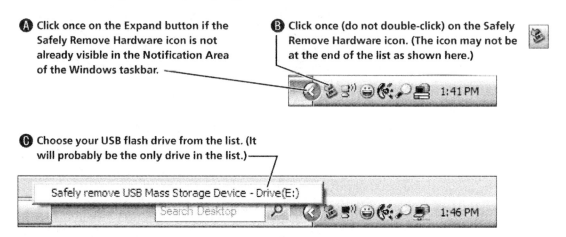

Ⓐ Click once on the Expand button if the Safely Remove Hardware icon is not already visible in the Notification Area of the Windows taskbar. —

Ⓑ Click once (do not double-click) on the Safely Remove Hardware icon. (The icon may not be at the end of the list as shown here.)

Ⓒ Choose your USB flash drive from the list. (It will probably be the only drive in the list.)—

Safely remove USB Mass Storage Device - Drive(E:)

Windows displays a prompt that you can safely remove the drive. Or, you will see a prompt that the drive cannot be removed and that you must wait.

ⓘ **Safe To Remove Hardware**   ✕

The 'USB Mass Storage Device' device can now be safely removed from the system.

2:05 PM

3. Gently unplug the USB flash drive from its port or extension cable.

Using the Documents Folder

NOTE!

Many computer labs do not allow students to use this folder.

Windows creates a unique Documents folder for each login ID. This folder resides on the main system drive (usually the C drive). The Office 2007 application programs provide a Documents navigation link in their Open and Save As dialog boxes for quick navigation to this folder.

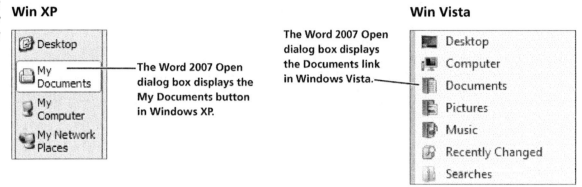

Win XP

The Word 2007 Open dialog box displays the My Documents button in Windows XP.

Win Vista

The Word 2007 Open dialog box displays the Documents link in Windows Vista.

Hands-On A.4   Download and Unzip the Exercise Files—Documents Folder

Follow these steps to download a copy of the student files necessary for this book.

1. Launch Internet Explorer.

2. Enter **labpub.com/learn/wdhtml** in the browser's address bar and tap ‾Enter‾.

3. Click the Student Exercise Files link below the Downloads heading.
   A prompt to run or save the student exercise files appears.

4. Click the Save button.

5. Follow the steps for your version of Windows:

   ■ **Win XP:** Choose My Documents on the left side of the Save As window.

   ■ **Win Vista:** If necessary, click the [⊙ Browse Folders] button, and then choose Documents on the left side of the Save As window.

   Now that you've shown Windows where to save the file, you are ready to download it.

6. Click the Save button.
   After a pause, the exercise file will begin downloading to your computer. Continue with the next step after the download is complete.

NOTE!   *If you are downloading the files via a dial-up modem connection, it will take several minutes or more for the download to be completed.*

7. Click the Open Folder button on the Download Complete dialog box.

   If the Download Complete dialog box closes after the download is completed, follow the step for your version of Windows to open a folder window to the Documents folder you used in step 5.

   - **Win XP:** Choose Start→My Documents.
   - **Win Vista:** Choose Start→Documents.

8. Double-click the wdhtml_student_files icon, as shown at right.
   Windows may ask if you wish to run the software. This confirmation helps protect your computer from viruses. In this case, you know the file is safe.

wdhtml_student_files.exe

9. Choose Run if Windows asks you if you are sure you want to run this software, otherwise continue with step 10.
   A prompt appears, telling you where the student exercise files will be unzipped.

10. Click the Unzip button.
    The self-extracting archive unzips all of the student exercise files for this book into the new folder. This should take less than one minute to complete.

11. Click OK to acknowledge the successful unzip process.

12. Click the Close button to close the self-extractor window.
    All of the files necessary to use this book are now unzipped to your file storage location. They are located in a new folder named Web Page Design.

    Since the zip file is no longer needed, you will delete it in the next step. (You can always download it again if you need fresh copies of the exercise files in the future.)

13. (Optional) Make sure that the wdhtml_student_files zip file is chosen, and then tap the Delete key on the keyboard. Click OK if you are asked to confirm the deletion.

Using a Network Folder

NOTE!

Your instructor or a computer lab assistant can tell you how to locate a network drive if this is where you are to store your files.

You may use a system connected to a network. There may be a folder on a network server computer in another location that is dedicated to storing your work. Usually, you will find this folder within the *My Network Places* (Win XP) or *Network* (Win Vista) folder of your computer. The Office 2007 application programs provide a Network link in their Open and Save As dialog boxes for quick navigation to this folder. You may have to navigate deeper into the folder to locate your personal network drive folder.

Win XP

In Windows XP, the Word 2007 Open dialog box displays the My Network Places button.

Win Vista

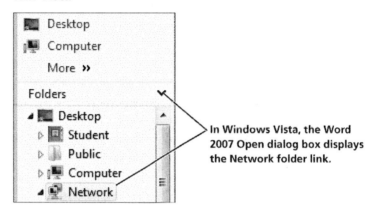

In Windows Vista, the Word 2007 Open dialog box displays the Network folder link.

Hands-On A.5   **Download and Unzip the Exercise Files— Network Drive Folder**

Follow these steps to download a copy of the student files necessary for this book.

1. Launch Internet Explorer.

2. Enter **labpub.com/learn/wdhtml** in the browser's address bar and tap `Enter`.

3. Click the Student Exercise Files link below the Downloads heading.
   A prompt to run or save the student exercise files appears.

4. Click the Save button.

5. Follow the steps for your version of Windows:

   ■ **Win XP:** Choose My Network Places on the left side of the Save As window, and then navigate to your network folder.

   ■ **Win Vista:** Click the menu button as shown at right, and then choose Network. Navigate to your network folder.

   Now that you've shown Windows where to save the file, you are ready to download it.

6. Click the Save button.
   The download begins. Continue with the next step after it is complete.

⚠ NOTE! *Downloading the files via a dial-up modem connection will take several minutes.*

7. Click the Open Folder button on the Download Complete dialog box.
   If the Download Complete dialog box closes after the download is completed, you will need to open a folder window to the file storage location you used in step 5.

8. Double-click the wdhtml_student_files icon, as shown at right.
   Windows may ask if you wish to run the software. This confirmation helps protect your computer from viruses. In this case, you know the file is safe.

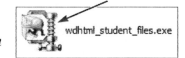
wdhtml_student_files.exe

9. Choose Run if Windows asks you if you are sure you want to run this software, otherwise continue with step 10.
   A prompt appears, telling you where the student exercise files will be unzipped.

10. Click the Unzip button.
    The self-extracting archive unzips all of the student exercise files for this book into the new folder. This should take less than one minute to complete.

11. Click OK to acknowledge the successful unzip process.

12. Click the Close button to close the self-extractor window.
    All of the files necessary to use this book are now unzipped to your file storage location. They are located in a new folder named Web Page Design.

    Since the zip file is no longer needed, you will delete it in the next step. (You can always download it again if you need fresh copies of the exercise files in the future.)

13. (Optional) Make sure that the wdhtml_student_files zip file is chosen, and then tap the [Delete] key on the keyboard. Click OK if you are asked to confirm the deletion.

Using a Floppy Disk with This Book

It is not recommended that students use floppy disks with this textbook. As you work through the exercises in this book, you will create numerous new files that must be saved. A floppy disk will not have enough storage capacity to hold all files created during this course. In addition, many computers no longer feature a floppy drive, and this trend should continue as USB flash drives take over the portable file storage role once filled by floppies.

APPENDIX B

Outlining Useful Development Resources

While a plain text editor such as Notepad is all anyone needs to code a valid web page, you have learned about a variety of software tools (free and commercial) and other resources that can help you to code more efficiently and aid in the overall creation of web pages. The following list summarizes the recommended free software and resources discussed in this book.

 See the web page for this book for links to the following websites.

- Crimson Editor—This freeware text editor features syntax coloring and line numbering in addition to many other features.

- Notepad2—This freeware text editor features syntax coloring and line numbering. Notepad2 is a standalone executable that can be run without being installed. Copy the executable to your USB drive and launch it on any PC.

- MultipleIE—This installer for Windows PCs installs several versions of the Internet Explorer browser. Be warned that you should have Internet Explorer 7 already installed before using this software. MultipleIE is not recommended for use with Windows Vista.

- Mozilla Firefox—This is a popular web browser.

- Web Developer toolbar—This is an add-on toolbar for Mozilla Firefox.

- Web Accessibility Toolbar—This is an add-on toolbar for Internet Explorer.

- IrfanView—This is a freeware image editor.

- PDPhoto.org—This is an Internet source for royalty-free and public domain images.

- MorgueFile.com—This is an Internet source for royalty-free and public domain images.

- CSSZenGarden.com—This is an Internet source for inspirational CSS designs and layouts.

- W3C Validator—This is an online validation tool from the World Wide Web Consortium.

APPENDIX C

Working with Character Codes

The following tables include the HTML character codes. Remember that character codes must begin with an ampersand (&) and end with a semicolon (;).

MATHEMATICAL SYMBOLS

Description	HTML Code	Glyph	Description	HTML Code	Glyph
Angle	&ang;	∠	Intersection	&cap;	∩
Asterisk operator	&lowast;	∗	Less than or equal to	&le;	≤
Asymptotic	&asymp;	≈	Logical and	&and;	∧
Ceiling left	&lceil;	⌈	Logical or	&or;	∨
Ceiling right	&rceil;	⌉	Masculine ordinal indicator	&ordm;	º
Circled plus	&oplus;	⊕	Minus	&minus;	−
Circled times	&otimes;	⊗	Multiplication	&times;	×
Congruent	&cong;	≅	Nabla	&nabla;	∇
Contains as a member	&ni;	∋	N-ary product	&prod;	∏
Degree	&deg;	°	N-ary sum	&sum;	Σ
Division	&divide;	÷	Not	&not;	¬
Dot operator	&sdot;	⋅	Not a subset of	&nsub;	⊄
Double prime (seconds, inches)	&Prime;	″	Not an element of	&notin;	∉
Element of	&isin;	∈	Not equal	&ne;	≠
Empty set	&empty;	∅	Partial differential	&part;	∂
Equivalent	&equiv;	≡	Perpendicular	&perp;	⊥
Exists	&exist;	∃	Pi symbol	&piv;	ϖ
Feminine ordinal indicator	&ordf;	ª	Plus/Minus	&plusmn;	±
Floor left	&lfloor;	⌊	Prime (minutes, feet)	&prime;	′
Floor right	&rfloor;	⌋	Proportional to	&prop;	∝
For all	&forall;	∀	Radical	&radic;	√
Fraction one-half	&frac12;	½	Similar to	&sim;	∼
Fraction one-quarter	&frac14;	¼	Subset of	&sub;	⊂
Fraction slash	&frasl;	⁄	Subset of or equal to	&sube;	⊆
Fraction three-fourths	&frac34;	¾	Superset of	&sup;	⊃
Greater than or equal to	&ge;	≥	Superset of or equal to	&supe;	⊇
Infinity	&infin;	∞	Therefore	&there4;	∴
Integral	&int;	∫	Union	&cup;	∪

ACCENTED LETTERS

Description	HTML Code	Glyph	Description	HTML Code	Glyph
Capital *A* with acute	&Aacute;	Á	Small *a* with acute	&aacute;	á
Capital *A* with circumflex	&Acirc;	Â	Small *a* with circumflex	&acirc;	â
Capital *A* with grave	&Agrave;	À	Small *a* with grave	&agrave;	à
Capital *A* with ring	&Aring;	Å	Small *a* with ring	&aring;	å
Capital *A* with tilde	&Atilde;	Ã	Small *a* with tilde	&atilde;	ã
Capital *A* with umlaut	&Auml;	Ä	Small *a* with umlaut	&auml;	ä
Capital *C* with cedilla	&Ccedil;	Ç	Small *c* with cedilla	&ccedil;	ç
Capital *E* with acute	&Eacute;	É	Small *e* with acute	&eacute;	é
Capital *E* with circumflex	&Ecirc;	Ê	Small *e* with circumflex	&ecirc;	ê
Capital *E* with grave	&Egrave;	È	Small *e* with grave	&egrave;	è
Capital *E* with umlaut	&Euml;	Ë	Small *e* with umlaut	&euml;	ë
Capital *ETH*	&ETH;	Ð	Small *eth*	&eth;	ð
Capital *I* with acute	&Iacute;	Í	Small *i* with acute	&iacute;	í
Capital *I* with circumflex	&Icirc;	Î	Small *i* with circumflex	&icirc;	î
Capital *I* with grave	&Igrave;	Ì	Small *i* with grave	&igrave;	ì
Capital *I* with umlaut	&Iuml;	Ï	Small *i* with umlaut	&iuml;	ï
Capital ligature *AE*	&AElig;	Æ	Small ligature *ae*	&aelig;	æ
Capital ligature *OE*	&OElig;	Œ	Small *n* with tilde	&ntilde;	ñ
Capital *N* with tilde	&Ntilde;	Ñ	Small *o* with acute	&oacute;	ó
Capital *O* with acute	&Oacute;	Ó	Small *o* with circumflex	&ocirc;	ô
Capital *O* with circumflex	&Ocirc;	Ô	Small *o* with grave	&ograve;	ò
Capital *O* with grave	&Ograve;	Ò	Small *o* with stroke	&oslash;	ø
Capital *O* with stroke	&Oslash;	Ø	Small *o* with tilde	&otilde;	õ
Capital *O* with tilde	&Otilde;	Õ	Small *o* with umlaut	&ouml;	ö
Capital *O* with umlaut	&Ouml;	Ö	Small sharp *s*	&szlig;	ß
Capital *S* with caron	&Scaron;	Š	Small thorn	&thorn;	þ
Capital THORN	&THORN;	Þ	Small *u* with acute	&uacute;	ú
Capital *U* with acute	&Uacute;	Ú	Small *u* with circumflex	&ucirc;	û
Capital *U* with circumflex	&Ucirc;	Û	Small *u* with grave	&ugrave;	ù
Capital *U* with grave	&Ugrave;	Ù	Small *u* with umlaut	&uuml;	ü
Capital *U* with umlaut	&Uuml;	Ü	Small *y* with acute	&yacute;	ý
Capital *Y* with acute	&Yacute;	Ý	Small *y* with umlaut	&yuml;	ÿ
Capital *Y* with umlaut	&Yuml;	Ÿ			

OTHER CHARACTERS

Description	HTML Code	Glyph
Acute	&acute;	´
Alef	&alefsym;	ℵ
Ampersand	&amp;	&
Arrow double down	&dArr;	⇓
Arrow double left	&lArr;	⇐
Arrow double left right	&hArr;	⇔
Arrow double right	&rArr;	⇒
Arrow double up	&uArr;	⇑
Arrow down	&darr;	↓
Arrow left	&larr;	←
Arrow left right	&harr;	↔
Arrow right	&rarr;	→
Arrow up	&uarr;	↑
Blackletter capital *I*	&image;	ℑ
Blackletter capital *R*	&real;	ℜ
Broken vertical bar	&brvbar;	¦
Bullet	&bull;	•
Carriage return	&crarr;	↵
Cedilla	&cedil;	¸
Circumflex	&circ;	ˆ
Copyright	&copy;	©
Dagger	&dagger;	†
Double dagger	&Dagger;	‡
Double left quote	&ldquo;	"
Double low quote	&bdquo;	„
Double right quote	&rdquo;	"
Em-dash	&mdash;	—
En-dash	&ndash;	–
Greater than	&gt;	>
Horizontal ellipsis	&hellip;	…
Inverted exclamation mark	&iexcl;	¡
Inverted question mark	&iquest;	¿

Description	HTML Code	Glyph
Left guillemet	&laquo;	«
Left single quote	&lsquo;	'
Less than	&lt;	<
Macron	&macr;	¯
Micro	&micro;	µ
Middle dot	&middot;	·
Non-breaking space		
Overline	&oline;	‾
Per mille	&permil;	‰
Pilcrow	&para;	¶
Quotation mark	&quot;	"
Registered trademark	&reg;	®
Right guillemet	&raquo;	»
Right single quote	&rsquo;	'
Script capital *P*	&weierp;	℘
Section	&sect;	§
Single left angle quote	&lsaquo;	‹
Single low quote	&sbquo;	‚
Single right angle quote	&rsaquo;	›
Small ligature oe	&oelig;	œ
Small s with caron	&scaron;	š
Superscript 1	&sup1;	¹
Superscript 2	&sup2;	²
Superscript 3	&sup3;	³
Tilde	&tilde;	˜
Trademark	&trade;	™
Umlaut	&uml;	¨
Lozenge	&loz;	◊
Spades	&spades;	♠
Clubs	&clubs;	♣
Hearts	&hearts;	♥
Diamonds	&diams;	♦

GREEK LETTERS AND SYMBOLS

Description	HTML Code	Glyph	Description	HTML Code	Glyph
Small f with hook	&fnof;	ƒ	Small beta	&beta;	β
Capital Alpha	&Alpha;	A	Small gamma	&gamma;	γ
Capital Beta	&Beta;	B	Small delta	&delta;	δ
Capital Gamma	&Gamma;	Γ	Small epsilon	&epsilon;	ε
Capital Delta	&Delta;	Δ	Small zeta	&zeta;	ζ
Capital Epsilon	&Epsilon;	E	Small eta	&eta;	η
Capital Zeta	&Zeta;	Z	Small theta	&theta;	θ
Capital Eta	&Eta;	H	Small iota	&iota;	ι
Capital Theta	&Theta;	θ	Small kappa	&kappa;	κ
Capital Iota	&Iota;	I	Small lambda	&lambda;	λ
Capital Kappa	&Kappa;	K	Small mu	&mu;	μ
Capital Lambda	&Lambda;	Λ	Small nu	&nu;	ν
Capital Mu	&Mu;	M	Small xi	&xi;	ξ
Capital Nu	&Nu;	N	Small omnicron	&omicron;	o
Capital Xi	&Xi;	Ξ	Small pi	&pi;	π
Capital Omnicron	&Omicron;	O	Small rho	&rho;	ρ
Capital Pi	&Pi;	Π	Small final sigma	&sigmaf;	ς
Capital Rho	&Rho;	P	Small sigma	&sigma;	σ
Capital Sigma	&Sigma;	Σ	Small tau	&tau;	τ
Capital Tau	&Tau;	T	Small upsilon	&upsilon;	υ
Capital Upsilon	&Upsilon;	Y	Small phi	&phi;	φ
Capital Phi	&Phi;	Φ	Small chi	&chi;	χ
Capital Chi	&Chi;	X	Small psi	&psi;	ψ
Capital Psi	&Psi;	Ψ	Small omega	&omega;	ω
Capital Omega	&Omega;	Ω	Small theta symbol	&thetasym;	ϑ
Small alpha	&alpha;	α	Upsilon with hook symbol	&upsih;	ϒ

CURRENCY

Description	HTML Code	Glyph	Description	HTML Code	Glyph
Cents	&cent;	¢	Pounds	&pound;	£
Currency	&curren;	¤	Yen	&yen;	¥
Euro	&euro;	€			

Working with HTML/XHTML Tags and Attributes

The following table lists the HTML/XHTML tags and attributes presented in this book. For a complete list of all HTML/XHTML tags and attributes, visit the website for this book. Deprecated tags and attributes should be replaced with CSS alternatives whenever possible.

Tag Name	Code	Required Attributes	Optional Attributes
DOCTYPE (Document Type Declaration)	`<!DOCTYPE>`	Defines the version of X/HTML used to code a page	
Anchor	`<a></a>`	None	coords, href, name, shape, target (deprecated)
Area	`<area />`	alt	coords, href, shape, target (deprecated)
Body	`<body></body>`	None	alink, background, bgcolor, link, text, vlink (all deprecated)
Bold (deprecated)	`<b></b>`	None	None
Break	` `	None	None
Caption	`<caption></caption>`	None	Align
Center (deprecated)	`<center></center>`	None	None
Definition data	`<dd></dd>`	None	None
Definition list	`<dl></dl>`	None	None
Definition term	`<dt></dt>`	None	None
Division	`<div></div>`	None	align (deprecated)
Emphasis	`<em></em>`	None	None
Font (deprecated)	`<font></font>`	None	color, size, face (all deprecated)
Form	`<form></form>`	action	method
Head	`<head></head>`	None	None
Heading 1–6	`<h1></h1>` through `<h6></h6>`	None	align (deprecated)
Horizontal rule	`<hr />`	None	align, noshade, size, width (all deprecated)
HTML	`<html></html>`	xmlns	None

Tag Name	Code	Required Attributes	Optional Attributes
Image	`<img />`	alt, src	align (deprecated), border (deprecated), height, hspace (deprecated), usemap, vspace (deprecated), width
Input	`<input></input>`	None	checked, maxlength, name, size, type
Italic (deprecated)	`<i></i>`	None	None
Label	`<label></label>`	None	for
Link	`<link />`	None	href, rel, type
List item	`<li></li>`	None	type, value (all deprecated)
Map	`<map></map>`	id	name
Option	`<option></option>`	None	selected, value
Ordered list	`<ol></ol>`	None	start, type (all deprecated)
Paragraph	`<p></p>`	None	align (deprecated)
Select	`<select></select>`	None	multiple, size
Span	`<span></span>`	None	None
Strong	`<strong></strong>`	None	None
Style	`<style></style>`	type	None
Table	`<table></table>`	None	align (deprecated), bgcolor (deprecated), border, cellpadding, cellspacing, summary, width
Table data	`<td></td>`	None	align, bgcolor (deprecated), colspan, height (deprecated), nowrap (deprecated), rowspan, scope, valign, width (deprecated)
Table header	`<th></th>`	None	align (deprecated), bgcolor (deprecated), colspan, height (deprecated), nowrap (deprecated), rowspan, scope, valign, width (deprecated)
Table row	`<tr></tr>`	None	align, bgcolor (deprecated), valign
Textarea	`<textarea></textarea>`	cols, rows	name
Title	`<title></title>`	None	None
Unordered list	`<ul></ul>`	None	type

Glossary

Accessibility   The measure of how many people with handicaps or using alternate devices can access your site

Active state   A hyperlink that is being clicked is said to be in the active state
See also Hover state, Link state, and Visited state

Animation   A feature of GIF image files where several frames are combined into a single image to create a crude flip-book style animation

Apache HTTP Server (Apache)   The most widely used web server software available; open-source and free from apache.org

Attribute   A characteristic of an HTML element; use an attribute to modify the behavior or presentation of an HTML element by specifying a value; in `<p align="center">`, the attribute is "align"
See also Value

Bandwidth   *See* Monthly transfer

Bookmark   A named anchor
See also Named anchor

Box model   The space containing an HTML element, including the margin, border, padding, content area, and width

Class selector   May apply to several elements on the page; the HTML class attribute is used to specify the class of an HTML element; the CSS selector must begin with a dot, such as `.highlight`

Color mode   The method used by an image to combine and create color; all web graphics must use RGB, while images in the print industry use CMYK

Container tag   An HTML tag that consists of an opening tag and a closing tag, such as `<p></p>`
See also Replacement tag

Data table   A table used to display tabular data, or data that makes sense to reside in a table

Declaration   A property-value pair in a CSS rule; declarations must be separated by semicolons

Dedicated hosting   A web hosting plan where only one website or hosting account resides on a server

Default document   A setting on a web server that defines what the homepage must be named; common default documents include index.htm and default.htm

Deprecated element   *See* Deprecated tag

Deprecated tag   A tag that still works but that is being phased out and is no longer officially supported; examples include the `<center>` and `<font>` tags

Descendant selector   A way to apply a CSS rule to an element that is a child of another element; descendant selectors are separated with a space

Dithering   A process used by GIF image files where tiny dots of varying color are packed closely together to create another color not in the GIF's color palette

Domain name service (DNS)   An Internet service responsible for associating a domain name with an IP address

Element   In X/HTML, anything that represents a structure, such as heading, paragraph, image, list, etc.; elements are created with tags
See also Tag

Email harvester   A spam harvester
See also Spam harvester

Embedded styles   CSS that is written inside `<style>` tags inside the `<head>`

External link   A hyperlink that references a page or file on a website other than yours

External styles   Styles that exist in a dedicated stylesheet that is linked to HTML pages

Font   A typeface in a specific size, weight, and style

Form handler   A file or program that processes the data from an HTML form when the form is submitted

Full comp   A full-color rendering of a web page design used by the developer to extract graphics and act as a guide while coding XHTML and CSS

Generated file   A file generated from a source file; for example, JPGs and GIFs are often generated from a Photoshop (.psd) source file

See also Source file

Grouped selector   A way to apply the same CSS declarations to multiple selectors; grouped selectors must be separated with commas

Hack   Additional code in the XHTML or the CSS that addresses inconsistencies among browsers

Hand-coding   The practice of writing HTML/XHTML/CSS code manually in a text or HTML editor as opposed to using a program that writes the code for you

See also Manual-coding

Hexadecimal color code   A way to reference a color by its hexadecimal color code, such as "#FF0000", by using a hexadecimal value; the first two values indicate the amount of red, the middle two values indicate the amount of green, and the last two values indicate the amount of blue

Hover state   A hyperlink that is being pointed to is said to be in the hover state

See also Active state, Link state, and Visited state

HTML editor   A file editor that reads and writes text files with support for syntax coloring, line numbering, and other features; popular HTML editors include Crimson Editor, Notepad2, and BBEdit

See also Text editor

Hyperlink   Text or an image that, when clicked, navigates to another page or file

Hypertext   Text that, when clicked, opens another file or location

Id selector   May be used only once on each page; the HTML id attribute is used to specify the id of an HTML element; the CSS selector must begin with a pound symbol, such as #footer

Image map   A mapping of areas to an image to provide several hyperlinks on a single image

Image slicing   Creating several small images from a larger one in a graphics editing program to be pieced back together in an HTML document

Inline styles   CSS that is applied directly to an HTML tag via a style attribute

Internet   A worldwide network of computers that offers many services, such as email and the World Wide Web

Internet Assigned Numbers Authority (IANA)   An organization responsible for allocating Internet Protocol addresses (IP addresses)

See also Internet Corporation for Assigned Names and Numbers (ICANN)

Internet Corporation for Assigned Names and Numbers (ICANN)   The organization that operates IANA

See also Internet Assigned Numbers Authority (IANA)

Internet Information Services (IIS)   Microsoft's web server software that is included free with current versions of Windows

Internet Protocol (IP) address   A number in the form xxx.xxx.xxx.xxx that uniquely identifies a website or a computer on the Internet

Layout table   A table that is used to accomplish a specific layout of elements

Line height   The vertical space between lines of text

Link state   A hyperlink that has not been clicked, is not in the state of being clicked, and is not being pointed to is said to be in the link state

See also Active state, Hover state, and Visited state

Liquid   When an element's width changes as the browser window narrows or widens, the element is said to be liquid; entire layouts are said to be liquid if they stretch and contract as the browser window narrows and widens

Local site root   The folder on your computer holding all the files for a specific website

See also Site root and Remote site root

Lossless   A method of image file compression where no image data is discarded during the compression process, but the color palette is reduced resulting in visible color dots; GIFs use lossless compression

Lossy   A method of image file compression where image data is discarded during the compression process, resulting in blurred areas of the image; JPGs use lossy compression

Manual-coding   *See* Hand-coding

Markup   Program code written in accordance with a set of rules

See also Syntax and Presentational markup

Meta-data   Information about information; for example, a web page may offer information about chairs and meta-data may be included within the document's HTML code that describes the web page as being about chairs, who authored the document, when it was last updated, etc.

See also Meta tag

Meta tag   An HTML tag that holds meta-data

See also Meta-data

Monthly transfer   The amount of data that can be transferred to and from your website in any given month; this amount varies by web host and by web-hosting service plan

Mystery meat navigation   Links that fail to identify their linked location; users must either point to the link or click it to see where it will go

Name resolution   The process of matching a domain name to an IP address

Named anchor   A specific location on a page that users can jump to by clicking a hyperlink

See also Bookmark

Named color   A way to reference a color based on the name of the color, such as `"red"` or `"blue"`

Navigation bar (Navbar)   A group of hyperlinks often used for navigating between the main pages of a website

Non-linear branching   The ability to navigate web pages in order rather than sequentially from "page 1" to "page 2" to "page 3," etc.

Notepad   The default text editor that comes with Microsoft Windows

See also Text editor

Page centric   Software that treats each web page as an individual entity with no knowledge of related pages

See also Site aware

Presentational markup   In X/HTML, code that affects the visual presentation of a document

See also Markup

Property   The portion of a CSS rule that determines the characteristic of the element to receive formatting, such as the color or background

Pseudo-class selector   A selector used to style the four states of a hyperlink: link, visited, hover, and active

Remote site root   The folder on the web server that holds all of the files for a specific website

See also Site root and Local site root

Replacement tag   An HTML tag that is replaced by something else when rendered in the browser; for example, the `<br />` replacement tag is replaced with a line break while the `<img src="my_image.gif" />` replacement tag is replaced by the image specified in the SRC attribute

See also Container tag

Resolution   The number of pixels a computer monitor can display; usually written as the number of pixels a monitor can display across times the number of pixels it can display down, such as 800×600

Royalty-free image   An image you can use on your website without paying usage fees; royalty-free images may not be free themselves, but once purchased, can be used without future royalty fees

Rule   The combination of a selector and declaration(s) creates a CSS rule

Runtime   When the HTML/XHTML/CSS code actually executes, or is rendered in a browser

Selector   The first part of a CSS rule that determines which HTML element receives the formatting

Shared hosting   A web-hosting plan where many websites reside on the same server

SimpleText   The default text editor that comes with Apple Macintosh OS9 and earlier
See also Text editor

Site aware   Software that is capable of dealing with related pages in a website and, thus, can help maintain links or consistency in layout and design between pages
See also Page centric

Site root   The folder that holds all of the files for a specific website
See also Local site root and Remote site root

Source file   A file used to generate other files; for example, a Photoshop file (.psd) can be the source from which to create GIF and JPG graphics
See also Generated file

Spacer GIF   A small transparent GIF used as a shim to accomplish a specific layout; spacer GIFs are non-essential graphics and should be replaced by CSS padding and margin

Spam harvester   A program that searches websites' HTML code for email addresses in an effort to send spam
See also Email harvester

Statement of purpose   A concise sentence or paragraph describing what a website will and will not accomplish

Syntax   The rules of a programming language, such as where to type certain characters or required punctuation
See also Markup

Syntax coloring   A feature of HTML editors where the typed code is color coded to help identify errors
See also Syntax highlighting

Syntax highlighting   *See* Syntax coloring

Tag   Constructs that mark the beginning and end of an element; HTML tags are enclosed in angle brackets, such as <body>
See also Element

Text editor   A program that reads and writes plain text files with no formatting
See also HTML editor

TextEdit   In Apple Macintosh OSX, TextEdit replaced SimpleText as the default text editor; however, TextEdit is not a true text editor as it can read and write Rich Text documents, which can contain formatting
See also Text editor

Transparency   A feature of GIF image files where a color can be made transparent so the web page background shows through

Type selector   Applies to a specific HTML tag

Typeface   A family of fonts, such as Times or Arial

Typography   The process of working with type (text and lettering)

Usability   The measure of how easy it is for visitors to use your site

Value   Describes how an attribute should affect an HTML element; in <p align="center">, the value of "center" aligns the paragraph to the center of its container
See also Attribute

Visited state   A hyperlink that has been clicked is said to be in the visited state
See also Active state, Hover state, and Link state

Web browser   Also called a web client; software used to view web pages; Microsoft Internet Explorer, Mozilla Firefox, and Apple Safari are all web browsers

Web page   A document written in a web language such as HTML or XHTML for display in a web browser

See also Website

Web host   A company that provides web servers and monthly or annual hosting plans to the public

Web server   A computer that houses web pages and makes them available via the Internet

Websafe color palette   The 216 colors that display the same on various older computer systems capable of displaying only 256 colors

Website   A collection of related web pages

See also Web page

Whois   An Internet service that allows you to check the availability of a domain name

Wire frame   A rudimentary sketch of a web page's layout

World Wide Web (WWW)   One of the many services available on the Internet; the web is used to share web pages and websites throughout the world

Wrapper   Any element that contains another element; a common use for a wrapper is to use a single DIV or table to wrap the entire contents of the body in order to limit page width

WYSIWYG editor   Abbreviation for *What You See Is What You Get* (pronounced "wissy-wig"); software that automatically writes code for you as you drag and drop page elements as you would in a drawing or page layout program; popular WYSIWYG editors for web design include Adobe Dreamweaver, Adobe GoLive, Microsoft FrontPage, and Microsoft Expression

XML (Extensible Markup Language)   A tag-based computer language similar to, but more advanced than, HTML; XML files are often used as configuration files for software or as flat-file databases for websites

Index

free resources
   form handlers, 399
   FTP clients, 434
   image editor software, 144–145
   images, 146
   web hosting plans, 425
FrontPage, 75
FTP (File Transfer Protocol), 428, 434
full comp design, 137

G
generated image files, 139
generic vs. country code top-level domains, 431
get method for form data handling, 400
GIF (.gif) file format, 138, 140–141, 143
GIMP (GNU Image Manipulation Program), 144
GoLive, 75
Google, 11
governing bodies for web, 7–8
Graphical User Interface (GUI) tools, 66, 70, 75–76
graphic images (*see* images)
graphics generation, 138
graphics interchange format (GIF), 138, 140–141, 143
Greek letter and symbol HTML codes, 495
grouped selectors, CSS, 291–292
GUI (Graphical User Interface) tools, 66, 70, 75–76

H
hacks, CSS, 462
hand coding, 45
head element, 36–37, 55, 284
headings, text, 55, 96–100, 106, 113
<head> tag, 55, 284
height attribute
   cells in tables, 242, 244, 246
   images, 176, 179–181
   tables on pages, 240
Hex-3 color codes, 280
Hex-6 color codes, 279–280
hexidecimal color codes, 279–280, 281
<h> (heading) tags, 55, 96–100, 113
hierarchy, web page, 22
homepage and multiple layouts, 15
hooks, CSS, 288, 289
horizontal ruled lines, 182–185, 187
horizontal scrolling, avoiding, 254
host address, FTP, 435

hosting, website, 424–430
hotspots and image maps, 213
hover link style, CSS, 295
href attribute, 202, 213
<hr /> (horizontal rule) tag, 183–185, 187
hspace attribute, images, 176, 181–182
HTML editors, 69–74
html element, 36–37, 43, 55
HTML (Hypertext Markup Language)
   (*see also* CSS (Cascading Style Sheet))
   character codes, 104–105, 492–495
   comments, 446–447
   introduction, 34–39
   knowledge of for GUI-based tools, 76
   and source code, 6
   standards compliance, 9
   summary, 55
   viewing code, 6, 35, 38–39
   vs. XHTML, 90
<html> tag, 55
.htm vs. .html extension, 52
hyperlinks
   <a> (anchor) tag, 201–204, 206–210, 211, 215
   clear text for, 12
   email, 208–210
   to external pages, 205
   to files, 215–216
   and hypertext, 35
   from images, 211–215
   named anchors, 206–208
   navigation bars, 200–201
   pseudo-class selectors for, 295–296
   text-based, 201–204, 210
hypertext, definition, 35
Hypertext Markup Language (HTML) (*see* HTML)

I
IANA (Internet Assigned Numbers Authority), 7
ICANN (Internet Corporation for Assigned Names and Numbers), 7, 431
Id attribute
   and CSS id selector, 290–291
   divisions, 111
   forms, 381, 384, 385, 388, 393, 395, 398
   image maps, 213–214
   value rules, 111, 206
Id selectors, CSS, 285, 290–291
IIS (Internet Information Service), 425